Y0-BXR-647

Religion and Violence in South Asia

September 11, the war in Iraq, bombing in cities from Bali and Madrid to London; there has perhaps never before been a time when the study of religion and violence have been so relevant to global society. It is a topic at once sensitive, complex, potentially offensive and of major importance.

In today's increasingly polarised world, religion has been represented by some as a primary cause of social division, conflict and war, whilst others have argued that this is a distortion of the 'true' significance of religion, which when properly followed promotes peace, harmony, goodwill and social cohesion. This collection looks beyond the stereotypical images and idealized portrayals of the peaceful South Asian religious traditions, which can occlude their own violent histories, in order to analyze the diverse attitudes towards and manifestations of violence within the major religious traditions of South Asia. An international team of distinguished contributors, led by **John Hinnells** and **Richard King**, engages with issues relating to both religion and violence in their classical and contemporary South Asian formations.

The book combines case studies with theoretical discussion, relating an up-to-date overview of current issues surrounding religious violence in South Asia to new ideas and their social, critical and cultural ramifications. Part One explores violence and the classical traditions of South Asia (Hindu, Sikh, Buddhist, Jain, and Islamic), while Part Two investigates religious violence in contemporary South Asia. The book concludes with three major chapters discussing the impact of globalization and the key theoretical issues informing contemporary discussions of the relationship between religion and violence.

Contributors: Balbinder Bhogal, Paul Dundas, Rupert Gethin, Robert Gleave, Peter Gottschalk, Christophe Jaffrelot, Richard King, Laurie Patton, Peter Schalk, Arvind-pal Singh Mandair, Ian Talbot.

Editors: John R. Hinnells is Professor of Comparative Study of Religions at Liverpool Hope University, UK. His specialist research area is Zoroastrianism and the Parsis, on which he has written, among others, *The Zoroastrian Diaspora* (2005). He is also the editor of various works, including *The Routledge Companion to the Study of Religion* (2005).

Richard King is Associate Professor of Religious Studies at Vanderbilt University, USA. He is the co-author (with Jeremy Carrette) of *Selling Spirituality* (Routledge 2005) and author of *Orientalism and Religion* (Routledge 1999), and *Indian Philosophy: An Introduction to Hindu and Buddhist Thought* (1999).

WITHDRAWN
UTSA LIBRARIES

Religion and Violence in South Asia

Theory and Practice

Edited by
John R. Hinnells and Richard King

Routledge
Taylor & Francis Group
LONDON AND NEW YORK

First published 2007
by Routledge
2 Park Square, Milton Park, Abingdon, Oxon OX14 4RN

Simultaneously published in the USA and Canada
by Routledge
270 Madison Ave, New York, NY 10016

Routledge is an imprint of the Taylor & Francis Group, an informa business

© 2007 John R. Hinnells and Richard King for selection and editorial material; individual contributors for their contributions

Typeset in Galliard by Taylor & Francis Books
Printed and bound in Great Britain by Antony Rowe Ltd, Chippenham, Wiltshire

All rights reserved. No part of this book may be reprinted or reproduced or utilised in any form or by any electronic, mechanical, or other means, now known or hereafter invented, including photocopying and recording, or in any information storage or retrieval system, without permission in writing from the publishers.

British Library Cataloguing in Publication Data
A catalogue record for this book is available from the British Library

Library of Congress Cataloging in Publication Data
A catalog record for this title has been requested

ISBN10: 0-415-37290-9 (hbk)
ISBN10: 0-415-37291-7 (pbk)
ISBN10: 0-203-08869-7 (ebk)

ISBN13: 978-0-415-37290-9 (hbk)
ISBN13: 978-0-415-37291-6 (pbk)
ISBN13: 978-0-203-08869-2 (ebk)

Library
University of Texas
at San Antonio

Contents

Contributors

Balbinder Singh Bhogal is Assistant Professor in South Asian Religions and Cultures, and co-ordinator of the South Asian Studies Program at York University in Toronto, Canada. His research focuses on South Asian religions and cultures in general, but with a specialist interest in Sikh Studies, especially the teachings and interpretation of the Guru Granth Sahib. Recent publications include 'Questioning Hermeneutics with Freud: How to Interpret Dreams and Mute-Speech in Sikh Scripture?' in *Sikh Formations: Religion, Culture and Theory* 1 (1): 93–125. He is currently working on a monograph provisionally entitled *Nonduality and Skilful Means in the Hymns of Guru Nanak: Hermeneutics of the Word.*

Paul Dundas is Reader in Sanskrit in the School of Literatures, Languages and Cultures, University of Edinburgh. He has published widely in the field of Jain history and sectarianism. His *History, Scripture and Controversy in a Medieval Jain Sect* is forthcoming with Routledge.

Rupert Gethin completed his Ph.D. at University of Manchester. Since 1987 he has taught at the University of Bristol where he is currently Reader in Buddhist Studies. Since 2003 he has been President of the Pali Text Society. His principal research interests are in the theories of early Buddhist meditation and Abhidhamma.

Peter Gottschalk is Associate Professor at Wesleyan University. He is author of *Beyond Hindu and Muslim* (Oxford University Press, 2000) and is co-designer of 'A Virtual Village' with Mathew Schmalz (http://virtualvillage.wesleyan.edu). Currently he is researching British information projects in India.

Robert Gleave is Professor of Arabic Studies at the Institute of Arab and Islamic Studies, University of Exeter. He specializes in Islamic law, Muslim hermeneutics and Shi'i Muslim thought.

John R. Hinnells is Research Professor in the Comparative Study of Religions at Liverpool Hope University; he was formerly at SOAS and Manchester

University. His research area is Zoroastrianism, specifically the Parsis. His major works include *Zoroastrians in Britain* (Oxford University Press 1996) and *The Zoroastrian Diaspora* (Oxford University Press 2005) and a selection of his articles was published by Ashgate in 2000. He has edited the *New Penguin Dictionary of Religions* and the *New Penguin Handbook of Living Religions* (1996 and 1997) as well as several books for Routledge including *Islamic Mysticism in the West* with Professor Jamal Malik (2006) and *The Routledge Companion to the Study of Religions* (2005).

Christophe Jaffrelot is Director of the Centre d'Études et de Recherches Internationales (CERI), Sciences Po (Paris) and Director of Research at the Centre National de la Recherche Scientifique (CNRS). He is an expert on South Asian politics and is the author/editor of a number of books including: *India's Silent Revolution. The Rise of the Lower Castes in North India* (2003), and *The Hindu Nationalist Movement and Indian Politics* (1996), both published by Columbia University Press.

Richard King is Associate Professor of Religious Studies and Senior Research Fellow in the Center for the Study of Religion and Culture at Vanderbilt University, USA. His main research interests include Hindu and Buddhist philosophical traditions, post-structuralist and postcolonial approaches to the study of religions, and the comparative study of mysticism and spirituality. He is the author of four previous books including *Early Advaita Vedānta and Buddhism* (State University of New York Press 1995), *Orientalism and Religion: Postcolonial Theory, India and 'the Mystic East'* (Routledge 1999), *Indian Philosophy: An Introduction to Hindu and Buddhist Thought* (Edinburgh University Press 1999/2000) and *Selling Spirituality: The Silent Takeover of Religion*, co-authored with Dr Jeremy Carrette (Routledge 2005).

Arvind Mandair teaches at the University of Michigan at Ann Arbor where he holds the SBSC Endowed Chair in Sikh Studies. His recent publications include: *Sikh Religion, Culture and Ethnicity*, co-ed. (Curzon Press 2001), *Teachings of the Sikh Gurus: Selections From the Scriptures*, co-ed. (Routledge 2005), and a monograph entitled *Religion and the Politics of Translation*. He is founding co-editor of the new journal *Sikh Formations: Religion, Culture and Theory* published by Routledge.

Laurie L. Patton is Winship Distinguished Research Professor in the Humanities and Chair of the Department of Religion at Emory University, USA. She is the author or editor of seven books: *Authority, Anxiety, and Canon: Essays in Vedic Interpretation*, ed. (State University of New York Press 1994); *Myth as Argument: The Bṛhaddevatā as Canonical Commentary*, author (Walter de Gruyter 1996); *Myth and Method*, ed. with Wendy Doniger (University Press of Virginia 1996); *Jewels of Authority: Women and Text in* *the Hindu Tradition*, ed. (Oxford University Press 2002); *Bringing the Gods to Mind: Mantra and Ritual in Early Indian Sacrifice*, author (University of California Press 2004) and *The Indo-Aryan Controversy: Evidence and Inference in Indian History*, ed. with Edwin Bryant (Routledge 2005). Her book of poetry, *Fire's Goal: Poems from a Hindu Year*, was published by White Clouds Press in 2003, and her translation of the *Bhagavad Gītā* is forthcoming from Penguin Press Classics Series. She has recently returned from India where she worked as a Fulbright scholar, completing research for her forthcoming book, *Grandmother Language: Women and Sanskrit in Maharashtra and Beyond.*

Peter Schalk is Professor in the Department of the History of Religions at Uppsala University in Sweden. Dr Schalk's main fields of research are ritual transmission of Buddhism in Sri Lanka, the religions of Fu Nan as state ideologies, the history of Buddhism among Tamils in Tamilakam and Ilam, Hinduism in Western exile, and the religious expressions of social-economical conflicts in present South Asia. His recent publications include 'Robert Caldwell's Derivation *īḻam < sīhala*: A Critical Assessment', in *South-Indian Horizons: Felicitation Volume for François Gros* (Institut Français De Pondichery, 2004); '*Īḻam < sīhala*? An Assessment of an Argument' in *Historia Religionum* 25 (2004); 'God as Remover of Obstacles. A Study of Caiva Soteriology among Ilam Tamil Refugees' in *Historia Religionum* 23 (2004).

Ian Talbot is Professor in British History at the University of Southampton where he is also Director of the Centre for the Study of Britain and Its Empire. His recent publications include *Pakistan: A Modern History* (Hurst revised edn 2005) and 'Pakistan in 2003: Political Deadlock and Continuing Uncertainties' in *Asian Survey* XLIV (1) January/February 2004.

Introduction

John R. Hinnells and Richard King

Studies of religion and violence are at once sensitive, complex, potentially offensive and of major importance. During the gestation period of this book there have been the horrendous events of 9/11 when Muslim 'extremists' flew aircraft into the twin towers of the World Trade Center in New York, the leaders of 'the free world', President Bush and Prime Minister Blair (both self-proclaimed Christians) led a coalition to invade Iraq, on one occasion even using the term 'crusade' in what has been widely interpreted by their opponents as a Christian assault on Islam. During this time there have been bombings in cities from Bali and Madrid to London and Mumbai, enacted, according to their perpetrators, in the name of their religion. Despite millennia of apparent 'religious violence', there has perhaps never before been a time where studies of religion and violence have been so important.

Many adherents of various religions depict their tradition as a force for peace, stability and virtue. It is not only the Christian image of 'Gentle Jesus Meek and Mild', but Hindus, notably Mahātma Gandhi, who have presented 'true Hinduism' as non-violent in nature. 'Love' is proclaimed by many to be the essential teaching of various religions. Conversely, people who disclaim any adherence to a religion sometimes argue that religions have been the greatest force for persecution, oppression, torture and murder, citing such diverse examples as forced conversion at different times and places in Christian and Islamic history. Another common explanation is to argue that religions are associated with violence only when they deviate from their ideals, that violence is perpetrated in the name of a religion, but does not truly reflect its ideals thus making violence an expression of religion that has 'gone wrong', or that the 'real' religion does not encourage violence but humans fail to live up to its ideals, as though a religion exists independently of those who practice it. Inevitably, the situation is more complex than any of these claims implies.

In a South Asian context this debate is played out in a number of ways. One trend for instance is the trope of inclusivist 'tolerance' that has become a key feature of the discourse of 'Hindu spirituality' that has developed since the nineteenth century. Similarly, the association of specific South Asian traditions (especially Hindu, Buddhist, Jain and Sufi) with the notion of non-violence (*ahiṃsā*) is commonplace, contributing as it does to an idealized portrayal of such traditions which occludes some of the more violent aspects of their own histories. Moreover, the discourse of 'non-violent' and 'spiritual' religions (usually, though not exclusively, identified with those traditions originating from the Indian subcontinent) is often pressed into service in order to contrast such traditions from those emphasizing notions such as 'the crusade' and '*jihad*' – which themselves are often seen as determinate features of the so-called 'religions of the book'. It is not so easy, however, to reconcile aspects of the *Dharma-śāstras* or the exhortation to battle in the *Bhagavad Gītā* with such ideals, Gandhi's hermeneutics notwithstanding. This volume of articles is designed to look beyond such stereotypical images and to analyze the diverse attitudes towards and manifestations of violence within South Asian traditions.

Contrary to the 'spiritualistic' image of Hinduism, violence of course has been an integral aspect of Hindu traditions. As Patton demonstrates, many different stances have been taken with regard to the practice of violence by Hindus. This complexity and diversity is no different in the case of all the traditions under consideration in this volume. Bhogal questions whether love and violence are necessarily mutually exclusive, a question addressed by Christians as well as Sikhs. Hindu images, both iconographically and metaphorically of Durga and Kali express vividly the idea that birth and death, violence and love are two sides of one reality or force. In Islam God is most frequently referred to as 'The Compassionate, the Merciful', but sanctions violence against individuals (Gleave) or opposing tribes. The question perhaps is not whether South Asian traditions condone violence but rather under what conditions do they do so and against whom is such violence inflicted?

Images of violence, indeed, can be found throughout the various religious traditions of the world. In Hindu art, the gods are portrayed with symbols of violence – sword and discus; key events are set in the midst of battles most obviously in the vision granted to Arjuna in the *Bhagavad Gītā* within the context of violent conflict. Not just Christian history but the Bible in general is replete with stories and parables of violence. Within the *Qu'ran* some verses call for violence against unbelievers, other *suras* state one should only use violence when attacked – which *sura* abrogates which is a matter of scholarly and religious debate.

The specificities of the debate about 'religion and violence' in South Asia are played out in a number of ways. The various papers in this volume attempt to look beyond standard stereotypical images and to analyze the diverse attitudes towards and manifestations of violence within the major religious traditions of South Asia. The volume is divided into three parts. Part One focuses on the ancient or 'classical' sources of South Asian traditions, particularly their sacred texts and major sources of authority. Although discussion of these sources is important, authors were encouraged to pay attention to the broader historical context of each tradition, as well as reflect upon the social, political and cultural factors pertinent to an understanding of the place and role of violence in relation to each tradition under discussion. It is hoped that these chapters will provide a useful overview and discussion of textual and historical resources for understanding violence, its legitimation and its condemnation by the major religious traditions of South Asia.

In Part Two attention turns to the contemporary context, with chapters exploring violence in Sri Lanka (Schalk), Pakistan (Talbot) and Gujarat (Jaffrelot). In the modern period we have also witnessed the transformation of South Asian traditions and cultures as a result of the end of European colonialism, the emergence of 'postcolonial' nation-states and regional conflicts both within and across national borders. New diasporic communities have emerged and old ones have begun to assert themselves in new ways. How have the ancient traditions responded to this new context and the issue of sectarian violence? Moreover, in the context of President Bush's 'global war on terrorism', we find the discourses of 'religion' and 'terrorism' becoming intertwined in new and quite complex fashions. In some cases, the newly valorized language of 'international terrorism' has become a powerful discourse for governments to repress internal opposition and the civil liberties of troublesome minorities. In cases such as the Gujarat riots of 2002, this new language of terrorism has provided an effective means for creating scapegoats, particularly when tapping into anti-Islamic sentiments in a post 9/11 era (Jaffrelot).

Finally, in Part Three, our contributors (Gottschalk, Mandair and King) offer a series of critical and theoretical reflections on the underlying presuppositions of the 'religion and violence' debate and the particularities of its unfoldment in the context of the study and representation of South Asian traditions and societies.

There are also a series of prior questions to consider about the conception of violence utilized in such debates. As Gyanendra Pandey (1992: 27) notes in his discussion of 'Hindu-Muslim' violence in India:

> Violence always appears as an absence ... because historical discourse has been able to capture and represent the moment of violence only with great difficulty. The 'history' of violence is, therefore, almost always about context – about everything that happens around violence.

In this way discussion of violence in modern Indian historiography tends to represent it as an aberration or an absence – 'an exceptional moment, not the "real" history of India at all' (Pandey, ibid.). Violence then only appears to us as a fragment, a splinter in what is seen as the otherwise peaceful flow of history. However, the representation of violence in terms of extraordinary events tends to render everyday, systemic and structural forms of violence invisible.

What counts as 'violence' then is also open to debate. Gleave, within the context of his discussion of a specific Islamic text, defines violence as 'the actual and intentional bodily damage carried out by an individual or individuals on another individual'. Within the context of that specific discussion such a definition is evidently reasonable. Within wider discussions, however, other forms of 'violence' merit consideration. An obvious example here might be cases of asceticism, for example fasting unto death in Jainism (Dundas), or the 'extreme' renunciatory practices taken by Hindu *sādhus* or Christian monks. These might be considered violent by outside observers. The Christian Crusades and the cult of martyrs idealized violence. Self-inflicted violence is common amongst Shi-ites at the festival of *Muharram*. Perhaps René Girard is right to argue that all traditions which include a doctrine of sacrificial offerings, real or symbolic, have violence at the very heart of their teaching and ritual practice whether the victim be a 'scapegoat' for sin or an offering to a god. Similarly, religions that envisage a cosmic struggle between good and evil often take up the imagery of violence, and sometimes have translated that into action against people thought to support, practice or be evil. As Schalk asks, does the 'end' (peace) justify violent 'means' (violence)? In much Sanskritic literature it is the duty, *dharma*, of some to fight – the *kṣatriya* (Patton, Dundas). In much of South (and East) Asia martial arts have religious associations (Dundas); although it may well be argued that what they teach is self control, violence nevertheless remains a feature of them in many forms.

The mainstream debate on religion and violence has also tended to proceed on broadly humanistic grounds – violence almost always denotes acts carried out upon other human beings. This seems to reflect a Christian/humanistic framing of the discussion. Why, for instance, is violence towards animals largely ignored in such debates? Any religion that permits the eating of meat thereby condones such violence. In traditional Zoroastrianism, a religion forged in the Asian steppes where a high protein diet was essential, there is the belief that Ahura Mazda created certain animals for food for humans, but there was a religious obligation to ensure that the creature died with merciful swiftness and so it was traditional for animals killed for food to be slain by a priest in the ritual setting, for that ensured a 'good' death. One suspects that this exclusion would be less prevalent if the Indian term '*hiṃsā*' functioned as the primary signifier in the debate rather than the English term 'violence'. One of the contributions that a consideration of the South Asian context surely should be to broaden the horizons of what counts as 'violence' in such debates.

Similarly, environmentalists might also argue that one should consider extending the scope of the term even further by considering acts of violence upon the planet and its eco-systems. Pollution, climate change and environmental degradation have consequences for humans (if we wish to continue to read violence in largely anthropocentric terms), but one might also consider the ongoing plundering and destruction of the planet's resources as within the remit of what counts as violence. To believe for instance, that current levels of environmental exploitation and mass consumption can be maintained indefinitely and on a global scale is to be influenced by a mythic capitalistic ideology that is as 'utopian' and idealistic as any apparently 'religious' worldview (King).

Most discussion within the literature on 'religion and violence' tends to ignore the existence of cultural, epistemic or symbolic violence. However, as Foucault reminds us in *The Archaeology of Knowledge*, the world does not present itself to us with a legible face, leaving us merely to decipher it. Rather, he suggests:

> We must conceive discourse as a violence that we do to things, or to all events, as a practice we impose upon them; it is in this practice that the events of discourse find the principle of their regularity. (1972: 229)

The decision to ignore epistemic or cultural violence ignores important historical factors that are relevant to a consideration of 'religion and violence' in South Asia. Not only is cultural violence an issue worthy of analysis in itself, it also remains a key factor in the unequal playing field of history that has so often served as the background to the irruption of physical acts of 'religious violence'. One cannot, for instance, understand the rise of 'anti-American' and anti-Western sentiments amongst many contemporary Islamist groups without taking into account the historical involvement of western nations in the colonial, political and economic domination of the Middle Eastern regimes. Similarly, hostile reactions to the American-led invasion of Iraq in 2003 cannot be understood without acknowledging the charge of injustice and hypocrisy that is frequently laid at the feet of the United States for what is perceived by some to be its largely uncritical military support of Israel against the Palestinians. As Chalmers Johnston (2004) has argued in his book *Blowback*, the failure to recognize the history of violence – both symbolic and material in nature – that has been enacted upon others by the powerful western nations is a major obstacle in any attempts to understand the structural and historical factors that have contributed to the contemporary rise of violent sectarian movements across the globe.

The papers by Bhogal, Mandair and Gottschalk attempt to address the question of symbolic, cultural or 'epistemic' violence by highlighting the role that western Orientalist assumptions about the category of 'religion' have played in conceptualizing what has been called 'the communalist problem' in South Asia. Those discussions therefore need not be rehearsed here. On this topic some commentators seem to imply that communalism and Indian nationalist are little more than a colonial construction or legacy of British imperial rule (Aditya Mukherjee, 1990; David Ludden, 1993: 266–68; Ronald Inden, 1990: 408). Thus, Aditya Mukherjee (1990: 165) has argued that:

> Indian society was not split since 'time immemorial' into religious communal categories. Nor is it so divided today in areas where communal ideology has not yet penetrated ... However, communalism as it is understood today, ... is a modern phenomenon, which took root half way through the British colonial presence in India – in the second half of the nineteenth century.

Anyone convinced that sectarian violence in South Asia is merely a 'western import' however need look no further than Christopher Bayly's work (1985) which discusses incidents of 'communal violence' that occurred long before the onset of British colonialism. It is easier to make such claims about India because of the prevalence of certain romanticized stereotypes about the non-violent and 'mystical' nature of South Asian (or at least 'Indic') traditions. The question of why such sectarian conflicts should be called 'religious' and also whether British colonial assumptions fed such pre-existing divisions, however, remains open for discussion. Several authors in this book question the usefulness of the term 'religion' when discussing violence and South Asian traditions (see especially Bhogal, Gottschalk, Mandair and King). One of the key issues here, of course, is how to represent complex social events within a historical narrative: what makes a riot 'communalistic' or 'religious' in nature, rather than economic or ethnic or class-based, etc.? There are multiple narratives that can be offered of any complex social phenomenon and it is not always clear why classifying them in terms of a universalized discourse of religion aids us in understanding either their specificity or their context. More profoundly, however, there are important epistemological and political issues to consider in relation to the application of a rigid dichotomy between something called 'the religious' and something called 'the secular' in the context of South Asian history and culture.

It is perhaps a quirk of the modern West that religion is seen as a 'private matter of belief'. From the perspective of modern liberalism it is often argued that when religions involve themselves in the 'secular' affairs of the state one is likely to find ideas of cosmic conflict translated into historical conflict – be that when Christianity became the religion of the Roman empire or Buddhist nationalists in modern Sri Lanka. As various authors in this volume demonstrate, South Asian traditions have commonly been an important element in sectarian politics, nationalism and war. With the possible exception of Jainism (Dundas), Buddhism has some of the most explicit ethical affirmations of 'non-violence', as Gethin shows, but this has not prevented Buddhists in several countries from using violence to achieve their goals (Schalk). Where 'state religion' exists, is it inevitable that the state will justify its violence through religious doctrine? Where, as in the case of Pakistan (Talbot), a nation is conceived as having religion as its boundary is it inevitable – rather than an abuse – that religious violence occurs? Such situations also highlight the issue of the grounds for claiming a 'just war'. Is violence justified if it is thought to lead to 'peace' (Schalk)? Who defines 'peace' in that context? Is religious revenge a justification for violence (Jaffrelot)? From a different point of view, does the focus upon 'religion and violence' as *the problem* (to be overcome presumably by a mediating secular state) create a smokescreen that effectively insulates modern 'secular' ideologies, institutions and regimes from the same level of critical analysis (King)?

Verbal and social violence are also issues (see Mandair's discussion of Derrida). It might reasonably be asked if the laws relating to purity and pollution in Zoroastrianism and other religions do violence to women as they are excluded from religious and traditionally from family life, during menstruation. Social injustice and poverty might well be considered a powerful form of structural violence (King). To many, the sense of guilt associated with various forms of religions, for example in Christianity, may well be seen as perpetrating a form of psychological violence. Might one even argue that the perpetrators of violence are themselves harmed through this process? Where does the boundary lie between 'harm' and 'violence' (Gleave)? In short, the term 'violence' is as multifaceted, or debatable, as the term 'religion'.

Although this book focuses on South Asia, the editors are well aware of omissions – Bangladesh, a study of the victims of violence, Indian Christianity etc. But restrictions of space required selection and we have focused on some of the traditions and regions most commonly discussed on this theme. The editors wish to express their gratitude for the grants given by the Society of South Asian Studies and the British Academy to facilitate the research workshop on which this volume is based and to James Newell for his typographical and editorial work on the final manuscript.

Cited works

Bayly, Christopher (1985), 'The pre-history of "communalism": religious conflict in India, 1700–1860' in *Modern Asian Studies* 19: 177–203.

Foucault, Michel (1972), *The Archaeology of Knowledge*, trans. A.M. Sheridan Smith, Tavistock Publications Ltd.

Inden, Ronald (1990), *Imagining India*, Oxford, Basil Blackwells.

Johnston, Chalmers (2004), *Blowback: The Costs and Consequences of American Empire*, 2nd edn, Owl Books.

Ludden, David (1993), 'Orientalist Empiricism: Transformations of Colonial Knowledge' in Carol A. Breckenridge and Peter van der Veer (eds), *Orientalism and the Postcolonial Predicament*, Philadelphia, University of Pennsylvania Press.

Mukherjee, Aditya (1990), 'Colonialism and Communalism', in Sarvepali Gopal (ed.), *Anatomy of a Confrontation: The Babri Masjid-Ramjanmabhumi Issue*, Calcutta and New Delhi, Penguin.

Pandey, Gyanendra (1992), 'In Defense of the Fragment: Writing about Hindu-Muslim Riots Today', in *Representations* 37: 27–55.

Part I

Classical approaches to violence in South Asian traditions

1 Telling stories about harm

An overview of early Indian narratives

Laurie L. Patton

Introductory thoughts

One of the most basic challenges for a teacher of Hinduism and the Indian traditions is constructing a fair narrative about the development of the concept of *ahiṃsā,* or non-injury. One of the easiest and most common ways to tell the story is that, while earlier sacrificers accepted violence in the form of victim immolation, the challenges of Buddhism and Jainism changed this view. After their emergence, Brahmin priests incorporated their own doctrines of *ahiṃsā*, which have been a hallmark of the classical Hindu tradition ever since. There are other, ancillary arguments to this story as well. These revolve around the nature and role (if any) of human sacrifice (*puruṣamedha*) in the early Indian and Indo-European worlds (Weber 1864; Hillebrandt 1887; Eggeling 1900; Oldenberg 1917; Kirfel 1951; Handiqui 1949; Shlinghoff 1969; Gonda 1975; Krick 1975; Thakur 1978; Witzel 1987; Schmidt 1997; Houben 2001).[1] They also address the internal changes and attitudes toward violence in brahminical Hinduism which may have interacted with external pressures from Buddhism and Jainism (Alsdorf 1962; Schmidt 1968; Tull 1996; Schmidt 1997; Houben 2001; Bodewitz 2001); about whether sacrifice should be understood as 'violence' at all (Oguibenine 1994; Bodewitz 2001).

While this historical debate is necessary, it is also important to locate debates about injury and non-injury within specific genres of early Indian texts, and to inquire about what is at stake concerning injury *within* those genres. In this article, I have chosen narrative genres about *hiṃsā* (and related terms such as *droha, apakāra* and *riṣ*),[2] rather than *ahiṃsā*, and some textual genres related to narrative, such as the *Dharma Sūtras*. These legal texts are not explicitly narrative, but implicitly so, in that they address and describe human situations of injury. I assume that violence is always a problem in any literary representation – an event that resists narrativization even as it might be justified and incorporated into the text. Therefore, stories about violence in early India should be studied and understood within their own environments as well as understood as 'doctrines' or 'proto doctrines' relating to *ahiṃsā*.

It is helpful (and not often done) to discuss recent theories about the narrative representation and violence in the context of ancient India. Writing about how people tell stories about terrorism and violence in Śri Lanka, E. Valentine Daniel outlines several forms of relationship between 'word' and 'thing' in theories of language, and by implication, theories of narrative representation: 1) language represents objects; 2) language constitutes subjective reality; and 3) following Taylor (1987), language responds to and expresses a match between internal and external realities. As Daniel writes, following William Connolly (1987), such theories consistently give hegemony to integration (Daniel 1987: 151).

> Regardless of which form it takes, it conceals the violence done to life when the recalcitrantly ambiguous character of lived experience is downplayed or swallowed up by even higher forms of compulsive ordering – an activity at which we intellectuals excel.
>
> (356)

Normalizing discourse contains (ignores, destroys, suppresses) that which deviates from it. In this way Connolly's thinking is parallel to Romila Thapar's notion in her 'Imagined Religious Communities', and other writings (1991, 1993), where facts about ancient India and the relationships between religions are homogenized in such a way as to make them more 'readable' in a Hindu nationalist present.

In contrast, there is one theory of language that does not conceal the violence to life – the genealogical mode. Daniel goes on: 'How then ought the story to be told in a genealogical mode? In its vocabulary and rhetoric, its own ambiguity must be made overt so as to caution those who read or hear to be wary of doctrines that glorify normalization' (2000: 360). Such narratives, frequently traced by Daniel in his fieldwork in Śri Lanka, employ multiple voices to relativize all the voices; they prevent any single voice from dominance. At times such stories lack resolution, and even clarity.

Gyan Pandey also refers to this dynamic of storytelling in the midst and aftermath of violence. In interviews with those who experienced the Partition violence, Pandey discusses the dynamics of remembering and forgetting. Partition survivors struggle between the 'will to truth' – where violence is actually remembered – and the suppression of actual memories in service of a larger, more peaceful narrative in which 'someone else' committed the violence 'in another town'. As Pandey puts it, 'the will to truth is commonly accompanied by the need to forget'. Such forgetting involves the basic human fact that one must try to render the incomprehensible comprehensible. And because remembering violence involves the recollection of the collapse of lived community, then there is necessarily a fragment of violence that cannot be integrated (1997; 2001: 177–182). This fragment remains at the margins of community, which cannot sustain it.

With these assumptions, I want to ask of early India, as one might of other societies: How do people tell stories about violence? What plots do they choose to construct about inflicting harm, and how do such plots create justification, or condemnation, or both in relation to violence? I will focus on the narrative and poetic moves where violence becomes an explicit issue within the text. Many of these passages have been discussed elsewhere, but the narrative emphasis is the key to my readings below. In each narrative situation, there is an implicit or explicit moment of self-reflection: what larger world view is imagined as normal and thereby kept whole, so that the physical body's wholeness becomes a subordinate issue, and physical harm becomes possible?

In early Indian narratives (and, I would argue, most other narratives) bodily injury is dealt with in a kind of 'back and forth' dynamic of ambivalence, whereby violence is transmuted into different kinds of normative languages within the story itself. Building on this approach, I will add a special note on the use and imagery of weapons – the tools of *hiṃsā* – in some of the classical texts, as a form of practical reasoning about violence in its own right. The rhetoric of weaponry can give us an excellent view of how instruments of harm were understood within the complex web of social relationships that necessitated them. To take a contemporary example, we can understand twenty-first-century debates about weapons – gun control – as significant lenses onto the role and nature of violence in our own time as well as the rights of the individual to inflict bodily harm.

First, I argue that the Vedic ambivalence toward violence is expressed in the attempt to balance truth and untruth, life and death, in the procedures of the sacrifice. Whereas other scholars have called this attitude a straightforward 'denial' of or 'embarrassment about' violence and death, I want to suggest a subtler dynamic, whereby violent death is admitted, experienced, and then normalized. Weaponry is seen as an extension, and sometimes as a metaphor, for sacrificial power. Some hymns use the imagery of the other world to balance and normalize the violence being done to the sacrificial victim itself. Second, the Upaniṣadic perspective on physical injury is expressed in the language of metaphoric transcendence. These texts focus on the body and perception as a site of meaningful transformation, in which bodily experience and perception of *hiṃsā* becomes something else, usually represented as insignificant in the light of the knowledge of Brahman. Violence is admitted in the rather straightforward language of competition and killing (see Grinshpon 2005: 132 on this point), but rendered small in the face of a larger metaphysic.

Third, the ambivalence of the epics toward war is expressed in several ways. In the *Mahābhārata*, war is frequently thought of as sacrifice, where warriors are containers, not glorifiers of force. While this has been a common observation in scholarship of late, the *Mahābhārata* text in particular also repeatedly warns about the cost of such force, just as a sacrificer might be aware of the cost of sacrifice. In addition, in the epics, *dharma* is a great 'integrater' of violence in the sense Daniel uses above. It acts as a controller of the excesses of *hiṃsā* as well as its legitimation: the epic *Rāmāyaṇa*'s discussion of Rāma's slaying of the monkey Vāli is an excellent illustration of this idea. Finally, the *Dharma Sūtras*' view of the control of physical harm is elaborately codified in a discussion of *kṣatriyadharma* as well as the appropriate use of weaponry. Violence becomes a function of appropriate duties according to *varṇa*. The legal texts describe human situations in which potentially non-integrated violent acts become normalized through specific acts of expiation. Here the human himself is the force of integration. The control of *hiṃsā* happens through the social control of the self, or the codification of social *varṇa* role.

Beyond doctrinal readings: the choice of narrative and implied narrative

I choose texts with narratives and implied narratives, such as the *Dharma Sūtras*, because they are closer to the human situation, and might well contain compelling and instructive portraits of ambivalence about *hiṃsā*. Moreover, the texts themselves refer to terms for 'story', or descriptions of human situations, such as *ithāsa* (legend), *purāṇa* (ancient story), and so on. Moreover, my own sense is that previous accounts of *ahiṃsā*, *hiṃsā*'s opposite, tend to focus only on whether certain early Indian passages give 'evidence' for certain 'attitudes' toward violence.[3] They are perhaps too simply read as containing doctrines when in fact, if they are good narratives, they would not only contain doctrine, but rather complex, and in this case, usually tragic, imagistic explorations around a particular theme. These stories of violence, like Daniel's narratives, threaten to have no clear resolution, and yet still make very real and perhaps successful attempts to create coherence with no clear resolution. Reading early Indian texts only with a view toward the development of *hiṃsā* or *ahiṃsā* is like reading the *Iliad* only for certain Greek attitudes towards war, rather than for the complex human epic that it is.

In thinking about these narratives, we might also call upon Northrop Frye's (1983) less recent but still important *dictum* that when one reads a classical religious text *as literature*, not as *theology*, one assumes polyvalent meanings, and not just theological or doctrinal ones. My choice of narrative for this article allows us to move toward polyvalency even more explicitly. Tatiana Elizarenkova has pointed to polysemy, or the exploitation of multiple meanings[4] as an explicit Vedic style, and I think it would do interpreters well to assume polysemy in post Vedic styles as well. Complexity, play, ambivalence, and irony make a classic text a classic text, and the Indian epics and the *Upaniṣads* and the *Dharma Sūtras* are no different. In the case of the *Dharma Sūtras*, where the narrative element is not so explicitly present, there is still a strongly implied narrative in which the human situation is thickly described and thickly explored. As recent scholars of literature and law have suggested, legal situations usually involve a kind of thin narrative of conflict or wrongdoing which might be addressed or resolved. Indeed, David Damrosch and other scholars have made an excellent case for reading legal texts such as *Leviticus* as literature, in terms of their internal structures, uses of metaphors,[5] and so on, and I think we can also make the same kind of case here.

The Vedic world: going on paths that are good to go on

In the Vedic period, violence dwells just under the surface of many sacrificial texts. These hints at injury and death, both human and animal, are theorized by

Jan Heesterman (1984, 1993, 1995). In his view, the early Vedic scenario was an elaborate 'cycle of violence' in which sacrificers compete with each other for wealth such as cattle in a series of deadly contests, sacrifices and counter sacrifices. This rudimentary scenario is hinted at in verbal contests called *brahmodyas*, questions and answers, in which vituperation is heightened, and reviling can reach a pitch where the loser must be silent or accept death.[6] Even when the reviling is absent, such as in the *rājasūya*, or royal consecration, the contest remains at a fever pitch with chariot races, dicing games, and so on, as a basic part of the proceedings (Heesterman 1985: 89). Heesterman and other scholars have observed that, while it is not an exhaustive idiom, much of this agonistic language is also expressed in terms of guest reception and hospitality exchange.[7]

For example, one passage in a Vedic ritual text mentions the passing of a car, or chariot, through someone else's sacrificial fires and ritual enclosure, thus signifying a kind of battle. And even in the most innocuous of Vedic rituals, the *agnihotṛ*, the sacrificer still retains a *vajra*, a sword, possibly as a remnant of self-defence. As Heesterman puts it, 'the need for food forces humans to enter into a violent contract with the sacred, and thus requires giving up what is obtained by transgression through the sacrificial offering'.

While Heesterman's original scenario is not universally accepted, his work points to the basic tone of the Vedic world, which address the terror of violence inherent in the sacrifice. Perhaps the most well-known story is that of Śunaḥśepa. In this story, King Hariścandra's rigid *tapas* finally persuades Varuṇa to give him a son, on the divine condition that the king sacrifice it back to the god. The king finds the Brahmin Śunaḥśepa to substitute for the sacrifice, and when Śunaḥśepa is about to be killed, he recites the correct *mantra*, showing his ritual knowledge. He thereby gains release of himself, the king and his son. Śunaḥśepa must be reincorporated into the Brahmin world, however, and is adopted by the sage Viśvāmitra. His adoption incurs rivalry and violence amongst his brothers.[8] The evil of death thus becomes transferred to the arena of Brahminhood.

The story of Śunaḥśepa is a good example of what the sacrificial victim might have felt like before he was actually given to the gods. Śunaḥśepa's symbolic death makes him an ambivalently charged 'remnant' who needs reintegration into society: one wonders if he has actually died or not in terms of sacrificial categories. The same ruminations about violence in the Vedic meditations about the sin of Brahmincide are introduced early in many hymns of the Vedas. Sacrifice involves death, and death involves sacrifice, and the brahminical/priestly management of this symbolic economy is one of the central preoccupations of the early Vedic texts. How can one integrate violent death into a narrative about something which is claimed as primordially creative?

As the narrative progresses, the normalization occurs in ways other than if the human victim actually had been killed. We have some very powerful examples of this ambiguity in the discussion of the human victim in the *Śatapatha Brāhmaṇa* (13.6.2.12–13). As Houben also notes, when this description of the sacrifice reaches the point where the victim is to be killed, the text switches to narrative mode, and past tense:

> Victims had the fire carried around them, but were not yet slaughtered. Then a voice says to the sacrificer and priests, addressing them as Puruṣa : 'Do not establish (*saṃtiṣṭhipo*) them [as victims], because if you did establish them, *puruṣa* would eat *puruṣa*'.
>
> (2001: 120)

The text goes on, 'After the fire had been carried around them, he set them free and offered oblations to the same divinities'. Houben sees here the beginning of embarrassment about killing; Schmidt (1997: 212) sees the beginnings of *ahiṃsā*. In the terms of this article, I would read here an issue of integration after potential or actual violence. For a time, at least, saved victims such as these, or Śunaḥśepa, will remain a remnant, and potentially 'non-integrated' and 'incoherent', in Daniel's terms. This status might be similar to the status of a 'survivor' today – someone who by virtue of their experience of violence is marked as outside in some significant way.

The portrayal of Śunaḥśepa as a kind of sacrificial remnant allows us to raise one of the basic questions that all of us ask in the dynamic of consumption involving violence: *whether something we consume is dead or alive*. There are other, very powerful images in early Indian sacrificial texts that also attempt to deal with the issues of violence and harm by claiming something is alive even as it is destroyed. The softer example of this is the question of the famous and all too often cited Puruṣa who is sacrificed in RV 10.90: nowhere does the hymn explicitly state that Puruṣa has died. He is simply divided. We will see another compelling example of this in RV 10.162.

The story of Sthūra and his companions provides a more direct and compelling example. A group of sacrificers started a long-term sacrificial session, called a *sattra*. Their leader, Sthūra, is defeated and killed in an encounter with a hostile band. The survivors, bereft and uncertain, mourn their slain leader. One of the members has a vision of the slain Sthūra passing from the place of sacrifice to the offering fire at the eastern end of the sacrificial arena, going upward from the fire and entering heaven. This member calls out, 'Do not lament; that one whom you are lamenting has gone upward from the hearth of the offering and entered heaven'. Thus, Sthūra's followers gain praise and honour.[9] This motif of the heavenly reward of the slain sacrificer is taken up again in the motif of the slain warrior in the *Mahābhārata*, which we will discuss below.

Even more intriguingly, however, this story of Sthūra shows that death is necessary for the gaining of a goal, perhaps even more necessary than sacrificial perfection or the appropriate performance of the ritual rules. Tellingly, the story of Sthūra illustrates the larger rule about appropriate times to conclude a long sacrificial session: these are the times when the sacrificers have reached a place called Plakṣa Praśravaṇa – close to the middle of the world.[10] They can end their sacrifice when the cows they have taken with them increase tenfold, or when they have lost all property, or when their leader dies. Notice that it is heightened abundance, or dramatic loss or death, which leads to the conclusion and appropriate end of the sacrifice'.

Sthūra's journey to heaven after violent death is also echoed in many Vedic hymns, most notably and movingly in the hymn to the horse. The controversy of Jha's recent book[11] aside, it is quite clear that the horse was ritually slaughtered in the *aśvamedha*, or horse sacrifice, according to specific rules and roles of various priests, including the 'butcher' priest.[12] In addition, *mantras* were sung to accompany this act. One of them was whispered to the horse as the sacrifice was being conducted; these *mantra*s counteract the fact of the horse's being slain and sectioned, and focus on his path to heaven instead. Verses 13–21 of RV 1.162 are particularly striking in this regard:

> 13 The small testing rod for the pot that cooks the flesh, the dishes for pouring the broth, the cover of the bowls to keep it warm, the hooks, the meat plates – all these wait for the horse.
> 14 Wherever he walks, where he rests, where he rolls himself, and the fetters on the horse's feet, and what he has drunk and the fodder he has eaten – let all of that be with you, even among the gods.
> 15 Let not the fire, smelling of smoke, cover you up, nor the glowing pot splinter. The gods receive the horse who has been sacrificed, worshiped, consecrated, and blessed with the cry of Vaṣat!
> 16 The garment that they spread beneath the horse, the upper garment, the golden trappings on him, the halter and the fetters on his feet – let these things that are dear hold fast to the horse among the gods.
> 17 If someone riding you spurred you on with heel or whip or by rushing, I make all these things well again for you with the sacred word, like the oblation's ladle in sacrifices.
> 18 The axe cuts through the thirty four ribs of the racehorse who is the companion of the gods. Keep the limbs uninjured and place them in the proper pattern. Cut them apart, calling out limb by limb.
> 19 One is the slaughterer of the horse of Tvaṣṭṛ; two restrain him. This is the rule. As many of your limbs as I set out, according to the rules, so many balls I offer into the fire.
> 20 Let not your dear soul hurt you as you go away. Let not the axe do durable damage to your body. Let no greedy butcher without skill treat the cut limbs in the wrong way with the knife.
> 21 You do not really die through this, nor are you harmed. You go to the gods on the paths pleasant to go on. The two bay stallions, the two roan mares are now your chariot mates. The racehorse was placed in the yoke of the donkey.[13]

In this hymn, the fact of death and harm is pushed against in a very direct way, and the images of injury are replaced by the imagery of chariots, all the best accoutrements of a horse's life staying with him, even among the gods (v. 14, 16). Indeed, verse by verse, each of the sacrificial acts of slaughter are transformed through prayer into forms of healing for the horse (v. 17, in particular).

Many have understandably read this hymn as a kind of explicit denial of death, an erasure of the fact of intentionally inflicted injury. But one might further ask, What kinds of denial (for there are many)? And is there only denial? Or perhaps even more subtly, What different understandings of violence – both integratable and non-integratable – are expressed in the hymn? If we take the hermeneutic principle of polysemy seriously, then we might assume this hymn, as in other Vedic hymns, contains several layers of meaning at once. As many have noted, we cannot know the full intentions of Vedic poets, but rather only the shadows of their intentions. However, even with such a play of shadows, complexity should be the hermeneutical principle of the day.

Let us examine some of this multiplicity in a little more detail. It is clear that the perfection of the horses' limbs as they are sacrificed is more important than its remaining a whole horse here on earth. Verse 15ab suggests that the horse does not make a sound, for we know from other texts that if he does an expiation rite is necessary (*mā tuvāgnir dhvanayīd dhūmagandhir mokhā bhrajanti abhi vikta jaghriḥ*). An alternative reading might suggest that the limbs themselves not boil too loudly so that the cauldron does not split. The second part of the verse 15cd, as well as the following one, 16, suggests that the gods only accept a horse which has been duly consecrated in this manner (*iṣṭaṃ vītam abhigūrtaṃ vaṣatkṛtaṃ taṃ devāsaḥ prati gṛbhṇanti aśvam*). Verse 16 mentions the covering, the head ropes, foot ropes, and golden trappings which should also attend his body. Even more significantly, in verse 18 the limbs of the horse must remain uncut, and whole (*achidrā gātrā*), while the pieces are named one by one (*paruṣ parur anughuṣyā*). In verse 20, the wholeness of the horse's body is protected against clumsy butchers, so that the body is not hacked in the wrong place (*mā te gṛdhnur aviśastātihāya achidra gātrāṇi asinā mithū kaḥ*). Note here, too, that *division* is necessary and not necessarily harmful, and mentioned throughout the verses of the hymn. However, *cutting*, particularly in the wrong place, is associated with harming.

And what are we to make of the verses of explicit denial that constitute verse 20 and 21? The language is intriguing here: in verse 20b, continuing the theme of the earlier verses, the poet states that the axe should not do lasting harm to the horse's body (*mā svadhitis tanva tanvā ā tiṣṭhipat te*). And yet the earlier part of the verse gives us a discussion of not mourning, or not burning the self, or the soul, as it goes on its journey (*mā tvā tapat priya ātmāpiyantam*). This language does not suggest straightforward denial, but rather an acknowledgment of a state of affairs which may be interpreted another way. The denial does not involve ignoring or being silent about the fact of injury or harm, but rather a straightforward struggle with the fact that one wishes it were not true. And in verse 20, you do not really die, nor are you harmed – emphatic *etan* singles out the fact of death – *na va u etan mriyase na riṣasi*. This sentence structure begs the question of whether, in fact, death is indeed involved and must be argued against. (The Vedic verb *riṣ*, here, is 'to be injured, suffer wrong', but related to and not always distinguishable from *riś*, 'to hurt, tear, or pluck off'.)[14]

A narrative reading of this hymn to the horse, then, might suggest verses partly tinged with pathos, or perhaps even tragic irony, in response to incontrovertible physical evidence of the division of a body. We cannot forget that the application of the hymn occurred during the divisions of the meat – clear evidence that the horse is no longer alive and has been violently killed. Other parts of the RV 10.162 (8bcd) suggest that the parts of the horse may also stick to the axe (*svadhitau*), the sacrificial post (*svarau*), or the hands and nails of the slaughterer (*yad dhastayoḥśamitur yan nakheṣu*). The poet asks that they, too, 'go to the gods' (*sarvāte api deveṣu astu*).

In other verses, we might read a triumphant argument with the fact of death, and other places may express a certain tragic wish that the harm done to the horse be ameliorated. The descriptions of violence in these verses need not be read only doctrinally, but rather more like one might read the famous Shakespearian phrase, 'Death, where is thy sting?' – a phrase to which Western tradition has imputed deep and multiple meanings. There is no real reason not to do so here as well.

Most importantly, we might return to the original formulation of this essay: what wholeness is greater than bodily wholeness? And how might the violence be made coherent? It is clear that the metaphorical wholeness of the horse as a symbol of the sacrifice, as well as the perfection of its divided limbs, is more important than the harm that might be done in actually dividing the horse here on earth. Like Sthūra, the horse's death is made coherent by its reintegration in the next life. But the fact that both harm and death are mentioned, even in forceful arguments against them, suggests not just a denial, but a deeper understanding of the cost than previous analyses have allowed.

Relatedly, our discussion of cutting and division above is relevant to our concerns with weapons, those knives that the butcher uses that are forms of 'practical reasoning' about violence. It should be an important and final note that the use of weaponry in the Vedic period is also charged with sacrificial imagery. The 'Hymn to the Weapons', RV 6.75,[15] is a powerful example of a hymn that is uttered either to the warriors protecting the horse in the *aśvamedha*, or to the weapons that are about to be used in battle. The protective armour is both physical armour and the protective power of the sacrifice (v. 1, 10); the bow allows the warrior to win contests similar to those of sacrificial contests and is the seed of Parjanya, the rain god (v. 3, 15); the wagon on which the weapons of transport are placed is called the 'oblation' and is compared to the oblation which carries the Soma to the gods in the sacrifice (v. 8). So too Agni is the carrier of the oblation and the wagon; Soma, the sacrificial drink, is also the armour which dresses the wounds (v. 18).

This hymn, compellingly constructed with many different kinds of metaphors, is an important image with which to think about violence in early India. Weapons and their use are tools of destruction but also tools of sacrificial regeneration. The hymn implies that their ethical use focuses on their ability to protect against wounding and to preserve the idea of the sacred order, or *ṛta*, which is assumed to be an ethical good in its own right. Their power derives, both metaphorically and actually, from their status as sacrificial tools. Thus, in continuity with our earlier discussion of the hymn to the horse, violence is imagined as necessary physical harm which the sacrifice itself can overcome.

The *Upaniṣads*: violence as metaphor

As is well known, the *Upaniṣads* departed from the basic elaboration of these ritual themes. Rather, they used sacrifice as a reference point, a metaphor, for the focus upon and realization of the self (*ātman*) and the identity of the self with the all-important force that animates the world (*Brahman*). Some scholars (including those discussed above) have called this process 'the internalization of the sacrifice'. It is important to note that this is not 'rejection of the sacrifice in favor of philosophy' as some earlier scholars have characterized the Upaniṣadic move. While Upaniṣadic perspectives differ from each other, all draw from a common stock of stories, dialogues, and metaphorical constructions involving famous kings and teachers from a broad geographic spread, covering the Gangetic plain from Kuru Pañcala in the West to Kośala Videha in the East. This Upaniṣadic way of life expressed a radically different social and political reality from the heyday of Vedic society. There is a strong presence of movement across kingdoms and a high level of trade amongst kingdoms. In addition, kings (*kṣatriyas*) are as strong as Brahmins in their theological prowess and concerns. However, while this strong presence has led some earlier historians to hypothesize that *kṣatriyas* may have been the authors of the *Upaniṣads*, it is fairer to say that the mutual relationship between the Brahmins and the *kṣatriyas* took on a new vibrancy as kings played a new role in the emerging urban landscape. As Olivelle and others have argued,[16] the consolidation of kingdoms led to their being a kind of town/wilderness split which fostered such institutions as celibacy and asceticism. This system could be supported by the more established kingdoms, as the Aryan tribes were no longer simply constantly on the move and concerned about their own survival.

That is not to say, however, that sacrifice and the question of bodily harm is completely superceded or ignored. In fact, it is quite clear that sacrifice is still part of the increasingly complex world that the *Upaniṣads* represent. *Chandogya Upaniṣad* 8.15 states the ideal of a virtuous life – one who lives in his teacher's house, does daily tasks for the teacher, and then returns to his own house and performs daily Vedic recitation in a clean place, rears virtuous children and draws all sense organs into himself and refrains from killing any creature except in the presence of sacrifices/holy places/worthy people (*tīrtha*); the one who lives this way all his life attains the world of Brahman and does not return again (*ahiṃsan sarvabhūtāny anyatra tīrthebhyaḥ/ sa khalv evaṃ vartayan yāvad āyuṣaṃ brahmalokam abhisāṃpadyate//*). The word *tīrtha* here is ambivalent, and can mean all three of the options I have given above. As Olivelle notes, the word could mean that one slaughters as one would in a sacrifice, or at a pilgrimage place, or for special food in preparation for a guest.

The refraining from killing here is important to note, for two reasons: first, it is a function of a life geared toward the perception of Brahman. *Ahiṃsā*, or non-injury, occurs here for the first time in combination with these other elements. Non-injury is part of the withdrawal of the senses and the well-lived life, rather than an ethical principle that stands apart from all other aspects of a well-lived life. Second, it is not a radical *ahiṃsā*, but one which allows for killing under certain kinds of circumstances. The results of a closer reading go against simply reading the passage as 'evidence' for a 'doctrine'.

Ahiṃsā appears again connected to sacrifice in *Chandogya Upaniṣad* 3.17.4. The passage mentions *ahiṃsā*, along with austerity (*tapas*), generosity (*dānam*), integrity (*ārjavam*), and truthfulness (*satyavacanam*) in a list of virtues listed metaphorically as 'sacrificial gifts' (*dakṣina*). Keeping in mind, however, the recently discussed Vedic hymn to the horse 1.162 (which is also from a chronologically later book of the RV, and therefore closer to the Upaniṣadic world view), it is clear that even sacrificing the horse was not conceived of as injury, but argued against as its opposite.[17]

In light of these rather ambivalent passages connecting householder sacrifice and *ahiṃsā*, one way of thinking about violence in this new Upaniṣadic context is the *prāṇāgnihotra* – the fire sacrifice of breath. It is, in a sense, the infusion of the meal and the sacrifice in a single person of the (metaphorical) sacrificer, who, in order to achieve transcendent goals, must remove himself from society. Whereas the earlier sacrificer (*dīkṣita*) wanted to return to society, the person performing the sacrifice of the breaths wants to keep himself removed from the toss and tumble of every day settled life, and turn away from the practical need for dependence on, or cooperation with, others.[18] Knowledge becomes the all-important goal, and in one who knows, all opposites become one in transcendent realization. As Bodewitz notes in conversation with Tull, just because something was defined as 'not killing' does not mean that such a definition would stop the killing (2001: 33).

Violence, then, becomes a matter of perception of the self. To return to the frame of this article, physical injury is integrated by becoming a metaphor, if one defines metaphor as Ricoeur (1979: 213) does, as a form of 'seeing as'.[19] As *Bṛhadāraṇyaka Upaniṣad* 4.1.3 states in the famous dialogue between Janaka and Yājñavalkya:

> If a man is afraid of getting killed when he travels somewhere, Your Majesty, it is because he loves his breath (*api tatra vadhāśaṅka bhavati yām diśam eti prāṇasyaiva samrāṭ kāmāya*). So clearly, Your Majesty, the highest Brahman is breath. When a man knows and venerates it as such, breath never abandons him, and all beings flock to him; he becomes a god and joins the company of gods.[20]

This fear of getting killed, then, is the platform upon which one can realize the nature of Brahman, and humanity's correct relationship to it. It is nothing else than love of breath, which one should hold dear. One holds breath dear not in order to cling to life unnecessarily, but to understand the ways in which the breath is the foundation of Brahman.

Later in the dialogue, Yājñavalkya compares the knowledge of the *ātman* to the kind of sleep where one has no desires and sees no dreams. So, too, the experience of violence and harm is a form of perception, of 'seeing as', which is not free from desire and sorrows. But with knowledge of Brahman, even violent acts in dreams are experienced differently:

> Now, when people appear to kill or vanquish him, when an elephant appears to chase him, or when he appears to fall into a pit, he is only ignorantly imagining dangers that he had seen while he was awake (*atha yatrainaṃ ghnantīva hastīva jinantīva vicchāyayati gartam iva patati yad eva jāgradbhayaṃpaśyati tad atrāvidyayā*). But when he, appearing to be a god or a king, thinks, 'I alone am this world! I am all!' – that is the highest world. Now this is the aspect of his that is beyond what appears to be good, freed from what is bad, and without fear.
>
> (4.3.20–22)[21]

Chandogya Upaniṣad (5.10.9) goes so far as to say that someone who knows the five fires which constitute Brahman are not tainted, even when they associate with someone who kills a Brahmin (*atha ha ya etān evaṃ pañcāgnīn veda na saha tair apy ācaran pāpamanā lipyate*).

In a final consideration, Indra and Prajāpati, as student and teacher respectively, debate on this very issue during the long years of tutelage in heaven amongst the gods. As Prajāpati has explained the same point as Yājñavalkya, that the person who goes happily about in a dream, free from desire, is the one who knows Brahman. However Indra also wonders:

> This self is clearly unaffected by the faults of the body – it is not killed when this body is slain or rendered lame when this body becomes lame. Nevertheless people do in a way kill it and chase after it; it does in a way experience unpleasant things; and in a way it even cries. I see nothing worthwhile in this.
>
> (*Chandogya Upaniṣad* 8.10.1–3)[22]

Prajāpati continues to teach transcendence, and the *Chandogya Upaniṣad* 8 concludes its lesson, and its entire teaching, with the passage discussed above – the meditation on someone who learns the Vedas, does daily Vedic recitation in a clean place, rears virtuous children, draws all sense organs into himself, and refrains from killing any creature except at a *tīrtha*. Someone who lives this way all his life attains the world of Brahman, and does not return again.

So, too, the treatment of weaponry in the *Upaniṣads* takes an extreme metaphorical nature – even more so than in the Vedas. In the *Kauṣītaki Upaniṣad* 4.7, Balaki discusses the person in the wind as the person to be venerated in the verbal dialogue between himself and King Ajataśatru. King Ajataśatru rejects this, and says, 'Don't drag me into a discussion about him! I venerate him only as Indra Vaikuṇṭha, the invincible weapon. Anyone who venerates him in this way will be victorious and invincible, and he will triumph over his adversaries'. Here, the weapon is part of a god, and part of the wind. But it is clearly only a part, and not the whole of Brahman, and to be used in a general way against adversaries.

So too, in the *Muṇḍaka Upaniṣad*, the teaching itself is revered as a weapon, to be used as the means by which to attain Brahman. The author admonishes the seeker:

> Take, my friend, this bow,
> this great weapon of *upaniṣad*;
> place veneration on it
> as the whetted arrow;
> stretch it with the thought fixed on the nature of thought;
> that very imperishable is the target, my friend.
> Strike it![23]

Here, the weapon becomes a cosmological tool, and its object is Brahman. The success of the weapon becomes the success with which the seeker finds, or strikes, Brahman.

These Upaniṣadic passages show that injury is made coherent through a very real process of training the mind to see harm as something other than, and less than, Brahman. Killing, being killed, and sleep are identified as the same psychic states. So, too, the weapons which, in the Vedic period, were powerful physical objects where pieces of flesh could stick, now become the mind itself. Death is a metaphor, and the weapon is the power of perception to make the metaphor stick.

Arthaśāstra and the pragmatics of the state

Despite their courtly dialogues, it is unclear what the Upaniṣadic sages' relationship was to the workings of the state. However, one could not end this section on pre-classical India without mention of the manual of statecraft, the *Arthaśāstra*, composed by Kauṭilya around the fourth century BCE. This text's attitudes toward violence are very similar to the *Dharma Sūtras*, but unlike those texts, Kauṭilya is in some ways equally concerned with affairs of the state as with affairs of caste. *Arthaśāstra* 1.3.13 includes *ahiṃsā* in the list for all people and classes, which also includes *satyam* and *śaucam*. As Bodewitz (2001: 37) also notes, *brahmacarya* and *aparigraha* are missing as elements – a fact which suggests that *ahiṃsā* had reached a larger audience than just the celibate practitioners.

Exact punishments for bodily injury are explained in 3.19, and physical injury itself is defined as 'touching (*sparśanam*)', 'menacing (*avagūrṇam*)', and 'striking (*prahatam*)'.[24] Distinctions are made between touching the upper body and the lower body, pressing, squeezing, causing hurt without blood, causing hurt with blood, breaking a limb, and so forth. Physical injury also involves theft, injury to property, as well as injury to small and large animals, and to plants and trees. Each carries their own specific punishment.

Of particular interest within the section on punishments is Kauṭilya's hierarchy of expiation (3.19.12). In cases of 'holding' (*avalembaneṣu*), the fine increases depending upon whether it is the feet (the lowest fine), the garment, the hand or the hair (the highest). So too the fine for a basic wound without blood (*duḥkhaṃ aśoṇitam utpāda*) is 24 *paṇa*s, whereas for causing bleeding (*śoṇitam utpādane*), the fine is double that amount. The lowest fine for serious beating is breaking the extremities, such as the hands, feet, teeth, ear and nose, or opening up wounds. The middle fine involves the thigh or neck, or the eyes, or obstructions in bodily movement or speech. And the highest fine involves wounding unto death. This basic graduated scheme also applies to animals (3.19.26) – presumably outside the sacrifice, and for trees, the idea of bleeding is transferred into the cutting off of branches (3.19.28).

Kauṭilya also argues with those who say that the court makes judgments in favour of those who run to the court first. In his view, witnesses alone should help decide the case, and if there are no witnesses, then the wounds themselves (*ghātaḥ*) or the signs of scuffle (*kalahopaliṅganaṃ*). Kauṭilya shows an intriguing view quite similar to our own 'forensic' perspective; that wounds and bodily marks can 'speak' in cases of adjudication, as can evidence from the site of the crime itself.

Equally significant, and markedly different from bodily injury, are the rules of whether to make war or peace. These are contained in the section on foreign policy (7.1). As the first verse of the chapter states, 'The six measures of foreign policy are peace (*saṃdhi*), war (*vigraha*), staying quiet (*āsana*), marching (*yāna*), seeking shelter (*saṃśraya*), and the dual policy of peace and war at the same time (*dvaidhībhāva*)'. Verses 6–12 explain, 'entering into a treaty is peace; doing injury is war. Remaining indifferent is staying quiet. Augmentation of one's powers in marching. Submitting to another is seeking shelter. Peace with one and war with another is dual policy' (*tatra paṇbandhaḥ saṃdhi/ apakāro vigraḥa/ upekṣaṇam āsanaṃ/ abhuccayo yānam/ parārpaṇaṃ saṃśrayaḥ/ saṃdhi-vigrahopādānaṃ dvaidhībhāvaḥ/ iti ṣaḍguṇāḥ*).[25]

Kauṭilya goes on to describe exactly when a king should decide on what is in his best interest, and what proper course of foreign policy to take. Most of the criteria for deciding the course depend on his assessment of his own and his enemies' relative positions, and whether he will be able to obtain equal results for him and his enemy. Significantly, the attitude towards violence in this case is that whatever is best for the kingdom justifies harm. Verse 7.3.15 gives a persuasive example of this kind of pragmatic thinking about state-initiated violence: 'Even in the case of simultaneity of calamities, if he were to see: "I am in a greater calamity, the enemy in a lighter calamity will easily overcome his own calamity, and attack"; even the stronger should make peace' (v. 15) (*vyasanayaugapadye 'pi 'guruvyasano 'smi laghuvyasanaḥ paraḥ sukhena pratikṛtya vyasanam ātmano 'bhiyuñjyād' iti paśyej jyāyān api saṃdhīyeta*). Or, if by resorting to peace or war, he were not to see the weakening of the enemy or increase in his own strength, then even the stronger should stay quiet (v. 16) (*saṃdhivigrahayoś cet parakarśanam ātmopacayaṃ vā nā 'bhipaśyej jyāyān apy āsīta*).[26] In the *Arthaśāstra*, we have a worldly contrast to the metaphoric attitude toward violence in the *Upaniṣads*. Not unlike present times, state interests and calculations determine the question of group violence.

Overall, Kauṭilya codifies injury in a pragmatic way. Because his main concerns are restitution and the restoration of social balance, he assumed that the members of the social whole will do things that undermine that whole. Particularly in cases of individual injury, Kauṭilya's concern with expiation is taxonomical, and not with the larger ideal for which it might be worth risking bodily injury. However, in its concern with the maintenance of the kingdom, there are clear allowances to be made for physical injury. In the terms set out earlier in this article, the kingdom is the ideal for which the integrity of the body might be sacrificed. Its laws tell very particular narratives whereby violence is normalized through exact measures of punishment in the case of the body, and exact calculations of risk in the case of the state.

The *Mahābhārata*: the ambivalent connection between *dharma* and violence

The classical period started perhaps with the advent of the epics whose final compilation occurred as early as the second century BCE. As is well known, this period witnessed the advent of devotional practices in the new pantheon of Śiva, Viṣṇu, Brahmā, and the pan-Indian goddess Devī. It also emphasized royal patronage of temples and the arts, culminating in the flowering of the Gupta empire in the fourth century CE. As the Mīmāṃsā, or ritual-philosophical thinkers also attest, this period witnessed the emergence of *dharma* as a central principle in Hinduism. Whatever *ahiṃsā*'s ultimate origins, as Alsdorf (1962) and Hans-Peter Schmidt (1968) suggest, during this period the idea of non-injury became incorporated into the *dharma* texts. (It is also important to note here that Mīmāṃsā authors are quite clear in their refutation of *ahiṃsā* as absolute authority.) More importantly for our purposes, sacrifice was set apart in an autonomous sphere of its own, and animal sacrifice was limited to appropriate place, time and purpose within exact social confines.[27]

Violence in the *Mahābhārata* emerges during the epic period – that time in which the doctrines of *ahiṃsā* have had full chance to grow and flourish, and be readapted into the brahminical milieu. In the *Mahābhārata*, we see several distinct approaches to violence: 1) the motif of war as the final sacrifice, as a kind of fatal doom, a *pralāya*, or dissolution, of time itself; 2) violence as a necessary but costly form of *dharma*; and 3) non-violence as the highest goal for the spiritual adept.

Several passages in the *Mahābhārata* refer to the war between the Paṇdava brothers as a kind of sacrifice, a war to end all sacrifices (*Mahābhārata* 1.2.12). One passage refers to the final battle as the ending of the warrior race (7.11.43). Several scholars (most recently Jatavallabhula 2001) have argued that the motif of the war in a kind of epoch-ending sacrifice is the central motif of the text.[28] So too, the *dvaparayuga*, or second to last *yuga*, is ended by the *Mahābhārata* war, as is also the practice of sacrifice. Thus, the violence is so great and all powerful, it is the ultimate end of certain forms of violent worship as we know them. The Bhārata war, then, is the sacrifice to end all sacrifices.

In one particularly telling passage in the *Sabhā Parvan*, Yudhiṣṭhira is both encouraged and warned by Narada to undertake the *rājasūya*, or kingly coronation sacrifice, for in doing so he will be able to go into that region of his ancestors which is inhabited by the chief of the immortals. But in doing so, he goes on to give a warning that the sacrifice is filled with many obstacles.

> There are Brahmin *rakṣasas*, who obstruct the sacrifice, and find the flaws. A battle follows therein, and in its purview, the destruction of the earth, and there will be a sign that causes destruction. Think about this, my Lord, and do what is appropriate. Always grow into the protection of the society of the four *varṇas*. Prosper, and be happy, and give gifts to the twice-born. (*Bahuvighnaś ca nṛpate kratur eṣa smṛto mahān/ chidrāṇy atra hi vāñchanti yajñaghnā brahmarākṣasāḥ// yuddhaṃ ca pṛṣṭhagamanaṃ pṛthivīkṣayakārakam/ kiṃ cid eva nimittaṃ ca bhavaty atra kṣayāvaham// etat saṃchintya rājendra yat kṣamaṃ tat samācara/ apramattotthito nityaṃ cāturvarṇyasya rakṣaṇe/ bhava edhasva modasva dānais tarpaya ca dvijān//*).
>
> (2.11.68–70)

Thus, in going ahead with this sacrifice, whose likely result is cataclysmic war, Yudhiṣṭhira is admonished by Narada to behave as dharmically as possible; being watchful and ready in protecting the four orders of his subjects, growing in prosperity.[29] Notice here that the prospect of world-ending violence is immediately juxtaposed with *dharma*, or right action, thus setting up one of the basic tensions of the entire epic.[30] This question gives rise to the many discussions on *ahiṃsā* in the *Mahābhārata*, such as the moving, and oddly familiar, statement of Bhīṣma's that one should always avoid the destruction of the lives of other creatures, and that one should not do to others what is abhorrent to the self (*yad anyair vihitaṃ necched ātmānaṃ karma pūruṣaḥ/ na ta tat pareṣu kurvitā jānann apriyam ātmanaḥ*) (12.251.19)[31] Yet it also gives rise to another question: How can one behave righteously, given the inevitability of violence and even its dharmic sanction?

We can see this question apparent even in the *Mahābhārata*'s episodes concerning weapons. Arjuna's travel to the land of Kailash involves a test by Śiva, in which Śiva kills an animal with his powerful weapon, Paśupat, at the same time that Arjuna kills it.[32] Arjuna queries who could have shot the animal at the same time as himself, a dharmic question. When Śiva appears, Arjuna understands that he has been undergoing a test. Śiva grants him the boon of the weapon of Paśupat to be used in the war against the Kauravas, and with the ability to use it at will. This small episode underscores the fact that one must prove oneself worthy of certain kinds of weapons. Later in the heat of battle, when Aśvatthama releases his world-destroying weapon, Kṛṣṇa tells Arjuna to release his Paśupat. The participants in the battle anticipate a cataclysmic effect, and begin to meditate. As a result, the world shifts in its orbit slightly, and the weapons fly off the face of the earth, never to return.[33] Catastrophe has been avoided.

Again, the episode implies that such weapons are not simply magical, but require contemplation.

Many have suggested that the frame of dharmic violence is the most appropriate way to read the *Bhagavad Gītā* – not as a sanction for war, but rather an answer to the questions raised so painfully by Arjuna in his dialogue with Kṛṣṇa. His question at the beginning of the dialogue is a version of the one we asked above: How can one behave according to *dharma* in the face of such overwhelming and inevitable kind of destruction? Rather, we read it as Van Buitenen does in his 1979 translation: in the *Gītā* there are no more happy warriors, only resigned ones'.[34] Thus, the *Gītā* itself might be read as an implicit critique of the excesses of sacrificial violence, even as the warrior *dharma* is, as Arjuna is instructed by Kṛṣṇa, to go ahead and fight.

The *Gītā* also uses metaphors of weapons quite similar to those of the *Upaniṣads*. As Kṛṣṇa counsels Arjuna in the fourth chapter: 'Son of Bharata, when, with the knife of wisdom, you have cut this doubt that lives in the heart, and begins in ignorance, then stand up – and go to yoga!' (4.42)[35] (*tasmād anjñāna saṃbhūtaṃ hṛtsthaṃ jñānāsinā 'tmanaḥ/ chittvainaṃ saṃśayaṃ yogam ātiṣṭhottiṣṭha bhārata//*). Both the spiritual and the physical actions of war are alluded to here, in a kind of double reference to *kṣatriya dharma*, which involves restraint, as well as skill with the spiritual weaponry of knowledge, the *Gītā*'s main arguments.

Relatedly, in 18.53, Kṛṣṇa also counsels Arjuna to relinquish force itself: 'Abandoning the ego – force, pride, desire, anger and grasping – without a sense of "mine", and at peace, then one is fit for the being of *Brahman*' (*ahaṃkāraṃ balaṃ darpaṃ kāmaṃ krodhaṃ parigrahaṃ/ vimucya nirmanaḥ śānto brahmabhūyāya kalpate//*).

How does abandoning force square with the idea of warrior *dharma*? Gandhi's interpretation of this tension in the *Gītā* involved two different moves: first is that for that time, warrior *dharma* was not seen as force if it was done for a righteous cause. Tilak, of course, took this one step further and wrote from his jail cell that for the twentieth century, too, such force was necessary in the service of a righteous cause against British oppression. The second is that the ideas about warriorhood should be taken as a spiritual exercise, as a kind of non-violent militancy. Space does not permit us here to repeat the myriad views of scholars on the issue; suffice it to say that in the *Gītā*, there is enough material similar to the two statements above, which combine a kind of dharmic restraint, spiritual use of warrior imagery, and exhortation to fight, to make these differing kinds of interpretations possible.[36] Following Daniel, we might see in the *Gītā* a genealogical impulse which challenges 'normality' of violence, in tension with the more theological impulse toward its integration.

Perhaps this multiplicity of views about violence within the epics makes it easier for epic texts to comment upon the violence within the story itself. This is certainly true of the famous episode in the *Kiṣkindhā Kāṇḍa* of the *Rāmāyaṇa*, involving Rāma's killing of Vāli. While in many ways, the *Rāmāyaṇa*'s battle is clearly a less ambiguous one, in which there is a clear victory of 'good' over 'evil' (see Jatavallabhula 2001: 102), its narratives still do possess tension and argument, where alternative voices are entertained and then discarded.

As the story goes, the monkey Sugrīva is in a battle over the kingship with his brother Vāli. Sugrīva assumes, after Vāli spends many months inside a cavern fighting the demon Mayavi, that Vāli has been vanquished and killed. Sugrīva takes over the kingdom and some time later Vāli returns alive. He is enraged at what his brother has done, and seizes Vāli's wife, and drives him out of the kingdom. Sugrīva takes refuge in a place which has been cursed by a sage to be out of bounds to Vāli, and pleads with Rāma to address the situation. Vāli and Sugrīva fight in a passionate battle, and Rāma finally intervenes, shooting Vāli from a place of hiding.

Before this scenario, Vāli explains that he has done nothing to deserve such an adharmic killing; he has not encroached upon territory, and did not commit an act of aggression. There is no land, gold or beautiful women to be had in this country; nor, he admonishes Rāma, is he allowed to be eaten by men, as it is dharmically forbidden. Accusing Rāma of breaking the code of morality, Vāli asks: 'Having perpetrated this crime of indiscriminate killing, what will you tell the holy men concerning yourself?'[37]

As he lies dying, Vāli questions Rāma on the *dharma* of his own violent act, and they engage in a discussion of when and how it is appropriate to kill in the manner that Rāma has chosen. Vāli says

> I have been slain by the elephant, Rāma. He has abandoned the elephant-goad of *dharma*, ignored the *dharma* of the virtuous ones, and broken the chain of good conduct. What will you say to the virtuous ones after you have returned to be in their company, after committing this impure, improper act, which anyone worthy would blame?
>
> (*chinnacāritryakakṣyena satāṃ dharmātivartinā/ tyaktadharmāṅkuśenāhaṃ nihato rāmahastinā// aśubhaṃ cāpy ayuktaṃ ca satām caiva vigarhitam/ vakṣyase cedṛśaṃ kṛtvā sadbhiḥ saha samāgataḥ//*)
>
> (17.44–45).

And later: 'Rāma, you are like a serpent who kills men when they are asleep; you are overcome by wrongdoing, and killed me, who am difficult to conquer, by keeping yourself out of sight in battle' (*tavyādṛśyena tu raṇe nihato 'haṃ durāsadaḥ/ prasuptaḥ pannageneva naraḥ pāpavaśaṃ gataḥ/* (7.47)).

Note here that the issue of violence is reflected upon with a different use of metaphors than the ones we read in the *Upaniṣads*. In the *Upaniṣads*, violence itself is like a dream when one was sleeping, and the weapons are the spiritual weapons of the self. Yet here, the violence is likened by Vāli to an elephant who has run amok, and *dharma* is likened to the tools used to control an elephant. In Vāli's eyes, not only is this lack of control evident in Rāma, but in addition, there is a cowardice in warfare when, like a snake who strikes when the victim is asleep, people strike others out of a hidden place.

In *Kiṣkindhā Kaṇḍa* 19, Rāma replies that Vāli does not know *dharma* and yet he blames him. Rāma goes on to reason, that, according to the code of righteousness, one should treat one's younger brother, or one's son, or one's disciple as one's own son (*jyeṣṭho bhrātā pitā vāpi yaś ca vidyām prayacchati/ trayasto pitaro jñeya dharma ca pathi vartinaḥ* (18.23)). And yet Vāli was living with his younger brother's wife, who is like a daughter to him. First, then, it is Rāma's duty as representative of the emperor to mete out the right punishment. Second, Sugrīva is his friend, and, on his honour, he has promised him to restore the kingdom. Third, Rāma explains that he did not fight directly with him, but killed him from a place of hiding because Vāli is of the same species as forest-dwelling animals, which can be killed in this way. 'Even royal sages who are knowledgeable in *dharma* go hunting and thus you were killed in the conflict by me with the shaft' (*yanti rājarṣayaścātra mṛgayāṃ dharmakovidāḥ tasmāt tvaṃ nihato yuddhe mayā vāṇena vānara* (8.40, ab)). Rāma goes on to say that because Vāli has accepted his punishment, he will ascend to heaven. Vāli apologizes for his lack of knowledge and dies with the full blessing of Rāma, and anticipation of heaven.

Much exegetical ink has been spilled over this exchange between monkey and man/god, and multiple interpretations have sprung up over the course of the millenia.[38] However, the important point for our purposes here is that Rāma and Vāli are here engaging in a debate about the ethics of violence itself, and the rules of proper conduct. The terms of their debate are not on the question of violence or nonviolence per se, but rather the question of how *dharma* might be infused into a seemingly senseless act of violence.

As in the *Mahābhārata*, the question of the ethical use of weapons is very important in this episode. Rāma proves himself and overcomes Sugrīva's doubts about his ability to defeat Sugrīva by affixing his missile to a weapon, and then firing it. It pierces the trees, the mountain itself, and the whole earth, then returns to Rāma. Its magic powers are proof of Rāma's abilities to vanquish Vāli, and what is more, proof of his dharmic potential of friendship with Sugrīva. Yet when Vāli is injured by Rāma's weapon, he does not die. The arrow thrown off from Rāma's bow illumined the path to heaven for the hero, and brought him to a supreme state (*tadsatraṃ tasya vīrasya svargamārgaprabhāvanam/ rāma-bāṇāsanakṣiptamāvahat paramāṃ gatim* (17.8)). Thus, the weapon itself becomes a statement about *dharma*, and the fusing of *dharma* and devotion. Vāli wins a place in heaven *both* because of his acceptance of his punishment and his being pierced by Rāma's weapon.[39]

Two important facts emerge in this brief look at significant episodes of physical injury in the epics. The first is that *dharma* is the normalizing force in the narratives; it allows certain acts to be told in such a way that they are not out of the realm of possibility for the epics' late Vedic or pre-classical world. In the *Mahābhārata, dharma* provides the occasion for reflection after an almost intolerable act of violence has been committed (Bhīṣma's being wounded, for example). Rāma's dharmic knowledge trumps Vāli's, even as he lies wounded, accusatory and near death. There is, however, also a significant point of difference in the two major epics. Unlike the *Mahābhārata*, the *Rāmāyaṇa* consistently gathers up the threads in which violence could remain a threatening memory. Notice that Vāli asks Rāma twice in this episode what Rāma will say to the wise ones when he returns; Vāli implies with his question that such an act could not possibly be counted as a legitimate, integratable memory.

Dharma Sūtras: the necessary conditions of violence, codified in caste

Also composed primarily in the early classical period (third to second centuries BCE), the *Dharma Sūtras* are more specific, non-narrative codes of law that state more abstractly the kinds of issues raised in the epics. These documents show important considerations of intentionality and the lack of intentionality, gradations of punishment, and so on, for violent acts committed.

Gautama (1.3.4) and *Āpastamba Dharma Sūtras* (2.13.7)[40] both focus on the fact that men of earlier times committed violence but did not suffer the consequences; they incurred no sin because of their extraordinary powers. But they warn that the person who tries to do the same in the present period, observing what their forefathers did, will perish. (This is the classical tradition of *kalivarjya*. This comment is a fascinating view of violence, in which the consequences of bodily harm in an earlier age are not the same as the present age. Thus, there is an awareness of precedent, as well as an awareness of changing circumstances in which violence may or may not be appropriate, and constitute the same amount of wrongdoing.

In addition, like the *Arthaṣāstra*, the *Sūtras* state general rules about killing. Many of of these discussions are prefaced by a general statement about *kṣatriyadharma*, whereby the law specific to a king is the protection of his subjects by use of weapons, and a king must obtain livelihood by these means. The *Āpastamba Dharma Sūtra* 1.19.2 argues that one who kills unintentionally reaps fruit of his own sin, but the sin is greater if done with forethought. It goes on to argue that killing in self-defence is admissible, for in that case, 'anger meets anger', and there is an equality of states. *Baudhāyana* 1.18.6 goes into greater detail, stating that a king should not turn his back in battle, nor strike with barbed or poisoned weapons. A warrior should not engage people who are afraid, intoxicated, delirious, or have no armour. Nor should he kill women, children, old people or Brahmins, unless they are trying to kill him. Even killing a teacher is permissible in the *Dharma Sūtras*, if that killer is an assailant. *Vāsiṣṭha Dharma Sūtra* 3.16.24–25 goes into even greater detail on this very point, and asks the question of what constitutes an assailant and justifies killing him? If one is a robber of possessions, a stealer of land, or a wife, wielding a weapon or poison, all of these constitute being an assailant, and therefore merit a counter-attack.

Even more interesting is that the *Dharma Sūtras* mete out punishment for killing according to *varṇa*, or caste. As *Āpastamba Dharma Sūtra* (1.25.11) states, killing a person of the first class if you are not of that class means that you yourself must be killed or offered in sacrifice. The author goes on to argue that the penance for killing certain animals is the same as that for killing a *śūdra*.

Gautama Dharma Sūtra 22.1–25 has an extensive section on the penances for killing which are entirely based on scales of purity relative to caste. *Vāsiṣṭha Dharma Sūtra* (20.23–47) makes a similar list, with the interesting exception that killing a *kṣatriya* or *vaiśya* who is in the middle of sacrificing is the same as killing a Brahmin.

The *Gautama Dharma Sūtra* passage 22.1–10 is intriguing for its understanding of justice and fair equivalencies in relationship to the *dharma* of killing, and is worth quoting here:

> A man who has killed a Brahmin shall emaciate his body and throw himself into a fire three times, or make himself a target during an armed battle. Or else, for twelve years he should live a chaste life and, carrying a skull and the post from a bed frame, enter a village only to beg for food while proclaiming his crime. When he sees an Ārya, he should get out of the road. In this manner he becomes purified, as he remains standing during the day and seated at night, and bathes at dawn, noon and dusk. He is purified also if he saves a Brahmin's life; he is defeated three times while attempting to recover the property stolen from a Brahmin, or if he takes part in the ritual bath at the end of a horse sacrifice or even of another sacrifice as long as it concludes with the *Angiṣṭut* offering.[41]
>
> (*agnau saktir brahmaghnas trir avacchātasya/ lakṣyam vā syāj janye śastrabhṛtām/ khaṭavāṅga pālapārṇrvā dvādaśa saṃvatsarān brahmacārī maikṣāya grāmam praviśetkarmā ''cekṣāṇaḥ/ pato'pakrāmet saṃdarśanād āryasya/ sthānāsanābhyāṃ viharansavaneṣūdakopasparśā śudhyet/ prāṇalābhe vā tan nimitte brāhmaṇasya/ dravyāpacaye tryavaraṃ pratirāddhaḥ/ aśvamedhāvabhṛthe vā/ anyayajñe' pyagniṣṭud antaścet/*)

Here, we have a very intriguing set of patterns, where bodily harm is counteracted by the giving of a body, in which the perpetrator himself becomes the sacrificial victim. He is actually required to chant a mantra offering his body to death while doing so, according to the *Vāsiṣṭha Dharma Sūtra*. (20.23) Battle, too, becomes a kind of sacrificial penance of death.

At the end of the passage, the sacrificial bath remains an option for penance, presuming a life of radical asceticism. If the perpetrator remains alive, he absents his own body in the presence of an Ārya; i.e., he literally disappears (*pato 'pakrāmet saṃdarśanād āryasya*). His crime, however, does not, as he must continue to proclaim it throughout his life of almsgiving. The crime is known, the person is not.

Finally, the *Dharma Sūtras* are very strict about the polluting power of weapons for Brahmins. *Āpastamba* 1.18.9 warns that a Brahmin should not eat the food of anyone practising a craft or using weapons, and later (1.29) argues that a Brahmin should not take a weapon in his hands, even to examine it. *Gautama* (7.26) however, argues that even a Brahmin can resort to weapons in the case of *āpad dharma* or the *dharma* of emergencies. This debate reveals that we have come a long way indeed from the celebration of weapons blessed by the priests in the Vedic arena. The possibility of violent harm, and therefore the shedding of blood, has become a potentially polluting act that must be avoided by Brahmins at all times.

Unlike the *Arthaśāstra*, then, in the *Dharma Sūtras*, expiations tend to be imagined in terms of conduct rather than payment. Their narratives are ones where counter-actions tell another kind of story – one other than the explicit normalization of killing. Indeed, the legal tale of the almsgiver proclaiming his act is never normalized, but always on the margins, always a fragment of society and never symbolic of its whole.

Concluding thoughts

The early Indian narratives of violence show different strategies incorporating and normalizing violence into the story. The diferent genres in which these narratives occur have a significant influence. The Vedic perspective is a ritual acceptance of violence, with precise instructions about killing, bloodshed, contestual striving, and the division of the body in sacrifice. Yet such acts are accompanied by forms of complex resistance to the eruptive nature of violence, such as hymns and songs which transport the facts of injury and death into another, safer world – whether it is Sthūra going to heaven or the sacrificial horse moving on paths that are good to go on. Violence is normalized through such moves. Vedic weapons, moreover, have a direct and powerful link to the instruments of sacrifice.

The *Upaniṣads* make images of violence into metaphors, in which the self, even if undergoing pain or death, does not really die, as it understands itself as Brahman. Its weapons are forms of knowledge, which can pierce through experienced reality in perceptive acuity. Violence is integrated through perceptual shifts.

The *Arthaśāstra* presents a series of sophisticated punishments, where the penances fit the crimes of injury, and where the views of violence are based on the interests of the harmony of the state. This same principle guides its understanding of the waging of war. Here, the risk to the state is the guiding 'normalizer' which justifies and narrativizes injury to the body.

The epics view war in a much less pragmatic way, but rather explore the many tensions between the all-encompassing nature of war and the dharmic actions of individuals within it. Further, in many episodes the epics focus on the ways in which the event of injury itself can be made into a narrative discourse on *dharma*. Yet the *Mahābhārata* never completely integrates violence into its narrative, despite the efforts of Yudhiṣṭhira and his brothers. The *Rāmāyaṇa*, on the other hand, attempts to do so through Rāma's perfection.[42]

Finally, the *Dharma Sūtras* codify violence as a function of caste purity, in which the harm is relative to the standing of the individual. Weapons are forms of impurity, not vehicles for devotion or magic. Yet their expiations are 'counter-narratives' in which violence of one individual is reintegrated through the actions of that individual. In other cases, that individual is permanently marginalized, and the counter-narratives reflect that status as well.

It seems that each genre of early brahminical texts transforms violence in some way, so that its basic horror is translated into another language – a language that can integrate injury on the text's own terms. This transformation could be achieved by the language of heaven, the language of metaphysics, the language of devotion, or the language of purity. Each early Indian genre thus achieves a way of perceiving violence differently. In this sense these texts perform the very human task of making violence something more tolerable, and perhaps even possible, in the muck and passion of everyday life.

Yet they never fully make violence coherent, and the echoes of such incoherent fragments remains. We never know if the pieces of the slaughtered horse are indeed picked off the axes. We can never say for sure if Brahman actually changes the dying man's perception. The challenge that Vāli gives to Rāma is, in some eyes, only partially answered by his dharmic discourse. The murderer in the Sūtras is never integrated, but remains a powerfully radiant 'fragment', doomed to proclaim his own marginality as he walks from village to village.

Notes

1 Bodewitz, in particular gives an excellent summation of the ways in which *ahiṃsā* comes onto the scene in the late Vedic period as a universal code of conduct which is named as part of a general virtue. It should be noted here, as Schmidt and Bodewitz and Houben all do, that *ahiṃsā* might also be viewed as a function of rebirth – the kind of conduct that might insure birth in a better womb, as *Chandogya Upaniṣad* 5.3–10; *Bṛhadāraṇyaka Upaniṣad* 6.2; *Jaiminīya Brāhmaṇa* 1.18; see also Schmitthausen 1991, 1994, 1995; and Bodewitz 1992, and 1996, as well as Houben 2001: 166, n17. The debate runs as follows: in 1962, Ludwig Alsdorf suggested that *ahiṃsā* was not a monopoly of Jains and Buddhists, but was a common Indian movement in which Brahmanism, Buddhism and Jainism equally shared (1962: 121). This hypothesis goes against the idea that Brahminism took over the idea from its competitors. In 1966, Louis Dumont argued that the Brahmin became vegetarian through a reaction against the Vedic animal sacrifice rather than a development from within it. In 1968, Schmidt begins a larger argument that there should be a continuity from Vedic to later classical doctrine of *ahiṃsā*. The Vedic celibate student, the *brahmacārin*, evolved into the figure of the renunciant *saṃnyāsin*. Dumont shares this opinion with Heesterman (1964: 1–31, and 1982: 251–271). Schmidt argued that Vedic sacrifices became interiorized in stages, whereby the presence of an animal sacrifice was replaced by a sacrificial procedure in which the victim became superfluous. This led to the classical stage of full renunciation outside of society and its sacrifices. In a later, responding article, Heesterman (1984) continues to agree with the Vedic origins of *ahiṃsā* thesis put forth by Schmidt, but further specifies that the move was even earlier than the Upaniṣadic texts, and to be found rather in the Vedic sacrifice itself. When the texts suggest that decapitation of the victim should be substituted with strangulation, this is the beginning of *ahiṃsā*. Moreover, vegetarianism is prescribed by the *dīkṣita*, or consecrated sacrificer, as he prepares for the sacrifice. Oguibenine (1994) also agrees with this idea, and focuses on the rhetoric of sacrificial language; Herman Tull (1996), in deepening this idea, argues that the Vedic resolution of killing is to deny the fact that it is killing at all, but rather direct transportation to heaven. Houben (2001) argues that Vedic sacrifice was

initially criticized by extra-Vedic principles; Bodewitz agrees, and shows the flaw in arguing that the critique could have been intra-Vedic. Houben goes on to say that the critique is later defended by traditional Hindu principles.

2 *Baudhāyana Dharma Sūtra* 2.6.23 refers to the non-injurious person as *adrohin*; also see *Manu Smṛti* 4.148: *adronheṇa ca bhūtānāṃ*. So too *riṣ* and related *riś* are used in Vedic contexts for 'to harm' as well as 'to cut'. Also see Bodewitz 2001: 18, n6 and 38, n29 as well as Schmidt 1986: 634.

3 Here I would differ with Bodewitz (2001: 32) who argues that Oguibenine offers 'nothing new' to the study of the historical origins of *ahiṃsā*. I see Oguibenine's introduction of the term 'rhetoric' and his subsequent discussion of the ambiguities of rhetoric as a real contribution. If one is primarily concerned with historical origins of a concept, one will necessarily have a different view of what counts as a contribution. (See my 'Beyond the Myth of Origins: Narrative Philosophizing in Vedic Commentary', 1993.)

4 Elizarenkova 1995: 29ff.

5 As Damrosch writes of *Leviticus*, the text

> is of great literary interest in itself, as the fullest expression of the Pentateuchal effort not simply to set the law within a narrative context, but actually to subsume narrative within a larger symbolic order. An attentive look at the laws shows how it was possible in the Priestly writers to intersperse law and story so readily; in their hands, law itself takes on narrative qualities.
> (1987: 66)

6 See, for instance, *Vājāsaneyī Saṃhitā* 23.50–60 for an early example; *Śatapatha Brāhmaṇa* 11.6.3.11 gives a series of *brahmodya* passages. For examples of exchange, see *Pañcavīṃśa Brāhmaṇa* 4.9.12 and 5.5.13, *Aitareya Brāhmaṇa* 5.25.22, *Kauṣītaki Brāhmaṇa* 25.4, *Taittiriya Brāhmaṇa* 2.3.5, and *Āpastamba Śrauta Sūtra* 21.11.12ff. Kuiper 1960 and Thompson's recent work on the *brahmodya* (1997: 13–37) are two of the more well-known examples. For further discussion, see Heesterman 1985: 78ff.

7 Heesterman 1993; Thieme 1957.

8 The story is told in *Śāṅhāyana Śrauta Sūtra* 15.17–19 and *Aitareya Brāhmaṇa* 13–18. Another classical work is Weller 1956. As Houben (2001: 121) notes, the story need not be an actual account of events, it says much about what was regarded as normal, exceptional, and unacceptable. The slaughter of a human as such was seen as unacceptable by the author or authors and the public.

9 *Jaiminīya Brāhmaṇa* 2.97–99; and Heesterman 1985: 85–87.

10 According to *Jaiminīya Brāhmaṇa Upaniṣad* 4.26.12, the centre of the earth is one span north of this spot.

11 D.N. Jha (2001) argued against the prevalent perspective that India has always been vegetarian. Many scholars of the last one hundred years have understood the basic and incontrovertible fact that meat eating was part of ancient Indian culture. See also the review by Wendy Doniger in the *Times Literary Supplement* (8 February 2002).

12 *Śatapatha Brāhmaṇa* 1.2.3.5–9 suggests that a rice cake is substituted for an animal victim at the New and Full Moon sacrifice (*paśur ha vā eṣa ālabhyate yat puroḍāśaḥ*). However, for the most part the killing of the animal victim is never spatially integrated into the arena. The *Śamitṛ* priest, or actual butcher, is best translated as 'the quietener', since he strangles the victim. The other priests also refuse the integration of violence by turning away from the victim. (ŚB 3.8.2.15; *Baudhāyana Śrauta Sūtra* 4.6–7 and 15.28). In addition, by this period, the animal was strangled with a cloth dipped in ghee (*tārpya*) so that it would not cry out (Dumont 1927: 175, 335; and Houben 2001: 118, n.21).

13 I have consulted Geldner (1923) and Doniger's translation follows Doniger 1981; 91–92 with modifications. See also Dumont 1927 and Jamison 1996. Jan Houben argues here that the first line is identical with *Taittirīya Brāhmaṇa* (TB) 3.7.7.14; and suggests that the TB mantra may well be as old if not older than the mantra in the *Ṛg Veda* (RV), especially RV 1.162.21 (Houben 2001: 118.)

14 Monier 2001: 881; Grassmann 1964: 1167.

15 See Renou (1956): 39–42 for a fuller treatment of this hymn.

16 See in particular Heesterman 1984; Schmidt 1997; Bodewitz 2001: 28–33.

17 Jan Houben (2001) notes both of these Upaniṣadic passages, but without connecting them specifically to sacrificial metaphors (pp.115–16). Along with Olivelle, he also notes the discussion of *tīrtha*: see Venkateswaran 1966, *Ṛg Veda* 10.114.7, Geldner's notes, *Ṣaḍvīṃśa Brāhmaṇa* 31.4–6; *Kauṣītaki Brāhmaṇa* 18.9. See also Olivelle 1998: 287 and 571.

18 See Heesterman's Vedic Sacrifice and Transcendence', in Heesterman 1984 for a full discussion of this issue, whereby *prāṇa* and other concepts are fleshed out in terms of interiorization.

19 As Ricoeur writes:

> Half thought, half experience, 'seeing as' is the intuitive relationship that holds sense and image together. How? Essentially through its selective character: 'Seeing as is an intuitive experience-act by which one selects from the quasi-sensory mass of imagery one has on reading metaphor the relevant points of such imagery'. This definition contains the essential points. Seeing as is an experience and an act at one and the same time... 'seeing as' quite precisely plays the role of the schema that unites the empty concept and the blind impression; thanks to its character as half thought and half experience, it joins the light of sense with the fullness of the image.
>
> (1978: 213)

20 I am following here Olivelle (1998: 105).

21 Ibid.: 115.

22 Ibid.: 283.

23 Ibid.: 445.

24 Following, with some slight modifications, Kangle (1972: 247).

25 Ibid.: 321.

26 Ibid.: 328.

27 See Heesterman (1962: 22–24).

28 Among many many other works, see specifically on this topic: Gehrts (1975: 162ff and 234ff); Geld (1935); Fitzgerald (1983: 611–30); Hiltebeitel (1972–1973: 95–135); Dandekar (1990); Sutton (2000). Sutton's work is a helpful inventory and analysis of doctrinal perspectives; yet it does not address the narratological perspectives I argue for here.

29 See also 46.7–17 for a similar kind of rhetorical juxtaposition between these two concepts.

30 I am not sure that it is fruitful to look for a single message in the *Mahābhārata*, or even a single tension to be resolved. (See Jatavallabhula 2001: 98.) With Daniel, I would argue that the epic shows constant anxiety about the non-integratable nature of violence, and constantly attempts to make it part of the normal record. The final *parvans* are, I think, more 'genealogical' in Daniel's sense, in their continuous questioning of violence, and their raising suspicion about the war rather than the need to legitimate it.

31 I am grateful to Arindam Chakravarty, personal communication, 2002, for this discussion of Bhīṣma's lecture. See also Chapple 1996.

32 See *Mahābhārata* 3.39–41, 7.57, and 172–73.
33 See *Mahābhārata* 7.170.
34 Van Buitenen's translation is a very wise assessment of these issues (1979: 5ff).
35 Translations are my own, from Patton (forthcoming) *Bhagavad Gītā*, Harmondsworth: Penguin Press.
36 See Agarwal's (1993) helpful discussion of Gandhi's interpretation of other verses, such as those on equanimity in Chapter Three, and those involving *lokasaṃgraha*.
37 Ibid.: 190.
38 See Lefeber 1994; also Freeman 2000 and Narayanan 2000.
39 Many of these epic themes about weaponry and devotion are present in the *Purāṇas*. As the later theological praises of classical Indian deities, they are even more pronounced in their transforming of weapons, and physical injury, into forms of devotion. The Purāṇic stories of Dadhīci (Dadhyañc) are quite powerful in this regard. The earlier Vedic story (based on RV 1.116) emphasizes the ways in which Dadhyañc gives a secret knowledge to the gods, and has his head replaced with a horses' head; later, Indra uses his bones as weapons against the demons. In the Purāṇic versions (*Śiva Purāṇa* 24.11–32; *Bhāgavata Purāṇa* 10.6–8; *Agni Purāṇa 7.1*), the sage becomes devoted to death so that Indra and the gods might be armed with his bones. In his mind, these bones would be more effective weapons than thunderbolts for the destruction of Vṛtra and the Asuras. In the *Śiva Purāṇa*, Śiva even grants this to him as a boon for his devotion. In other words, the story begins with a kind of punishment, in which bodily decapitation ends up serving the violent, if necessary, ends of Indra, who needs weapons. In the Purāṇic authors' hands, the story ends up as an intentional devotional act, in which the only way for the gods to win against the demons is if the sage sacrifices himself.

    In addition, the *Purāṇas* make violence a function of time. While this theme is hinted at in the *Mahābhārata* understanding of the end of the *dvaparayuga*, mentioned above, it is fully played out in the Purāṇic theory of the *yugas*, or ages. *Kūrma Purāṇa* 127: 16–57, for example, gives an elaborate description of the reasons for the degeneration of the ages. In the *Treta*, greed and passion arise such that people begin to steal, to do harm, and to destroy each others' homes. Thus it is necessary to institute the laws of behaviour according to *varṇa*, or caste, as well as practice of sacrifice without injury to cattle. Notice here that in the *Kūrma Purāṇa* it is precisely because of this violent, degenerative turn of events that non-violent practices are introduced. In the *dvaparayuga*, war is introduced as one of the clearest signs of the degeneration of the age.
40 For these references, I have consulted the following editions of the *Dharma Sūtras*: Buehler 1932; Mitra 1969; Furher 1930. I also worked with Olivelle 1999.
41 Here I am following Olivelle's translation (1999:115ff).
42 The *Purāṇas* pick up on the epics' attitude toward weapons, and make such instruments of violence actual instruments of passionate commitment to a deity. Moreover, war is a function of the degeneration of time, the herald of the next *yuga*.

Bibliography

Agarwal, P. (1993) *The Social Role of the Gītā*, Delhi: Urmila Agarwal.

Alsdorf, L. (1962) *Beiträge zur Geschichte von Vegetarismus und Rinderverehrung in Indien*, Wiesbaden: Franz Steiner.

Aufrecht, T. (ed.) (1879) *Aitareya-Brāhmaṇa*, Bonn; trans. A.B. Keith, *Rigveda Brāhmaṇas*, 1920.

Bodewitz, H.W. (forthcoming) 'The Hindu Doctrine of Transmigration: its Origin and Background', in *Felicitation Volume Bongard-Levin.*

Bronkhorst, J. (1993) *The Two Traditions of Meditation in Ancient India*, Delhi: Motilal Banarsidass, 2nd edn.

——(1993) *The Two Sources of Indian Asceticism*, Bern: Peter Lang; 2nd edn, Delhi: Motilal Banarsidass, 1998.

Buehler, G. (ed.) (1932) *Āpastamba Dharma Sūtra*, 3rd edn, Bombay Sanskrit and Prakrit Series 44, 50, Poona: Bhandarkar Oriental Research Institute.

Chapple, C. (1996) 'Ahiṃsā in the *Mahābhārata*: A Story, a Philosophical Perspective, and an Admonishment', *Journal of Vaiṣṇava Studies*, 4: 109–125.

Connolly, W. (1987) *Politics and Ambiguity*, Madison, Wisconsin: University of Wisconsin Press.

Damrosch, D. (1987) 'Leviticus', in Alter, R. and Kermode, F. (eds) *A Literary Guide to the Bible*, Cambridge, MA: Harvard University Press.

Dandekar, R.N. (1990) *Mahābhārata Revisited*, New Delhi.

Daniel, E.V. (1987) *Fluid Signs: Being a Person the Tamil Way*, Berkeley: University of California Press.

——(2000) 'Mood, Moment and Mind' in *Violence and Subjectivity*, (eds) V. Das and A. Kleinman, Berkeley: University of California Press, 333–67.

Deussen, P. and Strauss, O. (1906) *Vier Philosophische Texte des Mahābhārata*, Leipzig: Brockhaus.

Doniger, W. (1981) *The Rig Veda*, Harmondsworth: Penguin Press.

Dumont, P.E. (1927) *L'Aśvamedha: Description du sacrifice solennel du cheval dans le culte vēdique, d'après les textes du Yajurveda blanc (Vājasaneyisaṃhitā, Śatapathabrāhmaṇa, Kātyāyanaśrautasūtra)*, Paris: Paul Geuthener.

Edwards, E. (1913) 'Human Sacrifice (Iranian)', *Encyclopedia of Religion and Ethics*, vol. 6, Edinburgh: Clark, pp. 853–855.

Eggeling, J (1900) *Śatapatha Brāhmaṇa*, Vol.5, Sacred Books of the East, 44, Oxford; reprint Delhi: Motilal Banarsidass.

Falk, H. (1986) *Bruderschaft und Worfelspiel: Untersuchungen zur Entwicklungsgeschichte des vedischen Opfers*, Freiberg: Falk.

Fitzgerald, J. (1983) 'The Great Epic of India as Religious Rhetoric: A Fresh Look at the *Mahābhārata*', *Journal of the American Academy of Religion*, 51: 611–630.

Freeman, R. (2000) 'Thereby Hangs a Tail: The Deification of Bali in the Teyyam Worship of Malabar', in Richman (ed.) *Questioning Rāmāyaṇas*, Delhi: Oxford University Press.

Frye, N. (1983) *The Great Code: The Bible and Literature*, San Francisco: Harcourt Brace Jovanovich.

Furher, A.A. (ed.) (1930) *Vasiṣṭha Dharmasūtra*, 2nd edn, Bombay Sanskrit and Prakrit Series 23, Poona: Bhandarkar Oriental Research Institute.

Gait, E.A. (1913) 'Human Sacrifice (Indian)', *Encyclopedia of Religion and Ethics*, vol. 6, Edinburgh: Clark, pp. 849–853.

Garvin, L. (1956) 'Major Ethical Viewpoints', in Fern, V. (ed.) *Encyclopedia of Morals*, New York: Greenwood Press.

Gehrts, H. (1975) *Mahābhārata: das Geschehen und seine Bedeutung*, Bonn: Bouvier.

Geld, G. (1935) *The Mahābhārata: An Ethnological Study*, Amsterdam.

Gonda, J. (1975) *Vedic Literature, A History of Indian Literature*, vol. 1.1, Wiesbaden: Harassowitz.

——(1979) *The Ritual Sūtras, A History of Indian Literature*, vol. 1.2, Wiesbaden: Harassowitz.

Grassmann, H. (1964) *Wörterbuch zum Rig-Veda*, Wiesbaden: Harrassowitz.

Grinshpon, Yohanan (2003) *Crisis and Knowledge: The Upanishadic Experience and Storytelling*, New Delhi and New York: Oxford University Press.

Gune, J. (1994) 'Paśu-sacrifice in the Sūtras', *Annals of the Bhandarkar Oriental Research Institute*, 74: 153–167.

Hacker, P. (1958) 'Der Dharmabegriff des Neuhinduismus', *Zeitschrift für Missionswissenschaft*, 42: 1–15.

——(1965) 'Dharma im Hinduismus', *Zeitschrift für Missionswissenschaft*, 49: 93–106.

——(1978) *Kleine Schriften*, (ed.) L. Schmithausen, Weisbaden: Steiner.

Halbfass, W. (1988) *India and Europe: an Essay in Understanding*, Albany: SUNY Press.

Handiqui, K.K. (1949) *Yaśastilaka and Indian Culture*, Sholapur: Jaina Samskriti Samraksana Sangha.

Heesterman, J.C. (1962) 'Vrātya and Sacrifice', *Indo-Iranian Journal*, 6: 1–37.

——(1966) 'Review of Alsdorf 1962', *Indo-Iranian Journal*, 9: 147–149.

——(1984) 'Non-violence and Sacrifice', *Indologica Tauriensia*, 12: 119–127.

——(1985) *The Inner Conflict of Tradition: Essays in Indian Ritual, Kingship, and Society*, Chicago: University of Chicago Press.

——(1987) 'Self-sacrifice in Vedic Ritual', *Gilgul, Essays on Transformation, Revolution and Permanence in the history of religions: Dedicated to R.J. Zwi Werblowsky*, S. Shaekd, D. Shulman, G.G. Stroumsa (eds), Leiden: Brill, pp. 91–106.

——(1993) *The Broken Sword of Sacrifice: An Essay in Ancient Indian Ritual*, Chicago: University of Chicago Press.

Hiltebeitel, A. (1972) 'The *Mahābhārata* and Hindu Eschatology', *History of Religions*, 12: 95–135.

Houben, J. (1999) 'To Kill or Not to Kill the Sacrificial Animal (*Yajñapaśu*): Arguments and Perspectives in Brahmanical Ethical Philosophy', in J. Houben and K.R. Kooij (eds) *Violence Denied: Violence, Nonviolence, and the Rationalization of Violence in South Asian Cultural History*, Leiden: Brill.

——(forthcoming): 'On the Horse-sacrifice and the Changing Notion of *ahiṃsā*'.

Jamison, S.W. (1996) *Sacrificed Wife/Sacrificer's Wife*, New York: Oxford University Press.

Jha, D.K. (2001) *The Myth of the Holy Cow*, New York: Verso.

Kane, P.V. (1930–62) *History of Dharmaśāstra*, vols I (1930), II parts i and ii (1941), III (1946), IV (1953), and V part i (1958), Poona: Bhandarkar Oriental Research Institute.

Kangle, R.P. (1968) 'The Relative Age of the *Gautamadhamasūtra*', in *Mélanges d'Indianisme àla memoire de Louis Renou*, Paris: E. de Boccard, pp. 415–425.

——(1972) *The Kauṭilya Arthaśāstra*, vol. II, Delhi: Motilal Banarsidass.

Kashikar, C.G. (1964) 'The Vedic Sacrificial Rituals through the Ages', *Indian Antiquary*, 1: 77–89.

Kashikar, C.G. and Parpola, A. (1983) 'Śrauta Traditions in Recent Times', *Agni: and Vedic Ritual of the Fire Altar*, vol. II, ed. F. Stall, Berkeley: Asian Humanities Press, pp. 193–251.

Kirfel, W. (1951) 'Der Aśvamedha und der Puruṣamedha', in *Beiträge zur indischen Philologie und Altertumskunde* (ed.), Seminar für Kultur und Geschichte Indiens, Hamburg: Cram, de Gruyter, pp. 39–50.

Klostermeier, K. (1996) '*Hiṃsā* and *Ahiṃsā* Traditions in Hinduism', in Dyck, H. and Klassen, W. (eds) *The Pacifist Impulse in Historical Perspective*, Toronto: University of Toronto.

Krick, H. (1977) 'Nārāyaṇabali und Opfertod', *Wiener Zeitschrift für die Kurde Süd und Ostasiens* 21: 71–142.

Kuiper, F.B.J. (1960) 'Ancient Indian Verbal Contest', *Indo-Iranian Journal*, 4.

Kulke, H. and Rothermund, D. (1990) *A History of India*, revised edn, London: Routledge.

Kumarappa, B. (1934) *The Hindu Conception of the Deity as Culminating in Rāmānuja*, London: Luzac.

Lefeber, R. (1994) 'Introduction', *Rāmāyaṇa, Kiṣkindhā Kaṇḍa* vol. 4, trans. by R. Goldman, Princeton: Princeton University Press.

Mitra, R. (1881) *Indo-Aryans: Contributions Towards the Elucidation of the Ancient and Medieval History*, 2 vols, Delhi: Indological Bookhouse, 1969.

Mitra, V. (ed.) (1969) *Gautama Dharma Sūtra with Maskarin's Commentary*, Delhi: Veda Mitra and Sons.

Monier, M.-W. (2001) *English–Sanskrit Dictionary*, East Hanover, NJ: Laurier Books Ltd.

Narayanan, V. (2000) 'The *Rāmāyaṇa* and its Muslim Interpreters', in Richman (ed.) *Questioning Rāmāyaṇas*, Delhi: Oxford University Press.

Oguibenine, B. (1994) 'De la Rhétorique de la Violence', in *Violences et Non-violences en Inde*, Vidal *et al.* (eds), Paris: École des Hautes Études en Sciences Sociales, pp. 81–95.

Oldenberg, H. (1917) *Die Religion des Veda*, Stuttgart: Gotta.

——(1919) *Vorwissenschaftliche Wissenschaft, Die Weltanschauung der Brāhmaṇa-texte*, Goettingen: Vandenhoeck & Ruprecht.

Olivelle, P. (1992) *Saṃnyāsa Upaniṣads: Hindu Scriptures on Asceticism and Renunciation*, New York: Oxford University Press.

——(1998) *The Upaniṣads: Annotated Text and Translation*, Delhi: Munshiram Manoharlal.

——(1999) *The Dharmasūtras*, New York: Oxford University Press.

Pandey, G. (1997) 'In Defense of the Fragment,' in *Subaltern Studies Reader, 1986–1995*, (ed.) Ranajit Guha, Minneapolis: University of Minneapolis Press.

——(2001) *Remembering Partition: Violence, Nationalism, and History in India*, Cambridge: Cambridge University Press.

Patton, L.L. (2005) *Bringing the Gods to Mind: Mantra and Ritual in Early Indian Sacrifice*, Berkeley: University of California Press.

——(forthcoming) *The Bhagavad-Gītā*, Harmondsworth: Penguin Press.

Ramachandran, T.N. (1952) 'Aśvamedha site near Kalsi', *Journal of Oriental Research – Madras*, 21, 1–31.

Renou, L. (1956) *Hymnes spéculatifs du Rig Veda*, Paris: Librairie Gallimard.

Ricoeur, P. (1978) *The Philosophy of Paul Ricoeur: An Anthology of His Work*, (eds) C. Reagan and D. Stewart, Boston: Beacon Press.

Ritter, J. (1972) 'Ethik, I–VI', in *Historisches Wörterbuch der Philosophie*, vol. 2, Darmstadt: Wissenschaftliche Buchgesellschaft, pp. 759–795.

Schayer, S. (1925) 'Die Weltanschauung der Brāhmaṇa-Texte', reprinted in *O filozofowaniu Hindusiw: artykuly wybrane*, (ed.) M. Mejor, Warsaw: Pañstwowe Wydawnictwo Naukowe, pp. 325–331.

Schlingoff, D. (1969) 'Menschenopfer in *Kauśambī*?', *Indo-Iranian Journal*, 11: 175–189.

Schmidt, H.P. (1968) 'The Origin of *ahiṃsā*', in *Mélanges d'Indianisme àla memoire de Louis Renou*, Paris: Editions de Boccard, pp. 625–655.

——(1997) '*Ahiṃsā* and Rebirth', in *Inside the Texts – Beyond the Texts: New Approaches to the Study of the Veda*, (ed.) M. Witzel, Cambridge, MA: Harvard University Press, pp. 207–234.

Schmithausen, L. (1995) 'Man, Animals, and Plants in the Rebirth Passage of the Early Upaniṣads', *Journal of the Royal Asiatic Society of Śri Lanka*, New Series, 38: 141–162.

Sharma, G.R. (1960) *The Excavations at Kauśambī (1957–1959), The Defences and the Śyenaciti of the Puruṣamedha*, Allahabad: Allahabad University Press.

Smith, F. (1987) *The Vedic Sacrifice in Transition: A Translation and Study of the Trikāṇḍmaṇḍana of Bhāskara Miśra*, Poona: Bhandarkar Oriental Research Institute.

Sutton, N. (2000) *Religious Doctrines in the Mahābhārata*, Delhi: Motilal Banarsidass.

Thakur, U. (1978) *An Introduction to Homicide in India (Ancient and Early-medieval Period)*, New Delhi: Abhinav Publications.

Thieme, P. (1957) *Mitra and Aryaman*, New Haven: Transactions of the Connecticut Academy of Arts and Sciences.

Thompson, G. (1997) 'The Brahmodya and Vedic discourse', *Journal of the American Oriental Society*, 117: 13–38.

Tull, H. (1996) 'The Killing that is not Killing: Men, Cattle, and the Origins of Non-violence (*ahiṃsā*) in the Vedic Sacrifice', *Indo-Iranian Journal*, 29: 223–244.

Van Buitenen, J.A.B. (trans.) (1979) *The Bhagavad Gītā in the Mahābhārata*, Chicago: University of Chicago Press.

Venkatesananda, S. (1988) *The Concise Rāmāyaṇa*, Albany: SUNY Press.

Weber, A. (ed.) (1855) *Śatapatha-Brāhmaṇa (Madhyandina-śākhā)*, London.

Weber, Albrecht (1864) 'Uber Menschenopfer bei den Indern der vedischen Zeit,' *Zeitschrift der Deutschen Morgenlandischen Gesellschaft* 18: 262–87, reprint: *Indische Streife*, Band 1: 54–89, Berlin: Nicholaische Verlagsbuchhandlung, 1868.

Weller, F. (1956) *Die Legende von Śunaḥśepa, Aitareya Brāhmaṇa und Śāṅkhāyanasrautasūtra*, Berlin.

Wilson, H.H. (1852) 'On Human Sacrifices in the Ancient Religion of India', *Journal of the Royal Asiatic Society*, 8: 96–107; reprinted in *Works by the Late Horace Hayman Wilson*, vol. II, London: Trubner, 1862, pp. 247–269.

Witzel, M. (1987) 'The Case of the Shattered Head', *Studien sur Indologie und Iranistik*, 13–14: 363–415.

2 The non-violence of violence

Jain perspectives on warfare, asceticism and worship

Paul Dundas

The Kharatara Gaccha is a Śvetāmbara Jain subsect whose origins and early development from the eleventh century are to be located in western India within the area of what is now central and north Gujarat and south Rajasthan. Consciously attempting to reactivate the ancient and pure mode of disciplined mendicancy described in the Jain scriptures, the leaders of the Kharatara Gaccha and their followers defined themselves against the sedentary, so-called 'temple-dwelling' (*caityavāsin*) monks whom they saw as a corrupting influence on Jainism. Perhaps the earliest chronicler of this reforming group is Jinapāla (thirteenth century) who describes from a highly partisan perspective how various senior teachers of the Kharatara Gaccha triumphed in a succession of formal public debates with their opponents, often presided over by powerful potential supporters, and thus promulgated their own vision of the Jain path.

One of the longest of Jinapāla's accounts deals with the encounter in 1182 between Jinapatisūri, the chief ascetic of the Kharatara Gaccha, and Padmaprabha, a leading temple-dwelling monk from a rival subsect, the Ukeśa Gaccha. This debate was held in the court assembly (*sabhā*) of Pṛthivīrāja Cāhamāna, the last significant Hindu ruler of western India. As described by Jinapāla, things did not go well with Padmaprabha from the start of the proceedings and he floundered badly in the face of Jinapatisūri's command of Jain doctrine and general philosophical learning. He was then humiliated in a poetic contest that required the composition of a 'picture poem' (*citrakāvya*) in the form of a sword. Finally, realising that he was likely to be exiled from the kingdom as a public laughing stock, the demoralised Padmaprabha informed King Pṛthivīrāja that he was an expert in martial arts (*mallavidyā*) and wished to wrestle with Jinapatisūri in order to settle matters. The king, ignorant of the customs of philosophers, as Jinapāla puts it, looked at Jinapatisūri to see what to do. The Kharatara Gaccha leader replied:

> Your majesty, wrestling is not appropriate. Children grabbing each other by the throat excel at it, not great men; princes duelling hand to hand with weapons excel at it, not merchants; slatterns biting and shrieking at each other excel at it, not queens. So how can I accept Padmaprabha's challenge? Scholars excel in competing against each other with their

> powers of formulating question and answer. At that moment, the court scholars present at the debate said, 'Sire, we get our livelihood from you because of the quality of our scholarship, not our skill in martial arts'.[1]

Jinapatisūri confirms that he will engage in any form of literary or learned dispute with Padmaprabha but not in wrestling, which he describes as 'anti-social and contrary to his religion' (*lokaviruddhaṃ svadarśanaviruddham*). So the scholarly contest moved to its inevitable conclusion, with Padmaprabha exiled and Jinapatisūri proclaimed victor by Pṛthivīrāja who declared that no enemy would be able to attack his kingdom while that Jain teacher was living there.[2]

This particular event, the general historicity of which need not be doubted, took place on the eve of a decisive moment for medieval western India, since with Pṛthivīrāja's defeat by the Muslims a decade or so later, traditional Hindu polity and its attendant court culture of art and learning, while not totally disappearing, never flourished quite so resplendently again in that region of the subcontinent. Martial arts were, of course, a feature of the Indian courtly world, apparently from the beginning of the common era and before. So the Kalpa Sūtra, the earliest extended Jain scriptural biography of Mahāvīra, the historical 'founder' of what has come to be called Jainism, describes the great teacher's aristocratic father engaged in martial arts activities in the gymnasium and wrestling hall.[3] Padmaprabha's challenging of Jinapatisūri to a wrestling match, boorish and inappropriate as it might appear in the context of learned debate, in fact reflects an awareness of what was a natural, time-honoured court pastime, being an attempted formal enactment of the elaborate martial arts culture which was traditionally practised to a particularly high level in Gujarat.[4] Furthermore, *citrakāvya*, a genre of virtuoso Sanskrit court poetry involving the production of various elaborate visual shapes, a feat which apparently proved too much for Padmaprabha, seems to have had its origins in the realm of martial arts.[5]

Jainism as a way of heroism

While Padmaprabha's insistence on a wrestling match to settle his debate with Jinapatisūri was no doubt the result of frustration, it is also redolent of an Indian religious world in which holy men were expected both to be paragons of wisdom and sanctity and also, when necessary, to be capable of defending themselves against attackers. World renunciation of the sort followed by the Jains, Buddhists and other groups was an institution which entailed not so much the abandonment of social ties for a career of mendicant quietism as an entry into a heroic way of life which derived a great deal of its ethos, at least at its outset in the Ganges basin around the seventh or sixth centuries BCE, from an affinity with the early Indo-Āryan warrior brotherhoods, bands of young men who at certain times of the year engaged in raiding, concomitant violence and the purificatory practice of celibacy.[6] The Mallas, whose name was traditionally perpetuated in the discipline at which Padmaprabha claimed to excel (cf. Sanskrit *malla*, 'wrestler'), were in origin one such group, and both the Buddhist and Jain scriptures describe them as honouring the remains of Mahāvīra and the Buddha, both members of the warrior (*kṣatriya*) class.[7]

In this context, then, I would like to suggest that Jainism can profitably be regarded as exemplifying throughout its history what has been styled the 'path of heroism' (*vīryamārga*), a reconfiguration of warrior codes of bravery and physical control in the ascetic search for spiritual power and mastery, qualities which have led to Jain monks being much respected since medieval times by groups such as the Rajputs who identify their own background in martial terms.[8] The very designation 'Jain' (Sanskrit: *Jaina*), 'follower of the conquerors' (*jina*), obviously relates to the martial overcoming of enemies, whether internal or external. Mahāvīra in particular, the 'Great Hero', whose name has its origins in Vedic ritual, epitomises many of the qualities of the Vedic warrior god Indra and the legendary stories of his birth in particular evince obvious connections with divine power.[9] The worship of Mahāvīra and the other Jinas in later centuries no doubt had strong connections with the commemoration of dead heroes so common in Indian religiosity. The medieval memorials which can still be seen at celebrated holy spots such as Śravaṇa Beḷgoḷa in Karnataka to commemorate the valiant fasting to death (*sallekhanā*) of Jain ascetics are equivalent to the hero stones erected all over the subcontinent in honour of those who died a gallant death in battle.[10]

Jainism and non-violence

While it is well known that a martial arts culture flourished amongst Buddhist and Hindu renouncers, elements of which in the former case seem to have migrated into eastern parts of Asia,[11] there is unfortunately not so much evidence for the practice of martial arts amongst Jain monks. Jinapatisūri's rejection in Pṛthivīrāja's *sabhā* of his Jain opponent's invitation to engage in physical violence is thus an interesting piece of testimony. His disparagement of wrestling as anti-social no doubt reflects Jainism's perennial concern, as embodied in its textual tradition, for the public decorum of its renunciant adherents, which the reforming monks of the Kharatara Gaccha felt their temple-dwelling counterparts were failing to maintain. For anyone familiar with Jainism's well-known espousal of the principle of non-violence (*ahiṃsā*) and compassion to all living creatures, Jinapatisūri's claim that physical combat infringed the tenets of his religious path would thus seem highly predictable.

Certainly no religion identifies itself more closely with non-violence to living creatures (*ahiṃsā*) than Jainism. As exemplified by Jain ascetics, the enactment of it represents the highest form of heroism. According to the ancient *Sūtrakṛtāṅga Sūtra*, 'such heroes are free from passion, they destroy anger and fear, they don't kill creatures'.[12] The exact provenance of the idea of non-violence in ancient India remains a regular topic of scholarly debate. Early *ahiṃsā*, accurate discussion of which has often been obfuscated by anachronistic association with twentieth-century Gandhian notions of passive resistance,[13] is now generally, although not universally, regarded as having its origins in the practice of Vedic ritual and trends of reflection upon the nature of sacrificial violence which evolved within it.[14] Yet even within the ritual literature the term in its earlier manifestations did not have the same generalised significance which it came to assume at a later period, and a scenario can be posited in which the idea of ritual non-violence (it need not at this early period be regarded as a virtue) was subjected to some type of outside influence, possibly brahmanical or deriving from the non-brahman renunciatory milieu, which led to it being resituated in a broader ethical scenario.[15] In this context Schmithausen has concluded that in the early Jain (and Buddhist) sources *ahiṃsā* is motivated on the basis of two different arguments, namely that violence leads to unwanted results in this world and the next, and that all living creatures are essentially the same.[16]

Non-violence was undoubtedly a common feature of renunciatory religious practice in traditional India. Yet the pretensions of other religious paths to be non-violent have generally been deemed by Jain monastic intellectuals to be completely unsustainable on the grounds that they lack Jainism's particularly thoroughgoing analysis of reality as consisting at all levels of embodied souls or life monads (*jīva*), each of which has an intrinsic value and desire to avoid destruction. The Jain advocacy of non-violence is accordingly strongly linked to a particular mode of conceptualising reality, and religions such as Hinduism, Buddhism and Islam were accordingly stigmatised at various periods in Jainism's history as *hiṃsāśāstra*, pseudo-soteriological paths whose teachings inevitably promote violence on the grounds of their fundamentally misconceived grasp of the nature of living reality.[17] Non-violence in Jainism is thus not simply regarded as a simple refraining from harming living creatures, but is most profoundly conceptualised as both an ethical stance tied to a rigorous interpretation of reality as embodied in the basic constituency of the world, and a form of spiritual exercise necessary to make progress on the path to deliverance.

The Jain merchant as ambivalent figure in respect to violence

To return to Jinapatisūri's response to Pṛthivīrāja, and specifically his observation that combat is inappropriate for merchants. Without wishing to over-interpret this remark, I would suggest that Jinapatisūri is here voicing an awareness of the primacy of the business and trading role which the Jain lay community had begun to assume, largely to the exclusion of any other, from around the time of the decisive supplanting of Hindu polities in Gujarat by Muslim power from the twelfth century onwards. This role was, at least until the decline of Mughal hegemony in the late eighteenth century, only tangentially capable of influencing political authority through the occasional providing of finance in times of strife. From the circumstances prevailing in the early modern period seems to have emerged the stereotyped but nonetheless self-perceived and self-reinforcing image of the Jain *baniyā*, or merchant, as an upright and fair-dealing type with high public prestige based on scrupulous adherence to the dictates of non-violence in his own private, business and ritual life, regular engaging in meritorious social works and minimal participation in India's often turbulent public affairs.[18] No doubt it was this mercantile stereotype in nascent form to which Jinapati Sūri was referring. However, another stereotyped representation of the *baniyā* was to become prevalent from the early modern period in South Asia, namely as an inflicter of violence upon his fellow man, specifically through exploitation of an indigent peasantry by means of his characteristic business activities of money lending and attendant massaging of prices and the assisting of the authorities in the collection of taxes, practices which Hardiman subsumes under the general rubric of 'usury'.[19] Certainly, the *baniyā*'s adherence to the ideal of non-violence within private or community religiosity seldom seems to have allowed for any broader humanitarian perspectives towards the indebted in this mercantile context.[20] So pervasive was the stereotype of Jain mercantile greed and callousness that Jain renunciants were at times popularly perceived as supporting their lay *baniyā* followers in their exploitative violence by means of their supposed ability magically to control the monsoon rains and thus create food shortages.[21]

Furthermore, despite the tone of Jinapatisūri's rejection of participation in violence by merchants and the *baniyā*'s general perception of himself as being outside political affairs, adherence to a religious path which promoted the primacy of *ahiṃsā* did not always entail quiescence on the part of the Jain merchant in the face of social unrest or controversy. While it seems to have been unusual for the Jain laity to have been associated with large-scale communal violence in pre-British times, there is clear evidence of rioting and civil disturbance in Jaipur in the eighteenth century between Jains and Hindus, and also between rival sects within the Digambara Jain community.[22] The power and leverage accrued by regional Jain mercantile communities subsequent to the breakdown of Mughal authority also led to the sponsorship of anti-Muslim unrest in the eighteenth and early nineteenth centuries.[23] In the twentieth century, members of the Jain community in Rajasthan took up arms to defend themselves against the depredations of the militantly anti-*baniyā* Anūp Maṇḍal,[24] while violence, admittedly of a sporadic type, has not been slow to break out amongst Jains themselves in the course of disputes over internal matters as disparate as the ritual calendar and the ownership of sacred sites.[25]

My aim in this essay is not to examine further the ambivalent position of the Jain merchant in the modern period but rather to take some examples from Jainism's earlier history and consider how a religious path celebrated for its espousal of non-violence attempted to accommodate itself within a broader Hindu world where violence, particularly of the martial sort, was often conceived in positive terms. Specifically, I will refer to early Jain tradition's perspective on martial conflict, the internalisation of violence by Jainism in the form of ascetic practice and, in the wake of the Jain community's disconnection from serious political power in the late medieval period, the expression of concern about violence in two areas, the actions of the omniscient person and the performance of worship.

In anticipation of this, I now offer some brief consideration of how violence is envisaged in Jainism.

Jain views on the nature of violence

The great Gujarati Jain teacher Hemacandra, who lived just a little earlier than Jinapatisūri asserted that all correct religious and disciplinary practices, however correctly performed, are useless unless violence (*hiṃsā*) is abandoned.[26] However, despite such an apparently definitive statement and many others like it throughout Jain literature concerning what amounts to mental attitude as well as physical action, Jainism does not have an entirely monochrome attitude towards violence.

Given the Jain analysis of the world as being filled with myriads of life forms, violence would appear to be virtually inescapable at every turning. This is certainly the view of the oldest stratum of the scriptural tradition.[27] However, Jain teachers came in time to equate the taking of life with the concomitant presence of carelessness and lack of guarded attention to one's surroundings.[28] It is thus clear that killing and violence are not the same in Jainism. Taking life (*prāṇātipāta*) is merely the outcome of *hiṃsā*. An individual in a genuine state of watchfulness and mental restraint might inadvertently destroy minute life forms in the ground or air, yet not be deemed responsible for committing *hiṃsā*.[29] The removal of the mental knots which bring about passion-based activity effects the gaining of *ahiṃsā*.[30] Violence and the abandonment of it are at the most profound level issues which have bearing upon the self, not the external world. What derives from *ahiṃsā* is in actuality the spiritual result of purification of the self.

Violence gradually came to be classified in different ways in Jainism, depending on whether it related to minute organisms or to larger creatures such as animals or humans, or whether it was intentional or unintentional.[31] It also came to be held that violence in self defence (*virodhīhiṃsā*) was justifiable in certain circumstances. A classic scriptural example of the justifiability of violence in defence of a monk can be found in the twelfth chapter of the *Uttarādhyayana Sūtra*, which may date from around the third century BCE. This describes how Harikeśa, an untouchable who has become a Jain monk, is physically attacked by brahmans when he approaches a sacrificial enclosure seeking for alms. A deity intervenes on his behalf and beats the brahman into submission. Although the point of this narrative is to establish the superiority of Jain moral values over those of brahman ritualists and Harikeśa does not carry out any violence himself, it clearly demonstrates that the principle of non-violence need not necessarily pertain when there is a threat to monks.[32]

Much later, the influential text on monastic behaviour, the *Bṛhatkalpa Bhāṣya* of Saṅghadāsa (*c.* sixth–seventh centuries CE), which was produced at a time when Jain monasticism had become fully institutionalised, makes clear that violence on the part of monks to protect their fellow renunciants, most notably nuns, is justifiable. Even killing five-sensed creatures in the cause of defending the monastic group is not stigmatised, as in the narrative case of the monk who clubbed three lions to death while his companions slept.[33]

Jainism and war

In the light of the identification of violence as an internal issue relating primarily to purity of the self, it may not then be so striking that Jain writers, until relatively recent times, have not devoted any real effort to excoriating the practice of warfare,[34] but have instead concentrated upon the mental stance taken by those involved in conflict. What might be styled a scriptural template for the Jain perception of war and military violence is to be found in the largest text of the scriptural canon, the *Bhagavatī Sūtra*. While in its final redacted form this text dates from the early centuries of the common era, it may in part record material relating to an earlier period, although without any eyewitness status.

Bhagavatī Sūtra 7.9 describes two battles which supposedly took place during Mahāvīra's lifetime involving King Kūṇiya. There is no way of assessing the historicity of these events, but their large-scale violence suggests the world of conflict described in the *Mahābhārata*, whose core was probably approximately contemporary with that of the *Bhagavatī Sūtra*. In the 'Battle of the Thorns like Great Stones' (*mahāsilākaṇṭayasaṃgāma*), the intensity of which was such that the touch of thorns, leaves, twigs and the like were as severe to the protagonists as blows from great stones, King Kūṇiya defeats a tribal confederacy, amongst whom are the Mallas, leading to the death of 8,400,000 combatants. Mahāvīra comments upon this event, informing his disciple Gautama that as immoral and non-renunciant men the dead will be reborn in the lower realms of existence as hell-beings or animals.

The 'Battle of the Chariot with the Club' (*rahamusalasaṃgāma*) is described in more detail. In the course of this engagement, Kūṇiya effects a similar massacre to that in the previous battle, this time by means of an automaton-like chariot without horses or driver which careers about dealing out death by means of an attached club. The numbers of the slaughtered this time amount to 9,600,000. Of these, virtually all are reborn amongst lower forms of existence, with only one being reborn in heaven and another in a morally upright family.

Bhagavatī 7.9 then recounts how Mahāvīra's disciple Gautama invokes the general view that anyone who dies in any sort of combat is reborn in heaven. Mahāvīra challenges this and gives an account of the destiny of the advanced Jain layman Varuṇa of the city of Vaiśālī. Varuṇa, despite his intense religious life, was compelled by King Kūṇiya and the state authorities to fight in the 'Battle of the Chariot with the Club'. Prior to entering the fray, he took a vow not to attack anybody until he himself was attacked. Challenged in the battle by an opposing warrior, Varuṇa described the nature of his vow whereupon his infuriated would-be adversary gave him a bad wound from an arrow. Full of rage, Varuṇa shot an arrow back and killed his foe. Knowing that his own death was near, he left the battlefield and in a solitary spot paid homage to Mahāvīra and recited the monastic vows. He then took off his armour, removed the arrow and, fully prepared spiritually, died the religious death alone. An old friend of Varuṇa's, also mortally wounded in the battle, saw what he had done and himself took the lay vows immediately before death. Because Varuṇa's noble end was miraculously acknowledged by gods, raining down flowers and playing divine music, it was generally concluded that all warriors dying in battle are reborn in heaven. However, Mahāvīra makes clear that Varuṇa's resolve only to fight in self-defence and the piety of his death, as effectively a monk, led to his rebirth in heaven (he had in fact evinced wrath when fighting which seems to have precluded immediate human rebirth) and a subsequent final human rebirth which will bring deliverance. His friend was immediately reborn in a human family and will also eventually gain deliverance.[35]

Although this narrative purports to describe specific political events from around the fifth century BCE, there can be little doubt that in actuality it makes reference to the martial world portrayed in the Hindu epic where a glorious death in battle is reckoned to lead to heaven. Significantly, the *Bhagavatī Sūtra* conveys no outright condemnation of the waging of war as such; rather it makes clear that going into battle when commanded by one's leader is obligatory but also that to do so with the wrong, impassioned attitude, specifically one not informed by Jain values, leads to an ignominious rebirth. It is this attitude that may account for the regular presence of Jains amongst the officer corps in the modern Indian army[36] and informs the following statement about war by a contemporary Jain layman:

> Jain religion does not say you should be a coward. Jains are heroes. Religion first teaches you about duty. So if it is part of your duty to go to the front in war, you should do that. It is different for renouncers, but laymen should do that duty. There were always Jain warriors, and they were very religious. Jain warriors used always to stop when the time came for *samayik* (a meditational exercise performed by many Jains at the same time every morning) and perform their *samayik* on horseback.[37]

An inspection of the later medieval Jain versions of the Hindu epics and *purāṇas* also reveals an awareness that violence is at times necessary to maintain social morality.[38] The most striking example of this is the several Jain versions of the *Rāmāyaṇa*. Here, as is well known, the traditional story of Rama and his wife Sītā is put in a Jain framework in which the violence which is such a necessary part of the story is not perpetrated by Rāma, a pious Jain layman, but by his brother Lakṣmaṇa and blame for this is misogynistically ascribed to Sītā.[39]

However, the most marked example of the withdrawal from violence by the Jain warrior occurs in the famous story of Bāhubali. Found in its most celebrated form in the *Ādipurāṇa* by the eighth-century Digambara monastic poet Jinasena who was writing for the court of the monarch Amoghavarṣa Rāṣṭrakūṭa, this narrative describes how Bāhubali, in order to prevent a full-scale battle, engages in single combat with his half-brother Bharata for rulership over their father's kingdom and after bringing his opponent helplessly to his knees in front of him, refrains from killing him, leaving the battlefield for the forest in order to search for liberation.[40]

This story, which seems to have provided an idealised model for the Jain warrior aristocrat in medieval south India, can be read as a Jain riposte to one of the most famous Hindu justifications of the necessity of battle, that found in the *Bhagavad Gītā*. There the Pāṇḍava hero Arjuna is urged by his charioteer Kṛṣṇa to fight the Kauravas at the battle of Kurukṣetra, despite their army being filled with his relatives and friends, both because it is his obligation as a warrior to do so and because the warrior with true understanding of the eternal natures of the soul realises that in actuality nobody is capable of killing or being killed. The slaughter that ensues is of course horrendous and fatal to virtually all the main protagonists, although, in accord with one of the master themes of the *Mahābhārata*, it is also the harbinger of a new era of time. Jainism, however, does not subscribe to the creative and purifying role of battle as does Hinduism, and Bāhubali's abandonment of the kingdom to his brother without the loss of a single life demonstrates, at least at an ideal level, how Jain writers felt the requirements of warfare could be balanced by non-violence.

As to Kṛṣṇa's famous teaching in the *Bhagavad Gītā* of the ultimate impossibility of killing or being killed due to the immortality of the soul, the early Digambara Jain Kundakunda is clearly alluding to this in his *Samayasāra* when, in the course of a description[41] of how somebody engaging in martial arts exercise is or is not covered with dust (an analogy for karmic material) depending on whether he has been smeared with oil beforehand, he asserts: 'He who thinks I kill or am being killed by other beings is foolish and ignorant. The man of knowledge is at variance with this'.[42] However, Kundakunda then goes on to locate this teaching in the context of Jain karma theory which dictates that only the disappearance of that particular type of karma which determines length of life (*āyuṣkarman*) can bring about death:

> The Jinas have proclaimed that the death of living creatures comes about through the destruction of length of life karma. You [yourself] do not remove life karma. How then have you brought about the death of those living creatures? The omniscient ones say that a living creature has life through the arising of life karma. You do not endow it with life karma, so how can you have given life to them?[43]

The possible antinomian gloss justifying irresponsible violence which can be and has been given to Kṛṣṇa's teaching in the *Bhagavad Gītā* is neutralised by Kundakunda by means of the explanation that death and killing are not so much events which do not occur but rather are determined by actions in previous existences which are responsible for particular intensity of life-karma.

The monarch and the monk

In the same manner as Buddhism, Jainism from a relatively early period promoted the ideal of the *cakravartin*, the universal emperor who, after setting forth from his capital at Ayodhyā, conquers the subcontinent of Bhārata and, following a discus (*cakra*) which had floated out of the royal armoury, brings under his sway the various quarters of India without the use of violence. Scharfe has argued for the roots of *cakravartin* being in the nomadic world of the early Vedic chariot warrior and suggests that the wandering of world renouncing ascetics such as Jain monks and nuns are an echo of this ancient time.[44] Certainly this royal imagery was used as late as the seventeenth century when Meghavijaya in his *Digvijayamahākāvya* (Chapter 5) describes the monk Vijayaprabhasūri embarking on his wanderings as the universal emperor of ascetics setting forth in order to conquer delusion as he were a king marching to battle with his army.

Unlike the *cakravartin*, who was to represent little more than an ideal, the *vijigīṣu* ('desiring to conquer') king, a monarch conceived in ritual terms who was obliged to expand the boundaries of his kingdom by violent means, was very much a political reality in ancient and medieval India, and the Jain community had no difficulty identifying itself with such a figure.[45] Indicative of this is the fact that Jain texts from the first millennium CE are perfectly at ease with the important art of military prognostication, the prediction of success or disaster for aggressive and expansive kings embarking on an expedition (*yātrā*) against a neighbouring monarch. A good example of this is the *Bhadrabāhusaṃhitā* (in origin perhaps eighth or ninth centuries CE but drawing on earlier texts) which describes at length in its thirteenth chapter how Jain monks, operating in conjunction with brahman priests, should carry out the preliminary rituals prior to the expedition and interpret the relevant omens and astrological portents of possible victory or defeat for the invading army.

Among the last of many medieval Indian rulers who as enthusiastic soldiers and patrons of Jainism would have made use of such prognostic rituals were several prominent members of the Caulukya dynasty who ruled Gujarat during the eleventh and twelfth centuries. Occupying a central position in their public and private devotionalism was the Jina Ajita, the literal meaning of whose name, 'The Unconquered One', seems to have been particularly significant for this warrior family committed to the widening of the frontiers of its kingdom, and a remarkable temple dedicated to him was erected at the border fortress of Tāraṅgā in northern Gujarat.

The violence of asceticism

The *Sthānāṅga Sūtra*, a Jain canonical text dating probably from the early common era which groups various doctrinal, cosmographical and social categories under numerical headings, correlates four types of army with four types of monk. According to this typology, the first type of army is victorious and is not defeated, the second is defeated and is not victorious, the third is for various reasons both victorious and defeated and the fourth is neither victorious nor defeated because, according to the eleventh-century commentator Abhayadevasūri, it lacks an aggressive king to lead it (*avijigīṣutvāt*). The four types of monk are said to be similar to these armies in respect to their ability to deal with the *parīṣaha*, the tribulations and physical discomforts of the ascetic path. Of these, it is heroic individuals like Mahāvīra who overcome the *parīṣaha* without being perturbed by them. The other types of monk do not or sometimes do and sometimes do not succeed in conquering the *parīṣaha*, while the fourth type, presumably because of laxity in conforming to the disciplinary requirements of the path, does not experience them at all.[46]

The *parīṣaha* are an integral part of the ascetic life as lived out fully by the Jain monk or nun. Yet they are adventitious and not in any way willed in the manner of ascetic practices; as such, they do not function as central features of internal (that is, mental) or external asceticism (*tapas*), which in Jainism consists of regularly performed religious exercises and self-mortification in the form of fasting deliberately undertaken to ward off and destroy karma, in the same way as one consciously picks up a weapon to fight an enemy. The life of every Jain monk and nun is meant to embody through a system of controls and delimitations the very essence of heroic non-violence. It was the particular intensity of this dimension of Jain religious practice that struck early Buddhism, a tradition which attempted, not always successfully, to de-emphasise the role of asceticism, and led to the supposed judgement of the Buddha that Jain monks must be in the grip of some sort of evil karmic destiny to subject their bodies to such pains.[47]

This view of asceticism as a form of violence inflicted on a body conceptualised in inimical terms is a resilient one. So Olson has recently argued at length for the early Indian renouncer as being a violent type of individual, on the grounds that he inflicts violence not upon other people but upon his own body as a form of self-sacrifice in what, it is claimed, is a reconfiguration of the ancient Vedic ritual offering.[48] He considers the most marked manifestation of this to be the controlled fasting to death of *sallekhanā* which, as far as Jain scriptural ideology is concerned, is the only appropriate end for a monk.[49]

The details of Olson's pursuit of the Indian renouncer into the wider realms of masochism, eroticism and narcissism need not concern us here. However, it may be held that he significantly underemphasises the creative and universal dimension of asceticism in favour of its supposed violent aspects. In the light of the frequency of its occurrence in a wide variety of religious contexts, there is compelling evidence that asceticism in the sense of the experience of willed bodily and mental pain for spiritual purposes is a near-universal human propensity. Bronkhorst has suggested that 'the shared disposition to consider one's "self" different from one's body and mind'[50] and so by nature free from actions and mutability might well be the trigger which propels intense attempts by those with a heightened awareness of this, whether located in Indian soteriologies such as Jainism, Christianity or so-called primal religions, to effect a distance from the physical though control or suppression of bodily functioning. In a full-scale investigation of the role, motivation and physiology of ritually inspired pain, Glucklich offers a complementary interpretation:

> Modulated pain weakens the individual's feeling of being a discrete agent; it makes the 'body-self' transparent and facilitates the emergence of a new

identity. Metaphorically, pain creates an embodied absence and makes for a new and greater presence.[51]

The view that austerity plays a creative role in the production of such a new identity, or in the reconstruction of a pre-existing but hitherto occluded one, can be seen in Jain scriptures such as the *Bhagavatī Sūtra* where the expressions *bhāviyappā*, with 'self brought into being' or *bhāvei appāṇaṃ*, 'he brings the self into being', are continually used to convey a change of spiritual status effected by advanced ascetics. The term *sallekhanā* used of controlled fasting to death also seems originally to have had connotations of cleansing and purifying indicative of the re-emergence of the inner self. However, it should be acknowledged that discussions by Jain intellectuals do make clear that Jainism's uncompromising advocacy of asceticism as the necessary agent of radical transformation was consistently subjected in early India to the Olson-like criticism that it might involve violence.

The most eminent and incisive Jain defender of the integrity of asceticism was Haribhadra who most likely lived in the eighth century. In the eleventh chapter of his *Aṣṭakaprakaraṇa*, paraphrased here, he refers to the critical Buddhist judgement, that austerity involves suffering (*duḥkhātmakam*) on the grounds that it is connected with the arising of karma, as incorrect. If this were the case, Haribhadra argues, then every ascetic would experience suffering and also ought to be an inhabitant of hell since that place is of course characterised above all by suffering. However, those who practise physical and mental discipline do not experience suffering because their activity predominantly involves happiness that derives from quiescence of negative factors. There certainly does exist a type of bad or unpleasant austerity, but that must be given up because it generally harms the self through bringing about undesirable states of mind (*aśastadhyānajananāt prāya ātmāpakārakam*). The fact that the Jinas have continually advocated control of the mind and senses guarantees that this activity cannot involve any real suffering. Naturally there will arise some degree of physical pain from activities such as fasting, but that is just the equivalent of an illness. Anyway, such physical pain does not cause suffering when the goal of the religious path is achieved. Haribhadra concludes his defence of asceticism by confirming that it consists of various positive attributes, namely a particular type of knowledge, agitation at worldly existence and calm. In actuality asceticism is based the simultaneous destruction and quiescence of karma, rather that its arising, and consists of happiness free from pain.[52]

Asceticism in Jainism, then, is not seriously to be equated with violence. As Laidlaw has pointed out on the basis of observing lay ascetic practice today, fasting is celebrated by Jains because of the positive effects generated, not because it engenders any form of self-destruction. He criticises the view of fasting as being an attack upon a hostile body as a departure from the normal understanding of Jain practice, with the body being erroneously conceived as 'an ontologically distinct other, rather than a part of the self to be properly organized'.[53]

Another Jain intellectual of the eighth century, Akalaṅka, describes how the religious death of *sallekhanā*, in which the passions are gradually 'cleaned out' (*sallikhita*), is not a form of suicide involving violence to the body because of the fact that it involves joy (*prīti*) and also lacks the fault of carelessness (*pramāda*) which according to Jain prescription, as we saw above, is the necessary concomitant of any act of violence which removes life. A simple act of suicide would be motivated by the passions (strong attachment, hatred and delusion) which would inevitably exemplify themselves in the use of poison or weapons.[54] The Jain religious death of *sallekhanā*, on the other hand, is highly ritualised, involving consciously organised procedures such as the retaking of ascetic vows. As such, it is the heroic culmination of a disciplined physical and mental life rather than its 'violent' denial and will lead to a positive rebirth that will make the attainment of ultimate freedom from rebirth more imminent.

The violence of the enlightened and of worship

As the second millennium of the common era drew on, some groups within the Jain community became increasingly preoccupied with the possibility of violence manifesting itself in relation to that ideal human type regarded as the most elevated embodiment of the rejection of violence. This is the *kevalin*, the enlightened being who has gained omniscience, and, in particular, those *kevalins* who by particularly meritorious karma have become the Jinas or *tīrthaṅkaras*, the great teachers of the religion.[55]

The two main sects of Jainism, the Śvetāmbaras and the Digambaras, had argued since near the beginning of the common era about whether the *kevalin* was after his attainment of omniscience physically perfect or still subject to bodily needs such as hunger, thirst and fatigue. The Digambara espousal of the former position could not be seriously challenged inasmuch as it was in the last resort theoretical, since both sects concurred that nobody had become a *kevalin* since Mahāvīra's time. A dispute, which arose amongst the Śvetāmbaras in the sixteenth and seventeenth centuries, also involved this ideal type, but in terms of whether he was capable, even involuntarily, of inflicting violence. As we have briefly seen, in the course of the expansion of Jain monastic law a much clearer correlation between action and intention became permitted than found in the early scriptures so that it proved acceptable to excuse inevitable breaches of the vow of non-violence that ensued as wandering ascetics carried out their daily duties. Thus the inadvertent destruction of microscopic life forms in the air through hand motions when necessary religious duties were being carried out or in water as a river was forded could be pardoned on the grounds of its unintentional nature. However, would it be possible for a supposedly perfect *kevalin* to commit such breaches of non-violence, or had he reached the culminating moral point where even involuntary violence, such as killing life forms in the air through merely moving his body or blinking, would be impossible?

The view, associated with the teacher Dharmasāgara (second half of the sixteenth century), that the enlightened person cannot engage in any possible violent behaviour, however minor or involuntary, may be regarded as extreme and based on an often slanted reading of scriptural sources. The response to this position, also largely scripturally derived, makes clear that any external act of violence, which inevitably must be perpetrated by the *kevalin* through simple movement of the body, can only be judged in terms of the purity of the agent's inner state of mind. Just as a vigilant and careful monk does not bind new karma as a result of 'violent' actions carried out in the course of the religious path, so neither does the *kevalin*.[56]

A much more significant controversy concerning the nature of violence in relation to the ideal human being, this time in iconic form, was to preoccupy the Jain community throughout the second millennium CE, namely whether the performance of physical worship of the Jinas involved a breach of the principle of *ahiṃsā*. Devotional worship (*pūjā*) of the Jinas, the saving teachers, which usually takes place in domestic shrines or temples housing images, has been an important dimension of Jainism since near its very beginnings. Renunciants, male and female, have always been restricted to inner mental worship (*bhāvapūjā*) primarily on the grounds that their lack of possessions means that they have nothing which could be offered up in front of the image of the Jina. Physical worship (*dravyapūjā*) involving offerings of liquids, fruits, flowers and sweets, and direct contact with images can only be carried out by lay people, although with full encouragement by renunciants.

By around the fifteenth century it seems to have been claimed, perhaps by monks aware that the central core of old scriptures contains no reference to what in the earliest period had not immediately become a standard devotional idiom of Jainism, that *dravyapūjā* by its nature involved major acts of violence as defined by the Jinas themselves.[57] First, the construction of temples to house images of the Jinas, requiring the cutting down of wood for structural purposes and digging in the ground for foundations, acts forbidden to renunciants, would involve violence towards minute life forms. Second, the act of worship itself would also involve violence, in that fresh (that is, living) flowers and fruits would have to be cut for offerings and so be destroyed.

These criticisms came to be articulated most vociferously by the fifteenth-century Śvetāmbara teacher Loṅkā and two subsequent ascetic lineages still in existence today, the Sthānakvāsīs and the Terāpanthīs, have consistently maintained an anti-image-worship stance.[58] By strict scripturalist interpretation, this rejection of *dravyapūjā* on the grounds of the destruction involved at all stages might seem reasonable in the light of the basic and rigorous Jain insistence that spiritual progress can only be made by minimising violence towards life forms as much as possible. However, a more nuanced approach to the definition of violence can also be identified which would hold that a minor act of harming can be acceptable if it leads to a morally or devotionally positive outcome. The analogy used by Śvetāmbara Jain image-worshipping teachers is that of digging a well. Just as the exhaustion of those digging the well and the dirt which covers them are outweighed by the benefit to the large number of people who gain access to water, so the minimal amount of violence committed by worshippers cutting flowers to offer in front of images of the Jina is less significant than the devotion involved and its power to awake morally positive attitudes which have no connection with the passions that motivate the destruction of life forms.[59]

In other words, the ubiquitous Indian religious model of two truths, a higher soteriological level and a lower transactional level, is deployed to neutralise literalist interpretations of what might be involved in and entailed by violence. In this respect, a type of corollary can be pointed to, in that, for example, a man mistaking a rope for a snake and attacking it is guilty of violence from the internal, *bhāva* point of view, but not the external *dravya* point of view. A mental act of violence, while not involving killing, emphatically derives from a motion of the self driven by the passions.[60]

Conclusion

There has unquestionably been a ubiquitous connection in traditional South Asia between warrior and ascetic meditator, the conqueror of external enemies and the one who overcomes inner psychological foes.[61] Jainism's position as a religion of non-violence, which at the same time appealed to a warrior aristocracy throughout India up to the early centuries of the second millennium CE, need not then appear paradoxical, being most realistically explained by the central position within it of the quality, required by both ascetic and fighter, of intensely restrained control, and also by the promotion of a type of religio-political authority which in idealised form could encompass both the worldly and the soteriological. If Jainism did not condone political violence in all circumstances, often teaching that non-violence could be positively projected into situations involving conflict, it nonetheless was not at serious variance with the practice of warfare as a necessary component of a kingdom's capacity to expand or defend itself. Furthermore, inevitable manifestations of violence in the natural functioning of the human body and in the course of ritual could be neutralised by an appeal both to expediency and a higher level of meaning. For Jainism is a path not just for the heroic ascetic but also for the layperson grappling with the realities of living in the social world.

Notes

1 In translating I have condensed the original Sanskrit, which is couched in punning form.

2 Jinapāla, *Yugapradhānācāryagurvāvalī*, pp. 31–32.

Padmaprabha's penalty was less rigorous than that meted out to other defeated opponents in Jain tradition. Compare the physical chastisement of a Buddhist opponent at the end of a debate by the Digambara Jain monk Akalaṅka described by Prabhācandra (eleventh century) in his *Kathākoṣa*, story no. 2. Rather more ambiguous is the famous story of the great Śvetāmbara Jain scholar-monk Haribhadra who conquered the Buddhists in debate and then, to revenge his nephews who had previously been killed by them, compelled his adversaries to jump into a vat of boiling oil. Glorious as was this triumph over early medieval Jainism's arch-enemies, it was prompted by the negative mental traits of grief and anger, and some hagiographers of Haribhadra describe how the great teacher's huge scholarly production was an act of repentance for his earlier violence (Granoff 1989). Other Jains regarded this violence as acceptable and representing an act of service (*vaiyāvṛttya*) to the community that could subsequently bring about elimination of karma. Cf. the sixteenth-century Dharmasāgara's *Pravacanaparikṣā* 1.44 and 8.170, p. 227.

3 Jacobi 1895: 242. The *Kalpa Sūtra* most likely dates from the early centuries of the common era and may well have been composed in western India.

4 Roçu 1981: 436–37.

5 See Lienhard 1997.

6 Bollée 1981, Das 2000: 110–12 and Scharfe 1987: 306.

7 See Bollée 1981. Hinüber 2001: 200 is sceptical about whether *malla* is, as claimed by Bollée, a Middle Indo-Aryan derivative from Sanskrit *marya*, the term used for a member of a warrior sodality. There seems to have been in ancient India at the time of Mahāvīra and the Buddha a close connection both between the institution of renunciation and the practice of medical healing (Bronkhorst 1999) and between healing techniques with their knowledge of anatomy and martial arts (Roçu 1981).

8 Cf. Harlan 2003: 66 and Michaels 2004: 272–73.

9 See Bollée forthcoming.

10 Cf. Dundas 2002a: 224–25 and Thapar 2000: 680–95. Mailāra, a form of the Mahārāṣṭrian god Khaṇḍobā worshipped in Karnataka, seems to have been in origin a Jain who died bravely on the battlefield and was then deified (Sontheimer 1997: 99). In Rajasthan Jains venerate divine hero figures whose martial energy and concomitant disciplined control provide a basis for enacting the loftier ideal of non-violence (Harlan 2003: 66).

11 See Bouillier 1994, McFarlane 1994 and Roçu 1981: 446–48. The title of this essay is modelled on the title of Bouillier's paper and that of Granoff 1989.

12 Jacobi 1895: 251.

13 Cf. Babb 2004: 21 and Biardeau 1994: 125. Gandhi and his followers succeeded in promoting the non-violent values of western Indian trading castes to the extent that they have come to be accepted in recent times as components of a pan-Indian ideology.

14 See Obiguibénine 1994.

15 See Houben 2001.

16 See Schmithausen 2000.

17 Dundas 1999 and Granoff 1992.

18 I treat the Jain *baniyā* as most representative of the stereotype, although Vaiṣṇava Hindus also belonged to this caste. It should be noted that Jains in western India have defined themselves, as witnessed by their caste origin myths, in terms of rejection of brahmanical sacrificial ritual which is perceived to be inherently violent. At the same time, their non-violence rendered them dependent on others for protection and thus, given the regional prestige of martial values, often made them objects of disdain because of their supposed passivity and avarice. See Babb 2004: 141–84 and 219.

19 Hardiman 1996: 7–10

20 Vidal 1997: 158–66.

21 Cf. Babb 2004: 64 note 29.

22 Cort 2002: 61.

23 Bayly 1998: 229–30.

24 Singhi 1991: 157–58 and Unnithan-Kumar 1997: 238–47.

25 Carrithers 1988 and Cort 1999: 36–37. For a perpetuation of many components of this *baniyā* stereotype, compare Brass 1997: 58–96 who analyses the processes which led to communal violence concerning a supposedly stolen

image of Mahāvīra in rural Uttar Pradesh in the 1980s. Brass does not rule out the possibility that the violence which broke out may have been fomented by the Jains themselves hiring dacoits to retrieve the image and in some way manipulating events from a safe distance.

26 Hemacandra 2001: 36.

27 The root *hiṃs-*, from which the term *hiṃsā* derives, seems in origin to have had a desiderative sense of 'wish to strike, kill' (Malamoud 1994: 5 and Oguibénine 1994: 81). However Caillat 1993: 220–23 has shown that this sense cannot be found when *hiṃs-* and derivatives from it are used in the early Jain texts.

28 Compare Akalaṅka (eighth century CE), *Tattvārtharājavārttika*, p. 540, who asserts that when there are no careless mental, vocal or physical activities (*pramattayoga*) and merely taking of life, then there is no violence. Cf. Kundakunda, *Pravacanasāra* 3. 17: a monk who kills something on the way while taking care about his physical movements (*īryāsamiti*) is not guilty of violence.

29 Cf. Siddhasena Divākara (*c.* sixth century CE), *Dvātriṃśikā* 3. 16, who states that separating somebody from life does not necessarily entail the fault of killing. The strong ascetic view is that while violence towards lower forms of life is less significant than that towards higher forms of life, the person of discernment attempts to avoid both types. See Mahāprajña 1988: 38–39.

30 Mahāprajña 1988: 30.

31 Mahāprajña 1988: 78–79 and Zydenbos 1998: 197.

32 Jacobi 1884: 50–56.

33 Deo 1956: 388 and 425.

34 Cf., for example, Ryan 2000: 239.

35 See also Jaini 2004.

36 Cf. Babb 2004: 57.

37 Laidlaw 1995: 155.

38 Cf. Jha 1978: 38.

39 See Dundas 2002a: 238–40.

40 See Dundas 1991.

41 Kundakunda, *Samayasāra* vv. 252–61.

42 Kundakunda, *Samayasāra* v. 262.

43 Kundakunda, *Samayasāra* vv. 263–64.

44 Scharfe 1987.

45 Cf. Zydenbos 1998: 188–91.

46 *Sthānāṅga Sūtra* 292, pp. 369–70.

47 *Middle Length Sayings*, *Cūḷadukkhakhandha Sutta*.

48 Cf. Nayak 2000: 25.

49 Olson 1997.

50 Bronkhorst 2001: 414.

51 Glucklich 2001: 207.

52 Compare Haribhadra, *Anekāntajayapatākā* ch. 6, pp. 218–22, for a prose elaboration of this stressing a morally positive fame of mind (*kuśalapariṇāma*) as informing the performance of austerity in Jainism.

53 Laidlaw 1995: 238.

54 Akalaṅka, *Tattvārtharājavārttika*, pp. 550–51. The Jain here somewhat disingenuously suggests an inconsistency on the part of the Buddhist who while denying the existence of the self, also attacks the possibility of 'killing the self' (*ātmavadha*), the literal sense of the Sanskrit expression for 'suicide'.

55 In other words, all Jinas are *kevalins* who are in possession of an advanced form of karmic development which makes them Jinas, but by no means all *kevalins* are Jinas.

56 See Balbir 1999 and Dundas forthcoming: Chapter 5.

57 The Paurṇamīyaka order, originating with the Śvetāmbara monk Candraprabhasūri in 1102, objected to the role of senior monks in installing images, on the

grounds of the possible violence involved, although it did not take exception to image worship itself.

58 A similar minority strand can be found amongst the Digambara Jains.

59 See Dundas 2002b: 107–10.

60 See Mahāprajña 1988: 66 and 120.

61 Cf. Ryan 2000: 256 n. 105.

Bibliography

Primary sources

Akalaṅka, *Tattvārtharājavārttika*, two volumes, ed. Mahendrakumar, Kashi: Jnanapitha Murtidevi Granthamala 1953 and 1957.

Bhadrabāhusaṃhitā, ed. N. Śāstrī, New Delhi: Bharatiya Jnanpith 1959.

Bhagavatī Sūtra, ed. Muni Nathmal, in Aṃgasuttāṇi, Vol. 2, Ladnun: Jain Viswa Bharati, 1974.

Dharmasāgara, *Pravacanaparīkṣā*, two volumes, Surat, 1937.

Haribhadra, *Anekāntajayapatākā*, two volumes, ed. H.R. Kapadia, Baroda: Gaekwads Oriental Series 1940 and 1947.

Haribhadra, *Aṣṭakaprakaraṇa*, ed. K.K. Dixit, Ahmedabad: L.D. Institute of Indology 1999.

Jinapāla, *Yugapradhānācāryagurvāvalī*, ed. Muni Jinavijaya. Reprint in Vinayasāgar (ed.), Kharataragacccha-Bṛhadgurvāvali, Jaypur: Prākṛt Bhāratī Akādamī 2000.

Meghavijaya, *Digvijayamahākāvya*, ed. A.P. Śāh, Baṃbaī: Singhī Jain Granthamālā 1945.

Kundakunda, *Pravacanasāra*. In P. Sāhityācāra (ed.), Kundakundabhāratī, Paltan: Śrut Bhaṇḍar Va Granth Prakāśan Samiti 1970.

Kundakunda: *Samayasāra*. In P. Sāhityācāra (ed.), Kundakundabhāratī, Paltan: Śrut Bhaṇḍar Va Granth Prakāśan Samiti 1970.

Prabhācandra, *Kathākoṣa*, ed. A.N. Upadhye, Delhi: Māṇikcand Digambara Jain Granthamālā 1974.

Siddhasena Divākara, *Dvātriṃśikā*. In A.N. Upadhye (ed.), Siddhasena Divākara's *Nyāyāvatāra*, Bombay: Jaina Sāhitya Vikās Maṇḍal 1971.

Sthānāṅga Sūtra with the commentary of Abhayadevasūri, ed. Muni Jambūvijaya, Amadāvād/Bhāvnagar: Śrī Siddhi-Bhuvan-Manohar Jain Ṭrasṭ/Śrī Jain Ātmānand Sabhā 2003.

Secondary sources

Babb, L.A. (2004) *Alchemies of Violence: Myths of Identity and the Life of Trade in Western India*, New Delhi/Thousand Oaks/London: Sage.

Balbir, N. (1999) 'About a Jain Polemical Work of the 17th Century', in N. Wagle and O. Qvarnström (eds), *Approaches to Jaina Studies: Philosophy, Logic, Rituals and Symbols*, University of Toronto: Centre for South Asian Studies, 1–18.

Bayly, C.A. (1998) *The Origins of Nationality in South Asia: Patriotism and Ethical Government in the Making of Modern India*, New Delhi: Oxford University Press.

Biardeau, M. (1994) 'Le brāhmanisme ancien, ou la non-violence impossible', in D. Vidal, G. Tarabout and E. Meyer (eds), *Violences et non-violences en Inde*, Paris: Collection Puruṣārtha, Éditions de l'École des Hautes Études, pp. 125–39.

Bollée, W.B. (1981) 'The Indo-European Sodalities in Ancient India', *Zeitschrift der Deutschen Morgenländischen Gesellschaft* 131: 172–91.

——(forthcoming) 'A Note on the Birth of the Hero in Ancient India', in G.-D. Sontheimer (ed.), *The Concept of the Hero(-ine) in Indian Culture.*

Bouillier, V. (1994) 'La violence des non-violents, ou les ascetes au combat', in D. Vidal, G. Tarabout and E. Meyer (eds), *Violences et non-violences en Inde*, Paris: Collection Puruṣārtha, Éditions de l'École des Hautes Études, pp. 213–43.

Brass, P.R. (1997) *Theft of an Idol: Text and Context in the Representation of Collective Violence,* Princeton: Princeton University Press.

Bronkhorst, J. (1999) 'Is there an Inner Conflict of Tradition?' in J. Bronkhorst and M.M. Deshpande (eds), *Aryan and Non-Aryan in South Asia: Evidence, Interpretation and Ideology*, Cambridge: Department of Sanskrit and Indian Studies, Harvard University, pp. 33–57.

Bronkhorst, J. (2001) 'Asceticism, Religion and Biological Evolution', *Method and Theory in the Study of Religion* 13: 374–418.

Caillat, C. (1993) 'Words for Violence in the "Seniors" of the Jaina Canon', in R. Smet and K. Watanabe (eds), *Jain Studies in Honour of Jozef Deleu*, Tokyo: Hon-No-Tomosha, pp. 207–36.

Carrithers, M. (1988) 'Passions of Nation and Community in the Bahubali Affair', *Modern Asian Studies* 22: 815–44.

Carrithers, M. and Humphrey, C. (eds) (1991) *The Assembly of Listeners: Jains in Society*, Cambridge: Cambridge University Press.

Cort, J.E. (1999) 'Fistfights in the Monastery: Calendars, Conflict and Karma among the Jains', in Wagle and Qvarnström (eds), *Approaches to Jaina Studies: Philosophy, Logic, Rituals and Symbols*, University of Toronto: Centre for South Asian Studies, pp. 36–69.

Cort, J.E. (2002) 'A Tale of Two Cities: On the Origins of Digambar Sectarianism in North India', in L.A. Babb, V. Joshi and M.W. Meister (eds), *Multiple Histories: Culture and Society in the Study of Rajasthan*, Jaipur and New Delhi: Rawat Publications, pp. 39–83.

Das, R.P. (2000) 'Indra and Śiva-Rudra', in P. Balcerowicz and M. Mejor (eds), *On the Understanding of Other Cultures. Proceedings of the International Conference on Sanskrit and Related Studies to Commemorate the Centenary of the Birth of Stanislaw Schayer (1899–1941)*, Warsaw University, Poland, October 7–10, 1999. Warsaw: Oriental Institute, Warsaw University, pp. 105–25.

Deo, S.B. (1956) *History of Jaina Monachism*, Poona: Deccan College.

Dundas, P. (1991) 'The Digambara Jain Warrior', in M. Carrithers and C. Humphrey (eds), *The Assembly of Listeners: Jains in Society*, Cambridge: Cambridge University Press, pp. 169–86.

——(1999) 'Jain Perceptions of Islam in the Early Modern Period', *Indo-Iranian Journal* 42: 35–46.

——(2002a) *The Jains*, London and New York: Routledge (2nd revised and enlarged edn).

——(2002b) 'The Limits of a Jain Environmental Ethic', in C.K. Chapple (ed.), *Jainism and Ecology: Nonviolence in the Web of Life*, Cambridge, MA: Center for the Study of World Religions, Harvard Divinity School, pp. 95–117.

——(forthcoming) *History, Scripture and Controversy in a Medieval Jain Sect*, London: Routledge, 2006.

Glucklich, A. (2001) *Sacred Pain: Hurting the Body for the Sake of the Soul*, New York: Oxford University Press.

Granoff, P. (1989) 'Jain Lives of Haribhadra: An Inquiry into the Sources and Logic of the Legend', *Journal of Indian Philosophy* 17: 105–28.

——(1992) 'The Violence of Non-Violence: A Study of Some Jain Responses to Non-Jain Religious Practices', *Journal of the International Association of Buddhist Studies* 15: 1–43.

Harlan, L. (2003) *The Goddesses' Henchmen: Gender in Indian Hero Worship*, Oxford and New York: Oxford University Press.

Hardiman, D. (1996) *Feeding the Baniya: Peasants and Usurers in Western India*, Delhi: Oxford University Press.

Hemacandra (1931) *The Deeds of the Sixty-Three Illustrious Men, Vol. 1*, trans. Helen W. Johnson, Baroda: Gaekwad Oriental Series.

——(2001) *The Yogaśāstra of Hemacandra. A Twelfth Century Handbook on Śvetāmbara Jainism*, trans. Olle Qvarnström, Harvard University: Harvard Oriental Series.

Hinüber, O. von (2001) *Das ältere Mittelindisch im Überblick*, 2nd edn, Vienna: Verlag der Österreichischen Akademie der Wissenschaften.

Houben, J.E.M. (2001) 'The Vedic Horse-Sacrifice and the Changing Use of the Term Ahiṃsā: An Early Insertion in TB 3. 9. 8?' in K. Karttunen and P. Koskikallio (eds), *Vidyārṇavandanam: Essays in Honour of Asko Parpola*, Studia Orientalia 94, 279–90.

Jacobi, H. (1884) *Jain Sutras* (Part One), Oxford: Clarendon Press.

——(1895) *Jaina Sutras* (Part Two), Oxford: Clarendon Press.

Jaini, P.S. (2004) '*Ahiṃsā* and the Question of "Just War", in T. Sethia (ed.), *Ahiṃsā, Anekānta and Jainism*, Delhi: Motilal Banarsidass.

Jha, S. (1978) *Aspects of Brahmanical Influence on the Jaina Mythology*, Delhi: Bharat Bharati Bhandar.

Laidlaw, J. (1995) *Riches and Renunciation: Religion, Economy, and Society among the Jains*, Oxford: Clarendon Press.

Lienhard, S. (1997) 'Martial Arts and Poetics: Some More Observations on *Citrakāvya*', in S. Lienhard and I. Piovano (eds), *Lex et Litterae: Studies in Honour of Professor Oscar Botto*, Torino: Edizioni dell'Orso, pp. 343–59.

McFarlane, S. (1994) 'Fighting Bodhisattvas and Inner Warriors: Buddhism and the Martial Traditions of China and Japan', in T. Skorupski and U. Pagel (eds), *The Buddhist Forum: Volume III*, 1991–93, London: School of Oriental and African Studies, University of London, pp. 185–210.

Mahāprajña (1988) *Ahiṃsā Tattva Darśan*, Cūrū: Ādarś Sāhitya Saṅgh.

Malamoud, C. (1994) 'Remarques sur la dissuasion dans l'Inde ancienne', in D. Vidal, G. Tarabout and E. Meyer (eds), *Violences et non-violences en Inde*, Paris: Collection Puruṣārtha, Éditions de l'École des Hautes Études, pp. 53–60.

Michaels, A. (2004) *Hinduism: Past and Present*, Princeton and Oxford: Princeton University Press.

Middle Length Sayings, Vol. 1 (1976) trans. I.B. Horner, London: The Pali Text Society.

Nayak, A. (2000) *Religions et violences: sources et interactions*, Fribourg: Éditions universitaires.

Oguibénine, B. (1994) 'De la rhétorique de la violence', in D. Vidal, G. Tarabout and E. Meyer (eds), *Violences et non-violences en Inde*, Paris: Collection Puruṣārtha, Éditions de l'École des Hautes Études, pp. 81–95.

Olson, C. (1997) *The Indian Renouncer and Postmodern Poison: A Cross-Cultural Encounter*, New York: Peter Lang.

Roçu, A. (1981) 'Les marman et les arts martiaux indiens', *Journal Asiatique* 269: 416–51.

Ryan, J.D. (2000) 'The Heterodoxies in Tamil Nadu', in K.E. Yandell and J.J. Paul (eds), *Religion and Public Culture: Encounters and Identities in Modern South India*, Richmond: Curzon, pp. 232–57.

Scharfe, H. (1987) 'Nomadisches Erbgüten in der Indischen Tradition', in H. Falk (ed.), *Hinduismus und Buddhismus: Festschrift für Ulrich Schneider*, Reinbek: Verlag für Orientalistische Fachpublikationen, pp. 300–308.

Schmithausen, L. (2000) 'A Note on the Origin of Ahiṃsā', in R. Tsuchida and A. Wezler (eds), *Harānandalaharī: Volume in Honour of Professor Minoru Hara on his Seventieth Birthday*, Reinbek: Verlag für Orientalistische Fachpublikationen, pp. 253–82.

Singh, N.K (1991) 'A Study of Jains in a Rajasthan Town', in M. Carrithers and C. Humphrey (eds), *The Assembly of Listeners: Jains in Society*, Cambridge: Cambridge University Press, pp. 139–68.

Sontheimer, G.-D. (1997) *King of Hunters, Warriors and Shepherds: Essays on Khaṇḍobā*, New Delhi: Manohar.

Thapar, R. (2000) *Cultural Pasts: Essays in Early Indian History*, New Delhi: Oxford University Press.

Unnithan-Kumar, M. (1997) *Identity, Gender and Poverty: New Perspectives on Caste and Tribe in Rajasthan*, Providence/Oxford: Berghahn Books.

Vidal, D. (1997) *Violence and Truth. A Rajasthani Kingdom Confronts Colonial Authority*, Delhi: Oxford University Press.

Vidal, D., Tarabout, G. and Meyer, E. (eds) (1994) *Violences et non-violences en Inde*, Paris: Collection Puruṣārtha, Éditions de l'École des Hautes Études.

Wagle, N. and Qvarnström, O. (eds) (1999) *Approaches to Jaina Studies: Philosophy, Logic, Rituals and Symbols*, University of Toronto: Centre for South Asian Studies.

Zydenbos, R.J. (1998) 'Jainism as the Religion of Non-Violence', in J.E.M. Houben and K.R. van Kooij (eds), *Violence Denied: Violence, Non-Violence and the Rationalization of Violence in South Asian Cultural History*, Leiden/Boston/Köln: Brill, pp. 185–210.

3 Buddhist monks, Buddhist kings, Buddhist violence

On the early Buddhist attitudes to violence

Rupert Gethin

A problem of Buddhism in theory and Buddhism in practice[1]

In one early Buddhist text it is stated that it is impossible that the *arahat* or perfected Buddhist saint should knowingly deprive a living being of life.[2] In another text we find it stated that 'a man or woman who kills living beings, who is murderous, who has blood on his or her hands, who is given to blows and violence, who is without pity for living beings' will as a result be reborn 'in a state of misfortune, an unhappy place, a state of affliction, hell' (M III 203). A group of three texts (S IV 308–11)[3] relates how various professional soldiers approached the Buddha saying that they had heard it said that a soldier who is slain when striving in battle will be reborn among the gods. The Buddha counters that this is a mistaken belief (*micchā-diṭṭhi*); in fact they will be reborn in hell. Other texts describe how the Buddha himself 'refrains from killing living creatures, discards sticks and swords, and is considerate and full of concern, remaining sympathetic and well disposed towards all creatures and beings' (D I 3–4). And one who would follow the Buddha's teachings should turn away from violence towards all living beings in the world; he should not kill a living creature, not cause one to be killed, nor even allow others to kill one (Sn 394). To quote from the *Metta Sutta* or 'Discourse on Friendliness', a text which has been chanted in Theravāda Buddhist ritual to bring protection and safety (*paritta*) for perhaps more than 2,000 years:

> One should not wish another pain out of anger or thoughts of enmity. Just as a mother would protect with her life her own son, her only son, so one should cultivate the immeasurable mind towards all living beings and friendliness towards the whole world.
>
> (Sn 148–50)[4]

Yet, in a well-known passage from a text composed by a Theravāda Buddhist monk living on the island of Lanka[5] perhaps a little before 500 CE (and nearly a thousand years after the composition of the texts quoted above),[6] a group of eight perfected Buddhist saints – *arahats* – are described as flying through the air to comfort Abhaya Duṭṭhagāmaṇi – Fearless the Wicked Leader – who is (finally) distraught at the carnage he has wreaked in the course of his military campaign to become ruler of the whole of the island of Lanka. These *arahats* declare to the king (in Geiger's translation):

> From this deed arises no hindrance in thy way to heaven. Only one and a half human beings have been slain here by thee, O lord of men. The one had come unto the (three) refuges, the other had taken on himself the five precepts. Unbelievers and men of evil life were the rest, not more to be esteemed than beasts. But as for thee, thou wilt bring glory to the doctrine of the Buddha in manifold ways; therefore cast away care from thy heart, O ruler of men!
>
> (Mhv xxv 109–11)[7]

How did these *arahats* come to get their Buddhism so wrong? Or in more strictly scholarly terms, what was a Buddhist monk such as Mahānāma doing in so brazenly having a group of *arahats* brush aside the slaughter of 'millions' (Mhv xxv 103, 108: *akkhobhiṇī*) of human beings as of little consequence on the grounds that, not being Buddhists, they were less than human? For on the basis of the earliest Buddhist texts one might have thought that the slaughter of even millions of animals might have been of some consequence.

Part of the answer to this question lies in the simple observation that, *being* human, Buddhists are as capable of hypocrisy, double standards and special pleading as anyone else. One might conclude one's remarks on the Buddhist perspective on violence at this point: as followers of the teachings of the Buddha, Buddhists should not kill, but alas, being human, they do. But we can also attempt to come to a more nuanced and subtle understanding of the tensions between the Buddhist ideal and the historical reality. This paper is an attempt to go some way towards articulating such an understanding.

Buddhist first principles

The founder of Buddhism (the man whom the earliest sources look back to as the Buddha) was, to use the term that has become current in the modern scholarly discussion of Indian religion, a 'renouncer' (*saṃnyāsin*). This term perhaps reflects a brahmanical bias, and the preferred general term in the earliest Buddhist sources is *samaṇa* (Sanskrit: *śramaṇa*) or 'one who strives'. The English term 'renouncer' is used in the scholarly literature on Indian religion to refer to the practice of leaving ordinary society – the household life with wife (or in some cases husband) and family and some kind of gainful occupation – to embark on some form of spiritual or religious life which typically takes the form of a quest for knowledge that will bring freedom from this imperfect and unsatisfactory world, freedom from the interminable round of rebirth. The origins of ancient Indian renunciation are obscure, and the precise form the phenomenon took seems to have been diverse and varied. However, many renouncers seem to have shared a common set of values. One way these basic values find expression is in terms of four commonly held 'precepts' or 'rules of training' (*sikkhāpada*, to use the Buddhist terminology): (1) not to kill living creatures, (2) not to take what is not given, (3) to remain celibate, (4) not to speak falsely (cf. Dundas 2000: 157–60, 189). The fundamental Buddhist attitude to violence is encapsulated in the first precept, although aspects of the other precepts, especially the fourth, are also relevant. It should be added, though, that some groups seem to have been more accepting of killing and acts of violence, if we are to take the Buddhist accounts of their teachings at face value.[8]

Why does the early Indian renouncer tradition regard killing living creatures as problematic? The liberating knowledge that renouncers sought could only be gained as a result of a way of life that involved a certain kind of discipline and training. Most agreed that killing was simply incompatible with that lifestyle. To state the reason for this in its most general terms: certain kinds of action tend to entangle and bind one to the round of rebirth more tightly, other actions and modes of behaviour tend to weaken those ties. Most early renouncers agreed that killing was one of the worst, most harmful, kinds of action in this respect: killing and involvement in killing bind one ever more tightly to the round of rebirth. Moreover they tend to bind one in a particularly unpleasant and undesirable way: as a bad action, killing has unpleasant and undesired results. As indicated above, it leads to rebirth in painful and unpleasant circumstances.

For early Buddhist thought the problem of violence is basically a mental one. We are bound to the round of rebirth because our minds are afflicted by various defilements. The two most basic defilements are ignorance and craving. Working together these manifest themselves in the form of various other defilements. These defilements lead us to act in various unwholesome (*akusala*) ways which perpetuate the sorry state of affairs that is the round of rebirth. The act of killing is considered an expression of one of the fundamental defilements of the mind: hatred. Hatred is conditioned by ignorance and craving: frustrated in our desires in various ways we become angry, which eventually leads to acts of violence, including killing (D II 58–59). But as well as being afflicted by these defiling tendencies, the mind is characterized by other tendencies which oppose and counteract these defilements: summed up in the early Abhidhamma texts as lack of delusion (*amoha*) or wisdom, lack of greed (*alobha*) or generosity, and lack of hatred (*adosa*) or friendliness. Actions motivated by these tend to the weakening of the bonds of the round of rebirth. By the systematic cultivation of these wholesome roots of action, the mind can eventually arrive at a state where a transcendent knowledge may arise, liberating one from the round of rebirth. In the present context it is important to note that this knowledge, this experience of waking up, is regarded as a fundamental reintegration and transformation of the individual and personality. The person who gains this knowledge is no longer an ordinary person (*puthujjana*) but a 'noble person' (*ariya-puggala*), and, when the transformation is complete, an *arahat*.

While an *arahat* is free of the round of rebirth and will no longer be reborn, and thus at death will disappear from the world, in most cases, like the Buddha, he lingers for a while. The presence of *arahats* in society, as portrayed in the earliest Buddhist texts, is not entirely irrelevant to that society: they teach other members of society the way (as understood by Buddhism) leading to the cessation of suffering. But not only do they teach by the conventional means of words, they embody that way in everything they do, say and think. The knowledge they have gained, the experience of waking up, has the effect of eradicating all the defiling tendencies of the mind: from then on their minds are completely without these defilements, so none of their deeds, words or thoughts can be tainted by these defilements. Instead all of an *arahat's* deeds, words and thoughts are motivated by and rooted in the tendencies that are opposite in character to the defilements: non-attachment, friendliness, and wisdom. Thus it is said that it is simply impossible that one who is an *arahat* could kill another living being.

The earliest Buddhist texts (as represented by the Pali Nikāyas and Chinese Āgamas) thus take an uncompromising stand against violence: violence in all its forms is condemned, while the advantages of such qualities as friendliness and compassion are praised and extolled repeatedly. The one who wishes to put the teachings of the Buddha into practice must renounce all forms of violence.

Ascetic violence

When I say violence in all its forms is condemned, it might be objected that there is one form of violence that I have left out of the reckoning, namely what might be called 'ascetic violence'. If one wishes to argue, as some might, that *all* forms of asceticism are in essence forms of violence against the self, then clearly Buddhist asceticism must represent an instance of violence against the self. Nevertheless, equally clearly there are and have been more and less extreme forms of asceticism, and it seems worth passing some comment here on the nature of Buddhist asceticism.

Ancient Indian sources indicate a variety of approaches to religious asceticism, some more extreme than others. One early Buddhist text, the *Kassapasīhanāda Sutta* (D I 161–77), details a conversation between the Buddha and a naked ascetic (*acelaka*) Kassapa, in which the Buddha dismisses the idea that the undertaking of the various ascetic practices (*tapo-pakkama*) described there make being an ascetic or brahmin a difficult thing. What makes it difficult is something quite different: cultivating a friendly mind that is free of enmity and ill will, and, by the destruction of the defilements that taint the mind, liberating the mind through wisdom (D I 169). The opening of the *Kassapasīhanāda Sutta* makes it clear that early Buddhist ascetics felt sensitive to the charge of being somewhat soft on the ascetic front. As is well known, the Buddha is reported to have practised various forms of extreme asceticism that he later turned away from (see, for example, the *Bhayabherava Sutta*, M I 16–24). Whatever the historical value of such accounts for the life of the Buddha, they make it abundantly clear how early Buddhism wished to position itself with regard to the varieties of ascetic practice in ancient India. As the Buddha's first discourse famously puts it (S V 421), the Buddhist path is the middle way between sensual indulgence (*kāma-sukhallikānuyoga*) and self-mortification (*atta-kilamathānuyoga*): although it is a form of asceticism (that is, a form of renunciation of the household life) it is a moderate form (in ancient Indian terms, if not by the standards of modern Western societies).[9]

Of course, middle positions are susceptible from both sides. At the end of his ordination ceremony a Buddhist monk is informed that the four basic 'resources' (*nissaya*) that he can count on for his four 'requisites' (*parikkhāra*) of food, clothing, lodging and medicine are food offered to him as alms, robes made of discarded rags, the foot of a tree, and fermented urine respectively (Vin I 58, 96). That these four resources represented the norm for early Buddhist monks seems unlikely, yet one might see the four resources as setting boundaries and defining the extent of Buddhist asceticism: thus far and no further. But the general tendency of Buddhist monasticism in India would seem to have been away from the ascetic lifestyle, which came to be regarded as a specific path that a monk might or might not choose to follow. Thus from a relatively early date a more or less set list of ascetic practices (*dhutaṅga/dhuta-guṇa*) is elaborated in the literature: two to do with clothing (the refuse-rag wearer's and the triple-robe wearer's practices), five to do with food (the alms-food eater's, the house-to-house seeker's, the one-sitting eater's, the bowl-food eater's and the later-food refuser's practices), five to do with dwelling (the forest dweller's, the tree-root dweller's, the open-air dweller's, the charnel-ground dweller's, and the any-bed user's practices), and one to do with vigour (the sitter's practice).[10]

Again, this list is significant for setting definite boundaries on Buddhist asceticism: this is as ascetic as Buddhist asceticism gets. In commenting on the ascetic practices, the ancient Buddhist manuals such as the **Vimuttimagga* and *Visuddhimagga* state that indulgence in self-mortification is to be avoided (Vism II 84); the purpose of cultivating the ascetic practices is to improve one's meditation practice.

Interestingly, the fact that an extreme ascetic tendency might be driven by self-hatred seems to be acknowledged and confronted in these ancient manuals. The ascetic practices are presented as specifically countering greed (Vism II 84), and in considering what kinds of monastic requisite are suitable for the various character types, it is suggested that someone whose temperament is dominated by hatred should have a comfortable bed and dwelling, fine robes, a clean, polished alms bowl, and tasty food. This, it seems, will counteract the hate-type's natural tendency to anger which when directed towards himself will take the form of a wish to deny himself any form of pleasure. By way of contrast, someone whose temperament is dominated by greed should have a dirt spattered, dilapidated dwelling full of bats, a bug ridden bed, rough robes, an old cracked alms bowl, and tasteless food (Vism III 97–100). In this light it is perhaps not insignificant that the Buddha is represented in the *Kassapasīhanāda Sutta* as emphasising to Kassapa the need for the cultivation of friendliness (*mettā*) to the naked ascetic Kassapa (D I 169).

That ascetic zeal should be tempered by the cultivation of friendliness seems to be a concern of the commentarial tradition: it is apparent from the way the tradition seeks on occasion to link prima facie unrelated discourses. A discourse entitled 'The Simile of the Blaze of Fire' (A IV 128–35) has the Buddha ask a group of monks which they regard as better: to embrace and sit and lie by a blazing fire, or to embrace and sit and lie by a young girl. They opt for the latter. The Buddha responds that it would be better for a weak monk to embrace and sit or lie by a blazing fire than to embrace and sit and lie by a young girl; on account of the former he would suffer great pain, but on account of the latter he would suffer rebirth in hell. The monks are then given a number of other similar choices. We are told that while the discourse was being delivered 60 monks coughed up hot blood, 60 returned to the lay life, and 60 more gained arahatship. In an earlier section of the *Aṅguttara Nikāya* (A I 10–11) the Buddha states that a monk who pursues, develops and pays attention to friendliness (*mettā*) for even a finger's snap should be considered one whose meditation is not worthless, whose consumption of the country's alms is not useless. The commentary suggests that the Buddha was prompted to encourage the monks with this 'reason for feeling at ease' (*assāsa-karaṇa*) in the spiritual life because after he had delivered the discourse on the blaze of fire he had returned from a fortnight of seclusion to find the monks discouraged and their numbers somewhat depleted (Mp I 61–74; cf. Aronson 1980: 24–28).

Significantly the circumstances that are presented in the Vinaya as prompting the Buddha to declare the third rule involving expulsion of a monk (deliberately taking the life of a human being) concern not the general issue of murder but ascetic excess.[11] As a result of the Buddha's recommending meditation on the ugliness of the body, a number of monks develop a loathing (*jigucchati*) for their own bodies, and begin to take their own and each other's lives. Some eventually request a certain Migalaṇḍika (described as a *samaṇa-kuttaka* or 'sham ascetic') to help them in this task; he is said eventually to take the lives of 60 monks in a single day in the belief that he is helping them 'cross over' and gain liberation. The Buddha once again returns from a fortnight of solitary meditation to find his group of monks seriously depleted in number. Ānanda explains what has happened and suggests to the Buddha that it would be good if he were to instruct them in a different meditation practice. He duly delivers a discourse on the benefits of mindfulness of breathing. It seems to me that there is quite possibly *intended* humour in these accounts – humour that aims at ridiculing ascetic excess and suicide as foolish and misguided.

There are three other separate accounts of individual monastic suicide in the Pali Nikāyas.[12] The attitude to these is rather more ambivalent. They are not explicitly condemned by the Buddha, and in fact, in Buddhist terms, the outcome in each case can only be described as a good one: each of the monks in question is said to attain arahatship. Yet in each case the commentary is at pains to point out that at the moment of actually 'using the knife' the monk is not yet an *arahat*; arahatship is achieved in the moments after applying the knife as a result of insight meditation on the painful feeling that arises.[13] While this might be read as a scholastic device to preserve the tradition mentioned above – namely that the *arahat* cannot kill – it nevertheless indicates a reluctance on the part of the early Buddhist tradition to take the approach of these monks to the ascetic life as paradigmatic. The commentarial tradition here represents the mainstream: these suicides are the exception that proves the rule. We also perhaps once again see Buddhist asceticism positioning itself in relation to other schools of asceticism, and distancing itself from such practices as Jain *sallekhanā*, the ascetic fast to death.[14]

Early Buddhist monasticism's desire to distance itself from various forms of violence and what it perceived as the excesses of asceticism is witnessed by the general tone of the monastic rule set out in the Vinaya. Apart from prohibiting the monk from killing human beings and other living creatures,[15] the Vinaya also, for example, prohibits monks from damaging plants,[16] from striking each other,[17] and from going out to look at drawn up armies.[18] Furthermore, the use of physical violence as a punishment for breaking the rules of the monastic code seems nowhere to be endorsed in the early Buddhist vision of monastic life.

The ascetic as warrior and hero

Despite their clear rejection of all forms of violence early Buddhist writings, in common with the literature or other ascetic schools, do, of course, employ the metaphors of the warrior and war with reference to the ascetic and his struggle to overcome the defilements of the mind.[19] The most obvious example is the account of the Buddha's defeat of the armies of Māra.[20] Such an account presents a problem: are Māra and his armies mere metaphors or has the Buddha defeated real beings?[21] Whatever our conclusion, the significant point in the present context is that the Buddha does not win the battle by the use of conventional weapons, but by the power of the spiritual qualities that he has perfected over countless lifetimes – his wisdom and compassion. And his opponents are not entirely destroyed; they live to fight another day, if not the Buddha, at least lesser beings. While the metaphor of the ascetic as warrior is clearly present in the early texts, there is little if any evidence of Buddhist monks actively engaging in martial arts in the manner of some Indian ascetics or of their Buddhist brothers in East Asia.[22]

For those of us without the power to defeat our opponents by means of our own wisdom and compassion, the tradition offers protection in the form of certain discourses to be recited as protective charms (*paritta/rākṣa*) in order to keep potentially malevolent beings at bay.[23] While some of the texts chanted evoke the power of kindness (*mettā/maitrī*) to achieve their effect, others confront these malevolent beings in a more assertive way. The *Āṭānāṭiya Sutta* (D III 194–206) describes how a god presents the Buddha with a charm to protect monks and lay followers from malevolent demons. Having presented his charm, the god comments that if any such demon continues to bother someone who has learnt this charm, then that demon will be reviled by the other gods; they will place an empty, upturned bowl on his head; they will cause his head to split in seven (D III 203). Whether this constitutes precisely a threat of violence is not clear, since this warning is used in other contexts and may represent something of a stylised form.[24] When, for example, the Buddha suggests to a brahmin that if he refuses to answer his question for a third time his head will spit in seven (D I 95), it seems that this is not intended to represent the Buddha as making a threat so much as a statement of fact, of the way of things when a Tathāgata is refused in this manner, and in warning the brahmin, the Buddha is actually rescuing him from his predicament. Nonetheless the commentary to the *Āṭānāṭiya Sutta* seems to recognize the special power of the charm and suggests that it should only be used as a last resort after such charms as the *Metta Sutta* have failed.[25] A rather similar ambivalence relates to some of the inscriptions associated with gifts to the *saṃgha* which suggest that those who interfere with the gifts will suffer an unfortunate rebirth as an animal.[26] These might be seen either as curses or, perhaps, as simple warnings of the natural effect of bad karma. As a counterpart to the use of charms to protect oneself and one's works, we can also note Schopen's interpretation of certain passages in the Vinaya as evidence for the ritualized destruction of *stūpas* by Buddhist monks as a way of coping with the threat posed to their prestige by Buddhist nuns.[27]

One further aspect of ascetic violence requires some brief comment: the ascetic as sacrificial victim. One aspect of the argument that the Indian renouncer tradition has its origins within the complex of Vedic sacrificial ritual, rather than outside it, is the suggestion that renunciation is an extension of the sacrificial ritual: the renouncer's life is essentially a form of sacrifice and he himself is ultimately offering himself as the sacrificial victim. Certainly we can find examples of the Buddhist spiritual path being presented as a species of sacrifice (*yañña*) in early Buddhist texts, yet the principal concern in these contexts seems to be to present this as precisely a non-violent sacrifice in contrast to the bloodthirsty sacrifice of a living victim.[28]

The one context in early Buddhist literature where the limits on ascetic violence are to some extent lifted is that of the practice of the *bodhisatta* (Sanskrit: *bodhisattva*) path to perfect and complete buddhahood. One reason why this is possible is that, at least in the accounts of the career of the being who eventually became Gotama the Buddha, the stories are told of a *bodhisatta* who is *not* a Buddhist monk whose lifestyle is governed by the rules of the Vinaya. He is rather an animal, a householder, a king, a brahmin or a non-Buddhist ascetic. Above all he is a lone hero, striving over interminable aeons, ready to make whatever sacrifice is necessary to reach his goal. In such contexts the practice of what could be seen as violence towards one's own body is presented as integral to the *bodhisatta*'s practice. The practice of giving is thus to be perfected by making gifts of both external and internal things.[29] As an example of this there is the well-known story of the *bodhisattva* offering himself to the hungry tigress to enable her to feed her young.[30] Although this particular story appears to be unknown to the Pali tradition, other similar stories are. One famous story is that of King Sivi, who has a surgeon remove his eyes so that he can offer them to a blind brahmin (Ja IV 402). Sivi's eyes are later restored by the power of a 'statement of truth' (*sacca-kiriyā*), and such a story contains various levels suggested by the metaphors of blindness and seeing. Nevertheless when the Pali commentaries set out the path of practice to be followed by an aspiring Buddha, they state that each of the ten qualities that a *bodhisatta* must perfect has three levels: ordinary, further, and ultimate.[31] Thus ordinary giving is a matter of giving one's belongings; further giving, of one's own limbs (like Sivi); ultimate giving, of one's own life (as the *bodhisattva* did to the tigress). The tradition itself would emphasize the difference between this kind of practice, motivated by compassion and altruism, and self-mortification driven by ascetic disgust for the body. Yet devotional zeal is also sometimes the motive. In the *Lotus Sūtra* it is told how the *bodhisattva* Bhaiṣajyarāja offered his body to the Buddha by setting fire to it: if the one aspiring to buddhahood 'can burn a finger or even a toe as an offering to a Buddha-stūpa, he shall exceed one who uses realm or walled city . . . as offerings' (Hurvitz 1976: 295, 298). (This, incidentally, puts kings in their place.) This is from an avowedly Mahāyāna source, but similar examples do exist in the Pali materials. The *Birth-Stories of the Ten Bodhisattas* tells how the future Buddha Rāma once in a previous life as a *bodhisatta* took two pieces of cloth, 'soaked them in scented oil and wrapped himself with them from head to foot and then set fire to them with a torch as an offering to the Buddha'.[32]

Mahāyāna sources it seems are readier to use the motivation of compassion to justify acts of killing. The *Upāyakauśalya Sūtra* tells the story of how the *bodhisattva* in a life when he is indeed called 'Great Compassion' kills a man in order to prevent him from killing 500 others – also *bodhisattvas*.[33] The motivation for this act is compassionate on two accounts: by killing the man he prevents him from killing others and thus prevents him from committing an unwholesome act that would result in his being reborn and suffering in hell; the *bodhisattva* also by his act saves the lives of the 500 others. Interestingly the way in which the *bodhisattva*'s act of killing is presented seems to accept the mainstream Buddhist outlook: acts of killing are instances of unwholesome karma. Thus in deciding to kill the man the *bodhisattva* is presented as accepting that this is an unwholesome act, the unpleasant consequences of which he will have to suffer in hell. Thus the Sūtra does not, initially at least, try to justify the act as one that is wholesome (*kuśala*). However, the Sūtra goes on to relate how the *bodhisattva* in fact avoided the sufferings of rebirth in hell; much later, as a Buddha, he lets his foot be pierced by a thorn in *apparent* retribution for this act of killing.

The analysis of the act of killing in systematic Buddhist thought

While certain Mahāyāna sources go some way towards offering the motivation of compassion as a justification for some acts involving the killing of living beings, the condemnation of acts of violence in early Buddhist thought is maintained in the systematic literature of both the Theravāda and Sarvāstivāda Abhidhamma/Abhidharma. I have argued in some detail elsewhere that the possibility that an act of killing a living being can be motivated by wholesome (*kusala*) states of mind is simply not allowed in Abhidhamma Buddhist psychology; the intention to kill another being always crucially involves hatred or aversion

(Gethin 2004). While certain acts of killing may be manifestations of stronger and more intense instances of anger, hatred, or aversion, no act of killing can be entirely free of these. There can be no justification of any act of killing as entirely blameless, as entirely free of the taint of aversion or hatred. In Abhidhamma terms, acts of killing can only ever be justified as more or less *akusala*, never as purely *kusala*. This applies to acts of so-called mercy killing, and acts of war and suicide.

Buddhist kings: war and peace, crime and punishment

Steven Collins (1998: 419–20, 451–66) in his impressive and far-reaching study of the Buddhist vision of happiness has suggested that one strategy for interpreting the variety of attitudes to violence found in Theravāda Buddhist sources is to divide what he calls 'the protean category of *dhamma*' into two modes. In the first mode *dhamma* ('what is right') functions as a practical moral framework for justice in which, depending on circumstances, violence is allowed; the advice to kings, then, is 'not to pass judgement in haste or anger, but appropriately, such that the punishment fits the crime'. In its second mode *dhamma* functions as an ethic of absolute values that characterizes all forms of violence as wrong; the advice to kings is, then, not to be one and to renounce the world. This is a useful distinction but I would suggest that it is *dhamma* in the second mode that is normative for early Buddhist thought. The first mode is more characteristic of later, post-canonical texts; in the Pali canon it is restricted to certain Jātaka stories.[34]

In line with what has been said above, war and conflict is seen as ultimately an expression of *akusala* states of mind: there is no possibility of killing in war being *kusala*. Perhaps one of the most vivid accounts in early Buddhist sources, integrating the arising of conflict and war into the general Buddhist understanding of the arising of human suffering, is to be found in the discourse on 'the mass of suffering' (*Mahādukkhakkhandha Sutta*):

> With the objects of sense desire as the cause, the starting point, the reason, with only the objects of sense desire as the cause, kings quarrel with kings. . .friend with friend.. . .They attack each other with fists, clods, sticks, or knives and as a result come to their deaths and suffering that is like death.. . .With the objects of sense desire as the cause, the starting point, the reason, with only the objects of sense desire as the cause, men take swords and shields and buckle on bows and quivers, and they charge into battle massed in double array with arrows and spears flying, and swords flashing; and there they are wounded by arrows and spears, and their heads are cut off by swords, and as a result they come to their deaths and suffering that is like death.
>
> (M I 86)

And the way to avoid this? The removal of attachment to the objects of sense-desire, the abandoning of attachment to the objects of sense-desire (M I 87).

Such a passage is undoubtedly typical and exemplifies the general attitude of the texts to such matters. That soldiers are guilty of killing is reiterated in the Buddhist systematic texts such as the *Abhidharmakośa*.[35] One might characterize the overall attitude as, at a certain level, one of resignation to the inevitability of human conflict and war. A human society free of war and conflict is an impossibility. The beings who constitute the round of rebirth are inevitably prey to greed, hatred, and delusion; and since that is so it follows that conflicts and wars will arise. This attitude of resignation though, does not necessarily add up to one of total indifference. Premasiri (2003) has pointed to the *Saṃyutta Nikāya* accounts of the war between the *devas* and *asuras* as suggestive of a concern that if one is to engage in war, then one should at least try to minimize and contain the unwholesome acts of violence that it will inevitably involve.

Less plausible, it seems to me, has been the tendency to read the canonical accounts of the *cakkavattin* myth as intended as some sort of social blueprint outlining a formal theory of how kings should conduct themselves, or as being simple legitimations for state violence. Steven Collins has made the following important observations:

> [W]hile they can be read [. . .] as imaginatively possible eu-topias, they can also be read as ou-topias which comment, ironically and from a distance, on the actual. An externalist approach, which sees, correctly, that Theravāda ideology was appropriated and promoted by holders of political and military power in premodern Southern Asia but then reads these texts simply as 'legitimations' of kingship, underestimates the inside of them.
>
> (1998: 496)

As Schmithausen points out:

> [O]ne of the reasons for the frequency of war even in Theravāda Buddhist countries seems to have been that in these countries government and politics continued to be guided to a large extent by their own system of values, which, being derived from, or at least strongly influenced by, ancient Indian manuals of law, politics and administration, focussed on maintaining and extending power and were thus quite different from the Buddhist system of values.
>
> (1999: 52)[36]

To some extent these observations must also be relevant to the earliest period of Buddhism in that one must assume, I think, that the kind of ideal and the sorts of duties of kingship that are set out in the *Dharmasūtras* and *Arthaśāstra* are basically taken for granted. And while Buddhist ideas represent an implicit critique of some of those ideas, there is no attempt to develop a formal alternative theory or model of kingship in the Nikāyas. But as Collins's remarks suggest, we can perhaps see Aśoka as doing this to some extent, drawing in part on the Buddhist version of the *cakkavattin* myth and taking to heart certain Buddhist teachings on non-violence. But the fundamental Buddhist attitude seems to have been this: the duties of the king involve violence (either in expanding his kingdom or in meting out punishment and keeping society under control); therefore the duties of the king involve breaking precepts, involve unwholesome actions of one sort or another. According to the Abhidhamma commentaries, even when a king orders with a smile the execution of some criminal, he does so with a mind motivated by aversion, albeit momentarily; he thus generates unwholesome karma.[37] Appropriately both Collins and Schmithausen refer to the story of Prince Temiya who, horrified at the violence involved in being a king, prefers instead to become an ascetic.[38]

Ascetics and society

As a 'renouncer', the relationship of the Buddhist monk to society is in some ways an ambivalent one. To some extent his values and his very existence represent a critique of society – the Buddhist monk is one who goes 'against the stream' (cf. Collins 1982: 250), the current of greed, hatred and delusion that sweeps normal human society along. His values are self-consciously different from the values of the rest of us. At the same time these values are the universal values praised by the wise, and we – all of us – are encouraged to approximate to those values as best we can, even though until we reach the state of the 'noble person' (*ariya*) we must all – Buddhist and non-Buddhist alike – inevitably fail to a greater or lesser extent. Yet while the Buddhist renouncer represents a critique of ordinary society's values, the Buddhist monk is (according to the strictures of the monastic rule by which he has undertaken to live) dependent on that society for his day-to-day material needs: without society's support he cannot survive. Thus it is only to the extent that secular society acknowledges and aspires to the values of the Buddhist renouncer that he can survive. In other words, his critique of society has to be a constructive one: he needs to persuade the members of secular society that the renouncer's values are the ultimate values, even if society as a whole will not be successful in its attempts to live by those values. One might put it, then, that in terms of the classic Buddhist conception of the monk's role *in* society (having stepped *out* of society), his duty is to affect society with his values. The cynic would interpret this as self interest: unless the monk can persuade people to be generous, he will not get the material support that will enable him to complete the practice that ends in liberation. The faithful might counter that such cynicism is indicative of the extent to which the cynic has not understood the values of the renouncer. But inevitably, given that Buddhist monks by their own account are mostly not 'noble persons', but, like the rest of us, deluded 'ordinary folk' (*puthuj-jana*), subject to greed and hatred, it is the values of ordinary secular society that are always in danger of affecting the monk. What this means in practice, and where it is relevant in the present context, is that since the monk needs society's support in order to survive, he is likely on occasion to court its favour through motives that fall short of the values that he should in theory embody. And courting society's favour means seeking the support of (and in turn supporting) society's most powerful and wealthiest potential patrons of the *saṃgha*, namely its rulers. On occasion this is likely to include supporting (by legitimizing) such worldly aims as war. When extremely affected or infected (to use a metaphor of disease not alien to Buddhist thought) by secular society's values, the monk is no longer even seeking support for the practice of the spiritual life, but simply colluding in the aims of ordinary society. (This danger seems in part to be the reason for the concern shown in the texts at D I 5–12 with the wrong and right livelihood of monks 'while living on food provided by the faithful'.) Such a model seems to me sufficient to explain in broad terms the history of the relationship between *saṃgha* and state in South and South East Asian Buddhist societies. In this light let us turn to two rulers who illustrate different aspects of the problem of the relationship between Buddhism and the violence of the state: Aśoka and Duṭṭhagāmaṇi.

Aśoka and Duṭṭhagāmaṇi

In the case of Aśoka, we have, of course, two quite distinct sets of sources of evidence. The first is the set of exactly contemporary edicts and inscriptions that come, as it were, directly from Aśoka's mouth, but had remained unread for centuries until James Prinsep deciphered the Brahmī script in 1837. The second is the set of legends preserved in such Buddhist texts as the *Aśokāvadāna* and *Mahāvaṃsa*, which in the form they have come down to us date from five or more centuries after Aśoka's death.

Aśoka succeeded to the Mauryan throne in *c.* 269 BCE. As a good Indian king should, he expanded the territory of his kingdom, eastwards into Kaliṅga. In the 13th major rock edict he speaks of his remorse at the deaths of over 100,000 as a result of the military campaign, and bemoans the suffering caused by war. This statement of remorse is sometimes linked to a specific conversion of Aśoka to Buddhism, though to do so is somewhat speculative. However, we know from a rock edict that exists in several versions (Bloch 1950: 145ff) that Aśoka regarded himself as a Buddhist layman (*upāsaka*); he speaks of having been an *upāsaka* for two and a half years and in the last year of having drawn closer to the Buddhist *saṃgha*. Other inscriptions also indicate a particular devotion to and concern with Buddhism, but they also make clear that he himself offered support to Ājīvikas (Bloch 1950: 156), as well as the Buddhist community; he exhorts his subjects to support ascetics and brahmins in general and calls for tolerance and understanding among different religious groups (*pāṣaṇḍa*) (Bloch 1950: 121–24). More directly relevant to present concerns is that he speaks of conquest by means of *dharma*, as opposed to violence (Bloch 1950: 129–31); he repeatedly exhorts his subjects to avoid anger, and killing and injuring human beings and animals; he speaks of himself and his huntsmen as giving up killing, and it seems that he may have abolished capital punishment.[39]

However, there continues to be scholarly debate concerning the extent to which and sense in which Aśoka can and should be regarded as a specifically 'Buddhist' ruler. If Aśoka thought of himself as an *upāsaka* and as such approached the *saṃgha* for religious instruction, then it seems likely that this had some influence on how he approached the task of government. But it is no doubt inappropriate to think of Buddhism as the official 'state' religion of his empire. Rather Aśoka seems to have approached matters of religion in the spirit of protecting his subjects and *dharma* in general, as all good Indian kings should. Some thus point out that Aśoka's vision of *dhamma* does not seem specifically Buddhist; there is no mention of the four truths, the eightfold path, and *nibbāna*. Yet this is only to point out that Buddhist values have a certain amount in common with more general ancient Indian values. The spirit of tolerance shown towards different groups of 'ascetics and brahmins', the ethical slant of his vision of *dhamma* can quite easily be seen as deriving from early Buddhist materials such as passages of the *Sāmaññaphala Sutta* (e.g. D I 53, 62) and *Sigālovāda Sutta* (D III 180–93).

The Buddhist legends, however, paint a rather different picture of Aśoka. While it is not entirely incompatible with the edicts, let us note one aspect that is. Rather than a tolerant supporter of different religious groups, the Aśoka of the *Mahāvaṃsa* becomes an uncompromising and exclusive supporter of Buddhism, withdrawing his support from other religious groups.[40] The Sanskrit *Aśokāvadāna* has Aśoka condemn 18,000 Jains/Ājīvikas to death after one of their followers draws a picture depicting the Buddha bowing down at the feet of their master; he goes on to offer a reward to anyone who brings him the head of a Jain. It must be added, however, that the narrative of the *Aśokāvadāna* does not seek to condone such acts of violence against followers of other religious schools. In fact we are told that as a consequence of Aśoka's orders his own monk brother is mistaken for a Jain and killed, leading Aśoka never to condemn anyone to death again.[41]

Duṭṭhagāmaṇi came to the Lankan throne of Anurādhapura in 101 BCE (or 161 BCE according to an alternative chronology). However, in his case we have no equivalent of the Aśokan edicts, but only the specifically Buddhist monastic legend, composed it seems some six or seven centuries later, although R.A.L.H. Gunawardana (1985) has made an attempt to reconstruct the historical reality behind Duṭṭhagāmaṇi's campaign on the basis of epigraphical records, which once again demonstrate a certain disparity between the Buddhist legend and historical actuality. What is perhaps surprising is the frequency with which the *Mahāvaṃsa* account of Duṭṭhagāmaṇi's campaign is mentioned in passing in the secondary literature with little indication that it must be largely legendary. Indeed, the *Mahāvaṃsa's* early history of Lanka shares certain significant features in common with such fabulous histories as Geoffrey of Monmouth's twelfth century *Historia Regum Britanniae* ('History of the Kings of Britain'): by mixing myth and legend (e.g. Brutus's journey from Italy to Albion to become the founder of the British people, Brennius's and then Arthur's campaigns against Rome) with historical persons and events (e.g. Julius Caesar's invasion of Britain), it projects the concerns of a later age back into an imagined past. That the *Mahāvaṃsa* at crucial points relates a certain kind of mythic history is apparent from its accounts of the Buddha's three flying visits to Lanka and his subduing of the island's demonic *yakkhas* (Mhv I). Such a theme resonates with the more general Buddhist use of charms against hostile beings (as mentioned above), yet in the context of the *Mahāvaṃsa* can turn Duṭṭhagāmaṇi's campaign from a war driven by greed and hate into a heroic struggle to restore and maintain the *dhamma* against hostile forces (cf. Greenwald 1978: 22–23).

The earlier *Dīpavaṃsa*, which in its final form must date from the second half of the fourth century CE but must incorporate various earlier sources, makes no mention of a war specifically between Eḷāra and Duṭṭhagāmaṇi; the latter is merely described as having killed 32 'princes' (*rājan*) before becoming king. Eḷāra's reign is dealt with in four verses (VIII 49–52) in which he is described as avoiding the paths of greed, hatred, fear and delusion, and ruling righteously (*dhammena*) for 44 years. Abhaya Duṭṭhagāmaṇi's reign is dealt with initially in just two (VIII 53–54). A further six verses of the somewhat muddled 19th chapter deal with Duṭṭhagāmaṇi's good works in supporting the *bhikkhu-saṃgha* (XIX 1–4, 10) and his death and rebirth in the Tusita heaven (XIX 24).[42]

In reworking the material contained in the *Dīpavaṃsa* perhaps a century later, Mahānāma, the apparently monastic author of *Mahāvaṃsa*, inserts a more or less self-contained epic describing the heroic rise to power of Duṭṭhagāmaṇi, his pious deeds carried out in support of the *bhikkhu-saṃgha*, and culminating in the account of his death and rebirth in the Tusita heaven with a prediction that he will be the first disciple of the future Buddha Metteyya (Mhv XXXII 81). This epic comprises eleven of the *Mahāvaṃsa's* 37 chapters (Mhv XXII–XXXII), and extends to some 863 verses, amounting to something approaching one third of the total number (2,904 verses). To be sure, the substance of the Duṭṭhagāmaṇi epic may well have existed and been known to the author of the *Dīpavaṃsa*, as indicated by its allusion to Duṭṭhagāmaṇi as having a retinue of ten warriors, slaying the 32 kings and later being reborn in the Tusita heaven.[43] Two elements of the account, often alluded to in modern scholarly literature, are of some significance in the present context. Duṭṭhagāmaṇi is described as having had a relic (presumably of the Buddha) set in his spear (*kunta*) (Mhv XXV 1). As Geiger long ago pointed out, the spear here should probably be seen as the royal standard, always carried before the king, rather than an actual weapon used in fighting,[44] though this makes it no less a symbol of the Buddhist legitimation of violence and power. The last 16 verses of Chapter 25 recount Duṭṭhagāmaṇi's remorse at the fact that so many had been slain in the war, and how the eight *arahats* comforted him by pointing out that since they were not Buddhists, in effect only one and a half men had been slain; this was the passage I referred to at the beginning of this paper.

To return to the question I raised there: what are we to make of these *arahats* so out of keeping with the spirit and the letter of the canon and commentaries of Theravāda Buddhism? How could Mahānāma get his Buddhism so wrong?

The basic answer to this question lies, I think, in observations already made by others, in particular Hermann Kulke (2000). Although the *Mahāvāmsa's* account is often seen as an attempt to engender a sense of Sinhala Buddhist identity to be contrasted with the 'other' non-Buddhist Tamil identity, this does not in fact seem to be Mahānāma's immediate purpose. The fact that his text may in practice have had this effect, particularly in more recent times is, of course, another issue. As Kulke points out (2000: 133), the *Mahāvaṃsa* depiction of the Tamils is rather contradictory. While they are presented as the arch enemies of Duṭṭhagāmaṇi, the *Dīpavaṃsa's* characterization of Eḷāra as a just ruler is preserved, and in its legendary account of the origins of the Sinhala people, they are shown as descended from Tamil mothers. As Kulke goes on to suggest (2000: 134), the significant reason for Mahānāma writing 'his new chronicle appears to have been sectarian struggles rather than "national" considerations'. Kulke here is referring to the rivalry (at times acute) for patronage and esteem that existed between the three great monastic lineages of ancient Lanka: the Mahāvihāra, the Abhayagirivihāra, and the Jetavana. A century or so before the composition of the *Mahāvaṃsa*, the Mahāvihāra had experienced real threats to its prestige and even survival in the form of King Mahāsena's (334–62/272–302 CE) patronage of its rival institutions. Such threats were of much greater relevance for Mahānāma and his brethren of the Mahāvihāra than the temporary rule of some Damiḷa kings. None of them had dared to treat the Mahāvihara as badly as the Buddhist king Mahāsena and the 'wicked bhikkhus' of the Abhayagirivihāra (Kulke 2000: 134).

What needs to be borne in mind, then, is 'the hagiographic character of Mahānāma's Duṭṭhagāmaṇi epos and his intention to enhance the greatness and fame of Duṭṭhagāmaṇi by depicting him as a truly epic hero' (Kulke 2000: 133). I would add here: and celebrate him as a great Buddhist ruler and patron of Buddhism in the manner of Aśoka before him. The celebration of Duṭṭhagāmaṇi's patronage of the Buddhist *sāsana* does after all take up seven of the eleven chapters of the epic. As a great patron and supporter of the Mahāvihāra, no matter how badly he had in fact behaved, he had to be redeemed as an example of the archetypal Buddhist king.

One cannot help but speculate that the *Mahāvaṃsa's* account of Duṭṭhagāmaṇi amounts to an attempt to rehabilitate a warrior with a violent reputation ('Fearless the Wicked Leader') who having gained the throne subsequently instituted great public Buddhist works and was especially a great supporter of the Mahāvihāra. But a man known as 'Fearless the Wicked Leader' calls for desperate measures, and so the *arahats* from Piyaṅgudīpa are flown in to retrieve the situation.[45]

In fact I think Mahānāma's text reveals some awareness of mainstream Buddhist attitudes to violence. It is significant that the text falls short of explicitly claiming that in being the cause of the slaughter of millions of men Duṭṭhagāmaṇi has performed no unwholesome kamma. What the *arahats* say is that his actions need not be an obstacle to rebirth in a heaven realm. Such a statement has a scriptural basis in, for example, the *Mahākammavibhaṅga Sutta*, which points out that someone who kills living beings need not in all circumstances be reborn in a hell realm, but may even be reborn in a heaven realm (M III 209). Moreover, according to the systematic analysis of the act of killing in the Pali commentaries, a victim's lack of virtuous qualities *is* a factor that diminishes the weight of the always unwholesome act of killing.[46]

Lest I be misunderstood, this is not intended as a justification of Mahānāma's *arahats*, but rather as an attempt to articulate more clearly just what Mahānāma was doing, both consciously and unconsciously, and to understand how he could write in such a way in an explicitly Buddhist context as a Buddhist monk. Yet even if I am right to suggest that these passages offer a theoretical context for Mahānāma's *arahats*, it must remain the case that to infer from them that those who have not taken the Buddhist refuges and precepts should be regarded as less than human is a grotesque distortion of the spirit of both the Nikāyas and Pali commentaries.

In the final analysis, Collins's two modes of *dhamma* amount perhaps to two sides of the same coin. Absolute non-violence is the Buddhist ideal, exemplified by the Buddha and his *arahats*. This very fact means that it is not and cannot be for this world; those who live in this world are prey to greed, hatred and delusion and therefore have to accept that violence will be part of their lives. But, lest we lose sight of that ideal, of the *dhamma* that transcends this world, we are urged to keep it to a minimum in the spirit of that same *dhamma*. That Buddhists have not always succeeded in living up to their own ideals is of the nature of things.

Notes

1 Abbreviations: A = *Aṅguttara Nikāya*; Abhidh-k-bh = *Abhidharmakośa-bhāṣya* edited by P. Pradhan (Patna: Kashi Prasad Jayaswal Research Institute, 1967); As = *Atthasālinī*; Bv-a = *Buddhavaṃsa-aṭṭhakathā*; Cp-a = *Cariyāpiṭaka-aṭṭhakathā*; D = *Dīgha Nikāya*; It-a = *Itivuttaka-aṭṭhakathā*; Ja = *Jātaka*; M = *Majjhima Nikāya*; Mhv = *Mahāvaṃsa*; Mp = *Manorathapūraṇī*; Paṭis-a = *Paṭisambhidāmagga-aṭṭhakathā*; Ps = *Papañcasūdanī*; Pp = *Puggalapaññatti*; S = *Saṃyutta Nikāya*; Sn = *Suttanipāta*; Sp = *Samantapāsādikā*; Spk = *Sāratthappakāsinī*; Sv = *Sumaṅgalavilāsinī*; Vin = *Vinaya*; Vism = *Visuddhimagga*. Editions of Pali texts are those of the Pali Text Society.

2 D III 235 gives five things that it is impossible that an *arahat* might do, A IV 370 nine; in addition to killing, they include stealing, engaging in the sexual act, and lying.

3 Schmithausen (1999: n. 12) also gives a Taishō reference for this, T 2:227b–228a.

4 Translation adapted from Norman (2001).

5 I use 'Lanka' in preference to 'Sri Lanka', since the latter as the recently coined name of a modern state is clearly anachronistic (like speaking of 'the United Kingdom in Roman times'), while the former can at least claim to be one of the ancient, general names for the island.

6 The exact date of the composition of the *Mahāvaṃsa* is uncertain (v. Hinüber 1996: 91), as is the date of the composition of the earliest Buddhist texts, but at least 700 years must separate them.

7 Mhv XXV 109–11: *saggamaggantarāyo ca n' atthi te tena kammunā |dīyaḍ-ḍhamanujā c' ettha ghātitā manujādhipa || saraṇesu ṭhito eko pañcasīle' pi cāparo |micchādiṭṭhi ca dussīlo sesā pasusamāmatā || jotayissasi c'eva tvaṃ bahudhā buddhasāsanaṃ |manovilekhaṃ tasmā tvaṃ vinodaya narissara ||*

8 See, for example, the account of the teaching of especially Pūraṇa Kassapa as found at D I 52–53.

9 On Buddhist asceticism as a moderate form of ancient Indian asceticism cf. Bronkhorst 1993 and Oberlies 1997. The story of how the Buddha rejects

Devadatta's demand for a stricter rule for monks (Vin II 196–98; III 171–72) is also relevant.

10 For references and a discussion of these in various sources see Ray 1994, 293–323.

11 Vin III 67–70; for references to sources in the Chinese canon see Demiéville 1973, 263–64. Issues surrounding other types of murder are dealt with in other stories attached to the third rule concerning expulsion (*pārājika*).

12 Channa, M III 263–66 = S IV 55–60; Godhika, S I 120–22; Vakkali, S III 119–24. For references in the Chinese sources see Demiéville 1973: 265.

13 The relevant passages are: Ps V 83–84 and Spk II 373 for Channa; Spk I 183–84 for Godhika; Spk II 314–15 for Vakkali. On suicide in Buddhism see also Demiéville 1973: 263–65, nn. 7ff; Lamotte 1949: 740–42, n. 1; Keown 1996.

14 Dundas 2000: 179–81, though, as Dundas points out, Jain tradition shows resistance to the notion that *sallekhanā* is equivalent to an act of 'suicide'.

15 Pārājika 3 prohibits the intentional killing of human beings: Pruitt and Norman 2001: 9; Prebish 1975: 50–51. Theravādin Pācittiya (= Mahāsāṃghika Pācittika = Mūlasarvāstivādin Pāyantika) 61 prohibits the intentional killing of any living being: Pruitt and Norman 2001: 69; Prebish 1975: 86–87.

16 Pācittiya (Pācittika/Pāyantika) 11: Pruitt and Norman 2001: 49; Prebish 1975: 76–77; cf. Schmithausen 1991.

17 Pācittiya 74/75(= Pācittika 58/59 = Pāyantika 48/49): Pruitt and Norman 2001: 75; Prebish 1975: 83, 86.

18 Pācittiya 48 (= Pācittika 55 = Pāyantika 45): Pruitt and Norman 2001: 63; Prebish 1975: 81, 86.

19 A clear and extended example of this is found at A III 89–100 (cf. Pp 65–69). See also M I 121, 242, where the forcible controlling of the mind is likened to a strong man grabbing a weaker man by the head or shoulders, and holding him down and overwhelming him. Bronkhorst (1993: 15, 79), however, argues that this violent image always describes a non-Buddhist form of meditation.

20 See for example Ja I 71–75, *Lalitavistara* chapter 12, *Buddhacarita* chapter 13.

21 Cf. Gethin 1997.

22 Roçu 1981; see also Lorenzen 1978.

23 Skilling 1992 and Gombrich 1991: 236–46.

24 See Syrkin 1984 for various examples from Buddhist texts as well as brahmanical parallels.

25 Sv III 969–70; cf. Rahula 1956: 279. The commentary does interpret the placing of an upturned bowl on the demon's head as involving violence: the other gods proceed to strike the bowl with an iron bar (Sv III 968); on the mistranslation of D III 203, 21–22 by Rhys Davids and Walshe see Norman 1997: 9–11.

26 The cover of Schopen 1997 cites the example of an eleventh- or twelfth-century inscription from Bodh-gaya. See *Epigraphia Zeylanica* V 146 for a similar twelfth-century inscription from Lanka. (I am grateful to Dr Mudagamuwe Maithrimurthi for drawing my attention to this reference.)

27 'The Suppression of Nuns and the Ritual Murder of their Special Dead in Two Buddhist Monastic Codes' in Schopen 2004: 329–59.

28 The *locus classicus* is the *Kūṭadanta Sutta* (D I 127–49). See also Olson 1997: 123–64; Freiberger 1998.

29 Cp-a 303–5, translated in Bodhi 1978: 289–91; cf. Schalk 1988.

30 The story is well known from Conze's translation from the *Suvarṇaprabhāsā* (see Conze 1959: 24–26); it is also found in *Jātakmāla* chapter 1 (Khoroche 1989: 5–9).

31 Cp-a 320–21, translated in Bodhi 1978: 312–13.

32 Saddhatissa 1975: 63; cf. Ja I 31; Bv-a 143–44.

33 See Williams 1989: 144–45; Chang 1983: 456–57. The incident is said to have taken place during the era of Dīpaṃkara, so is placed close to the bodhisattva's vow.

34 Collins 1998: 419–20, 451–66.
35 Abhidh-k-bh IV 72 (p. 240); cf. Schmithausen 1999: 48–49.
36 With reference to Bechert 1966: I 24.
37 Sp 463–64; Sv 1050 = Ps I 202 = Spk ii 148 = Paṭis-a I 223 = As 102; It-a ii 54.
38 Collins 1998: 423–36; Schmithausen (1999: 51) cites also the example of the Mahāsīlava Jātaka.
39 As Norman (1990) argues, though this interpretation has been disputed by Guruge (1997).
40 Mhv V 34–36, 73–74; Geiger (1912, 32) suggests that the latter two verses are suspicious since the *ṭīkā* fails to comment on them, but in the present context, *when* they were incorporated in Mhv is less important than the simple fact that they were incorporated.
41 Strong 1983: 232–33; cf. Strong 1994: 104.
42 Cf. Oldenberg's comments (1879: 208, n. 1).
43 von Hinüber 1996: 89: 'it seems that Dīp always needed some accompanying explanation in a similar way as an *ākhyāna*'.
44 Geiger 1912: 170, n. 1; Trainor 1997: 109–13.
45 The *Mahāvaṃsa's* explanation (XXIV 7) of how Abhaya came to be called 'the Hateful' (*duṭṭha*) – because he became angry (*kujjhitvā*) with his father when he refused to let him wage war on the Damiḷas – stretches the meaning of *duṭṭha* (Sanskrit: *duṣṭa*) by taking advantage of the assimilation of Sanskrit *doṣa* (fault) and *dveṣa* (hatred) in Pali *dosa*; it is thus somewhat contrived and can perhaps be seen as part of the attempt at rehabilitation. Nevertheless, it is not impossible that quarrelling with his father and waging war with his brother (Mhv XXIV) contributed to Abhaya being called 'the Wicked'.
46 Sv 69–70 = Ps I 198 = Spk II 144 = As 97; cf. Gethin 2004.

References

Aronson, H.B. (1980) *Love and Sympathy in Theravāda Buddhism*, Delhi: Motilal Banarsidass.

Bechert, H. (1966–73) *Buddhismus, Staat und Gesellschaft in den Ländern des Theravāda-Buddhismus*, 3 vols, Wiesbaden: Harrassowitz.

Bloch, J. (1950) *Les Inscriptions d'Aśoka*, Paris: Les Belles Lettres.

Bodhi (1978) *The Discourse on the All-Embracing Net of Views: The Brahmajāla Sutta and its Commentaries*, Kandy: Buddhist Publication Society.

Bronkhorst, J. (1993) *The Two Traditions of Meditation in Ancient India*, Delhi: Motilal Banarsidass, 2nd edn.

Chang, G.C.C. (ed.) (1983) *A Treasury of Mahāyāna Sūtras: Selections from the Mahāratnakūṭa Sūtra*, University Park: Pennsylvania State University Press.

Collins, S. (1982) *Selfless Persons: Imagery and Thought in Theravāda Buddhism*, Cambridge: Cambridge University Press.

——(1998) *Nirvana and other Buddhist Felicities: Utopias of the Pali Imaginaire*, Cambridge: Cambridge University Press.

Conze, E. (1959) *Buddhist Scriptures*, Harmondsworth: Penguin Books.

Demiéville, P. (1973) 'Le bouddhisme et la guerre: post-scriptum à l'"Histoire des moines gueriers du Japon" de G. Renondeau' in Paul Demiéville, *Choix d'études bouddhiques*, Leiden: E. J. Brill, pp. 261–299.

Dundas, P. (2000) *The Jains*, London: Routledge, 2nd edn.

Freiberger, O. (1998) 'The Ideal Sacrifice: Patterns of Reinterpreting Brahmin Sacrifice in Early Buddhism', *Bulletin d'Études Indiennes*, 16: 39–49.

Geiger, W. (1912) *The Mahāvaṃsa or the Great Chronicle of Ceylon*, London: Luzac & Co. for the Pali Text Society.

Gethin, R. (1997) 'Cosmology and Meditation: From the Aggañña Sutta to the Mahāyāna', *History of Religions*, 36: 183–219.

——(2004) 'Can Killing a Living Being ever be an Act of Compassion? The Analysis of the Act of Killing in the Abhidhamma and Pali commentaries', *Journal of Buddhist Ethics*, 11: 167–202.

Gombrich, R.F. (1991) *Buddhist Precept and Practice: Traditional Buddhism in the Rural Highlands of Ceylon*, Delhi: Motilal Banarsidass, 2nd edn.

Greenwald, A. (1978) 'The Relic on the Spear' in *Religion and Legitimation of Power in Sri Lanka*, (ed.) B.L. Smith, Chambersburg, PA: Anima, pp. 13–35.

Gunawardana, R.A.L.H. (1985) 'Prelude to the State: An Early Phase in the Evolution of Political Institutions in Ancient Sri Lanka', *The Sri Lanka Journal of the Humanities*, 8: 1–39.

Guruge, A. (1997) 'The Evolution of Emperor Aśoka's Humanitarian Policy: Was Capital Punishment Abolished?' in *Recent Researches In Buddhist Studies: Essays in Honour of Professor Y. Karunadasa*, A. Tilakaratne and K. Dhammajoti (eds), Colombo: Karunaratne, pp. 258–275.

Harvey, P. (2000) *An Introduction to Buddhist Ethics*, Cambridge: Cambridge University Press.

Hinüber, O. von (1996) *A Handbook of Pāli Literature*, Berlin: Walter de Gruyter.

Hurvitz, L. (1976) *Scripture of the Lotus Blossom of the Fine Dharma*, New York: Columbia University Press.

Keown, D. (1996) 'Buddhism and Suicide: The Case of Channa', *Journal of Buddhist Ethics*, 3: 8–31.

Khoroche, P. (trans.) (1989) *Once the Buddha Was a Monkey: Ārya Śūra's Jātakamāla*, Chicago: University of Chicago Press.

Kulke, H. (2000) 'Sectarian Politics and Historiography in Early Sri Lanka: Wilhelm Geiger's Studies of the Chronicles of Sri Lanka in the Light of Recent Research' in *Wilhelm Geiger and the Study of the History and Culture of Sri Lanka*, Ulrich Everding and Asanga Tilakaratne (eds), Colombo: Goethe Institute & Postgraduate Institute of Pali and Buddhist Studies, pp. 112–136.

Lamotte, É. (1949) *Le Traité de la grande vertu de sagesse*, Vol. ii, Louvain: Bureaux du Muséon.

Lorenzen, D.N. (1978) 'Warrior Ascetics in Indian History', *Journal of the American Oriental Society*, 98: 61–75.

Norman, K.R. (1990) 'Aśoka and Capital Punishment' in *Collected Papers*, Oxford: Pali Text Society, I, pp. 200–213.

——(1997) *A Philological Approach to Buddhism*, London: School of Oriental and African Studies, University of London.

——(trans.) (2001) *The Group of Discourses*, Oxford: Pali Text Society, 2nd edn.

Oberlies, T. (1997) 'Neuer Wein in alten Scläuchen: Zur Geschichte der buddhistische Ordensregeln', *Bulletin d'Études Indiennes*, 15: 171–204.

Oldenberg, H. (1879) *The Dīpavaṃsa: an Ancient Buddhist Historical Record*, London: Williams and Norgate; reprinted, Oxford: Pali Text Society, 2000.

Olson, C. (1997) *The Indian Renouncer and Postmodern Poison*, New York: Peter Lang.

Prebish, C.S. (1975) *Buddhist Monastic Discipline: The Sanskrit Prātimokṣa Sūtras of the Mahāsāṃghikas and Mūlasarvāstivādins*, University Park and London: Pennsylvania State University Press.

Premasiri, P.D. (2003) 'The Place for a Righteous War in Buddhism: An Enquiry Concerning the Current Sri Lankan Conflict in Terms of Pali Canonical Buddhism': 'Bath Conference on "Buddhism and Conflict in Sri Lanka"', *Journal of Buddhist Ethics*, 10. Available online at http://jbe.gold.ac.uk

Pruitt, W. (ed.) and Norman, K.R. (trans.) (2001) *The Pātimokkha*, Oxford: Pali Text Society.

Rahula, W. (1956) *History of Buddhism in Ceylon: The Anurādhapura Period (3rd Century* BC *to 10th century* AD), Colombo, MD: Gunasena & Co.

Ray, R. (1994) *Buddhist Saints in India: AStudy in Buddhist Values and Orientations*, New York: Oxford University Press.

Roçu, A. (1981) 'Les *marman* et les arts martiaux indiens', *Journal Asiatique*, 269: 417–451.

Saddhatissa, H. (1975) *The Birth-Stories of the Ten Bodhisattas Being a Translation and Edition of the Dasabodhisattuppattikathā*, London: Pali Text Society.

Schalk, P. (1988) 'Buddhismens lära om *adhyātmikadāna*', *Religio*, 12: 131–150.

Schmithausen, L. (1991) *The Problem of the Sentience of Plants in Earliest Buddhism*, Tokyo: International Institute for Buddhist Studies.

——(1999) 'Aspects of the Buddhist Attitude to War' in *Violence Denied: Violence, Non-Violence and the Rationalization of Violence in South Asian Cultural History*, in J.E.M. Houben and K.R. van Kooij (eds), Leiden: E.J. Brill, pp. 45–67.

Schopen, G. (1997) *Bones, Stones, and Buddhist Monks: Collected Papers on the Archaeology, Epigraphy, and Texts of Monastic Buddhism in India*, Honolulu: University of Hawai'i Press.

——(2004) *Buddhist Monks and Business Matters: Still More Papers on Monastic Buddhism in India*, Honolulu: University of Hawai'i Press.

Skilling, P. (1992) 'The Rakṣā Literature of the Śrāvakayāna', *Journal of the Pali Text Society*, 16: 109–182.

Strong, J.S. (trans.) (1983) *The Legend of King Aśoka*, Princeton: Princeton University Press.

——(1994) 'Images of Aśoka: Some Indian and Sri Lankan Legends and their Development' in *King Aśoka and Buddhism: Historical and Literary Studies*, (ed.) A. Seneviratna, Kandy: Buddhist Publication Society, pp. 99–125.

Syrkin, A. (1984) 'Notes on the Buddha's Threats in the *Dīgha Nikāya*', *Journal of the International Association of Buddhist Studies*, 7: 147–158.

Trainor, K. (1997) *Relics, Ritual, and Representation in Buddhism: Rematerializing the Sri Lankan Tradition*, Cambridge: Cambridge University Press.

Williams, P. (1989) *Mahāyāna Buddhism: The Doctrinal Foundations*, London: Routledge.

4 Crimes against God and Violent Punishment in *al-Fatāwā al-ʿĀlamgīriyya*

Robert Gleave

Violence and its justification in Islamic Law

At the centre of popular conceptions of Islam as a violent religion are the punishments carried out by regimes hoping to bolster both their domestic and international Islamic credentials. Pakistan under Zia and more recently the Afghan Taliban provide two South Asian examples of violence justified by reference to the implementation of Sharīʿa law.[1] The punishments of stoning for adultery and amputation for theft do indeed receive attention in the classical works of Islamic law. They belong to a class of punishments called *ḥudūd* (sing. *ḥadd*, literally 'boundaries' or 'limits'). For classical jurists, God has laid down in the Qur'ān and through his Prophet that certain crimes attract these *ḥudūd*, though the severity of the punishments also means that the standard of proof required to convict a criminal is demanding in these cases.[2] Once proven, the judge has no choice but to implement the *ḥadd*, as it is a non-negotiable divine prescription. What has been explored less in both the popular and academic literature is the conception of these punishments in works of law (*fiqh*) and the complex of ideas which underpin the theoretical elaboration of the *ḥudūd*. In this paper, I examine how Muslim jurists, despite the rigid demands of the *ḥudūd* regulations, have developed a sophisticated system whereby the *ḥudūd* are (semi-) rationalized and their implementation controlled, using as an example text a well-known Indian compendium of Islamic law. As such, this text represents an example of how pre-modern Muslim intellectuals engaged in discussions about violence and its justification. An analysis of a small portion of its contents enables me to make some tentative comments about the manner in which violence is discussed and legitimized in classical legal texts.

Ultimately, for classical Sunnī Muslim jurists, any action is justified through reference to 'indicators' within revelation (the Qur'ān and the Sunna of the Prophet).[3] These indicators point towards a particular rule being part of the law which God has decreed for humanity, the Sharīʿa. Hence violent acts, like any other, are justified through reference to the indicators found in texts which represent God's revelation to humanity. That God did not simply reveal a set of unambiguous laws is seen as proof that he wishes humanity to investigate the sources in order to discover the Sharīʿa; that is, human beings have been given an ability to rationalize, as far as possible, the information found in the texts in order to present God's law to the best of their ability. This schema brings a certain amount of ambiguity into the law, as jurists debate over whether a particular text is an indicator of a particular rule. Most jurists have accepted that there will be different opinions over the correct formulation of God's law, and that such dispute is a 'mercy' provided by God to take account of human inability to interpret the Sharīʿa in an infallible manner.[4]

This uncertainty concerning the law, however, does not prevent the law from being implemented. God has revealed procedures for a system of justice which includes rules of evidence, witnesses, confessions and oaths. This system may not be implemented in such a manner that justice will be infallibly served, but it does give the decision of the judge legal validity. There is a distinction, then, between a true judgement and a legal valid one. The former is known to God alone; the latter is all that judges can hope for in this world. For this reason, many modern jurists have felt uneasy about the easy adoption of *ḥadd* penalties by states who are unwilling to recognize that the punishments are only legally valid if the procedures of evidence have been scrupulously followed by the court. Even with this legal validity, the judgement may still not be the 'truth' about God's opinion concerning the law, and this humility concerning knowledge of the Sharīʿa, they argue, needs to be recognized.[5]

The immediate problem for an investigation of the justification of violence within Islamic legal texts involves a delimitation of parameters. What counts as violence?[6] Muslim jurists have not been unaware of this problem, though a single term which encompasses the various connotations of the English term 'violence' is not present in works of law (*fiqh*). Alternatively, Muslim jurists often take a general term (such as killing, *qitāl*)[7] and examine those occasions on which it is justified, and those occasions when it is not permitted and judicial proceedings are necessary to rectify the damage caused by an unjustified killing. Furthermore, there does exist a concept of 'harm' (*ḍarar*) in some Muslim legal traditions. The avoidance of harm is said by some to be an underlying intention (*maqṣad*) of the Sharīʿa.[8] When implementing a legal rule which causes an immediately recognizable harm (considered to frustrate the general intentions of the Sharīʿa), the legal rule should be suspended and a more benevolent rule set in its place. Such a procedure, which appeals to a jurist's (personal) understanding of God's aims and intentions in instituting the Sharīʿa, was highly controversial in the classical period; for some jurists it gave fallible human judgement a decisive and regulatory role over God's law. They argued that both our knowledge of God's intentions and our ability to determine the harm are products of a jurist's deductive and empirical reasoning. That God instituted the Sharīʿa for the benefit of humankind is not disputed; that humankind can always recognize what that benefit may be was not unanimously agreed upon by Muslim legal theorists. 'Harm' which arises through the enforcement of God's law is not, in truth, 'harm' at all. It is merely a benefit which it is difficult to discern. In any case, 'harm' is an element in the casuistic justification for a departure from the strict letter of the law; it is not the same as violence. The rule which is promoted in the name of 'preventing harm' may be more violent than the suppressed rule.

The Ḥanafī tradition, to which most Muslims of the Indian sub-continent belong, did not usually appeal to the underlying principles (*maqāṣid*) of the Sharī'a in order to justify a departure from the apparently clear rules of the Sharī'a. The Ḥanafīs had their own means of controlling the simple and possibly unjust application of a seemingly straightforward Sharī'a rule. They called it *istiḥsān* (literally, 'deeming something appropriate or better') and they used it to prevent what they considered the 'inappropriate' results of the application of rulings.[9] Instances of *istiḥsān* are found throughout *al-Fatāwā al-'Ālamgīriyya* (hereafter *al-Fatāwā*), the authoritative seventeenth-century Ḥanafī legal work of the Mughal period and the text used in this paper. For example, in the section dealing with the punishment for theft, the basic regulations are delineated. The punishment for the first offence of theft is amputation of the right hand; for the second, the left foot. A simple extension of the rule would dictate that the third offence would be punished by the amputation of one of the remaining limbs (indeed other schools of Muslim law demand such a simple extension of the rule).[10] However, the compilers of *al-Fatāwā* state:

> If he steals for a third time, then he does not undergo amputation, but he remains in prison until he repents. This is *istiḥsān*. He is also subject to a discretionary punishment. ... The leader [of the state, the *imām*] may have him killed for political reasons, since he has instigated corruption in the land.[11]

Now one might reason here that, by simple analogy (*qiyās*), additional offences entail additional amputations. The compilers of *al-Fatāwā*, however, state that prison is the appropriate punishment. Why might this be so? I offer here a tentative exposition of the legal reasoning. The results of analogical reasoning are rejected in favour of a solution which is deemed more appropriate (i.e. *istiḥsān*). The underlying legal presumption here could be that the punishment of amputation of the right hand is equivalent to the punishment of amputation of the left foot. However, to amputate the left hand of a man who has already lost his right hand and left foot is a much more serious punishment than the first two amputations. Reducing a third-time offender to having only a solitary right foot is an excessive punishment and, legally speaking, the enforcer oversteps his rights: the criminal suffers a punishment out of proportion with the other amputations for the same crime. On the other hand, it might be argued that imprisonment pending repentance is not equivalent to the loss of the right hand or left foot. Hence, additional provisions of punishment are made available to the enforcer, but these additional punishments are 'discretionary' (*ta'zīr*), and refer to punishments decided by the judge (or the state) on a case-by-case basis. By definition, discretionary punishment is not a *ḥadd*, for the judge has no discretion over the implementation of *ḥadd* punishments. Included in this category of 'discretionary punishment' for Ḥanafīs generally (and consequently for the authors of *al-Fatāwā* specifically) is the 'political' (*siyāsatan*) execution of the offender. The reason for execution being permitted here lies not in the act of theft itself, but in the threat to public order which a serial thief represents.

The manner in which the legal technique of *istiḥsān* operates illustrates well that Ḥanafī jurists did not necessarily call on *istiḥsān* in order to reduce the violence inherent in the implementation of Sharīʿa rules. They permitted more violent punishments to take the place of amputation for the third offence of theft: in an extreme case, these replacement punishments included execution. Rather, the jurists' concern is legal symmetry. In each case of amputation, a proportionality should be observed; this proportionality is compromised in the case of the amputation of the third limb. However, the occurrence of a third offence brings other legal considerations into play. Here one has a person who is a danger to society at large, and therefore execution may be necessary.

The case of amputation, and the introduction of the concepts of *taʿzīr* and political considerations (*siyāsa*) highlight a fundamental distinction in Islamic penal law which has important consequences for an analysis of violence in *al-Fatāwā*. If, as Weber argued, the state is 'a human community that (successfully) claims the monopoly of the legitimate use of physical force within a given territory',[12] then state violence displays no uniformity of justification in *al-Fatāwā*. The violence utilized by the Muslim state (represented by the judge or the *imām* in *al-Fatāwā*) against its citizens (primarily as punishments for crimes) is not gratuitous or unregulated; neither is it justified by a simple appeal to a single cause. The punishments of amputation and execution mentioned above are quite different types of violence, justified by quite different processes. The former is justified because the criminal has committed an act directly proscribed by God (i.e. one of the *ḥudūd*), and God has delineated the appropriate punishment in the Qur'ān. It is these 'crimes against God' and their punishments which form the main subject matter of this paper. The execution punishment is not due to 'a crime against God'; it is justified by political expediency and the preservation of public order. Of course, this could be considered the prevention of future unruly behaviour by thieves, and God decrees that society be orderly (and hence, this might be a crime against God). By 'crime against God' here, I mean a crime for which God has specified a punishment. If one draws the boundary too broadly, any crime could be considered 'against God' in a strict sense, as God, for Muslims, has ordered that society operates in a particular manner, and crimes (by definition) contravene this decreed mechanism.

Here we have two examples of how the state can justify its violent acts: through an appeal to a crime against God (the *ḥudūd* punishments), and an appeal to the public good (in this case the preservation of order). This does not, however, exhaust the justifications for violence within Islamic legal texts. The state can also enact violence against external enemies (the *jihād*).[13] Furthermore, Islamic legal texts sanction individual acts of violence in self-defence, and also as acts of retribution. In the latter case, the relatives of a murdered person have the personal right to kill the murderer; this violence is supposed to be conducted under the supervision of the state, but, unlike Western penal law, the state has no power to decree that the murderer be killed until after the relatives have made their decision, and then not as a *ḥadd* but as a discretionary punishment justified for political (*siyāsa*) reasons. Acts such as murder or bodily harm are subject to a complex compensatory scheme in Islamic legal texts and function more like torts than criminal offences. Intentional and unintentional damage (including murder) are treated with similar processes, and there is no strict category distinction between criminal and accidental damage.[14] Finally, for some schools of Islamic law, there is justified domestic violence. The Qur'ān appears to allow the husband to 'beat' his recalcitrant wife (*nāshiza*).[15] There is much debate about the meaning of this verse and its implications for the physical rights of the husband over his wife's body. For some schools, certainly, it permits the husband to exact physical violence upon his wife in cases where she refuses to obey his command. A full examination of the legal reasoning behind these various instances of justified violence in *al-Fatāwā*, conducted by both the state and individuals, is beyond the scope of this paper. In what follows, I examine the manner in which this Indian Ḥanafī text of Islamic law (*al-Fatāwā*) presents the state enactment of violent punishments upon individuals deemed to have committed 'crimes against God' (the *ḥudūd*).

Islamic legal reasoning

Consider the following passage, taken from our text, *al-Fatāwā*:

> If the thief has palsy of the left hand, or it has already been amputated, or if his right foot has been amputated, then he does not undergo amputation. The same rule applies if his right foot has palsy. The same rule applies if the thumb on his left hand has been amputated or has palsy, or indeed if two of the fingers of the left hand, other than the thumb, are like this. If one finger other than the thumb has been amputated or has palsy, then he does undergo amputation. . . . If his right hand is palsied or missing digits, then he does undergo amputation.[16]

Note the precise delineation of the circumstances in which the criminal avoids the specific punishment of amputation. The body can be excused the violence that legally flows from the commission of the crime through an examination of its corporeal history. The punishment due is amputation of the right hand for the first offence, and of the left foot for the second. However, if the left hand has been disabled by palsy or has been amputated through some other set of circumstances, the amputation procedure cannot take place. There is, perhaps, an implicit assumption that the intention of the punishment is to render the right hand of the criminal unusable; however, if the left hand is already unusable due to a set of circumstances entirely unconnected with the crime (through palsy, for example) then this disability substitutes for the amputation. The punishment had, in a sense, occurred before the crime had even taken place. The intention of the punishment was to make the criminal effectively 'one-handed'.

This has been achieved previously, through other means, and hence there is no reason to implement the punishment procedure. This also reveals that the act of amputation is not considered to be the punishment. The pain which the criminal may feel during the process of becoming 'one-handed', is not the punishment; living as a 'one-handed' person is the punishment. If the same effect can be achieved without immediate pain (i.e. through palsy or deformity), then that substitutes for the amputation.

Also of interest is that exact equivalence between the potential disability inflicted on the criminal and his actual disability is not required. Whilst a fully able thief will face the amputation of his right hand, a disabled thief, with a crippled or missing left hand, retains his right hand. Even a palsied or missing right foot can substitute as a punishment for theft. The intention of the punishment must now be formulated for a second time with more precision: it is not to amputate a limb per se, but to make the criminal 'three-limbed'. However, there seems to be a specificity about which limbs might substitute for the potentially amputated left hand. A (disabled or missing) left hand, or a right foot of similar description have this ability, but a palsied or missing left foot (it appears) does not. Their affliction appears to act vicariously, replacing the need for amputation.[17]

Exactly why disabled (or missing) left hands and right feet present a legal reason to be excused amputation of the right hand is not explained by the text. A possible explanation might be that the loss of functionality in any one of these three limbs is considered an approximately equal inconvenience for the criminal. Or to put it more precisely, to amputate the right hand when the criminal already has lost the use of his left hand or right foot would be a punishment beyond the demands of justice. The intention of the amputation punishment (one might formulate the proposition for a third time) is to inflict the level of inconvenience upon the criminal that comes about from having three limbs instead of four; to inflict this punishment upon an already three-limbed criminal is to render him, in effect, two-limbed. The enforcer of the punishment, it would seem, does not have the right to make the criminal 'two limbed' on the occasion of his first offence of theft (he may only do this on the second offence).[18] To carry out the amputation in such circumstances leads to a rights violation by the enforcer upon the thief: if the enforcer were to do this, then he would be overstepping his prescribed legal powers. It is clear that a palsied or missing left foot does not have a similar legal effect.[19] It is also clear that the enforcer is not permitted to amputate the left hand or the right foot in place of the right hand or the left foot. The regulations do not permit the enforcer to vire the punishment between limbs; the punishment is specific to the amputation of the right hand (or on the occasion of the second offence, the left foot).

Also of interest in the above passage is the stipulation that a level of affliction lower than mere amputation or palsy of the whole left hand may still bring into being a legal reason for the suspension of the amputation procedure. A missing or palsied thumb on the left hand has the same legal consequences as a missing or palsied left hand. Here, perhaps, we have an implicit definition of the use or ability of a hand. Without the thumb the hand is deemed (legally) unusable (or disabled). This reveals an inadequacy in our third formulation of the intention behind the amputation punishment. It is not simply that the punishment aims to reduce the criminal to being three-limbed on the occasion of his first offence. Rather, the intention is to inflict upon the criminal the inconvenience of having only three *able* limbs, with the definition of 'able' being linked to the operation of the thumb in the case of the hand. The definition of an able foot is given later in the passage: 'If his right foot is missing toes, then if he is able to stand and walk upon it, his hand is amputated. If he is not able to walk upon it, then he does not undergo amputation'.[20] The case described in this passage relates to whether a disabled right foot might have the legal effect of suspending the implementation of the amputation of the right hand. The answer is that it may, but only if the level of disability is such that the criminal is unable to walk using the right foot.

Returning to our opening text, there is also an indication that digits are differently valued. A single disabled or missing finger on the left hand is not equivalent to a similarly afflicted thumb on the said hand. The hand is still classified as able with a single disabled finger, and since it is able, it cannot act as a legal obstacle to implementation, and is legally incapable of preventing amputation of the right hand. However, two disabled or missing fingers are judged to be equivalent to a thumb. With two disabled or missing fingers, the hand is classified as disabled and hence does present an impediment to the implementation of the amputation punishment.

Finally, it seems that the classification of the right hand due for amputation on the occasion of the first offence of theft (i.e. whether the hand is classified as able or disabled) is irrelevant; the hand is amputated.[21] My fourth formulation of the intention of the punishment of the amputation of the right hand on the first offence is confirmed by such a statement. The intention appears to be to inflict upon the criminal the inconvenience of having only three able limbs ('able' having been previously defined for both hands and feet). It is not merely to deprive the criminal of the use of his right hand; and it is certainly not to inflict pain upon the criminal through amputation. This intention is fulfilled by amputating the right hand, be it able or disabled (this presumes, of course, that the criminal's other three limbs are all in full working order).[22]

I present these observations to illustrate first the nature of the discourse in texts of Muslim jurisprudence (*fiqh*) generally, and second the discussions concerning the occasions when and for whom the violent punishments are justified courses of action. *Al-Fatāwā* is a composite text, made up of citations of previous works of jurisprudence (*fiqh*) of the Ḥanafī school. The two elements omitted from the passage cited at the start of this essay (indicated by ' . . . ')[23] are actually references to previous works. The first omitted wording attributes the position just described to Burhān al-dīn Abū al-Ḥasan al-Marghīnānī, as laid out in his *al-Hidāya*. Al-Marghīnānī was a twelfth-century Central Asian jurist, whose *al-Hidāya* was probably the most influential of the Ḥanafī law compendia to be used in Mughal India before *al-Fatāwā*, and became one of the principal sources of 'Muhammadan Law' for the judges of British India. The second omitted wording makes reference to the *Tabyīn al-Ḥaqā'iq* of 'Uthmān b. 'Alī al-Zayla'ī (d. 1342). The second position (i.e. that the palsied left hand still undergoes amputation) is that laid out in the *Tabyīn*. As is the case with most sources cited within *al-Fatāwā*, these are not Indian sources.

The compilers of *al-Fatāwā* were a group of scholars commissioned by Awrangzīb to produce a work of *fiqh*, which would provide easy reference for Indian Muslim scholars. They completed their task, under the leadership of Shaykh Nāẓim, between the years 1662–1672. The authors/compilers, however, identified strongly with the broader Ḥanafī (Transoxanian and Middle Eastern) heritage, and make few concessions (or references) to the Indian context in which they were working. This is unsurprising considering the nature of works of *fiqh*. The supposed 'timelessness' of the prose, and the lack of reference to legal reality (such as specific cases occurring at the time of the author or specific policies of the government under which the writer is composing his work)[24] are general characteristics of the genre. This is not to say that later works cannot be distinguished from earlier works even though both utilize a style which makes rare reference to contemporaneous events. The history of Ḥanafī *fiqh* can be quite carefully charted (the same can be said for the other schools of Muslim jurisprudence), and the vocabulary, commentarial style and reference to previous works of *fiqh* can be used to date a work whose provenance is in doubt.[25] *Al-Fatāwā* (the provenance of which is not in doubt) makes little reference to the historical context of its writing: the legal rules it presents are not peculiarly 'Indian'.[26] It is, however, an obviously late work, not merely because it cites earlier sources, but more importantly because it presents a unified and developed Ḥanafī legal tradition through reference to the luminaries of the early period of the school. These include Abū Ḥanīfa (d. 767, the founder of the Ḥanafī school), his famous pupils al-Shaybānī (d. 805) and Abū Yūsuf (d. 798) and numerous other past masters of Ḥanafī legal scholarship. It is perhaps surprising that *al-Fatāwā*, composite and arguably derivative as it is, constitutes the Indian Ḥanafīs' most important contribution to the Ḥanafī tradition. Later Ottoman and Egyptian Ḥanafi writers produced a greater number of works of greater legal and literary significance.

The above passage presents an abstracted conception of Muslim law. The rules concerning palsied or missing hands and feet substituting for the limb designated to be amputated are, primarily, of theoretical concern. Underlying *al-Fatāwā* (and most other works of *fiqh*) is a theological commitment to the all-embracing nature of the Sharī'a, God's law for his creation (and particularly, created human beings). God has a rule for every situation: no area of existence (human or otherwise) has been left untouched by divine edict. The literary origins of the discussions concerning palsied or amputated limbs (the *Sitz im Leben*, if you like) described above are unlikely to be actual 'hard' cases of two-right-handed thieves faced by judges in Mughal India or elsewhere. They are more likely to be the result of the back and forth of questions within an academic environment in which scholars test their colleagues' positions through the presentation of hypothetical cases which challenge the asserted norm. Works of *fiqh* (*al-Fatāwā* included) are, in the main, the product of this scholarly exchange. This is not to say that 'hard' cases (or practice more generally) had no influence on the formulation of norms within the works of *fiqh*; merely that the dominant process whereby *fiqh* norms were formulated was academic dialogue.[27] This dialogue was inspired by a thirst on the part of the scholarly elite of Islam (the *'ulamā'*) to present their version of the Sharī'a (or more precisely, their *fiqh*) as their best attempt at describing the law of God.

Justified *ḥudūd* punishment in *al-Fatāwā al-'Ālamgīriyya*

As mentioned at the outset, theft is one of the categories of crimes which attract *ḥadd* punishments. These crimes, of which there are normally five listed by Muslim jurists,[28] are mentioned in the Qur'ān (and in the case of the adultery of married persons, in the Sunna of the Prophet) and have specific punishments attached to them.[29] All of the punishments involve physical bodily harm, and therefore should be considered violent.[30] The special status of these crimes stems from the fact that God saw fit to mention them and their punishments in his Word. They are best considered 'crimes against God', or even violations of God's law, which enable him to make a claim against the individual through his agents here on earth (the state and its functionaries). Exactly why these five offences are peculiarly abhorrent to God is unclear, and the punishments for their commission are non-negotiable. Why amputation is an appropriate punishment for theft is, in a theological sense, undiscoverable.[31] They are elements of the law that are resistant to legal reasoning. Just as the reasons for the impure status of dogs or pigs, or the reason why the fast occurs in Ramaḍān (and not another month, or, come to think of it, every month) are indiscernible, so the peculiar character of these crimes are taboos. It is, perhaps, elements of the legal system such as these which prompted Weber to remark that the 'cultivation of the ancient juristic thinking in Islam' has 'been unable to prevent the idea of rational law from being overgrown by theological forms of thought'.[32] The *ḥadd* punishments, then, lack the rational justification demanded by modernity. Furthermore there is no attempt to establish an equivalence between the crime and the punishment (a fundamental feature of modern Western criminal procedure). Drinking wine is considered a crime against God, whilst murder or the destruction of another's property are not so categorized. The latter are still crimes (and subject to a separate criminal procedure), but lack what might be called the particular moral abhorrence of the Almighty.

The *ḥadd* crimes are not, however, free of all justification, in the sense that their justification lies in the general Muslim conception of the authority of God's command. However to say that these elements of the law are totally resistant to Weber's process of rationalization ignores the ingenuity and detail with which the Muslim jurists applied legal reasoning to the elaboration of these punishments (an example of which is the rules outlined above for the substitution of the amputation punishment). This is a feature of Muslim juristic discourse which *al-Fatāwā* demonstrates well. Furthermore the role for bodily damage in the execution of *ḥadd* punishments makes them of particular interest as examples of how the state (or its agents) might exact justified violence upon its own populace in *al-Fatāwā*. Take the following passage concerning the correct execution of the lapidation of adulterers:

> It is recommended that the *imam* order a group of Muslims to be present to carry out the stoning. . . . It is necessary that the people line up, as they line up for prayer. Whenever one group [i.e. one line] has stoned, they go to the back, and as others come to the front, they then stone [the criminal]. . . . It is permitted for every person who throws [a stone] to aim to kill [the criminal], except for his close relatives.[33] It is not recommended that [one of them] be responsible for his death. . . . If the stoning has become necessary due to the testimony of witnesses, then it is obligatory that the witnesses commence [the stoning], followed by the *imam*, followed by the people.[34]

The idealized picture of the stoning penalty outlined by the compilers of *al-Fatāwā* may have little relation to the actual punishment practice of the Mughals.[35] This is not crucially relevant for understanding the meaning of justification of the violent punishment here described. As intimated already, the *ḥadd* punishments display certain ritual characteristics. These include the attention to detail, the consequences of the failure of correct performance and the irreducibly irrational connection between the punishment and the crime. The stoning ritual described in this passage further confirms the ritualisation of this punishment. The *imām* gathers a group of Muslims together to perform the punishment, and so the community shares in the enactment of God's justice. The writers of *al-Fatāwā* are specific: it is the Muslims who participate in the punishment (and, hence, no other element of society can act as agents, restoring God's justice here).[36] The stipulation that the people form lines as they do for prayer is (surely) more than a simple description of the geographical positioning of the participants. It hints that what is about to be performed is a divinely ordained act, sharing features with acts of worship. The liminal quality of the impending experience is emphasized. The stoners are divided into groups: the witnesses, the *imam*, the close relatives of the criminal and the 'people'. Each has his or her part to play in the drama; each performs different functions. *Al-Fatāwā* states later in this section that if any witness is absent, or has died since his testimony, or falls sick, or is subsequently convicted of a *ḥadd* offence (i.e. convicted between his testimony and the execution of the stoning penalty), then there is no stoning.[37] The lack of witness participation in the stoning penalty not only undermines the admissibility of the testimony. Their participation in the stoning assumes an almost sacerdotal role,[38] and though the legal reasoning is not explicitly stated, it seems that their being the first to stone the criminals is an assurance of the legal validity (and hence divine approval) of the punishment. Furthermore, as *al-Fatāwā* states elsewhere, the witnesses must be *'adl* (a quality which lies somewhere between just and righteous):[39] so the righteous witnesses to the crime must begin the stoning punishment. Without them, the punishment cannot be carried out.

After the witnesses, the representative of the state, the *imām* stones, thereby affirming the state's sanction of the proceedings and giving it a ceremonial quality. Finally the community as a whole joins in, but not in a disorderly scrum; in ordered lines, stoning with the precision of ritual observance. A taboo is also mentioned, giving the punishment further ritual flavour: the relatives of the criminal should participate, but not aim to kill the criminal. The text of *al-Fatāwā* mentions merely that it is not recommended that a close relative be responsible for the criminal's death.[40]

Elements of the execution serve more than the mere mechanistic application of principles of justice. Consider the public nature of the event, the prescription of the participants' behaviour and actions, and the taboos which are observed. Combined with the general lack of rationally detectable correlation between crime and punishment (beyond the fact that the correlation is dictated by God), one has a breakdown of the rational means–ends relationship expected in legal processes. A simple private stoning, carried out by professional lapidators would surely fulfil the demands of justice, yet the authors of *al-Fatāwā* demand a public participatory event.

The discrete and incommensurate nature of the *ḥadd* punishments further enhances their ritual status. This quality is exemplified by the fact that *ḥadd* punishments, for the compilers of *al-Fatāwā*, cannot be subject to comparison and combination:

> It is not permitted to administer lashing and stoning together [in one act of punishment]; nor can lashes and banishment for the *bikr*[41] be joined together. If the *imam* thinks that there is benefit in [banishing the criminal], banish [them] in a manner he sees fit. However this is not a *ḥadd*, but a discretionary punishment (*ta'zīr*) and a political act (*siyāsa*), and not for use exclusively in cases of illicit intercourse. Rather it is permitted for any crime, and it is the *imam*'s prerogative ... [elsewhere] it is explained that banishment can mean being thrown into prison, and this is best. It is a more effective means of quelling rebellion than banishment to another area.[42]

Lashing and stoning cannot be combined in one punishment, even if the criminal is guilty of both the relevant crimes. Each *ḥadd* has its own ritual character and one cannot be compensated by another (as would be the case in a so-called 'rational' system, where imprisonment, say, can be excused through monetary payment). The compilers of *al-Fatāwā* do not wish to combine the *ḥadd* with any other punishment (keeping them pure and sacred); in particular they affirm the established Ḥanafī position that fornicators (i.e. unmarried persons who have engaged in illicit sexual intercourse) are subject to 100 lashes, but that the additional punishment of banishment for one year (proposed by other schools of law) is invalid and inappropriate. *Ḥadd* punishments are complete in themselves and stand in no need of supplementation. However, if the state (i.e. the *imam*) deems it necessary to banish the fornicators, then it may do for political reasons. That is, banishment (which includes imprisonment) can be used to subdue rebellions or for any other benefit (*maṣlaḥa*) the *imām* considers necessary. The compilers of *al-Fatāwā* are quite clear though that these measures are not to be considered connected with the *ḥadd* punishment, and cannot compensate for any element of it. This incommensurability springs from the *ḥudūd*'s divine origins, and is linked to their lack of legal-rational justification. The sacred character of the *ḥadd* is thereby preserved from consequentialist moral reasoning which might make the *ḥudūd* merely punishments of deterrence, reform or retribution.

If we are dealing in the case of stoning with an example of ritualized violence, then, following Turner, we have here a 'contingent ritual' which takes place in response to a community crisis.[43] The crisis, one might imagine, is a violation of God's decreed 'limits' ('limit' being one translation of *ḥadd*). The adultery (and this could be applied to other *ḥadd* crimes) disrupts the imagined close relationship between the community and God. The stoning ritual (it may be misleading to continue to call it a 'punishment') fulfils the community's need to re-establish the relationship.[44] The adulterers are both criminals and sacrificial offerings, and the stoning is the ritual whereby an effective sacrifice is offered. Whilst this may seem a rather ambitious interpretation of the stoning penalty, I would argue that it accords with the description of the punishment found within *al-Fatāwā* and outlined above.

The contemporary Western revulsion towards the examples of state-sponsored violent *ḥadd* punishments is partly due to liberal ambivalence concerning alleged crimes of adultery and drinking wine. When the *ḥadd* refers to an act considered criminal in the liberal tradition (that is, when a right has been violated as in theft and highway robbery),[45] the abhorrence relates to the allegedly deficient rules of evidence, or the punishment being inappropriate to the crime. Considering the *ḥudūd* as part-ritual, part-legal enactments of the Sharī'a may not eliminate the abhorrence, but it may produce a more sophisticated understanding of these legal phenomena. The modern revulsion at such religiously sanctioned violence can also be traced to changes in Western attitudes concerning the function of punishment. This has been authoritatively examined by Foucault,[46] who traces the putative 'humanizing' progress of punishment from the public executions of *ancien régime* France and the Revolution to the dominant idea of punishment as reform through incarceration in the nineteenth century. Foucault's analysis explains the reasons for the modern repugnance of punishments carried out in modern Muslim states, but it also points towards an alternative means of understanding the bodily nature of the violence sanctioned in the *ḥudūd*.

One could argue that the prevalence of Cartesian dualism allowed a certain licence to harm the body in pre-modern punishment, as exemplified by the excessive violence enacted on Damiens in 1757 and graphically described in the opening section of *Discipline and Punishment*.[47] The ideological changes which come under the aegis of modernism saw a rise in the importance of the 'soul' in discussions of punishment (not in the sense of a disembodied spirit, but the psychological constitution of the individual). The criminal is humanized; the restraint of the body (i.e. imprisonment) and the imposition of physical demands (i.e. forced labour) are punishments aimed at reforming the individual's spirit.[48] The attitude towards the body in the enactment of *ḥadd* punishments is, however, complex and does not entirely accord with Foucault's portrayal of the role of the body in pre-modern criminal justice.[49] The punishments all include violence against the body: stoning (for adultery, discussed above), amputation (for theft), death by crucifixion or the sword (for highway robbery with murder) and a specified number of lashes (for drinking wine, false accusation of illicit sexual intercourse and the illicit sexual intercourse of unmarried persons).[50] The actual enforcement of the penalties is not chaotic, but regulated (see the above description of the performance of the stoning punishment).[51] Another example of this regulated performance is found in the section of *al-Fatāwā* dealing with the manner in which *ḥadd* may be performed (*kayfiyyat al-ḥadd wa-iqāmatihi*) and relates to the performance of the lashes:

> For [lashings administered as part of] both *ḥadd* and *ta'zīr*, the man is stripped and whipped wearing a single piece of cloth. This is how it is done for the *ḥadd* for drinking wine. However, he is not stripped for the *ḥadd* of false accusation of illicit sexual intercourse, but he must take off any pelts or stuffed clothing. . . . [52] The woman is not stripped, except of her pelts and stuffed clothing . . . if, however, she has no [clothing] other than these, she does not take them off. She is lashed sitting. If she is buried for the stoning penalty, this is permitted. If one does not [bury her], then there is no harm in this, though burying her is better. She should be buried up to the chest. The man is not to be buried. He is hit standing for all the *ḥudūd*.[53]

The decorum of the dress is to be observed even when the individual is undergoing punishment, and the deportment of the criminal is carefully regulated. The man must wear a single piece of cloth and the woman must not be stripped. The gender differentiation in punishment regulations reflects the gendered nature of Islamic legal discourse generally.[54] Here the female criminal, through the preservation of the dress regulations, gains some advantage (the protection afforded by clothing). The dress code takes precedence over regulations concerning the female criminal's attire, even if this means breaking the usual rules as she wears pelts and stuffed clothing. Similarly, for the stoning penalty, she is buried up to her chest, thereby concealing much of her body under the ground and reducing the danger of exposure of taboo areas. Burying her may also hasten death (and further lighten the severity of the punishment), though this is a compromise worth making to preserve the regulations concerning bodily exposure. The rules concerning proper dress take precedence over the rules for the *ḥadd*, even if this means that the severity of the punishment is reduced for the woman.

This precedence could be interpreted as signifying the non-liminal nature of the punishment (since everyday rules of dress apply even during the *ḥadd* punishment); alternatively though it could be understood as preserving the sacred nature of the event, since an event where dress rules were relaxed would necessarily reduce the event's sanctity. If the *ḥadd* punishments are to be considered as sharing some features with rituals, then they clearly do not induce what Turner refers to as communitas.[55] They are perhaps best seen as events where a liminal status is achieved (the dry description of the jurists should not deflect us from understanding the ritual nature of the event described) through careful control of the ceremony. This must be so if it is to serve its purpose (that is, the restoration of the correct relationship with God for the community generally, and the criminals in particular).

The dress code reflects the value placed on the human body in *fiqh* texts. Ironically, the respect due to the body is not suspended by the judicial decision to punish. Even in the act of mutilating the body through lashes or stoning, the sanctity of the body is maintained. The evaluations of which limbs may (and may not) substitute for the *ḥadd* punishment cited earlier are also an indication of the attention paid to the valuation of the body generally, and body parts in particular. In the next section of *al-Fatāwā* one finds additional evidence of this 'body valorization' which runs through much of Islamic legal understanding:

> If a *ḥadd* is obligatory upon the sick person, then if that *ḥadd* is stoning, it is carried out in this condition. If [the *ḥadd*] is lashes, then it is not carried out until he resembles himself [in good health] again (that is, he is well, and in sound health). However, if he is sick and there is no hope of recovery [i.e. he is terminally ill], then it is carried out. If the sickness is such that there is no hope of it disappearing, such as palsy, or if he was prematurely born such that his constitution is weak, then in our opinion he should be lashed with a branch (*ʿithkāl*) of one hundred date stalks and he is hit only once. Every date stalk must come into contact with his body, and hence it is said that it must be a widely woven binding.[56]

First, the capital punishment of stoning is carried out on the sick person. The reasoning here resembles the reasoning concerning the palsied right hand which is amputated.[57] Previous damage to the body (or body part) which is to be subjected to punishment does not prevent the punishment from taking effect. However, it is interesting that the person who is to receive lashes as his punishment must not be sick. Here a different set of rules apply to the sick person due to be stoned and the sick person due to receive lashes. Why might this be? What might be the reason behind this distinction? One possible explanation could run as follows: the intention of the *ḥadd* punishments is to achieve a bodily state in the criminal such that the body can be accurately described as 'having been subjected to the appropriate *ḥadd* punishment'. The presence of sickness in the individual hinders this aim in the case of lashes, but not in the case of stoning. The aim of the stoning penalty is to render the body lifeless through the ritual of stoning described above. This aim is not thwarted by the criminal's sickness. The aim of the lashes penalties must be more than merely to enact a specific act of physical violence upon the criminal's body. It could be formulated as 'to enact a specific act of physical violence (lashes in specified number) upon the body of the criminal *in its healthy state*'. The sickness of the criminal thwarts the last part of this formulation of the intention; hence there is a delay until the criminal is well. Now, if the criminal is terminally ill, there is little point in delaying the punishment – to delay it would hinder the justice of God. Hence, in cases of terminally ill criminals, the lashes *ḥadd* is carried out. This leads us to a yet another reformulation of the intention: 'to enact a specific act of physical violence (lashes in specified number) upon the body of the criminal *in its normal state*'. The body's normal state may be full physical health, or it may be terminal illness. What of the person who is not terminally ill, but who is permanently disabled (through paralysis or weak constitution)? *Al-Fatāwā* states that he should receive the 100 lashes due to the fornicator, but, interestingly, in an almost symbolic manner. He is lashed once with a whip of 100 date stalks, rather than 100 times with a single date stalk.[58] Now the presence of this symbolic lash for the palsied criminal should alert the reader, yet again, to the ritual nature of the *ḥadd* punishments. The lashes can *effectively* be carried out with a binding of 100 stalks in certain situations; the 100 lashes are suspended in these circumstances. The end result is the same in both circumstances: the body has received the physical punishment appropriate to the crime.

The status of the body within these punishments is, then, of vital importance to the right performance of the punishments. Just as the effectiveness of a ritual sacrifice is often dependent upon the physical state of the victim (the sheep for the *ʿīd* should be healthy, for example),[59] so the correct enactment of God's justice is, in part, dependent upon an assessment of the bodily state of the criminal. An incorrect assessment would lead to the overstepping of God's limits (*ḥudūd*) and would, in turn, need to be rectified. The sanctity of other parts of the body not covered by the *ḥadd* ordinances is clear in *al-Fatāwā*. For example, when discussing the correct procedure for amputation, the compilers state:

> If the executioner cuts off [the thief's] right foot [instead of his right hand], then the executioner must pay compensation for it (*diyatihā*), and the thief must pay compensation for his act of theft. . . . If he cuts off both hands at the same time, then the right hand is for the theft and the executioner must pay compensation to the thief for the left hand . . . if he cuts off both his hands and his feet, then he must pay compensation for the left hand and the two feet.[60]

The reasoning here appears simple: the executioner is permitted to amputate the right hand. Any amputation other than this does not act as a *ḥadd*.[61] The executioner must pay the thief compensation for the loss of a limb according to the compensatory system of justice found in other, non-*ḥadd* cases of criminal law.[62] Amputation of any other limb is damage, performed by the executioner which must be made good through compensation (*ḍamān*). However, returning to our definitions of the intention of *ḥadd* punishments given above: the intention of the *ḥadd* punishments is to bring about a particular bodily state in the criminal. This bodily state can be death (as in stoning), or the description 'this body has received a specified number of lashes whilst in its normal state' (as in wine drinking), or the description 'this body is three-limbed' (as in the case of theft). If these descriptions can be reached through other means, then the punishment has already been effectively carried out.[63] The executioner's amputation of the criminal's right foot (accidental or otherwise) achieves this end.

Emerging from this complex of legal definitions and qualifications is a general evaluation of the body and the violence which can be performed against it in the name of the *ḥudūd*. The criminal retains ownership of his body. The violent punishment to be exacted upon them is limited and specific. Any other harm which results from the executioner's error or vindictiveness is a crime. The *ḥudūd* are not torture, in the normal meaning of the term. In torture, the victim's body becomes (in Kantian terms) a mere means for the torturer; he achieves his ends through the victim's body. In the *ḥudūd* the criminal's body is an end – or rather, the intention of the *ḥadd* punishment is not to divest the criminal of ownership of his or her body, but to give him or her ownership of a body appropriate to his or her criminal history.

Conclusions

The *ḥudūd*, as described in *al-Fatāwā*, are legal constructions which display a level of complexity greater than their media image might indicate. Their intention is not to inflict physical pain upon the criminal. As we saw in relation to the legal obstacles to amputation, the punishment can be cancelled under certain circumstances. The intention of the *ḥudūd* is to bring into being a particular bodily state in the criminal, and if this bodily state has already been achieved, the punishment is cancelled. In the case of amputation, the punishment is not cancelled out of mercy for the criminal, but out of a recognition that the state's right to punish is limited here. The state has the right to make the criminal three-limbed; it does not have the absolute right to amputate the criminal's right hand.

Which bodily state is appropriate to which crime is, for the compilers of *al-Fatāwā*, not open to question. The correlation between crime and punishment has been laid down by God. In enacting the punishment, the believers submit to God's supreme authority over the operation of the Muslim community. The punishment is, then, a religious act, which establishes, strengthens or restores the relationship between God and his people. It has, then, elements common with sacrificial rites, and can be analysed as such. Indeed, the fact that the punishments are not entirely susceptible to the logic of legal rationalism heightens the ceremonial flavour of punishment described in *al-Fatāwā*. Some of the descriptions of the punishment procedures incorporate symbolism, such as the one lash with a 100 stalk binding to replace the 100 lashes, or the insistence that it be the right hand that is amputated. In a sense, the punishment is not merely inflicted upon the criminal. Inevitably the criminal is most directly affected by the punishment, but the community as a whole, through its participation (either directly as in the stoning ritual, or indirectly as an audience) is implicated in the punishment act. After the punishment, the community is changed; it now must incorporate the criminal within its midst. In the case of capital punishment, the community must incorporate the experience of the public stoning or public crucifixion (one of the available penalties for highway robbery with murder). The boundaries of the community have been delineated through these punishments (at times, literally, through the specification that the event takes place outside the community's geographical settlement). It is, perhaps, no coincidence that the capital *ḥadd* offences (such as highway robbery and illicit sexual intercourse of a *muḥsan*) are marked by a greater level of community involvement. These factors indicate the ritualized character of the violence in the *ḥudūd*, which makes them impervious to the usual reasoning which accompanies an examination of penal sanctions.

The sanctioned violence which forms part of *al-Fatāwā*'s depiction of the *ḥudūd* enables us to make some general comments concerning violence and its justification within the Islamic legal tradition. Obviously, justified violence is a highly regulated phenomenon, with care being taken to ensure that the victim is not only the rightful recipient of the violence, but also that he or she experiences an appropriate level of violence. The appropriate level is determined by the ends the violence is designed to serve, and any excess on the part of the perpetrator is subject to compensation, and, in some cases, retribution. The regulation of violence is not merely a reflection of a desire for legal exactness; it represents a religious commitment to obedience of God's law in a manner which enables the community (both collectively and individually) to be more perfect servants of God. If violence is necessary in the achievement of that aim, the Muslim legal tradition embraces that obligation; if the same ends can be met without recourse to violence (see the palsied limbs case above), then violence becomes a forbidden tactic. The *ḥadd* penalties present a peculiar case within these general mechanisms for the justification of violence. For the *ḥudūd*, the intention is to produce a body which has particular qualities (or a particular history), and these qualities can usually only come about through acts of violence supervised by the state. However, even within the rules imposed upon the jurists by the *ḥudūd*, the compilers of *al-Fatāwā* were able to construct a legal system which enabled a judge to avoid the more serious violence implied in God's revelatory texts.

Notes

1 On the punishments under Zia see the articles by Kennedy 1992: 769–787 and Kennedy 1988: 307–316; for an interesting analysis of the Taliban's policies, including their criminal 'law' (such as it was), see Cole 2003: 771–808.

2 See Schacht 1964: 175–187.

3 On the functioning of 'indicators' (*dalā'il*) see Weiss 1992: 151–160.

4 The well-known statement (sometimes attributed to the Prophet) that 'difference of opinion is a mercy for the community' (*ikhtilāf ummatī raḥmatun lil-nās*) has been seen as justifying the emergence of the four Sunnī legal schools (*madhāhib*): Mālikī, Ḥanafī, Shāfi'ī and Ḥanbalī. It is the Ḥanafī school which concerns us in this paper. On the emergence of the four schools, see Melchert 1997.

5 See, for example, Coulson 1969: 58–76.

6 In the late 1960s, a series of competing philosophical discussions concerning violence emerged in Western academic circles. Wolff argued that violence was best defined as 'the illegitimate or unauthorised use of force to effect decisions against the will or desire of others.' See Wolff 1969: 601–616 (this definition appears on p. 606). By tying illegitimacy into his definition of violence, Wolff rules out any discussion of justified, or legitimate violence. The Sunnī Muslim authors are not uninterested in the question of legitimacy, particularly legitimacy of the state, though it does not directly impinge upon the discussions of the *ḥudūd* in works of *fiqh* (this is not true of the Shī'ī legal tradition, however). Galtung's definition of violence as 'the difference between potential and actual, between what could have been and what is' (Galtung 1969: 167–191; this quote is from p. 168) is geared to allow structural violence being included in his analysis. Neither really enables us to analyse the Muslim legal tradition and its thoughts on violence with any added nuance. If I must define violence for the purpose of this paper, then I offer the following as my working definition: 'violence is the actual and intentional bodily damage, carried out by an individual or individuals on an individual or individuals'. This, I recognize excludes psychological violence, primarily because the classical Muslim legal texts are almost entirely silent concerning the harm caused by psychological violence.

7 See the discussions in the text under discussion, *al-Fatāwā al-'Ālamgīriyya*, accessed online at: http://feqh.al-islam.com/Display.asp?DocID-73&MaksamID-292&ParagraphID-7509&Sharh-0 and the following pages. This text has been published many times: for example: *al-Fatāwā al 'Alamgīriyya* 1865: lithograph, 3 volumes and the more modern edition using its alternative title: *al-Fatāwā al-Hindiyya fīmadhhab al-imām al-a'ẓam Abī Ḥanīfa al-Nu'mān* 1977. I have made comparisons with both printed editions and the online texts, and there are no major discrepancies.

8 The *Maqāṣid* are famously associated with the Andalusian jurists, Abū Isḥāq al-Shāṭibī (d. 1388), on whom see Masood 1989.

9 On the *istiḥsān* controversy in early Ḥanafī thinking, see, Hallaq 1997: 107–111.

10 On the amputation punishment generally, see the interesting (but ultimately limiting) analysis of Souryal, Potts and Al-Obeid 1994: 249–265. The authors are perhaps too interested in justifying amputation as a criminal justice policy.

11 Accessed on line at: http://feqh.al-islam.com/Display.asp?Mode-0&MaksamID-286&DocID-73&ParagraphID-7423&Diacratic-0.

12 Weber 1921: 396–450, translated as Weber 1946: 77–128 (this quote from p.78)

13 See the various writing of Peters, collected in Peters 1996. The state can also act with violence against rebels within its own territory. See Abou El Fadl 2001.

14 See Anderson 1951: 811–828.

15 The Quranic verse used is Q4.34.

16 Accessed at: http://feqh.al-islam.com/Display.asp?Mode-0&MaksamID-286&DocID-73&ParagraphID-7423&Diacratic-0.

17 One has here a complex combination of possible substitutions for the limb to be amputated. It gives the punishment a certain 'sacrificial' quality. Reducing the

criminal to three-limbed status is not dictated by some notion of the punishment 'fitting' the crime in the mind of the judge; nor of some 'reform' of the criminal; nor of a 'deterrent' justification for the offence (if it were intended as a deterrent by the authors of *al-Fatāwā*, then this fails for thieves with unusable left hands; they will suffer no punishment for their first offence). Ultimately the reason why the right hand is needed to restore the disruption caused by the theft is inscrutable. This is why the insistent and uncompromising demand for its loss in classical Islamic legal texts seems sacrificial. I elaborate on this further in note 43.

18 As is stated at the start of the section: 'On the manner in which amputation may take place: Its enactment is by amputating the right hand of the thief. ... For a second theft, the left foot is amputated.' Accessed online at: http://feqh.al-islam.com/Display.asp?DocID-73&MaksamID-286&ParagraphID-7422&Sharh-0.

19 The precision with which the left hand and the right foot are described as possible substitutes in the text would seem to indicate that a disabled or missing left foot does not substitute for the amputation of the right hand. The reason, perhaps, is that the left foot is reserved as a potential amputated limb for a second offence, and in the case of the limb to be amputated being disabled or missing, different rules apply. If a missing or disabled left foot were to substitute for an amputated right hand, then on the second offence, the missing or disabled left foot would act as a substitute for a second time. This would prevent the justice of the punishment being carried out, for the disabled or missing left foot would have taken the place of a legally binding punishment on two occasions, leaving the criminal three- rather than two-limbed, and hence frustrating the whole intention of the amputation punishment for the second offence of the criminal (which is, as I have outlined already, to render the thief two-limbed).

20 Accessed at: http://feqh.al-islam.com/Display.asp?Mode-0&MaksamID-286&DocID-73&ParagraphID-7425&Diacratic-0.

21 This seems indefensible considering the principles outlined up to this point. Surely if a disabled left hand or right foot can substitute for a right hand, then a disabled right hand should do so. The compilers of *al-Fatāwā* maintain it cannot. The commitment to the amputation of the right hand if all other limbs are healthy is preserved even when that hand is itself disabled. This non-rational demand for the amputation of even a disabled right hand represents a commitment to a legal taboo which indicates an imposition of religious consideration on the legal process.

22 That my formulation here may be in need of yet further revision is perhaps indicated by the dispute between scholars mentioned in the next paragraph of the text. The dispute concerns what to do with the criminal who (probably by some genetic deformity) has two hands attached to his right wrist. Some scholars say both should be amputated together. Such a position would indicate that the intention of the punishment is to reduce the number of able limbs of the criminal to three; whether he started out with five is immaterial. The crucial point for these scholars is that the criminal with healthy feet and a left hand should lose the use of *any* right hand he may have. Leaving a two right-handed person with both right hands defies the aim of the punishment. Other scholars say that one should amputate the main (*aṣliyya*) hand of the two right hands, leaving the other right hand intact. If it is not possible to identify the 'main' right hand, then both should be amputated. This latter group appear to be arguing that the main right hand is a sufficient candidate for amputation. Unless one assumes that the other right hand is so disabled as to be irrelevant, there seems little sense to their position. Furthermore, why should both right hands be amputated if the main one cannot be identified? To me at least, their position seems impenetrable.

23 I use this convention in the citations in this paper. One who wishes to ascertain which sources the compilers of *al-Fatāwā* are citing may refer to the text directly. The identity of the sources of the rulings is of secondary interest to my argument here, as it is the process of compilation and, occasionally the description of juristic dispute within the tradition, which is my primary interest here.

24 There are Muslim legal works which make such references – the collections of *fatāwā* of which there are a number from the Mughal period and which serve as a useful source for the history both of legal thought and pre-modern India. They are not, however, the focus of my interest in this essay. *Al-Fatāwā al-ʿĀlamgīriyya*, despite its title, is not a collection of *fatāwā* but a collection of the authoritative opinions found in works of *fiqh* of past Ḥanafī jurists. A mistake is to consider it a collection of *fatāwā* (see, for example, West 1900: 27–44; 'The *Fatāwa al alangiri* [sic] is one of the greatest and most esteemed of [*fatwā*] collections.', p.36). This mistake is repeated on the website used in this article to access the text, where it is classified, with other *fatwā* collections '*al-Fatāwā al-Hindiyya*', a common variant name of the work. On the title of the collection, see Schacht 1971: 475–478.

25 Meron 1969: 73–118 and Wheeler 1996.

26 A rare, possible, reference to Indian practice is found in the section under examination here. The compilers of *al-Fatāwā* state that spreading out on the ground 'as is done in our time' is permitted for the person about to be lashed. See *al-Fatāwā*, accessed at: http://feqh.al-islam.com/Display.asp?Mode-0&MaksamID-275&DocID-73&ParagraphID-6959&Diacratic-0.

27 The influence of practice upon the formulation of works of *fiqh* has been much debated recently in the secondary literature on classical Islamic law. From different perspectives see the work of Hallaq and Calder: Hallaq 1994a: 17–15 and Hallaq 1994b: 55–83; Calder 1995 and Calder 2000: 215–228.

28 Apart from theft, they are unlawful sexual intercourse, false accusation of unlawful sexual intercourse, consumption of wine and highway robbery (which may or may not involve the death of the victim).

29 The debate around the stoning penalty for adultery and its absence from the text of the Qur'ān is particularly complex, involving the relative probative powers of the Qur'ān and Sunna, and the possibility of Quranic verses which have been lost or dropped from the text as we have it today. Burton has written extensively on the subject; see Burton 1990 and the references therein.

30 See note 6 above.

31 A linkage between theft and the hand which has performed the theft can be postulated, drawing on a common Christian Heritage ('If your right hand offends you, cut it off', Matthew 18, v.8 and Mark 9.43). But here the right hand is amputated even if it was the left hand which performed the crime; and on the second offence the left foot is amputated, though the foot was not directly involved in the crime. The right hand and the left foot appear to adopt a symbolic role in the proceedings. They must be given up in order to restore the right relationship of the criminal (or perhaps, the community more generally) with God. I explore this peculiarly sacrificial nature of the *ḥadd* punishments below.

32 Weber 1946: 93.

33 The exact term is the *dhū raḥam maḥram*, which refers to both those who are related to the adulterer from the female line and would be due inheritance, and those who are related in such a proximity that he would not be permitted to marry them if they were female. The same regulations apply to the female adulterer.

34 Accessed at: http://feqh.al-islam.com/Display.asp?Mode-0&MaksamID-275&DocID-73&ParagraphID-6945&Diacratic-0 and following pages.

35 The operation of Mughal law remains to be fully studied. A rather limited attempt has been made by Jain 1970.

36 Erikson 1966: 196: '[D]eviant persons often supply an important service to society by patrolling the outer edges of group space'. The manner in which the community deals with deviants defines and re-enforces the community's boundaries. The adulterers, through suffering a divine ordained death, are reincorporated into God's plan. Their death is in accordance with God's law whilst their act of adultery was a clear violation of that law. The adulterers, at the end of the process, are enabled through the punishment to be (once again) obedient subjects of God.

37 Accessed at: http://feqh.al-islam.com/Display.asp?Mode-0&MaksamID-275&DocID-73&ParagraphID-6948&Diacratic-0 and following pages.

38 'Just as the king takes on priestly functions ... sometimes it happens that the executioner appears as a sacrosanct character who represents society in different religious acts' Caillois 1979: 241–242.

39 See the discussion at http://feqh.al-islam.com/Display.asp?Mode-0&MaksamID-475&DocID-73&ParagraphID-11520&Diacratic-0 and following pages.

40 One legal reason why the relatives should not be responsible for the criminal's death relates to inheritance (if a killer is also an inheritor, he loses his right to inherit). However, this does not explain why the relatives are not barred absolutely from participating in the stoning. The implication seems to be that they should participate, for this performance cements the community, but that they should not aim to kill as this offends some other (unspecified) element of the ideal structure of the Muslim community.

41 This term, meaning virgin, refers to one who is non-*muḥsan*. See note 49.

42 Accessed online at: http://feqh.al-islam.com/Display.asp?DocID=73&MaksamID=286&ParagraphID=7332&Sharh=0.

43 Turner 1972: 1100–1105. Contingent rituals are 'held in response to individual or collective crisis' (p. 1100).

44 Some of the *ḥadd* crimes have no discernable injured party (drinking wine, for example), and though the spouse of the adulterer might be considered an injured party, he or she receives no specific compensation. When there is an injured party (as in the case of theft), the thief is required to compensate the victim in addition to undergoing the *ḥadd* penalty. This demonstrates that the *ḥadd* punishments are not concerned with making good a right which has been violated. The obvious victim in these crimes is God, who has a divine claim on human behaviour and whose rightful claim has been violated by the *ḥadd* crimes. The punishments, decreed unilaterally by God, are a means of compensating God for the violations.

45 The *ḥadd* crime of false accusation of illegitimate sexual intercourse (*qadhf*) could also be considered a case of right violation; slander is treated as a right violation in most Western legal traditions. However, it is slander over a particular moral transgression and not a general prohibition on speaking ill of others. The particular attention paid to false accusation of illicit sexual intercourse in the *ḥudūd* may be rationalized as linked to the severity of the penalty, but could also be viewed as a legal manifestation of a taboo, and an attempt to discourage public discussion of illicit sexual acts. On the link between law and taboo generally, see West 1986: 817–82 and Caudhill 1991: 651–697.

46 Foucault 1977. See particularly his discussion of public executions on pp. 32–69.

47 Foucault 1977: 3–6.

48 Foucault 1977: 77.

49 Foucault argues that one element of pre-modern criminal justice (such as torture and violent executions) is the promotion of a 'political technology of the body', whereby the body, through its modification or incarceration, displays the

marks of power (Foucault 1977: 25–27). As I outline below, the criminal's body is not conceived of as an entirely 'owned' object in the discussion of the *ḥudūd*. The concern about excessive and inappropriate punishment of the criminal, and the requirement of compensation due on such occasions, implies that the criminal does not cede his body to power in the absolute manner implied by Foucault.

50 The unmarried fornicators are described as non-*muḥsan* (a complex term, on which see Burton 1974) and their punishment is, according to the Ḥanafīs (and hence the authors of *al-Fatāwā*) 100 lashes. Other schools add banishment for one year for the non-*muḥsan* fornicator; the Ḥanafīs refuse this for reasons which become clear below.

51 That is, whilst the ritual has a liminal quality, and might therefore be considered as an element of an 'anti-structure' (*pace* Turner), it does not display the characteristics of 'communitas'; the community is liberated from its structural constraints. See below, note 53.

52 The rationale for more lax regulations concerning the *ḥadd* for *qadhf* may represent a ranking of the associated crimes. According to the Ḥanafīs, both crimes require punishments of 80 lashes (giving them parity in this respect), though the clothing allowance made for *qadhf* might indicate a relative ranking lower than the drinking of wine.

53 See Abou El-Fadl 2001: 209–263.

54 Accessed online at: http://feqh.al-islam.com/Display.asp?DocID=73&MaksamID=286&ParagraphID=7422&Sharh=0

55 Communitas, as Turner conceives it, is the community spirit effected through 'the liberation of human capacities of cognition, affect, volition, creativity, etc., from the normative constraints incumbent upon occupying a sequence of social statuses' (Turner 1990: 44). In the rituals described here, the rules concerning gendered differentiation (Turner's 'structure') are not significantly disturbed. See Turner 1974: 231–271.

56 Accessed online at: http://feqh.al-islam.com/Display.asp?DocID=73&MaksamID=286&ParagraphID=7383&Sharh=0.

57 This follows an analogous legal argument concerning the suspension of the amputation of the right hand when the left hand is palsied; the intention of the amputation is to leave the body in a state of 'three-limbedness' and this has already been achieved by a natural cause.

58 *Al-Fatāwā*, unfortunately, does not state whether the number of stalks should be reduced for the disabled slanderer (due 80 lashes) or the wine drinker (also due 80 lashes).

59 See also Leviticus 16, where the (unblemished) scapegoat takes on the sins of Israel.

60 Accessed online at: http://feqh.al-islam.com/Display.asp?Mode-0&MaksamID-286&DocID-73&ParagraphID-7427&Diacratic-0 and the following pages.

61 It may, however, render the *ḥadd* cancelled (see below, note 63).

62 see note 14 above.

63 Note that the compilers of *al-Fatāwā* state: 'If he cuts off the left foot, then the executioner pays compensation for it, and the right hand of the thief is amputated'. If the executioner amputates the left foot instead of the right hand, he must pay the compensation for the left foot *but* the right hand is still amputated. If the intention was simply to render the criminal three-limbed, then the amputation of the left foot would surely be an effective means of achieving this intention. However, there is more to the left foot than being a simple limb. Rather, the left foot is the limb to be amputated on the commission of a second act of theft. For the same reason that a palsied left foot cannot substitute for a right hand, the executioners amputation of the left foot cannot act as a substitution for the *ḥadd*. See above, note 19.

Bibliography

Abou El Fadl, K. (2001) *Rebellion and Violence in Islamic Law*, Cambridge: Cambridge University Press.

——(2001) *Speaking in God's Name: Islamic Law, Authority and Women*, Oxford: One World.

al-Fatāwā al-ʿĀlamgīriyya. Available online at http://feqh.al-islam.com

al-Fatāwā al ʿAlamgīriyya (1865) Lucknow: Nawal Kishawr.

al-Fatāwā al-Hindiyya fīmadhhab al-imām al-aʿẓam Abī Ḥanīfa al-Nuʿmān (1977) Peshawar: Muḥammad Fāqir Nūrānī Kitābkhānah.

Anderson, N. (1951) 'Homicide in Islamic Law', *Bulletin of the School of Oriental and African Studies*, 13: 811–828.

Burton, J. (1974) 'The Meaning of "*Ihsan*"', *Journal of Semitic Studies*, 19: 47–75.

——(1990) *The Sources of Islamic Law: Islamic Theories of Abrogation*, Edinburgh: Edinburgh University Press.

Calder, N. (1995) 'Exploring God's Law: Muhammad b. Ahmad b. Abi Sahl al-Sarakhsi on zakat,' in Ch. Toll and J. Skovgaard-Petersen (eds), *Law and the Islamic World: Past and Present*, Copenhagen: University of Copenhagen Press.

——(2000) 'The Uqūd rasm al-Muftī of Ibn 'Ābidīn', *Bulletin of the School of Oriental and African Studies*, 63 (2): 215–228.

Caillois, R. (1979) 'The Sociology of the Executioner' in D. Hollier (ed.) *The College of Sociology (1937–1939)*, Minneapolis: University of Minnesota Press, pp. 241–242.

Caudhill, D. (1991) 'Freud and Critical Legal Studies', *Indiana Law Journal*, 66 (3): 651–697.

Cole, J. (2003) 'The Taliban, Women and the Hegelian Private Sphere', *Social Research*, 70 (3): 771–808.

Coulson, N. (1969) *Conflicts and Tensions in Islamic Jurisprudence*, Chicago: University of Chicago Press.

Erikson, J. (1966) *Wayward Puritans: A Study in the Sociology of Deviance*, New York: John Wiley and Sons.

Foucault, M. (1977) *Discipline and Punishment: The Birth of the Prison*, London: Penguin.

Galtung, J. (1969) 'Violence, Peace and Peace Research', *Journal of Peace Studies*, 5 (1): 167–191.

Gethin, R. (1998) *The Foundations of Buddhism*, Oxford, New York: Oxford University Press.

Hallaq, W. (1994a) 'From *Fatwās* to *Furūʿ*: Growth and Change in Islamic Substantive Law', *Islamic Law and Society*, 1 (1): 17–15.

——(1994b) 'Murder in Cordoba: Ijtihad, Ifta and the Evolution of Substantive Law in Mediaeval Islam', *Acta Orientalia*, 55: 55–83.

——(1997) *A History of Islamic Legal Theories*, Cambridge: Cambridge University Press.

Jain, B. (1970) *Administration of Justice in Seventeenth Century India (A study of Salient Conceptions of Mughal Justice)*, Delhi: Metropolitan Book Company.

Kennedy, C. (1988) 'Islamization in Pakistan: Implementation of the Hudood Ordinances', *Asian Survey*, 28 (3): 307–316.

——(1992) 'Repugnancy to Islam: Who Decides? Islam and Legal Reform in Pakistan', *International Comparative Law Quarterly*, 41 (4): 769–787.

Mandair, A. (2003) 'What if religion remained untranslatable?' in *Difference in Philosophy of Religion* (ed.) Phillip Goodchild, Aldershot: Ashgate, pp. 87–100.
Masood, M. (1989) *Islamic Legal Philosophy*, Delhi: Jameel ur-Rahman.
Melchert, C. (1997) *The Formation of the Sunni Schools of Law, 9th to 10th Centuries* CE, Leiden: Brill.
Meron, Y. (1969) 'The Development of Legal Thought in Ḥanafī Texts' *Studia Islamica*, 30: 73–118.
Peters, R. (1996) *Jihad in Classical and Modern Islam*, Princeton: Markus Weiner.
Schacht, J. (1964) *An Introduction to Islamic Law*, Oxford: Clarendon Press.
——(1971) 'On the Title of the *Fatāwāal-'Ālamgīriyya*' in C.E. Boswoth, *Iran and Islam: A Volume in Memory of Vladimir Minorsky*, Edinburgh: Edinburgh University Press, pp. 475–478.
Souryal, S., Potts, D. and Al-Obeid, A. (1994) 'The Penalty of Hand Amputation for Theft in Islamic Law', *Journal of Criminal Justice*, 22 (3): 249–265.
Turner, V. (1972) 'Symbols in African Ritual' *Science*, 179 (March 16): 1100–1105.
——(1974) *Dramas, Fields and Metaphors*, London: Cornell University Press.
Weber, M. (1921) 'Politik als Beruf', *Gesammelte Politische Schriften*, Dunker und Humblodt: Munich.
——(1946) *From Max Weber: Esssays in Sociology*, New York: Oxford University Press.
Weiss, B. (1992) *The Search for God's Law*, Salt Lake City: University of Utah Press.
West, R. (1900) 'Mohammedan Law in India', *Journal of the Society of Comparative Legislation*, 2 (1): 27–44.
West, R. (1986) 'Law Rights and other Totemic Illusions', *University of Pennsylvania Law Review*, 134 (4): 817–882.
Wheeler, B, (1996) *Applying the Canon in Islam: Authorization and Maintenance of Interpretive Reasoning in Ḥanafī Scholarship*, Albany: State University of New York Press.
Wolff, P. (1969) 'On Violence', *Journal of Philosophy*, 66 (19): 601–616.

5 Text as sword

Sikh religious violence taken for wonder

Balbinder Singh Bhogal

Loving-devotion (*bhagati*) of Hari[1]
is the sword (*kharag*) and armour of the True-Guru ...
(*Ādi Granth*: 312 G. Ramdas)

I bow with love (*hit*) and attention (*cit*)
to the Holy Sword (*srī kharag*) ... [2]
(*Dasam Granth*: 39 G. Gobind)

Sikh texts and traditions: love's hidden violence

Popular media representations of the Sikh tradition flash the image of a bearded, turban-wearing Sikh male with sword as a negative icon symbolizing religious violence and separatism. Although only a minority engaged in the struggle for an independent state (Khalistan) during the 1980s, the whole Sikh tradition was regularly depicted as a separatist movement comprised of 'extremists' and 'terrorists'. This discursive formation, which reads Sikhs as a violent people, rises out of a complex process inflected by the power and politics of representation as well as the specific histories of particular leaders, rulers and events. Yet the causes of this recent and violent history are attributed to the past of the Sikh Gurus, particularly the 'martyrdoms' of Guru Arjan in 1606 and Guru Tegh Bahadur in 1675, and Gobind Singh's establishment of the Khālsā ('Pure Ones') – a 'military' order in 1699.[3] It is often argued that the change in policy of the Mughal rulers, from Akbar's (1556–1605) tolerance to Jahangir's (1605–1627) and Aurangzeb's (1658–1707) intolerance towards non-Muslims, necessitated a military response to safeguard Hindu and Sikh traditions from forced conversion, tyranny and obliteration.

Scholarly discourse, via a particular reading of Sikh history, is somewhat complicit in the production of these media stereotypes. The historical narrative of a 'break' in the Guru Period (1469–1708) from 'pacifism' to 'militancy' that led to the transformation and/or displacement of 'saints' into 'soldiers' has been widely accepted by scholars – with the implication that there was a shift from 'religion' to 'politics'. This break is seemingly evidenced by the change in attire, architecture and style of leadership of the Gurus. Little is made of the Sikh Guru's own understanding of two principles that connect these pairs within a broader religious cosmology, symbolized most clearly by the sixth Guru's donning of two-swords, representing worldly and spiritual (*mīrī-pīrī*) power simultaneously – and that violence is understood as a last resort, viable only after all other means have been exhausted (*Zafaranāmah*, DG: 1389–1390, verse 22).

This assumption of a break in Sikh tradition operates on a simplistic and modern dichotomy that ignores the constant innovation of the Sikh tradition as reflected in the vocabulary, metaphors and themes of its scriptures. This paper explores the discrepancies and misreadings of the transformation thesis, charting its relations to a modern polarized understanding of 'love' and contra 'violence', 'religion' and contra 'politics'.

The Sikh tradition stresses the loving praise of Akāl Purakh 'Timeless Being', conceived as a nameless non-dual singular reality approached through a variety of personal names (Hari, Allah) with attributes (*sarguṇa*). Yet it also understands this Being impersonally without attributes (*nirguṇa*) as a becoming, a praxis and state (*sahaj*, *sunnu-samādhi*) of truthful living (*sacu karaṇī*). The central desire of Sikh *bhagati* is geared to a life lived in accordance with Akāl's Will, Order and Command (*hukam*) as it is 'written' in daily life and activity. A perception of hukam is seen as impossible without first sacrificing the ego (*haumai*). Like much of the *nirguṇa-bhakti* (devotion to a Formless Being) teaching across north India, Sikh praxis is anti-ritual, anticaste, anti-scripture/ Sanskrit, but it is also a world-affirming householder (*girahī*) tradition, promoting an egalitarian ethos, gender equality, social justice and welfare.

The title of this chapter[4] then requires explanation, for 'text as sword' signals the idea that Sikh scripture and practice, ostensibly about the *love* of Akāl through relationships with others, simultaneously concerns *violence*. How can a 'religion' of love be violent? This is the peculiar predicament we find ourselves in assessing violence within the Sikh tradition; there seems to be a conflation between peace and war, compassion and justice, love and violence *internal* to the Sikh tradition itself. The concurrence is hard to countenance; a much easier, though inevitably superficial, reading is to separate them in time, as McLeod does (below), and postulate a 'break' or 'transformation' in the tradition – words which often function as pseudonyms for a 'fall'.

In contemporary scholarship the Sikh scriptures of the *Ādi Granth*, 'Original Book' compiled in 1604 by the Fifth Guru, Arjan, and the *Dasam Granth*, 'Book of the Tenth (Guru)' collated by Mani Singh in the early eighteenth century, become iconic symbols of this 'break' in tradition. It would seem, as has been consistently interpreted by various scholars since the colonially inspired Sikh reform movements (1870s to 1920s), that there was and is a radical disjuncture between the obvious *nirguṇa-bhakti* of the AG's melodious though didactic lyrical praise and the battle cries of the DG's 'Hindu' epic myths of gods defeating demons.[5]

Rather than read militarization after the sixth Guru's martyrdom as a *break* in tradition (amounting to a loss of the 'religious') as 'outsider interpreters' do, or claiming a *continuity* of the same 'Nanakian' essence throughout Sikh history as 'insider exegetes' are wont to do, I argue for a 'continuity-in-difference'. Here, a Buddhist logic is implied: the present is neither the same nor different from the past – with the implication that conservation requires, rather than denies, innovation. That is to say, neither is Guru Nanak (as read in the AG) *identical* with Guru Gobind (as read in the DG), for this would deny the passing of time and context; nor is Guru Nanak (AG) *different* from Guru Gobind (DG) for this would deny obvious lineage and guruship between them. This continuity-in-difference does not signal a diachronic movement of some essence or its loss, but relates more a pattern, style, and creative resonance or echo related across the Gurus via different words and actions.

The following consists of two parts: the first, reflects on the theoretical and methodological issues concerning the motif of love's hidden violence and its key terms: 'religion' (*dharam*), 'love' (*bhagati*) and 'violence' (*hiṃsā*). These terms are re-evaluated and situated within their medieval contexts. The second part then focuses on the Sikh tradition as a continuation, conflation, and critique of strands charted earlier, especially those that figure *bhagati* as *violent*-devotion – thus upturning romantic and/or liberal constructions of 'religion' as pacifist and apolitical. It concludes with the suggestion that perhaps we do not know what violence is and underestimate our relation to it; and that likewise, our notion of love may not be devoid of inexplicable and harmful actions.

PART 1: RE-UNDERSTANDING 'RELIGION' AND '*BHAKTI*'

The metaphors and practices found in the writings of the Sikh Gurus are inseparable from the rhetoric and practices of the wider socio-political contexts of foreign Rule. The 'discursive formation' of Sikh identity and tradition discloses a constant interaction that telescopes a minority movement struggling for survival in often hostile environments of various rulers (the Lodhi Sultanate, the Mughals Emperors, British and Hindu governance).

A modern incapacity: polarized imaginations and the misreading of *bhagati*

According to McLeod (1984, 1989, 1997), Madan (1994), and Fenech (2000), this 'transformation' is assumed to be from 'pacifism' to 'militarism', from *interior* 'love' to *exterior* 'violence'. Such a view seems to have been inherited verbatim from the first orientalist observers of the tradition (see Singh, 1999: 91). Even those opposed to British colonial rule espoused similar views. M.K. Gandhi perceives 'Guru Govind Singh' amongst others (Shivaji, Pratap, Ranjit) as 'misguided and therefore, dangerous patriots' (1967: 487, 491) because he believes the Indian 'masses, unlike those of Europe, were untouched by the warlike spirits' since war 'never was the normal course of Indian life' (1967: 488). Gandhi's belief in literal non-violence led him to an 'abhorrence of the method'; he states 'I do not regard killing [war generally]...as good in any circumstances whatsoever' (1967: 489).

However, the epigraphs opening this chapter suggest a different Indic history and a 'continuity' between the terms and ideas of the early and late Gurus, the AG and the DG, since both groups and texts equate love (*bhagati*, *hit*) with violence/sword (*kharag*). The continuity within the Sikh tradition and its texts is best understood as a rhetoric of self-sacrifice – making Sikh *bhagati* a devotion of '*violent*' love. This is hard to comprehend and some balk at the conflation and ask, like McLeod, how can a 'religion of interiority' assume a martial politics of 'an overtly exterior identity'? (1989: 36). Yet the question reveals a peculiarly modern, secular standpoint that 'religion' and 'politics', 'pacifism' and 'militarism' entertain, and *should* entertain, contrary positions. This assumption leads to the 'inevitable' split in Sikh tradition and texts – predisposing McLeod to argue that the two texts are 'in fact completely separate' (1984: 6). The complexity and continuity-in-difference of the 'violence' of the believer and the 'affection' of the warrior is therefore missed.

An example of a recent work on martyrdom in the Sikh tradition continues McLeod's misreading, sending the modern scholar in search of a text to bridge the supposed divide:

> We should note that within the martyr tradition, both forms of martyrdom, those in which violence is appropriated as a last resort and those in which the sword is withheld, are revered and that there seems to be no text attempting to discriminate between the two.
>
> (Fenech 2000: 94)

The classificatory and disciplinary desires to look for an explanatory text in the first place, something obviously foreign to the tradition itself, may reflect a suspect methodology as well as a certain modern, humanist incapacity to read religious violence otherwise than as corruption.

According to Sikh tradition, the AG was transformed by the tenth Guru, Gobind Singh, into the 'living' *textual Guru* shortly before his death in 1708. This is significant because the wonder of the 'Word of Akāl' is synonymous for Sikhs with the 'Word of the Guru', but crucially the Sikh Gurus did not monopolize Akāl's Speech, given their belief that Akāl speaks through a multiplicity of voices, including non-Sikh ones, many of which are incorporated into the AG. Yet these wonders of the Word are also communicated as a Sword, and in the DG Akāl is also named All-Steel (*sarab-loh*), i.e. Sword and All-Death (*sarab-kāl*) – continuing Guru Nanak's vision of the absolute as having both personal and impersonal forms.

It is argued here that the change in Mughal policy that metamorphoses the AG's Hari into the DG's Sword, does not by itself 'create' the Sikh response, 'transforming' them into violent warriors. There is a radical openness to the teachings of the Sikh Gurus contained within the AG that does not rule out the possibility of violent behaviour as 'just' and 'pleasing to Hari'. It is the significance of these teachings which are central to Sikh thought that have been overlooked. I therefore chart and reflect upon the AG's rhetoric of the Sword *before* the militarization of the Sikh *panth* (community), as well as the rhetoric of love that continues *after* the 'break' even *during* the dark hours of war, as evidenced in the DG. In other words, underpinning both texts is a constant, devotional but violent rhetoric of self-sacrifice, which continues differently throughout Sikh history.

The milieu that predisposes modern scholars, like McLeod, to see a 'break' in tradition rather than a 'continuity-in-difference' dates back to British colonial rule and its orientalist legacy. Though this chapter does not directly disrupt the neat but problematic polarizations between *religion*-contra-*secularism*, and *tradition*-contra-*modernity*, it is quite clear that the identifications of religion with tradition as pre-modern, as well as reason with the secular as modern, are ones ill-suited to the worldview of the Sikh Gurus. The complexity of contemporary discourses on the rise of 'religious nationalisms' with attendant discussion of the politics of translation and the problematics of postcolonial representation prohibit any simplistic discussion of the Sikh tradition.[6] As van der Veer argues, 'Nationalism has to be connected to *secularism* to be truly *modern and enlightened*. Therefore "politicized religions" threaten both reason and liberty' (1996: 256).

This dichotomy between religion (as an apolitical spirituality) and violence is foreign to pre-colonial Sikh tradition and as such presents a misreading of both the AG and DG that is integral to colonial reconstructions of tradition as religion contra secular modernity.[7] This is, in part, an effect of a 'discursive construction of Western modernity, in which a modern construction of public and private makes religion a private matter of the individual' (van der Veer 1996: 269). From the perspective of modern colonial consciousness, co-opted but also co-created by Sikh reformers, this structural distortion brings into currency a chain of polarized pairs headed by a reflection on scripture where the AG (due to its 'monotheism') becomes a Western mimete and the DG (given its 'polytheism') remains the orientalist's other:

AG	DG
Religious	Political
Non-violent	Violent
Private	Public
Pacifism	Militarism
Love/Erotic	Violence/Sword
Moral	Immoral
Rational	Mythic
One Hari	Avataras of Hari
Sikh	Hindu

The Singh Sabha reformers (1870–1960), given their project of constructing a Sikh identity in contradistinction to the Hindu and in mimesis of the ruling British (and Protestant Christian) power, only managed to re-inscribe such dichotomies. Thus a firm wedge was placed between the religious and the political, private and public.

> The post-Enlightenment urge to define religion as an autonomous sphere, separate from politics and economy, is, of course, at the same time also a liberal political demand that religion 'should' be separate from politics. . . .The economic and political pieces constitute the real elements, while the religious is relegated to the unreal.
>
> (van der Veer 1996: 256, 269)

What is overlooked by such a modern, secular, liberal consciousness is the possibility that the 'unreal' can become a site for socio-political change. Van der Veer notes, 'it is precisely the effect of the normalizing and disciplining project of secular modernity that religion becomes so important as source of resistance' (1996: 256). That is to say, within the Sikh context, defending the self violently (if need be), as well as non-violently in acts of passive resistance, both conducted to the point of physical death, is not separated from 'killing-the-ego-self' metaphorically, emotionally and mentally through *bhagati*. This is because the pre-colonial Sikh context does not separate so neatly the religious from the political, the loving from the violent. It is incumbent upon us then to re-understand *religious love* and *political violence* as two moments of the same action that also speak a *political love* and *religious 'violence'*.[8]

McLeod's understanding of the difference between the AG and the DG as symbolic of the transformed tradition from early to late Gurus, then becomes a veiled critique of the tradition's turn from 'pacifism to militarism' given his contemporary, secular perspective. McLeod expresses a sense of perplexity in his analysis if not disappointment and in so doing unknowingly plays out a modernist polemic of polarities (1997: 111).

McLeod reduces 'religion' to an internal, subjective space of the 'mind/spirit', and limits politics to an external, objective realm of the 'body'. He therefore assumes that Guru Nanak's 'interior religiosity' is naturally opposed to Guru Gobind's Akāl army with their external uniform, disciplinary rituals and political 'aspirations'. However, the Gurus themselves, as well as close observers of the tradition, were well aware of such changes, *but saw them as innovations conserving tradition not displacing it.* Navdeep Mandair writes:

> This conflation of quietism and militancy signals the inadequacy, indeed, the spuriousness, of conceiving (Sikh) religious identity in terms of a dichotomy between interiority and exteriority, but also puts into question the idea, written into this dichotomy, that the interior religious experience constitutes religion's proper mode of expression.
>
> (2003: 108)

Both conceptions of a *religious* love and a *political* violence show themselves, in the literature on the Sikhs and their tradition, to be impositions, overwriting indigenous understandings within a modern secular frame that privatizes the religious and 'secularizes' the political. The task here is to 'recover', or at least re-think, notions of love and violence, religion and politics together, as a necessary response to the rewritings of the colonial reform period.

This chapter therefore argues that, in order to comprehend McLeod's orientalist quandary, a different set of questions, central to the textual tradition, have to be posed: is Guru Nanak's scriptural Word itself violent as well as loving?[9] Should the religious Text also be read as a Sword? Can *violence* in the AG and *love* in the DG be found? Furthermore, if the Guru's Word is inherently quietistic *and* militant then the modern, humanist anxiety over the Sikh's wonder over religious violence is misguided, and the supposed break in tradition a colonial misreading. If Sikh scripture and tradition point to a 'conflictual ontology'[10] representing a 'thematization of the "divine" as violent presence', then 'to posit Sikhism as commensurable with the contours of a transcendental conception of religion, one which privileges a pacific engagement with the world, seems unjustifiable', where 'every announcement of its militant ontology is always already informed by a whisper of regret, an inscrutable rhetoric of apology' (Mandair, N. 2003: 105–6). How then to read and hear Hari's/Nanak's Word as love *and* violence, without this modern whisper of regret?

The rhetoric of self-sacrifice: *bhagati* as violent-love

> But what is a Sikh without sacrifice?
>
> (*The Khalsa Advocate*, 18 March 1910, p.2. [cited by Fenech 2000: 210])

The foundational continuity that is differently expressed throughout the Sikh tradition is the idiom of sacrificing the self which implies a violent-love. It is commonplace to read Sikh *bhagati* as violent-love under the motif of the *living* martyr, whether in non-violent or violent resistance. C.F. Andrews (1871–1940), an Anglican missionary, wrote:

> It was a strangely new experience to these [Sikh] men, to receive blows dealt against them. . .and yet never to utter a word or strike a blow in return. The vow they had made to God [at the Akāl Takht] was kept to the letter. I saw no act, nor look of defiance. It was a true martyrdom for them as they went forward, a true act of faith, a true deed of devotion to God. They remembered their Gurus how they had suffered, and they rejoiced to add their own sufferings to the treasury of their wonderful faith.
>
> (cited by Fenech 2000: 270)

It is clear from this witness and other similar accounts that the act of sacrifice is as much an act of 'religion' as it is a radical 'political' gesture. The fact that a tradition – which has supposedly transformed itself from 'pacifism' to 'militarism' – would resist the warrior's nature to fight, and adopt the mode of a non-violent saint, reveals the 'break-in-tradition' thesis to be at least suspect. Furthermore this violent/non-violent open attitude of self-sacrifice can be traced back before the supposed break in tradition occurs. Indeed, Guru Nanak saw each existential moment of life (even if not recognized as such) as one of terror and inevitable violence: 'Behind, a terrifying tiger; ahead, a pool of fire' (AG: 1410); from the perspective of the self-centered ego (*haumai*) life cannot be lived without violent encounters – which can make the everyday extraordinary.

If every moment should be understood as an encounter with death, then one cannot avoid a narrative of violent-love, or a rhetoric of sacrifice (*hau vārīā̃*) which obviously implies a way of death, (*āpu māre*). Guru Nanak's statement that 'there is no Hindu nor Muslim' after his first mystical encounter with Hari already depicts a sacrifice of his Hindu identity, if not an identity crisis. This loss of a socially named and embedded self underlies the whole of Guru Nanak's 'religious' ideas. 'Loving-devotion' to Hari then, simultaneously implies a violent encounter wherein the ego-self must be murdered if Hari is to be seen and His Way (*bidhi*) lived.

It seems, just from this brief overview, that this 'violent-love' is an unformulatable mode of becoming given in the moment of acting that can be expressed and released through a variety of means, ranging from the *non-violent* (prayer, meditation, service, singing, passive resistance) to the *violent* (self-denial, asceticism, ritually curtailed living, armed self-defence). In this respect no (moral) limit or calculation can prejudge what the (socio-political) moment demands. In other words the religiosity of Sikh *bhagati* always carries with it a socio-political content: the way (of 'internal' sacrifice) cannot be walked without an 'external' situated life-context, nor is it to be found by transcending the timebound context, but living that context through time without 'I'.

To substantiate the argument for a 'continuity-in-difference' of the existential notion of Sikh *bhagati* as a context-bound movement of violent-love, (i.e., self-sacrifice) it is argued that militarism, rather than arising out of the 'martyrdoms' of Gurus Arjan and Tegh Bahadur alone, existed not only in the language and actions of the early Gurus but within the wider medieval milieu they inherited. This simultaneously shows a different configuration of 'religion' vis-à-vis 'politics'. Three aspects of this pre-Nanak milieu will be charted albeit in a cursory manner: first, the fact that even the most esoteric 'religious' language contains *metaphors* that express socio-political concerns; second, how the concept of *violent-love* pre-dates Guru Nanak; and third, how these metaphors become *ambiguous* within the context and phenomenon of ascetic-warriors.

Medieval times: metaphor, violent-love and ambiguity

> Seekers of the Way. . . .Kill anything that you happen on. Kill a patriarch or an arhat [Enlightened/Worthy disciple of the Buddha] if you happen to meet him. Kill your parents or relatives if you happen to meet them.
>
> (I-Hsüan (d.866) in Chan 1973: 447–448)

This is a Buddhist metaphorical injunction relating the need to transcend attachment to names and forms. Yet the arresting style with its violent imagery is not uncommon throughout the classical and medieval periods. The *Mahābharāta*'s *Bhagavadgītā* and *Śāntiparvan* is a noteworthy example. In the epic war and violence are pursued, sometimes deceitfully and regardless of the human cost. The *Bhagavadgītā* narrates the dialogue on dharma between Kṛṣṇa and Arjuna on the eve of war in the middle of the battlefield *not* in a hermit's cave. Kṛṣṇa, (the incarnation of Viṣṇu) engages in a pro-war dharmic ('religious') rhetoric that concludes with the paradigmatic expression of *bhakti* as a devotion constituted by 'violent-love': all actions, including violent ones, if sacrificed to Kṛṣṇa through *bhakti*, are deemed not only acceptable and worthy but also liberating. Whilst the dialogue of the 'Song of the Lord' precedes the outbreak of war, the 'Book of Peace' comes after the war. It is delivered by a highly revered Warrior-Prince (Bhishma). Despite being sworn to the *adharmic* 'evil/violent' side of the Kauravas, Bhishma lectures the leader of the Pandavas, Yudhisthira (the son of God Dharma no less) about the intimate relationship between the *dharma* of kings (*rājadharma*) and liberation (*mokṣadharma*). The *Mahābharāta*'s complex narrative reveals a fertile discourse that interweaves political governance with religious freedom awakening.

Davidson (2002: 2) argues that there are many examples of 'the intersection of the religious and the socio-political realms in early medieval India'. Advancing a bold and 'surprising' thesis based on metaphor, he argues that the political can be seen in the most esoteric of religions in the early medieval period (*c.*500 to 1200 CE) in north India and the Deccan. Startlingly, he claims, 'esoteric Buddhism is the most politicized form to evolve in India', its defining metaphor being the monk as the 'Supreme Overlord (*rājādhirāja*) or the Universal Ruler (*cakravartin*)'. That is to say, even the most 'interior' of traditions makes 'an attempt to sacralize the medieval world' to 'transform the political paradigm into vehicles of sanctification' (Davidson 2002: 4–5).

Arguing for a 'culture of military opportunism', Davidson shows how metaphors of violence and rule permeate all levels and areas of the Buddhist socio-religious imaginary (2002: 121). Citing examples of textual mimesis where Buddhist texts map the monk's 'ritual behaviour' onto the king's 'royal behaviour', Davidson reveals that for both this behaviour 'varies from pacific to destructive' (2002: 122).

One of the most conspicuous expressions of a 'violent-love' can be found in the metaphors of the *Periyapurāṇam* ('The Great Story').[11] This is a South Indian Tamil text composed in the twelfth century which explicitly relates extreme acts of violence performed by 63 saints of the Hindu god Śiva' in the name of *bhakti*. A 'child saint cuts off his father's feet', and another 'gleefully kills and cooks his son at the request of a visiting Śaiva ascetic' (Monius 2004: 113–114). These heinous crimes of violence are presented as (radical) 'expressions of love for Śiva' (115). Commentators argue that the 'violent-love' (*vannanpu*) demonstrated by these saints mimic Śiva's own propensity toward violence where death is crucial to regenerate life (2004: 123). Another South Indian text, the *Tirukkaḷiṟṟupaṭiyār* (1178 CE) attributed to Tēvanāyaṉār, classifies the effort involved in *bhakti* as of two kinds, 'gentle action (*melviṉai*) and harsh action (*velviṉai*)' and that both of these 'are the *dharma* of Śiva' (v.16. Monius 2004: 124).

Over time, with the spread of *bhakti* movements right across India, these metaphors became increasingly ambiguous. Davidson (2002: 177) argues that the shift was instigated not by Buddhist but heterodox Śaivite groups who promoted 'a discourse of the legitimization of otherwise illegitimate conduct':

> The siddha traditions also imported a politics of dominion and control, but for the benefit of the single siddha and not necessarily for the betterment of the surrounding community. Buddhist siddhas both developed radical meditative techniques not seen before in the Buddhist world and wrapped them in language that was simultaneously playful and ferocious, erotic and destructive.
>
> (Davidson 2002: 337)

Sikhs, being householders, not ascetics, are less vulnerable to the individualism implied by Davidson. The householder base also grounds Sikhs more firmly within the socio-political context as 'citizens', rather than ascetics 'dead to the world'. Yet both of these orientations contain the trace of this challenging love.

Contrary to Madan's orientalist/modernist view, Pinch notes the absence of 'tolerance' and 'pacifism' in soldier-monk traditions of the eighteenth century:

> Let there be no mistake: the evolution of a powerful martial tradition within Indian monasticism was very real, the battles fought between monastic orders at the Kumbh were ferocious and deadly, and the mercenary service undertaken by soldier monks in the eighteenth century was extremely dangerous and lucrative. Tolerance and pacifism were ancillary to the world of the soldier monk. And indeed, as recent scholarship in intellectual and cultural history has demonstrated, neither pacifism nor tolerance was given in Indian religious traditions prior to the eighteenth century. Both were brought to the fore to respond to ideological needs in the colonial, nationalist era.
>
> (1996: 141)

Apart from the modern construction of what 'religion' should be, i.e., inherently tolerant, loving, increasingly private and pacifist, this desire of the colonial 'ought' also operated as a strategy of exclusion and containment. Van der Veer notes that during the nineteenth century the countryside was 'demilitarized' which led to 'de-politicized' roles for such militant Sadhus and Faqirs resulting in the 'laicization of institutionalized religion' (1996: 260). Just as it is anachronistic to rewrite the past soldier-monks as purely 'religious' figures given their martial involvement in winning political battles, so is it wrong to see Gobind's Khālsā as indicating a loss of past religiosity displaced by militarism. It could also be argued that just as one does not gain religiosity by mere fact of renunciation, nor does one simply lose it by donning arms. The move from the religious (read pacifist) AG to the political (read military) DG then operates within a modern construction of religion contra politics, and is further inscribed within the context of religious communalism and traditionalism as opposed to secular liberal modern democracies. Thus the devotee-cum-householder Sikh's socio-political engagement does not displace his or her religious commitments. However, as we can see from the foregoing discussion, the medieval milieu out of which the Sikh tradition grows was already predisposed to view the divine as well as devotion as a double-edged sword, where religion spoke politics and politics courted religion, and where worship often came with weaponry. To establish and maintain *dharam* both, it seems, are required.

PART 2: THE SIKH TRADITION: METAPHOR, AMBIGUITY AND REALITY

> Everything is under Your Power; You are the True King (*sacā sāhu*).
> (AG: 556 G. Nanak)

> Those who realize the Truth, they alone are the true kings (*sacu rāje*).
> (AG: 1088 G. Nanak)

Not only is Hari the True King but also those who realize Hari. It is clear that the master metaphor that Davidson detects in esoteric Buddhism of the Ruler Supreme is widespread and recurrent, not only throughout the DG but also within the AG – both of which 'attempt to sacralize the medieval world' and 'transform the political paradigm into vehicles of transformation' (2002: 4–5). The political metaphors inherent within the AG are missed by McLeod, Madan, and Fenech – revealing a handicap to their reading of Guru Nanak's thought as a 'pacifist religion'. Guru Nanak's vocabulary alone incorporates many words from the Persian, Arabic as well as Indic sources (Shackle 1981). This reveals a desire to appreciate, reconcile but also transcend the Hindu (ascetic, dharmic) and Muslim juridico-political worldviews. For example he uses both Sanskritic and Persian namings of heaven (*surag*, *bhisat*) and hell (*narak*, *dojak*). This compound style leads Guru Nanak to make many similar and ingenious conflations (see Bhogal 2001). One such conflation that speaks to the present critique of the 'interiorization' of Guru Nanak's 'religion' is his juxtaposition of the Hindu Yogi's esoteric Tenth-Door *within* (*dasa-duār*) with the Muslim divine Door (*dar*) of God's Court (*darabār*) *without*. Similarly he conjoins the ascetic (*jogī*) with the sensualist (*bhogī*), householder (*girahī*), and servant (*sevak*) – that is, the inner and asocial world with the 'worldly' and socio-political world.

AG metaphors: violent and ambiguous

Guru Nanak's phrase of the True King (*sacce pātisā*), initially of Hari, gets mapped onto the True-Guru, and through the Bhatts (panegyrists in the AG) mapped onto the Sikh Gurus themselves.[12] The metaphor of rulership is therefore an integral part of the AG and the early Sikh Gurus' vision of social reality. As kings had their court-poets so did the Gurus, as reflected in the very structure of the AG's compilation which contains the writings of six of the Sikh Gurus (90.4 per cent), 15 Bhagats (8.2 per cent) as well as 17 Bhatts (1.4 per cent). These latter court-poets, writing before Guru Arjan's 'martyrdom', eulogized the Gurus as the 'warriors of the Word' (*sabad sūra*) (AG: 1391), as kings whose rule is eternal (AG: 1390), and as warriors of truth, wielding the power of humility (AG: 1393) fighting the battles of *dharam*:

> Wearing the armour of (yogic) absorption,
> (the Guru) has climbed and mounted (the horse) of wisdom.
> Holding the bow of Dharma,
> the fight of devotion and morality has started.
> He is fearless in the Fear of the Permanent Hari;
> He has thrust the spear of the Guru's Word into the mind.
> (AG: 1396 Sal)

The battle of love is superimposed on to the battle of warriors. The socio-political context of these writings reveals a growing and increasingly wealthy Sikh community who looked to the Guru for leadership in testing times. Unlike the Buddhist Siddhas, Jains, and Tantrikas (be they Vaiṣṇava, Śaiva or Śakta), the Sikh root metaphors for social virtue, righteousness and justice, as well as those of true rule and administration, are enacted in the actual activities of the Sikh Gurus and their followers. They built wells, wrestling grounds, sacred pools, temples; they founded cities, appointed representatives to collect tithes, held assemblies in the style of Mughal courts, instituted free 'kitchens' (directly challenging caste boundaries and social constructions of impurity and pollution), and voiced critiques of rulers in power. In short the Gurus began a project of social innovation and organization that was provocatively independent of Mughal administration (Grewal 1998: 28–61; Fenech 2000: 73–92). The early Gurus certainly did not confine their vision to an inner, private domain; they were seen as pillars of 'religion' (*dīn*) and increasingly the 'world' (*dunyā*) (Grewal 2001: 39 fn.25).

In this wider perspective the presumed break in tradition ignores a wealth of social and cultural growth. To reduce this multidimensional social movement to the category of 'interior religion' misreads early Sikh 'religiosity', which is so clearly orientated to a qualified relationship with the social world as reflected in both metaphors and practices of true royalty, heroism and rule, as well as welfare and charity.

On the theme of religious violence, the AG has much to say. The Sword is variously visualized as the Word, Name, Hari, Guru, Wisdom, but also as the loving-devotion of Hari as the opening quote indicated. The purpose of the Sword of Wisdom (*giān-kharag*) is to slay duality, the false-self and its desires and delusions. Relating *bhagati* through a deadly battle scene forces the reader to re-evaluate their notion of divine love to include an unsparing rhetoric of violence. The DG's re-reading of loving the divine through weapons and warfare is first seen in the AG where Guru Nanak portrays *bhagati* as a warrior's arsenal and lifestyle, outlining an active battling rather than a passive indifference:

> The understanding of Your way (is) horses, war harnesses, girths, gold.
> The appetite for virtue (is) bow, arrow, quiver, spear, sword belt.
> With honour manifest (as) cavalry and military bands, Your action is my caste.
> O Baba, the pleasure of other rides is false.
>
> (AG: 16)

Bhagati is not only about a romantic love swooning to Hari's flute, but also and always a matter of life and death where to love ultimately is to sacrifice one's life. A hugely popular expression of this form of the idea of violent-love, of *bhagati* involving the ultimate sacrifice of one's head, is iconized and lionized in the narratives surrounding the eighteenth-century figure of Baba Dīp Singh.[13]

Within the AG life is framed by violence and love and these constitute the fabric of one's past *karam*. The 'Sword of Death' (*jam-kharag*) hangs over each head (AG: 1087 G. Amardas). Violence is sanctioned by Hari: 'When it pleases You, they wield swords cutting off heads [of their enemies] as they go' (AG: 145 G. Nanak). Indeed, Hari Himself is violent: 'He Himself kills and rejuvenates' (AG: 1034 G. Nanak). Justice is the violent recompense of one's 'bad' deeds. Each moment must be recognized as the possible speaking of the Guru-Word, which includes, inevitably, the striking of the Sword of Death.

The first Mughal ruler, Babur (1483–1530), invaded India in the 1520s. These violent invasions were witnessed by Guru Nanak and commentated upon in four hymns. In one, Guru Nanak rationalizes that 'those whom the Creator would destroy – He (first) strips them of virtue' (AG: 417). Accepting Hari as all-powerful and violence integral to His Will, Guru Nanak seems to justify his own powerlessness, later stating that those who died were destined to die. He ends with a blunt tone of abject resignation that barely lifts itself to praise, noting that pleasure and pain occur by His will and none can change this: 'what is written [by Hari], is to be received' (AG: 418). It is this 'resigned' tone that changes in the later Gurus – though not the teaching itself for in the wider context of his hymns it is clear that for Guru Nanak love is itself a form of violence. The death of the mental ego is actively sought in all interaction. In other words the discipline of true devotion has to demonstrate a 'path along a double-edged sword' (AG: 918 G. Amardas) whatever that path happens to be.

Contrary to the break-in-tradition thesis, the 'external' and 'royal' nature of the early Gurus is attested by the third Mughal emperor, Jahangir (1605–1627) himself. He notes that the fifth Guru, Arjan, 'had noised himself about as a religious and worldly leader' (in Madra and Singh 2004: 4). Indeed Guru Arjan's stature is not as a passive saint, locked away in the interiority of divine contemplation, but rather as a figure of dynamic social presence and power.[14] Furthermore

Grewal argues that all the Gurus, not only the later ones, were referred to as True Kings (2001: 8 fn.25). Indeed, Guru Nanak's verses are read as barely veiled critiques of these 'earthly kings' (Lodhi Sultanate and Emperor Babur) who should not be praised since they will depart, for only Hari the eternal is worthy of praise (AG: 1088). Within this context of religious authority the works of some influential commentators explicitly reflect the political crossings between Mughals and Sikhs. For example, Bhai Gurdas Bhalla (1558–1636), who was Guru Arjan's amanuensis for the AG and intimate with the early Gurus, writes in his influential and authoritative *Vārs* (historical and exegetical reflections in verse):

> The True-Guru is the True King (*pātaśāh*);
> all other worldly kings (*bādaśāh*) are fake ones ...
> The True-Guru is the real banker; other rich persons cannot be believed.
> The True-Guru is the true physician ...
> (*Vār* 15.1. tr. Singh, Jodh 1998: 367)

Notice here that Gurdas contrasts the Punjabi vernacular for true king (*pātaśāh*) with the Persian courtly language of the Mughals for false king (*bādaśāh*) – making his point politically relevant and cutting. In addition, he frames the Sikh Gurus as trust-worthy bankers revealing an independent and growing economic structure of wealth and power.

Furthermore, Gurdas's witness bridges the apparent chasm between the AG's love (*prem*) and the DG's violence, symbolized by the Sword (*kharag*) – even whilst observing an apparent change in style of leadership between the early and later Gurus:

> The earlier Gurus sat peacefully in *dharamsalas*; this one roams the land.
> Emperors visited their homes with reverence; this one they cast in gaol.
> No rest for his followers, ever active; their restless Master has fear of none.
> The earlier Gurus sat graciously blessing; this one goes hunting with dogs.
> They had servants who harboured no malice; this one encourages scoundrels.
> Yet none of these changes conceals the truth; the Sikhs are still drawn as bees to the lotus.
> The truth stands firm, eternal, changeless; and pride still lies subdued.
> (*Vār* 26.24, tr. McLeod 1984: 31)

Whether this constitutes a 'fundamental change in policy and practice' as McLeod argues (1984: 30), however, is debatable. It is significant that whilst Gurdas finds the changes surprising he nonetheless concludes by 're-understanding' the notion of the 'religious' (*dharamsālas*, blessings, sitting) to include those of 'secular-state' activities (roaming, hunting, ever-active, gaol). In other words he sees a continuity-in-difference. Given the foregoing discussion it is hard not to think that this re-understanding was largely informed by his acute awareness of the Gurus and the contents of the AG rather than in spite of that knowledge. As we have seen the *mīrī* (King) – *pīrī* (Saint) formulation may be relatively new but the idea is certainly not; the underlying ambiguity of a violent-love is present even before Guru Nanak and Guru Hargobind's *mīrī* (violent) *pīrī* (love).

Love and real violence in the DG

> Reverently I salute the Sword with affection and devotion ...
> Thee I invoke, All-conquering Sword, Destroyer of evil, Ornament of the brave.
> Powerful your arm and radiant your glory, your splendour as dazzling as the brightness of the sun.
> Joy of the Saints and Scourge of the wicked, Vanquisher of vice,
> I seek your protection.
> Hail to the world's Creator and Sustainer, my invincible Protector the Sword!
> (DG: 39 *Bacitra Nāṭak*, G. Gobind, tr. McLeod 1984: 58, adapted)

As martial imagery and metaphors of the sword abound in the AG, so too is there blissful devotionalism in the DG, as the above hymn titled the 'Wonderful Drama' shows. The key difference, however, is that in the DG the sword is granted an original and ontological status as another epithet of Hari:

> (Akāl) first created the Double-Edged Sword (*khaṇḍā*), then the whole world.
> Having created Brahma, Vishnu and Mahesh, He made the entire play of Nature.
> (DG: 119 G. Gobind)

From the preceding scriptural quotes it becomes clear that for the Sikh tradition the Sword is not simply a metaphor but an icon of Sikh faith, a sign to act in the name of Akāl and a symbol indicating a reality to participate in.[15] Indeed, the icon partakes in the reality it represents. The existential engagement Guru Gobind Singh (Lion) himself relates in the DG, in a number of biographical reflections, mixes metaphorical violence with real violence of actual battles:

> There I hunted and killed many lions, antelopes and bears.
> Fateh Shah, the local ruler, angered by my presence, attacked me without cause ... [60]
> When [Harichand's] arrow struck me it roused me to anger.
> Seizing the bow I returned the fire, loosing a hail of arrows.
> The enemy turned and ran as the arrows showered upon them.
> Taking aim I shot again, despatching another of their number ...
> And so they fled from the field of battle, running in fear of their lives.
> Victory was mine, the enemy crushed by the grace of the Lord [Kāl] ...
> ... the saints sustained and the evil destroyed.

The wicked were slain, rended limb from limb,
dying like dogs the death they deserved.[16]

(DG: 60, 62–63 tr. McLeod 1984: 62–63, adapted)

A Saint that angers, kills and presents his violence as just retribution is worth pondering. According to Guru Gobind Singh, such details occur within a grander scheme of Akāl's cycles of violence and death where all arise from and return back into Akāl (DG: 19–20). In the DG Guru Gobind's conception of Akāl Purakh is filled with both violent and loving aspects (mirroring Shaivite and Muslim namings):

Salutations to the Death of all; Salutations to the Ever-Benevolent. ...
Salutations to the Annihilator of all; Salutations to the Nurturer of all.

(DG: 2)

The violent-love of Akāl is clear: the Annihilator is the Nurturer, creating and destroying is His mode of becoming. Akāl is not only the 'bliss of the devout' and 'vanquisher of vice' but more importantly the 'Scourge of the wicked', the 'Destroyer of Evil'. The 'field of battle', which had always been the struggle with every day psycho-social world, during the later Gurus' times becomes an actual fight in a real battlefield. It is undeniable, however, that there is a 'shift' towards overt militarism, although this occurs not at the expense or displacement of the earlier Gurus' 'religious' ethos but precisely because and out of it. It is however certainly not a shift from inner subjective to outer objective realm. Guru Gobind's battle combines the *ascetic* death of the mind with the warrior's *bloody* death of the body, slaying the demons of the passions as well as the 'demonized' Muslims and their 'injustices'.

Jeevan Deol argues that within the DG, *dharam* is reinterpreted and understood within a puranic metanarrative where the endless cycles of good versus evil take on cosmological proportions. At the centre of this culture of loving-violence is 'the worship of weapons and the perception of partaking in the Guru's mission to re-establish *dharma*' (Deol 2001: 33). However the puranic scene is not unfamiliar to the AG, especially when we consider that before Gobind's time Bhai Gurdas, whose *Vārs* are seen as the key to comprehend the AG, also framed the AG and its authors in a similar puranic fashion; Guru Nanak, like Guru Gobind, was also divinely commissioned to restore *dharam* (*Vār* 1.22–24). Furthermore the puranic conception of the four degenerating ages (*yugas*) is one accepted by the early Gurus and is internal to the AG. There are also retellings of puranic myths in the AG. Kabir (AG: 1194, *Basantu*) and Guru Amardas (AG: 1133, *Bhairau*) both relate the story of the prideful King, Haraṇākhas, who threatens to kill his own son Prahilād if he does not stop thinking of 'Hari'. The king, however, is brutally devoured by Hari who responds to the boy's prayer – relating all-too graphically a violent-love.

The Sikh 'saint-soldier' (*sant-sipāhī*) is a working householder who has social responsibilities to others. The Khālsā's spiritual regime is not performed in private isolation on the fringes of society, but actually dramatizes daily life as the locus of spiritual growth; the ascetic's silent cave and warrior's battlefield co-inhere with the responsibilities of the householder's social realm. The divine is re-understood within the heat of historical action, and is no longer defined in the cool ascetic denial and transcendence of time.

Sikhs therefore continue the *Bhagavad Gītā's* argument that inaction cannot be achieved by attempting to refrain from action. Inaction-within-action only occurs when one acts in accordance with a cosmic, though unwritten, Command (*hukam*). That which creates *karam* is instrumental will; that which creates *dharam* is sacrificing action in accordance with Akāl's Will (*hukam, bhāṇā*). The Sikhs therefore read violence otherwise than pain; the Guru martyrs Arjan and Tegh Bahadur, as well as a whole legion of martyrs that follow (Fenech 2000), are depicted as welcoming their torture and suffering (as they would pleasure) with equanimity, demonstrating their adherence to Hari's Will over their personal desires. One would assume that this violence could only be accepted if one was immersed in the sacrificial love of the divine.

The violent-love of the AG is re-understood as loving-violence of the DG – both understood as a part of Akāl's Will, both lending expression to *bhagati* as self-sacrifice or the art of dying. Sikh religious violence is taken for wonder because there is an unavoidable violence to 'religious' (dharmic) knowledge and action. This is the 'sword' of love: to love one's self as Akāl, one has to kill the self that resists that love, for the ego cannot love, because it always loves another (*duja bhāu*). Time as event is gift and judgement (otherwise known as the law of *karam*, reaping what one sows). Thus the Sikh way (of violent-love, *mīrī-pīrī*) is not to transcend the event of time, but hear and learn from its teaching. Celebrating time's ('good-and-bad') events as gifts requires a paradoxical logic wherein a song can become a battlecry and a melody a march.

Chandi as Sword and Flute

> Salutations to the Wielder of Weapons ...
> Salutation to the Mother of the world.
> (DG: 3 G. Gobind)

At places in the DG, God becomes Goddess: the Great Mother is the 'bringer of Death', 'Hurler of Missiles' Annihilator, as well as the 'giver of Life', 'Nurturer', and the most 'Beautiful'. According to Sikh male imaginings the Goddess is 'Beauty incarnate', and is wholly seductive (DG: 81–82). Even the blood dripping from her mouth is compared to a 'beautiful maiden spitting after chewing betel-leaves' (DG: 94, v.194. tr. Singh, Jodh 1999: 265). In the climax of Chapter 6 of the *Caṇḍī Caritra*, the demon Nisumbh is slain:

> At that time Chandi, in a fit of rage, held firmly her sword. She charged it with full strength at the head of Nisumbh and it went through his body – from head to toe. Who can truly appreciate that moment? The two pieces

> of his body fell down on the ground as pieces of soap fall down when the maker of soap cuts it into pieces with iron-wire.
>
> (DG: 95, v.202. tr. Singh, Jodh 1999: 269)

This violent-love aesthetic and rhetoric, however, must be set in a wider Indic context to make sense. This Sikh violent-love arises from the conflation of Vaiṣṇava and Śakta traditions, that is, the love of Krishna's flute and the violence of Kāli's blood-dripping sword:

> Kṛṣṇa wearing a garland of wild flowers with a flute
> in hand becomes Kālī with a sword ...
>
> (Ramprasad in Kinsley 2000: 151)

> I see my Mother ... now taking up the flute instead of the sword,
> or again seizing the sword instead of the flute.
>
> (Avalon 1960: 600)

As Ramprasad (1718–75) shows it matters little whether one starts with Kṛṣṇa or Kālī for each implies the other. The AG reflects the Flute, with Vaiṣṇava names (Hari, Ram), and the DG invokes the Sword, with Śakta names (Sri Bhagauti, Sarab-loh). Guru Gobind names his Sword after the Goddess, *Caṇḍī* (Skt. 'vicious, fierce, violent'). Whilst the Kṛṣṇa-as-Flute and Kālī-as-Sword reveal 'many central truths' to Hindu mythology, Kinsley is intrigued by their juxtaposition and ponders whether 'there is an ultimate truth of the tradition that lies somewhere in an unimaginable combination of the two' (2000: x). It is clear that the Sikh texts and traditions conjoin Hari (flute) with the Sri Bhagauti (the sword), compassion (lotus) with wisdom (thunderbolt and sword), just as in Tantra Shiva (spirit) is united with Shakti (matter).

Guru Gobind's saint-soldiers and Guru Hargobind's two-swords, are not inventions alone but innovations that conserve Guru Nanak's own ideas. For example they play out Nanak's own use of the Tantric compound of Śiva and Śakti (*siva-sakatī*) – which connects to the wider Saṃkhyan categories of Puruṣa and Prakṛiti (*puraku* and *kudarati*) – denoting a passive spirit (love) and active material power (violence). Both elements constitute the reality of creation (AG: 1096 G. Arjan; AG: 1056 G. Amardas). Hari as the 'One' is a constant interplay of two opposite but complimentary forces. Conjointly both express Hari's Order and Will (AG: 920 G. Amardas; AG: 1027; 1037 G. Nanak). Trying to contain 'religion/*bhagatī*' within the realm of a passive and subjective Śiva (de-linked from Śakti and her often violent action) is the mistake of a modern prejudice.

The Sikh Gurus, following Guru Nanak's masterful lead, communicated a very broad understanding of the truth; accepting and conflating its plurality led them to an intercultural ethic of reconciliation that manoeuvred across polarized traditions and their ideas. Their insight was to be at the border-crossing, at the confluence of Vaiṣṇava and Śakta (not to mention Nath-Jogi) and Sufi rivers. The Sikh Gurus were determined to innovate a pragmatic religio-political (nondual) movement from the bifurcated traditions of the Vaishnava and Shakta, Sheikh and Sant, priest and warrior, ascetic and householder, ruler and ruled. Whilst Guru Gobind employs the puranic myths in the DG, he not only 'invokes' the Goddess, he does so as a real sword, and thus maps the myth of goddesses defeating demons onto a real battlefield occurring in his life. This enables him to demonstrate a 'religiosity' otherwise than *ahiṃsā*. Religion as non-violence is something Guru Nanak also rejects. The Sikh re-reading of *ahiṃsā* is closely related to their re-reading of renunciation and the whole world of ascetic extremism. For Sikhs physical violence is sublimated as a mental violence, as physical ascetic practices and renunciation are re-read as an internal struggle. It is a nondual re-reading:

> If one accepts (the concept of) impurity (*sūtak*), then there is impurity everywhere [in cow dung, wood has worms, in grains of corn, in water by which everything comes] ... O Nanak, impurity cannot be removed this [physical] way; it is washed away only by [mental] gnosis (*giān*).
>
> (AG: 472 G. Nanak)

The impurities of the mind cannot be cleansed by ritualizing physical acts. What follows from this is that 'true' or mental *ahiṃsā*, may actually require 'compassionate-violence' to promote less suffering overall; gangrene of the foot requires the violence of amputation in order to save the whole body. Similarly the death of one tyrant in society may save a whole community (a form of reasoning prevalent in other traditions, especially Mahāyāna Buddhism; see Gethin pp. 228, 230, 264.[17] As renunciation cannot be attained by simply removing oneself from society, so too physical restraining not to cause harm may not always guarantee non-injury.

Those following McLeod, Madan and Fenech read the melody of Guru Nanak's flute of 'pacifism' as interrupted, displaced, and usurped by Guru Gobind's violent 'storm of swords' – rather than as an intensification of an Indic continuity-in-difference.[18] The strong suspicion is, of course, that the Sword will split the flute, that violence will corrupt love. In other words such scholars can not, and for very good reason, 'wipe out the forms and think of her sword as his flute' (Ramprasad in Kripal, 1998: 45). To think both together would be to postulate a 'Janus-faced ontology' of loving-violence. Understanding the Sword of the DG's 'tough' *bhagati* as also the Flute of the AG's 'mild' *bhagati*, yields an aesthetics of war.

By overlaying the gruesome violence of real battle scenes with well-known mythic narratives as seen in the *Caṇḍī Caritra*, Guru Gobind was able to 're-vision' the slaughter of war. The horror of war was not seen for what it was but for its re-enactment of a universal mythic narrative of Good versus Evil. Through this 'scriptural superimposition' the dreadfulness of violence is mollified and may even elicit aesthetic appreciation. The *Mārkeṇḍaya-Purāṇa's* mythic episodes, that express martial valour, skill and strength, were used by Guru Gobind to inspire Sikhs to fight. Not merely to fight nor take pride in the righteousness of the dharmic cause, but to appreciate the violence of battle as a martial art of divine love. Yet the early Gurus in the AG educe a similar chill:

Humility is my spiked club.
My double-edged Sword is the dust of all men's feet.
No Sinner can withstand these weapons.
The Perfect Guru has given me this understanding.
(AG: 628 G. Arjan)

This chapter has sought to question the general assumption that violence should always be negatively construed within the context of an ethical and disciplined religious praxis which is ostensibly about loving-devotion (*bhagati*). McLeod's totalizations of the Sikh tradition into Guru Nanak's 'eirenic aspect' of 'rapt devotion' of the Name, to a 'second variety' of Guru Gobind's military 'heroism', and finally to Dīp Singh's 'martyrdom', makes an unwarranted move from inner to outer, saint to soldier, love to violence – which the tradition itself rejects. The above has also questioned the totalizing leaps that polarize war and peace, sword and flute into mutually exclusive realities. Yet the question retains an urgency, how *can bhagati* be about the sword and the flute? That love and violence are mutually constituted requires careful reflection, for who can truly appreciate the poisoned dart in the flute, the music of the sword?

The only violence there is: forgetting the name

The above discussion of 'violent-love' must be understood within the wider context of Guru Nanak's major claim that there is really only one violent act. This is a crucial point because it brings into view two orders of violence, one false and one true:

Saying it, I live; forgetting it, I die.
(AG: 9 G. Nanak)

Forgetting the Name–Word–Guru produces mental death; only those who 'remember' the Name–Word–Guru are truly alive. All suffering, delusion and desire arise from this forgetting (*visāri*). Simply put, one commits violence against oneself and others in forgetting the Divine/Truth, which is synonymous with forgetting to be true. This forgetting is a violence that constructs a/the world (*saṁsāra*) in all its layers and diversity. Those who forget Hari have to suffer the pain of physical death repeatedly. The duality (*dubidhā*) of Hari *and* 'me' is the primal and only violence. There is no violence apart from this separation; 'forgetting' (to love the) Name, to be true, constructs a world of violence. Sikh religious violence is taken for wonder when it destroys this world/self that exists without the Word (i.e., false being).

I would cut myself into pieces for the Blessed Vision of Your Darshan;
I am a sacrifice to Your Name.
(AG: 557 G. Nanak)

At the core of Sikh *bhagati* love, is the concept of a serious and violently imagined sacrifice. To remember the Name is to kill the self 'moment by moment, bit by bit' (AG: 660 G. Nanak). The purview of the True-Guru then is to kill you or help you kill yourself (AG: 183 G. Arjan). But why kill the self? Guru Nanak answers: 'I am a sacrifice (*kurabāṇī*) to the Embodiment of Bliss (*ānand-rūp*)' (AG: 1342). Simply put, killing the ego-self produces the cognitive bliss of *sahaj* (effortless becoming without I) that reveals one's true nature: 'He kills the self (*āpu māre*), then finds the Name' (AG: 153 G. Nanak). This whole complex, is repeated and intensified by Guru Gobind Singh, and the rare bliss it promotes can be felt over and above physical torture. This yogic state (of *sahaj*) is one that allows extraordinary transcendence of pain and brutality: even joy (born out of love of Hari) has been expressed in the midst of horrific violence. This is what links the violent-love of the AG with the loving-violence of the DG: a mystic state of devotional bliss – violence and love envisioned otherwise.

Guru Nanak's non-dual thought often turns our world upside down revealing our 'knowledge' to be ignorance, our pleasure to be pain, our physical sufferings to be divine blessings. He places a 'spiritual' scale over events that we simply cannot fathom and which turns our human scale into a form of blindness:

> If my body was to suffer in agony and
> come under the influence of the two evil planets;
> (if) blood-thirsty kings were to stand over my head and rule and
> (if) I were to remain in this state, still I would continue to chant your praises.
>
> (AG: 142 G. Nanak)

> Look what is sweet [sugar cane] is cut down, slicing and cutting its feet are bound.
> Having placed them between the rollers (strong) farmers give that (bundle) (due) punishment.
> Its juice and marrow is put into a large iron cauldron heated and weeps bitterly.
> Even the left-over cane is taken care of; given to the fire (and) burnt.
> Nanak (says), 'come, O people, see (how) the Sweet are ill-treated'.
>
> (AG: 143 G. Nanak)

Guru Nanak's prophetic verse seems to outline the historical scenarios that plagued later tradition.[19] For example during the eighteenth century many Sikhs were forced into exile by government persecution. Taru Singh (1720–1745) was one of those who risked their lives to secretly feed and clothe these Sikh warriors in hiding. The governor of Lahore, Zakariya Khan, having caught Taru via his spies, ordered the scalping and execution of Taru Singh were he to refuse conversion to Islam. Taru's martyrdom, having chosen death over losing his hair (symbolic of a Sikh's faith), turns Nanak's metaphors into reality:

> The more the Turks tortured [Taru] Singh the rosier a hue did the Singh's face take on. The more they starved him and kept him thirsty the more did he display contentment. ... In contentment and composure he bowed his head joyfully to the Guru's will.
>
> (Ratan S. Bhangu's *Prāchīn Panth Prakāś* 1841: 287 cited in Fenech 2000: 195)

For contemporary Sikhs, such verses cannot help but remind them of past and recent memories; Guru Arjan's torture and martyrdom in the first year of Jahangir's reign (1605) marking a dramatic turn of fate for the Sikh *panth*, and the atrocities executed by Indian police after 1984 – with their tactics of rolling heavy wooden and/or iron logs over the legs of Sikh 'separatists/terrorists', mangling them beyond use and recognition.[20] But they may also point out an uncommon, if not wondrous, logic: the more one is violated, tortured, the more content and composed one becomes; the severer the violence, the sweeter the love. There are many accounts of this logic throughout Sikh history summarized by the popular eighteenth-century couplet: 'Mir Mannu [governor of Lahore] is our sickle and we the fodder for him to mow. The more Mir Mannu harvests, the more the Sikhs will grow' (Fenech 2000: 41). This phenomenon carries on right up to contemporary testimonies of Sikhs tortured at the hands of the Indian security forces (Pettigrew 1995; Mahmood 1996). Yet it is grounded first and foremost in the religious teachings of the AG:

> A fish is caught, cut and cooked in many different ways.
> Bit by bit it is eaten, but still, it does not forget the water.
>
> (AG: 658 Bhagat Ravidas)

Guru Nanak demands violence from those who seek love: 'If you want to play the game of love (*prem*) approach me with your head on the palm of your hand' (AG: 1412). It is this theme of self-sacrifice that Guru Gobind strategically plays upon in his call to establish the Khālsā (Singh 1997: 283). The Birth of the Khālsā is predicated on the full cognizance of the love inherent in this violence; if no one stood up to sacrifice themselves, there would be no *real* army. The *real* army is composed of those already dead (the point of Nanak's 'religious' quest), which is why the Khālsā are so formidable, there being nothing more to lose. The movement from Guru Nanak's prophetic metaphors, via Guru Gobind's ambiguous performative re-staging to the real Khālsā Army, through to the contemporary Sikhs (Akālis) who fought non-violently in India's Independence struggle, and the Gurdwara Reform Movement, reveals a continuity-in-difference of violent-love.[21]

However Guru Nanak holds the final s/word: '*If* the ego does not die then the heroic death of the warrior is not approved by God' (AG: 579). As with any activity then, *dharamic* or *adharamic*, religious or political, violent or loving, 'without the Name' (which simultaneously implies the death of ego) it becomes futile and empty; certainly no singular activity can always secure Hari's pleasure:

> One is not steeped in Hari/Truth
> by fighting and dying a brave warrior in battle.
> (AG: 1237 G. Nanak)

It should be clear then that throughout Sikh scripture no particular action is legislated into a principle, always being true regardless of the context in which it occurs – except, of course, the wholly open-ended 'law' to remember Hari by losing the ego. Just as the soldier chastises the saint that does not act in the world, so too does the saint condemn the soldier's instrumental violence. Just as the renouncer criticizes the householder for his worldly attachments, so does the latter censure the ascetic for selfishly neglecting his duty to society. Rather than doctrinal laws, the Gurus leave us with a questioning dialectic that seeks to confront all ideologically based thinking (*duramati*, lit. dualistic, false thinking). Neither militarism nor pacifism were taught by the Gurus, nor asceticism or pleasure-seeking. Their task was to pass on a cultivation of the in-between, a mode of living-in-the-Way (*jugati-samāi, hukam rajāi calañā*). The aim was to be led by an understanding, always incomplete, context-based and provisional, (more of an unknowing than a knowing) that spontaneously arose from an immersion in the Way. *True* action (loving or violent, *dharamic* or not) cannot be guided by rules and codes, but only by the unbroken rapture of devoted self-loss.

Conclusion: Guru Gobind's martial art of love

From the foregoing discussion it seems clear that the break-in-tradition thesis should be reassessed – a new interpretive frame is needed. The framework of martial arts is a far better paradigm to comprehend the fighting art (*gatka*), and strategic 'dance' (*paiṅtaṛā*) of the Khālsā than merely reading Sikhs as 'soldiers'. Given the centrality of *bhagati*, self-sacrifice, self-defence, nonduality, and an 'ever-rising spirit' (*chaṛḍi-kalā*), it seems much more fitting to think about Guru Gobind's 'saint-soldier' in terms of a 'martialization' rather than a 'militarization', where the former carries the discipline, devotion and ethics of a martial art. The founder of Aikido, Morihei Ueshiba, writes:

> In true *budo* [Way of enlightened activity] there are no opponents. In true *budo* we seek to be one with all things, to return to the heart of creation. In real *budo*, there are no enemies. Real *budo* is a function of love. The way of a Warrior is not to destroy and kill life but to foster life, to continually create.
>
> (Stevens 2002: 72)

The shift from the military to the martial provides the conceptual framework in which to read violent-love as not destructive but restorative of *dharam*: the Wielder of Weapons is the Mother of the World; Guru Nanak's Flute is Guru Gobind's Sword. The ideal Sikh warrior was no mere soldier, subservient to the command of secular rulers, but a slave to the martial art of love:

The lover enjoys King Rām;
within the battlefield he fights having killed the mind.
(AG: 931 G. Nanak)

When the continuity that underpins the 'break' is seen, then the Sikh tradition is understood as an ongoing experiment with love that is simultaneously a politics of social duty, welfare and transformation. As religion is often viewed as the nemesis of modernity, so too has mysticism been figured alien to politics. From the continuity-in-difference argued for here this polarized separation seems fetishistic. There seems to be a non-dual relation between love and violence which signifies a new hermeneutic wherein the Sikh tradition's violent-love can be read as a political mysticism. This is why the Sikhs are constantly misperceived as either exclusively religious or militant by a secular, rational, modern consciousness. The ambiguity of a text-as-sword is not seen as a wonder, but only strikes terror and fear. This seems to be a missed opportunity.

Notes

1 The Sikh Gurus use many personal and impersonal names for 'God/Absolute/Truth', ranging across traditions. Nanak's most frequent is the Vaishnava name 'Hari' whereas later tradition assumes 'Akāl-Purakh'. Punjabi spellings are used for common Indic terms: *karam* not *karma*; *dharam* not *dharma*; *bhagati* not *bhakti* etc. In addition to the Guru Granth Sahib/after the *Ādi Granth* (hereafter AG) and the *Dasam Granth* (hereafter DG), there is a third Sikh scripture, that directly substantiates the Sikh 'Text as Sword', and that is the *Sarab-loh Granth* (The 'All-Steel Book', or 'All-Sword Book'). This text is popular among contemporary *Nihangs* (Sikh warriors) and claimed by them to be the work of the tenth Sikh Guru, Gobind Singh. The work is, however, almost certainly after Gobind's time (see McLeod 2003: 139) and for this reason will not be consulted here. Translations are mine, though Trumpp (1989) and Sant Singh Khalsa's (2003) translations of the AG, and Jodh Singh's (1999) and S. S. Kohli's translations (2003) of the DG have been consulted and sometimes adapted. In addition to the editors, I would like to thank Sophie Hawkins for reading a draft of this chapter and making many sound suggestions.

2 Of course there is nothing unique, from a comparative perspective, in seeing the divine Word or God as a Sword, nor in seeing the spread of God's message by the physical Sword of judgement as part of the same idea. Within the Judeo-Christian tradition alone compare: 'Indeed the word of God is living and active, sharper than any two-edged sword' (Hebrews 4:12), and 'I have not come to bring peace, but a sword' (Matthew 10:34), and Jeremiah to Judas 'Take this holy sword, a gift from God, with which you will strike down your adversaries' (2 Maccabees 15:15). The Word/Text has often been understood as both a spiritual and physical sword, one that carries God's love and violent justice simultaneously (Holy Bible 1989).

3 The Sikh initiated into the Khālsā has to wear and keep five items as a part of his or her military regalia: uncut hair (*keś*), steel bracelet (*kaṛā*), sword or dagger (*kirpān*), shorts (*kach*) and comb (*kaṅghā*).

4 The title consciously echoes Homi Bhabha's (1997) title, 'Signs Taken for Wonder'.

5 We must note that the coherence and continuity between these texts have been and still are disputed; see Oberoi (1994) and Harbans Singh (1992). It is clear that the DG shared a greater standing in the past than it has done since the Singh Sabha reforms. Yet both are seen as scriptures by orthodoxy, and hymns from both form the selected set of prayers each Sikh has to recite morning and evening.

6 The 1870s onwards saw the rise of various reform movements. Through a process of intercultural mimesis, 'Hindus', 'Sikhs' and 'Muslims' re-constructed their 'ways of life' into mutually exclusive *religious* communities (Ludden 1996).

7 Modernity has a variety of readings of 'religion', and of course there have been many 'violent religions'. The modern definition implied here disciplines 'religion' as that which opposes the present in its backward gaze to tradition, and is essentially superstitious in comparison to secular science. It is a modern desire and demand that religious traditions put down their arms and stop behaving like 'savages'. For similar arguments see A. Mandair (Ch. 6), and N. Mandair (Ch. 7) in Goodchild 2003.

8 However, discussing 'religious violence' must obviously be done with care marking a clear distinction from 'terrorist violence' that often employs and/or usurps an overt 'religious' rhetoric to legitimize its murderous crimes. None of what is argued for here could nor should be construed as supporting such terrorist violence or ideology. Similarly, any discussion about 'violent-love' must be clear to distinguish itself from the obvious reading of it as rape.

9 Madan (1994: 613) misses this question and provides a common misreading with this claim: 'there can be no denying that Guru Hargobind made a radical departure from past practice. . . . The first Guru's teaching that a true Sikh's only weapon should be the holy word had thus been set aside.'

10 Private communication with Arvind Mandair.

11 Full title is the *Tiruttoṇṭarpurāṇam*, the 'Ancient Story of the Holy Servants'.

12 Although it is clear that Akāl does not incarnate in any one particular form, given the orientation towards a Formless and Attributeless Being (*nirguṇa-bhakti*), Akāl is also identified with the True-Guru (*satiguru*) given that 'there is no Other'. Those that realize this, and see Hari as Satiguru everywhere, are known as Gurus. There is then an easy identification between Guru, Satiguru, and Akāl. Such non-dual identifications justify the 'slippage' from Akāl as the True-King to Guru as the True-King.

13 See Fenech (2000: 95–102) for details of Dīp Singh, who supernaturally carries his own decapitated head for 15 kilometres en route to Amritsar to fulfil his 'religious' vow.

14 The missionary and later Persian scholar Father Jerome Xavier, who spent 20 years in the Mughal court of Akbar and Jahangir, notes: 'Guru [Arjan], who amongst the gentiles (i.e. non-Muslims) is like the Pope amongst us' (in Madra and Singh 2004: 7).

15 Lakoff and Johnson (1980) argue that metaphors are not simply ornamental – decorating what essentially could be said in literal fashion – but are cognitive models and structures that shape the way we think and live.

16 This is a description of the battle of Bhagani in 1688.

17 For example in the Skill-In-Means (*Upāyakauśalya*) Sutra the captain of a ship of 500 merchants, after gaining insight decides to murder a thief who was bent on killing all the merchants: 'the captain Great Compassionate protected those merchants by deliberately slaying that person (who was a robber) with a spear, with great compassion and skill in means' (Katz 1994: 74)

18 'The root of Muslim rule has decayed,' he declared, 'but the tree will not fall unless it is cut down or unless it is shaken by a mighty storm. A storm of swords will now assail it and thus it shall be felled.' Ratan Singh Bhangu's (*Prāchīn Panth Prakāś*, McLeod 1984: 72–73)

19 See Fenech (2000) who details many accounts and testimonies of Sikh violent and non-violent martyrs.

20 From personal testimonies of close friends. An Amnesty International report corroborates these testimonies:

> Reports of torture by Punjab Police continue, although they are less frequent than during the period of violent political opposition. The methods are similar. They often include kicks and blows with sticks and leather belts. Detainees have been strung up, usually with their hands behind their back or their head down. They have been subjected to the roller, a wooden pole or iron rod rolled over their legs by several police officers leaning on it with their full weight, which leads to a crushing of muscle tissue and subsequent kidney complaints. Detainees have been tortured with electric shocks to the genitals and other sensitive areas such as ear lobes and fingers. They have been beaten on the soles of their feet (*falanga*), burned with a hot iron or boiling water, and had chilli peppers applied to their anus or eyes. Police officers have threatened to kill them. As a result of torture, victims have suffered serious physical disabilities, deep states of depression, disturbed sleep and nightmares.
>
> (*Amnesty International* January 2003: 18)

I would like to thank Prabhsharandeep Singh for this information. There are many independent agencies that have charted the human rights abuses Sikhs have suffered, see Mahmood (1996: 277) for a comprehensive list. There have also been more recent reports (Kumar *et al.* 2003; Kaur 2004) – the latter analyses impunity and over 600 specific cases of 'extrajudicial execution and disappearances by Indian security forces'.

21 Of course this high ideal is not always achieved and must be sharply distinguished from its total opposite in the terrorist acts of the 1980s – the assassination of the Nirankari Guru, Baba Gurbachan Singh on April 1980, in retaliation to those murdered in the 'orthodox' Khālsā–Niraṅkāri confrontation in April 1978; the killings in the early 1980s of Lala Jagat Narain, chief editor of *Punjab Kesari* and his son Ramesh Chander, amongst many others, show this all too clearly. Furthermore, it is significant that there seemed to be no condemnation issued by the Akali (Sikh political) leadership of these cold-blooded killings – nor did any denounce Bhindranwale. However reading the Government of India's White Paper on Punjab Agitation one would get the impression that 'Sikh Extremists' are solely to blame for the violence in its black and white depiction of the events in the recent history of Sikhs (Kaur, Amarjit *et al.* 2004: 197–217).

Bibliography

Primary sources

Bhangu, Ratan Singh (1982 [1841]) *Prāchīn Panth Prakāś*, (ed.) Vīr Singh, Delhi, 5th edn.

Khalsa, Sant Singh (trans.) (2003) *Sentence By Sentence English Translation & Transliteration of Siri Guru Granth Sahib*. Phonetic transliteration by Kulbir Singh Thind, MD, Tucson, AZ: Hand Made Books. Available online at http://www.sikhs.org/english/frame.html (accessed 1 May 2005).

Kohli, S.S. (trans.) (2003) *Sri Dasam Granth Sahib*, 3 vols. Birmingham, UK: The Sikh National Heritage Trust.

Śabadārath Srī Gurū Granth Sāhib jī (1992 [1930]) text of the AG with partial commentary, 4 vols., Delhi: Sikh Gurdwara Parabandhak Committee, Hamdarad Printing Press, Jalandhar.
Singh, J. and Dharam Singh (trans.) (1999) *Sri Dasam Granth Sahib: Text and Translation*, 2 vols, Patiala, India: Heritage Publishers.
Singh, Jodh (trans.) (1998) *Vārāṅ Bhāī Gurdās: Text, Transliteration and Translation*, trans. Patiala, New Delhi: Vision and Venture.
Trumpp, Ernest (trans.) (1989 [1877]) *The Ādi Granth or The Holy Scriptures of the Sikhs (translated from the original Gurmukhī)*, New Delhi: Munshiram Manoharlal, 4th edn.

Secondary sources

Amnesty International (January 2003) *INDIA: Break the Cycle of Impunity and Torture in Punjab.* Available online at http://web.amnesty.org/library/Index/engASA200022003?OpenDocument&of=COUNTRIES%5CINDIA (accessed 26 September 2005).
Avalon, A. (ed.) (1960) *Principles of Tantra: The Tantratattva of Shrīyukta Shiva Candra Vidyārṇava Bhattacārya Mahodaya*, Madras: Ganesh & Co.
Bhabha, H.K. (1997) *The Location of Culture*, London: Routledge.
Bhogal, B.S. (2001) 'Nonduality and Skilful Means in Nanak: Hermeneutics of the Word', unpublished thesis, School of Oriental and African Studies, University of London.
Chan, Wing-tsit (trans. and compiler) (1973 [1963]) *Sourcebook in Chinese Philosophy*, Princeton, NJ: Princeton University Press.
Davidson, R.M. (2002) *Indian Esoteric Buddhism: A Social History of the Tantric Movement*, New York: Columbia University Press.
Deol, J. (2001) 'Eighteenth Khalsa Identity: Discourse, Praxis and Narrative', in *Sikh Religion, Culture and Ethnicity*, (25–46) (eds) Christopher Shackle, Gurharpal Singh and Arvind-pal Mandair, Richmond, Surrey: Curzon Press.
Fenech, L.E. (2000) *Martyrdom in the Sikh Tradition: Playing the 'Game of Love'*, Oxford: Oxford University Press.
Gandhi, Mahatma (1967) 'My Friend, The Revolutionary' *(9-4-1925)*, in Vol XXVI (January–April 1925) Ahmedabad: Navajivan Trust, of *The Collected Works of Mahatma Gandhi,* Delhi: Publications Division, Ministry of Information and Broadcasting, 1958–1997.
Goodchild, P. (ed.) (2003) *Difference in Philosophy of Religion*, Aldershot: Ashgate.
Grewal, J.S. (1998 [1990]): *The Sikhs of the Punjab: The New Cambridge History of India II.3,* Cambridge: Cambridge University Press.
Grewal, J.S. and Irfan Habib (eds) (2001) *Sikh History from Persian Sources: Translations of Major Texts*, New Delhi: Indian History Congress.
Holy Bible, New Revised Standard Version (1989) New York, Oxford: Oxford University Press.
Katz, M. (trans.) (1994) *The Skill in Means* (Upāyakauśalya) Sūtra, Delhi: Motilal Banarsidass.
Kaur, Amarjit, J.S. Aurora, Khushwant Singh, M.V. Kamath, Shekhar Gupta, Subhash Kirpekar, Sunil Sethi and Tavleen Singh (2004 [1984]) *The Punjab Story*, New Delhi: Lotus Collection, Roli Books.

Kaur, Jaskaran (2004) *Twenty Years of Impunity: The November 1984 Pogroms of Sikhs in India*, A Report by ENSAAF June 2004, UK: Nectar Publishing.

Kinsley, D.R. (2000 [1975]) *The Sword and the Flute: Kālīand Kṛṣṇa, Dark Visions of the Terrible and the Sublime in Hindu Mythology*, Berkeley: University of California Press.

Kripal, J.J. (1998 [1995]) *Kālī's Child: The Mystical and the Erotic in the Life and Teachings of Ramakrishna*, Chicago: University of Chicago Press, 2nd edn.

Kumar, R.N. *et al.* (2003) *Reduced to Ashes: The Insurgency and Human Rights in Punjab*, Nepal: South Asia Forum for Human Rights.

Lakoff, G. and M. Johnson (1980) *Metaphors We Live By*, Chicago: University of Chicago Press.

Ludden, D. (ed.) (1996) *The Making of Hindu India: Religion, Community, and the Politics of Democracy in India*, Delhi: Oxford University Press.

Madan, T.N. (1994 [1991]) 'The Double-Edged Sword: Fundamentalism and the Sikh Religious Tradition', in *Fundamentalisms Observed*, (eds) Martin E. Marty and R. Scott Appleby, Chicago and London: University of Chicago Press, pp. 594–627.

Madra, A.S. and Parmjit Singh (eds) (2004) *Sicques, Tigers, or Thieves: Eyewitness Accounts of the Sikhs (1606–1809)*, Hampshire, UK: Palgrave Macmillan.

Mahmood, C.K. (1996) *Fighting for Faith and Nation; Dialogues with Sikh Militants*, Philadelphia: University of Pennsylvania Press.

Mandair, N.S. (2003) 'Virtual Corpus: Solicitous Mutilation and the Body of Tradition', in *Difference in Philosophy of Religion*, (ed.) Phillip Goodchild, Aldershot: Ashgate, pp. 101–113.

McLeod, W.H. (trans. and ed.) (1984) *Textual Sources for the Study of Sikhism*, Manchester: Manchester University Press.

——(1989) *The Sikhs: History, Religion, and Society*, New York: Columbia University Press.

——(1997) *Sikhism*, London: Penguin Books.

——(2003) *Sikhs of the Khalsa: A History of the Khalsa Rahit*, New Delhi: Oxford University Press.

Monius, A.E. (2004) 'Love, Violence, and the Aesthetics of Disgust: Saivas and Jains in Medieval South India', *Journal of Indian Philosophy*, 32: 113–172.

Oberoi, H.S. (1994) *The Construction of Religious Boundaries: Culture, Identity, and Diversity in the Sikh Tradition*, Oxford: Oxford University Press.

Pettigrew, J.M. (1995) *The Sikhs of the Punjab: Unheard Voices of State and Guerilla Violence*, London and New Jersey: Zed Books Ltd.

Pinch, W.R. (1996) 'Soldier Monks and Militant Sadhus', in *The Making of Hindu India: Religion, Community, and the Politics of Democracy in India,* (ed.) David Ludden, Delhi: Oxford University Press, pp. 140–161.

Shackle, C. (1981) *A Nanak Glossary*, London: School of Oriental and African Studies, University of London.

Shackle, C., G. Singh and A. Mandair (eds) (2001) *Sikh Religion, Culture and Ethnicity*, Richmond, Surrey: Curzon Press.

Singh, Darshan (ed.) (1999) *Western Images of the Sikh Religion: A Source Book*, New Delhi: National Book Organization.

Singh, Harbans (ed.) (1992–1998) *The Encyclopedia of Sikhism,* vols I–IV, Patiala, Punjab: Punjabi University.

Stevens, J. (ed.) (2002) *Budo Secrets: Teachings of the Martial Arts Masters*, Boston and London: Shambhala.

Van der Veer, P. (1996) 'Writing Violence', in *The Making of Hindu India: Religion, Community, and the Politics of Democracy in India*, (ed.) David Ludden, Delhi: Oxford University Press, pp. 50–269.

Part 2

Religion and violence in contemporary South Asia

6 Operationalizing Buddhism for political ends in a martial context in Lanka

The case of *Siṃhalatva*

Peter Schalk

Introduction

In Lanka, there is not only the Pāli canon as a source of inspiration for thinking, speaking and acting in private and public life. A second inspiring source for Buddhists is the Vaṃsic or Chronical tradition formed in Lanka during part of the colonial period. A third source is foreign traditions representing religions, political ideologies, evaluations of life and worldviews. Among these, we find racial, racist/racialist ideas which were applied to and internalized by Tamils and Siṃhalas from the late nineteenth century onwards.

My main question is how these sources have been used in a situation of martial conflict in Lanka by political Buddhists.[1] It is first necessary to define the concept of 'political Buddhism'. Political Buddhism has the ultimate *political* aim to operationalize/instrumentalize Buddhist values, concepts, rituals, texts, etc. Political Buddhism should be distinguished from Buddhist politics[2] which aims at introducing Buddhist values in society. There is nothing odd about Buddhist politics; the Buddha himself was a Buddhist politician. Political Buddhism, however, is controversial because it subordinates Buddhist values to political values. The ultimate political aim may vary, but usually it is formulated in terms of state formations. In our specific context, the unitary, united, federal, con-federal and independent states appear in political/religious discourses. Political Buddhism ranges over a scale from the political extremist left to the extremist right. There are some political monks defending the view of the Communist and Trotskyite parties and others who are associated with Fascist organizations – to indicate the extremes.

Here, I shall focus on one special kind of political Buddhism in Lanka. It defends the integrity and sovereignty of the unitary state.[3] Its character is ethnic homogenization and political centralization. Here, we have to do with an anti-democratic or totalitarian form of political Buddhism, whose self-designation is *Siṃhalatva*, '(ideology of) Siṃhalaness', or *jātika cintanaya*, 'national ideology'. As outsiders we would say Siṃhala-Buddhist ethno nationalism. Some scholars and Buddhist enthusiasts, who normatively select pure or original Buddhism only, say that this kind of 'Buddhism' is not Buddhism at all. As a historian, I would argue that there is not only one kind of Buddhism, Judaism,

Christianity or Islam, but several kinds of each religion. One kind of Buddhism is political Buddhism. Buddhism today should be defined from the viewpoint of a historian as a syncretic conglomerate of different and even incompatible strands of ideals from the past and present.[4]

Long-term goals can change, as in the case of the scholar monk Walpola Rahula, who from his original quest for sovereignty of the island, which was incompatible with British colonialism, to his quest for the integrity of the island, which was and is – in the present historical situation – incompatible with the quest by Tamil militants for an independent state of Tamiḻīḻam. Towards the end of his life, he openly supported the war-for-peace idea, which he had (in a subtle way), as pointed out by Tessa Bartholomeusz,[5] already done in his *Heritage of the Bhikkhu* from the 1940s. He, together with ten outstanding Buddhist organizations, rejected peace talks in 1992 (which nevertheless took place in 1994/95). On 1 February 1992 he wrote in *The Independent* newspaper: 'Until this war is successfully concluded, no peace talks should be held'.[6] This was the precursor to the popular slogan 'war for peace' in the 1990s. Here, my focus is not on war slogans used by martial Buddhists, although they are important to study as genuine expressions of a martial situation. Instead, I focus on the process by which ideologues reverse civil values into martial values in a given martial context. Their reversal is an adaptation to, and expression of, the prevalent circumstances. They operationalize/instrumentalize ethnic categories, including religious categories, to preserve, rather than achieve, an ultimate political aim, in this case the unitary state of Sri Lanka. The unitary state is affirmed in the present Constitution of the island.[7] This is the moral and legal strength of the *Siṃhalatva*, which is the ideology of a Siṃhala-Buddhist ethno-nationalist centralized state.

The process of reversing pacifist civil values into martial values is not easy. Both sides of the conflict represent strong cultures that restrict the use of violence to achieve political goals. Both parties are aware of, and are strongly influenced by, restrictions going back to Gandhism, also to the enduring and silent martyrdom of a Christian tradition, to the explicit distancing of all violence by the Buddha (even for self-defence), and to modern secular concepts of human rights. It is not simply that Murukaṉ inspires Tamils only and the Buddha inspires Siṃhalas only, both are inspired by a complex of the same non-violent traditions, with, however, different emphases on them. My point is that these traditions reinforce each other in the minds of individuals. It is not easy to kill even a demonized enemy with all these cultural restrictions. This voice of conscience has to be silenced or marginalized by ideologues. The use of violence has to be rationalized, or at least scruples about using violence have to be reduced, by for example dressing violence in the garb of traditional Siṃhala culture. Bruce Kapferer has pointed to symbolic action in the form of exorcism as precursor to, and model for, anti-Tamil pogroms.[8] If a pogrom has the character of exorcism it can be seen as part of traditional Siṃhala culture. Reversed martial values can be made plausible by, for example, classifying them as offshoots of a valued historical tradition like the Vaṃsic tradition. The

Gandhian principle concerning the character of the 'means' determining the character of the 'ends', about peace not being attainable by war, has to be deliberately marginalized by ideologues. We shall see in the following discussion some variations on how to silence the voice of conscience in a martial situation.

In what follows I use as one of my main sources conference papers on Buddhism and Conflict in Sri Lanka at Bath, 2002. They are now published in both English and Siṃhala.[9] In this place of high symbolic value – it is a spa – an experiment took place between 27 and 30 June 2002. Scholars, Buddhist enthusiasts and political partisans from both sides were brought together to discuss the concept of violence within Lankan Buddhism, past and present.

Siṃhalatva

Siṃhalatva is an ideology of a unitary state based on Buddhism. It has different names, *jātika cintanaya* or *Siṃhalatva* as internal terms, and as an outsiders term, Siṃhala-Buddhist ethno-nationalism, a form of political Buddhism or Buddhist fundamentalism.[10] *Siṃhalatva* is an analogue to 'Hindutva' thereby emphasizing the view that what is regarded as 'Indian' (=Hindu) has to be monopolized by the 'Indians'. These include Hindus, Buddhists, Jains and Sikhs, but not Muslims, Christians, Parsis or Jews. In the case of *Siṃhalatva*, the so-called Siṃhala heritage has to be monopolized by the state. One of the more militant organizations within the *Siṃhalatva* movement is called *siṃhalaurumaya*, 'Siṃhala heritage', which established itself as a political party in the parliamentary elections of 2 April 2004 and gained 5.97 per cent of the votes and nine seats in Parliament under the name of *Jathika Hela Urumaya*,[11] 'National Siṃhala Heritage'. The nine MPs are monks. It is a clear deviation from the *Vinaya* for a monk to take up a political post.

Siṃhalatva leaves no place for other groups to share power. A multi-ethnic society is rejected. Again, the strength of *Siṃhalatva* is that it has the support of the Constitution when defending the concept of a unitary state. I have elsewhere coined the expression *dharmacracy* to describe the concept of a totalitarian Buddhist state being projected by *Siṃhalatva*.[12]

In the 1980s, I counted more than 100 organizations having *Siṃhalatva* as their ideology.[13] It is possible to follow some of them back to the beginning of national independence in 1948. Some of them have changed names, leaders have come and gone, methods of the propaganda work have changed from verbal to physical injuries, but the ultimate aim remains, the establishment of the unitary state, and the main method to operationalize Buddhist concepts for this aim, remains unchanged.

Siṃhalatva is a political ethno-nationalist ideology with a strong base also in the Sri Lanka Freedom Party, which houses a special identifiable section known as the *Siṃhalatva kavandaya*, 'the *Siṃhalatva* body',[14] but *Siṃhalatva* is mostly spread anonymously among individuals and represented by Buddhist militant organizations for example *siṃhala urumaya* and other Siṃhala/Buddhist organizations. Its strength is not evident merely from the numbers of public persons, but by the overt consent of members of other parties and above all by the silent consent of many anonymous persons in civil life. This party received 552,724 votes on 2 April 2004.[15] *Siṃhalatva* representatives, however, avoid describing the conflict in ethnic terms of Siṃhalas against Tamils because that would play into the hands of the stereotypes constructed by the *Īḻavar*. *Īḻavar* is an emic term that refers to those who support the establishment of Tamiḻīḻam.[16] These emphasize victimization on the grounds of ethnicity. Tamils are allegedly persecuted because they are Tamils. *Siṃhalatva* therefore makes a distinction between Tamils and 'terrorists' and directs its struggle against the latter in public statements. They do not use the designation *Īḻavar* which is a modern self-designation by Tamils relating to a new emerging identity.[17] They may, however, speak in English about 'Ealamists', which is a pejorative term and connotes terrorists.

The unity of the unitary state is conceptualized as Buddhism-cum-territory-language-race in a classical formulation going back to Anagārika Dharmapāla and is exploited by *Siṃhalatva* which is represented in modern times by the late Buddhist monk Maḍihē Paññasīha, *mahānāyaka*. His ideal of a man is Anagārika Dharmapāla. This monk Maḍihē Paññasīha published one of the best-known biographies in Siṃhala, *Vīra carita*, ('the life of the hero'), about Anāgarika Dharmapāla.[18] There is a direct line of ideological dependency from Anāgarika Dharmapāla to Maḍihē Paññasīha, who in this biography quotes the key formula of *Siṃhalatva*, coined by Anagārika Dharmapāla in Siṃhala:

> *magē raṭa, magē jātiya, magē āgama, magē bhāṣāva yana me mahā anargha ratna satarak mata tibē. mē ratana satara ārakṣā karagänīma magē yutukamaki.*[19]
>
> 'My country, my race, my religion, my language have become to me a group of four great invaluable jewels. It is my duty to make these jewels of four the protection.'

Here, not only religion, but also the country, the (Siṃhala) *jātiya*, and the (Siṃhala) language take the position of a *ratna*, 'jewel', i.e. the position of one concern in a cluster of concerns. These together constitute the ideological unity of the island. The official translation of *jātiya* in passports is 'race'.

Siṃhalatva is metaphysics: it presumes the existence of *siṃhalatatva(ya)*, 'Simhalaness' that is a racial essence, as a result of belonging to the Siṃhala race. *Siṃhalatatvaya* has been consciously shortened to *Siṃhalatva* to correspond to Hindī *Hindūtva*. *Siṃhalatva* is a neologism that has been heavily launched in Lankan tabloids like *The Island* and *Divayina*. Its ideologues alternate in their use between *jātika cintanaya* and *Siṃhalatva*. *Cintanaya* is 'ideology' and *jātika* can be translated in different ways as 'racial' or 'national'. German has 'völkisch', rich in connotations, which would correspond closely to *jātika*.

This ideology, which is identified with a special ethno-nationalist form of political Buddhism, focuses on those who question the integrity and the sovereignty of the unitary state and who are seen as traitors. Seen as such antagonists are the representatives of *yudev cintanaya*, 'Jewish ideology', which is a characterization of Western science and of Western politics including non-government organizations (NGOs) and the Norwegian mission, to facilitate negotiations between the conflicting parties. They are allegedly *vi-jātika*, 'anti-national'. An important aspect is that *Siṃhalatva* exploits the theory about the clash of cultures on the specific situation, where *yudev cintanaya* and *jātika cintanaya* allegedly fight a (cosmic?) battle. *Yudev cintanaya* is Western because it was constructed by Western, mainly American, Jews. Western ideology is dominated by Semitic ideas. It stands against *jātika cintanaya,* which is Aryan.

For *Siṃhalatva*, there is no radical change in history. Within the canonical, Vaṃsic, colonial and post-colonial tradition there is no break. There is allegedly a continuity constituted by the concept of the island as *dhammadīpa*, which is understood (wrongly) as 'island of the *dhamma*'. It is connected with the concept of *sīhaḷadīpa*, 'island of the Siṃhalas' and together they form the idea that the island has been a Buddhist island for the Siṃhalas only, since the arrival of Buddhism.[20] This modern anti-canonical and even in part anti-Vaṃsic interpretation of the concept of *dhammadīpa* is projected anachronistically into the past to form a continuity.[21] We see differences: there is a *tāyakam*, 'motherland', for the *Īḻavar*, and there is a *mavbima*, 'motherland', for *Siṃhalatva* enthusiasts.[22] Both parties operationalize/instrumentalize the same type of concept, but there is an ideological/religious surplus or overhang on the *Siṃhalatva* side among the Lankans. The *Īḻavar* follow a secular tradition of arguing for territory as *tāyakam*, 'motherland'.[23] Their main categories of instrumentalization are not race, but language, history and human rights which provide 'peoples' with a right of self-determination. Therefore, there is no symmetry in relation to the other party, to the *Siṃhalatva* movement. This latter movement operationalizes/instrumentalizes religion and race. Simhalatva representatives among the Lankans and *Īḻavar* do not 'meet' on the same level. This is important for judging the prospects of success in negotiations. *Siṃhalatva* representatives believe in a religiously defined island as *dhammadīpa,* which, by being religious, is lifted above all negotiations, because it is made the ultimate aim. All experiences about scruples of their stand taken have been eliminated by superimposing a religious interpretation on the concept of *mavbima*.

In the Vaṃsic tradition to be a Buddhist means much more than to have a religious conviction. There was no such concept as 'religion only' in the *Mahāvaṃsa*. The *buddasāsana* was the religion of the state; it was a royal state ideology. To be anti-Buddhist implies, therefore, being an enemy of the state. If I destroy a *stūpa*, rob the alms bowl, and smash the tooth relic, I also become an enemy of the state. Religious and political issues cannot be separated in the Vaṃsa tradition, which affects the evaluation of anti-Buddhist activities. It was easy to be classified as anti-Buddhist. Every action against the state was potentially an anti-Buddhist act, and *vice versa*. This idea is still living today and is fully exploited in the armed struggle by the *Īḻavar*. When some of them attacked the *bodhi*-tree of Anurādhapura in 1984, the Temple of the Tooth in Kandy in 2001 and the Nāga vihāra in Yāḻppaṇam city in 1985, their aim was not the destruction of the teaching of the Buddha, but the destruction of political Buddhism as a state ideology. In response, *Siṃhalatva* operationalizes/instrumentalizes these acts as anti-religious acts, as being directed against the pure teachings of Buddhism. Again, there is no symmetry in their respective motives. *Īḻavar* respond by ascribing to the Siṃhala army the motive of being anti-Hindu when they destroy Hindu temples, which has happened on several occasions, but from the army's side these may just be acts of revenge, racism or strategic destruction. Hindu temples are sometimes suspected to be refuges for the LTTE resistance. The LTTE (Liberation Tigers of Tamil Ealam) is the leading military organization of the *Īḻavar*.

The Vaṃsic sectarian Theravāda view, which was also anti-Mahāyāna, was reasserted by *Siṃhalatva* in the twentieth century, but combined with an additional new view, namely that Buddhism is the racial trait of the Siṃhalas only. It combined sectarianism with racism and made it impossible for Tamils to convert to Buddhism. In addition to reasserting Vaṃsic sectarian anti-Tamil xenophobia, Siṃhalas were not only regarded as a linguistic group, but also as a twentieth-century race. Buddhism became the religion of a race, and inversely and symmetrically, Caivam was related to the Tamil race, not by the Tamils, but by *Siṃhalatva*. Religion became a racial factor like the colour of the skin that cannot be changed. Under these circumstances, the idea of there being Tamil Buddhists is impossible.[24]

Siṃhalatva has two ideological pillars. One is the interpretation of *dhammadīpa* as an island of the *dhamma* for the Siṃhalas only.[25] The other is the formula *īḻam* < *sīhaḷa*, which is interpreted in an anti-Tamil way. It states that the old Tamil toponym *īḻam* is not Tamil, but is a derivation through stem mutation from *sīhaḷa*. Therefore, having no Tamil toponym, the Tamils have allegedly no founding tradition of early settlements, but are represented as latecomers to the island.[26]

Since 2001, the open military confrontation on the island has been replaced by a ceasefire, but the earlier slogan of the *Siṃhalatva* group, 'war for peace', is still promoted, as became clear in the Bath Conference in June 2002. The Ven. Dr Akuratiyē Nanda, a Buddhist monk, presented a paper entitled 'An Analysis of the Selected Statements Issued by the *mahānāyakas* on the North-East Problem of Sri Lanka'.[27] He distributed documents in Siṃhala as authentic sources for the views of the *mahānāyakas*. In his presentation, one could feel intensely the collision between two value systems. The monk believed that he presented the noblest Buddhist ideas of the Mahāsaṃgha. The Ven. Samitha, however, rose and made clear that the Mahāsaṃgha is divided on the acceptance of the statements by the *mahānāyakas*. He rejected the impression that the Ven. Akuratiyē Nanda spoke for all monks. The Ven. Samitha was the first monk to become a Member of Parliament and was a member of a Trotskyite Party. He lost his seat in the Parliamentary elections of 2 April 2004.

The Ven. Dr Akuratiyē Nanda distributed these official statements by the *mahānāyakas* to show that they were against the peace process. The ethnic problem is allegedly nothing but a terrorist problem. Norway was represented as a foreign power that supported terrorism. Peace talks, he asserted, would bring disaster. Even a federal system is detrimental to the country, nation and to Buddhism. The government was requested to crush terrorism. The peace process, he alleged, was a subtle strategy towards achieving a separate Tamiḻīḻam. C. R. de Silva, his respondent, succeeded in finding one statement by the *mahānāyakas*, not known or perhaps neglected by the monk, in which a more positive attitude to the peace process was discernible.

A *mahānāyaka* is a leader of a Buddhist order, of which there are several in Lanka. He is not elected by all the monks of his order, but by a special *sabhā*. His position does not necessarily have the confidence of all the monks of his order, and in a situation of conflict, disloyalties become evident. He is elected for his lifetime, but he has no formalized power. He has, however, status, which can be translated into terms of power or authority when making public statements. When asked about his order's views, he speaks not on behalf of himself but for his order. Politicians regularly visit such figures to 'inform' them, which implies getting their approval for political action. The Akuratiyē Nanda's performance at the conference was an illuminating incident, because he made clear to all listeners what the *mahānāyakas* really thought, and he documented it also. It is now published.[28] He had anticipated the objection by the Ven. Samitha. In his distributed paper, we read that the *mahānāyakas* are the most venerated leaders of the *saṃgha*. He also added that the possibility of individual monks having opposing views does not undermine the validity of the opinion expressed by the *mahānāyakas* not only regarding the matter of war and peace but all other matters.

The organizers of the Bath conference distributed a paper by an absent Buddhist monk called Ven. Bengamuvē Nālaka Thera. The title was 'The Origins of Tamil Racism and its Evolution'.[29] As this paper was covered with the logo and name of the conference organizers, it can be considered an official paper from the conference. The author presented himself as 'Secretary of the Patriotic Buddhist Front'. This organization is well known in the island as a centre for the cultivation of *Siṃhalatva*. In his paper, he condemned international conferences on 'the so called ethnic crises', and consequently he did not come to participate himself. He evidently wanted no dialogue. His paper is an excellent document for the study of *Siṃhalatva* at a grass-root level. His view can be summarized with a quotation: 'the responsibility of duly elected governments is but the deployment of troops and forces when "peace talks" is but a phoney war of terrorists'.

Finally, *Siṃhalatva* is responsible for launching a number of stereotypes about the Siṃhalas and the Tamils, which are widening the conflict. Some of these stereotypes have been internalized by both parties, and by the media and Western observers.

Justifying violence

Stereotypes are often ideologies reduced to *mantras*. They have in common an emphasis on the distance between the two parties. This usually results in the glorification of their own party and in a demonization of the other, which again justifies the use of psychological and physical violence in so-called self-defence. During the 1990s, the battle cry of political Buddhists, including prominent monks, was 'war for peace'. Already this unsophisticated slogan is a justification of war based on the universal principle that the 'end', here peace, justifies the 'means', here war.

There are more sophisticated ways of launching slogans to provide violence with a *raison d'ętre.* P. D. Premasiri from Peradeniya wrote a paper on 'The Place for a Righteous War in Buddhism: An Enquiry Concerning the Current Sri Lankan Ethnic Conflict in Terms of Pali Canonical Buddhism'.[30] The title can be misunderstood because it seemingly gives a place to the concept of a righteous war in Buddhism. That would not be very sophisticated. The speech and paper gave no such place. He asserted: 'there is no room for the concept of a righteous war in the canonical teachings' and 'participation in any kind of violence is absolutely out of question for those who seriously pursue the goal of Nibbana'. The professor was very certain of his conclusion and I have no objection. It implies that the justification of waging a war today by reference to the Buddhist canon is not valid. His paper contrasted with the outspoken paper of the Ven. Nālaka Thera.

Let us, however, look closer at Premasiri's paper. It speaks about exceptional cases, about those who seriously pursue the goal of *nirvāṇa*. For them no violence is even thinkable. What about all the 'normal' cases who suspend *nirvāṇa* or who are not serious in their pursuit? These cases probably constitute the majority. The paper by Premasiri is interesting also for what it alludes to. Having stated categorically that there is no room for a righteous war in the canonical teaching, he adds: 'However, war is sometimes recognized as a necessary evil'. Buddhists can claim today that there are no exceptional cases, they are just 'normal', and that they face a condition where war has to be recognized as a necessary evil. Furthermore, he says that 'the canon admits that in conducting mundane affairs of life even pious Buddhists may sometimes engage in war'. By this limitation, his general statement about the canon being totally pacifistic is invalidated. Taken in a formal way, all these reservations contradict the statement that there is no room in Buddhism for any war at all. They come close to a defence of a righteous war. Even if we leave out 'righteous', we still have a justified war. The result is, again, the universal formula that 'ends' may justify the 'means'.

There are here three universal ways of justifying violence. First, there is the distinction between what is valid for an elite, that in a Buddhist context means people who are striving for *nirvāṇa*, and what is valid for ordinary people who are concerned only with mundane affairs. It implies a double standard of ethics. Second, there is the distinction between what is valid now and what is valid in the distant future. In both cases we have a de-eschatologizing of religion, one that is applied to social strata and to time, that rationalizes violence. The eschaton, *nirvāṇa*, is currently suspended for the non-elite. I shall return to this in the conclusion of this paper. It is important to note that canonical Buddhism

Modi ~~175~~, 180-3
189

Hindutva 174, 183-84

Gujarat 173-90

Godhra 174-5, 180-1, 189

Communalism 45, 117, 155, 62, 173-86
195-7, 206-7, 244

makes a distinction between what is *lokika*, 'worldly' and what is *lokuttara*, 'beyond worldly' (=*nibbāna*), but it never amounts to a recognition of an autonomy of the two contrasting alternatives. On the contrary, the eschatological perspective expressed in the *lokuttara* concept, should be connected with the *lokika*-aspect. Third, we find the universal principle that 'ends' may justify the 'means' in the evaluation of war as a *necessary* evil.

Another sophisticated way of paving the way for violence is historical revisionism. The Vaṃsic tradition that is retrieved by *Siṃhalatva* goes back to state chronicles that were compiled from the fifth to the eighteenth century CE. It stipulates that the Theravāda tradition of the Mahāvihāra monks is the ultimate truth and that a true human is a Buddhist.[31] This sectarian, but not yet racial and racist/racialist view belongs to the early and middle Anurādhapura period. The passage 25: 101–11 in the *Mahāvaṃsa* from the fifth century CE, conveyed two ideas: (1) Tamils who were not belonging to the *buddhasāsana*, 'dispensation of the Buddha', were regarded as *micchādiṭṭhi*, 'wrong believers' and *dussilā*, 'evil-doers', and *pasumā*, 'like beasts'.[32] This is the rejectionist aspect of this passage, but there is another affirming side also. The passage implies (2) that Tamils could become humans, albeit gradually, if they turned systematically towards the *buddhasāsana*. If they accepted the refuge formula, they could become half-humans, and if they accepted the precepts, they could become full humans. Modern adherents of *Siṃhalatva* have closed this opening of the path to humanity for Tamils. For them Buddhism is a racial characteristic. If Buddhism is a racial characteristic of the Siṃhalas, you cannot convert to Buddhism as a Tamil, because it is not possible to change your skin. This is not the view of the Vaṃsic tradition, not even of the late one, but Vaṃsic tradition is interpreted in the light of racialism in the *Siṃhalatva* movement.

A historical revisionist approach to the Vaṃsic anti-Tamil xenophobic sources is not uncommon among monks today. Bhikkhu Dhammavihari presented a paper in the Bath conference called 'Sri Lankan Chronicle Data-Recording, Translating, and Interpreting: A Re-scrutiny of Erroneous Assumptions Regarding the History of Sri Lanka'.[33] He rejected the *Mahāvaṃsa* itself when it classified people as beasts, half-humans, and humans depending on their degree of having become Buddhists. Instead of acknowledging the fact that there has been conflict in creating passages in the *Mahāvaṃsa*, which have been fully exploited in anti-Tamil pogroms throughout history, Bhikkhu Dhammavihari wanted to change the *Mahāvaṃsa* and rewrite history. His approach to his sources was clearly normative.

There is another way that revisionism reinterprets uncomfortable historical data instead of denying them. During the Bath Conference Lorna Dewaraja distributed a paper called 'Religious and Ethnic Amity in Pre Modern Sri Lanka'.[34] We find both kinds of historical revisionism in her paper. She emphasized that Lankan Buddhist rulers have been tolerant towards other religions in the manner of the Buddhist Asoka. I want to make the following comments: to pinpoint rulers alone is misleading. Leading Buddhist monks, however, who have documented their views in texts such as those of the Vaṃsic tradition, are more significant examples. We know how these monks evaluated Abhayagirivāsins, Vetullavādins (Mahāyanists), Jains, Śaivas and Christians in the history of Lanka up to the eighteenth century, namely as 'heretics'. A study of the concept of 'heresy' being applied by the Mahāvihāravasins to other religionists would be very useful.

Nobody denies the facts that Lorna Dewaraja presented about these rulers, but to call them 'tolerant' is a euphemism and an anachronism. It is an anachronism because the concept of tolerance, based on the concept of the human right to express any religious idea, is a modern concept, no older than the Enlightenment and the French Revolution. It is also an instance of 'Orientalism', because it is the application of a Western concept to Eastern conditions. Instead of characterizing these rulers as tolerant, they should be characterized as pragmatic. They had economic, social, and political interests in keeping good relations with representatives of other religions, even at the Court itself. This pragmatism is *not* derived from Buddhism, but from reason. It calculates material gains against losses. Pre-modern insular Buddhist state formations co-operated regularly with Tamils, but not with anti-Buddhist Tamils. It co-operated with the Pāṇṭiyas, Cōḻas, Portuguese, Dutch, and British, but not with anti-Buddhist, Pāṇṭiyas, Cōḻas, Portuguese, Dutch, and British. There were numerous conflicts with the colonial powers due to an alleged anti-Buddhist attitude on their part. The Buddhists, including Tamil-speaking Buddhists, felt selected for a privileged destiny to transmit the *dharma* as the light on the island from generation to generation. Finally, even Asoka's 'tolerance' had limits. He deeply disliked post-Vedic sacrificial traditions and rejected them. This pragmatism we find worldwide. It has nothing to do with Buddhism in the Lankan case, but is nevertheless interpreted as Buddhist by modern historical revisionists.

This calculating political pragmatism combined with the occasional suspension of religious commitment can also be found among dedicated *Śaiva* rulers in Tamilakam, the Tamil land in South India, who built Buddhist monuments in the areas under their control for pragmatic reasons and at the same time devastated Buddhist monuments in Lanka, again for pragmatic reasons. Even Western rulers' religiosity can determine the religion of the people; pragmatism has been demonstrated in questioning the religious monopoly of Christianity. The Jews were accepted for pragmatic reasons in medieval Europe. This had nothing to do with the Christian concept of *agape*, 'love', nor was it simply modern liberal tolerance, but as *Duldung*, more specifically as *Judenduldung*, 'endurance of the Jews'. This endurance could stop at any time and be replaced by persecution when Christian anti-Jewish stereotypes were launched. We call this reaction Christian anti-Semitism to emphasize the religious character of this anti-Jewish attitude, albeit the reason for the persecution may have been fear of economic competition in national and international trade. Similarly we could speak of a Buddhist anti-Tamil attitude, though the reason for this xenophobia is sometimes political, social or economic. The Tamil invasions in the late Anurādhapura period triggered the identification of Tamils with anti-Buddhists. This idea, based on repeated experiences of war and conflict, was in the *Cūḷavaṃsa* abstracted from this martial experience and transformed into a stereotype, depicting the Tamils as anti-Buddhist. Being classified as anti-Buddhist, there was no space for them in the island having exclusively the *dhamma* as its light. The extension of this idea is that Buddhism in the island is transmitted by and for the Prakrit-Eḷu-Siṃhala speaking people only, and indeed even serious scholars accepted this view in the twentieth century. They projected this idea back to the beginning of historical time. A work by Senerat Paranavitana from as late as 1970 states: 'Buddhism in Ceylon had, from the earliest times, become a Sinhala Buddhism, adapted to the conditions of life of the people in this Island',[35] a view he held throughout his long career.

Conclusions

A reversal of civil values is made possible and plausible in a time of martial conflict. Then, ideologues actualize ways of integrating violence into non-violent traditions. I have referred to five ways of rationalizing violence that have global parallels.

The first way is the well-known and popular reasoning about the holy 'end' that justifies the less holy or even profane 'means'. It is so common in martial politics that no attention is paid to it any more. This reasoning reverses, however crudely, both Gandhian and some Buddhist principles which require that the 'means' should be of the same quality as the 'end'. From these perspectives it is not possible to achieve peace through war, but it is possible to achieve peace through non-violent means like *satyāgraha* and/or *satipaṭṭhāna*. *Siṃhalatva* of the Lankans and the *maṟavar* and martyr ideology of the *Īḻavar*, both being martial ideologies, presume the possibility of achieving peace through war. They have had to marginalize their own culture (being influenced by a Gandhian and Buddhist super-ego) for it to become plausible to themselves and their followers.

The second line of reasoning points to an alleged connection between the present and past idealized persons or events. An ideal past is invoked and connected with acts that in a situation of peace would be classified as immoral, like the use of violence in political life. Both *Īḻavar* and *Siṃhalatva* Lankans are sophisticated in this kind of justification of violence.

The third way of rationalizing violence introduces a de-eschatologizing distinction about preliminary and final 'ends', which are different from the distinction of 'means' and 'ends' mentioned above. The distinction between preliminary and ultimate 'ends' implies that the final 'end', for example *nirvāṇa*, is temporarily suspended. By 'suspended' I do not mean eliminated, but preserved. This creates a space for action. In the here and now, other conditions prevail, which force us to focus on preliminary aims, for example to establish a unitary state. This way of thinking was also a favourite rationalization of violence among German Christians who said that Paul's statement about there being no Greeks and Jews refers only to the future. Now, however, there are Greeks and Jews and there is a war of the races for domination. The aim was to bring the Aryan race to domination.[36] In this case it is evident that de-eschatologizing rejects the anticipation of a promising alternative future.

A fourth way is to make a distinction between an elite and the common people who are not capable of following the noble principles of the elite. They are 'mundane' and therefore the canonical literature allegedly recognizes that they engage in war. This is another way of de-eschatologizing Buddhism, by reserving the eschatological aspect for an elite. These preliminary 'mundane' aims can be political aims promoted during the period when the final aims are suspended for one social class. Political Buddhism, especially *Siṃhalatva*, presumes such reasoning when it de-eschatologizes Buddhism as a soteriology and transforms Buddhist concepts into political stereotypes. These are used as tools in street fighting, in pogroms, and in political discourse in the Lankan Parliament. True, this process of de-eschatologizing is already part of historical Buddhism (and of other religions) for example the *lokika/lokottara* distinction. But this aspect has been fully exploited, inflated and forged by political ideologues and activists in Lanka in a martial context.

A fifth and final method, which is rather unsophisticated, is historical revisionism. Its radical forms deny that violence has been used against ethnic minorities. Such a reaction to accusations is a model for future apologetics and is a *carte blanche* for the future use of violence, yet its existence is denied. Recognition of these historical conflicts is, however, a necessary precondition for reconciliation.

Notes

1 For more about political Buddhism see Harris (ed.) 1999; Bechert 1988; Phadnis 1976; Seneviratne 1999; Tambiah 1986 and 1992.
2 For this distinction see Schalk 2001c.
3 Schalk 1988a.
4 Schalk 2005a and 2005b.
5 Bartholomeuz 1999: 179–80.
6 See also Schalk 1981: 42–45 for the context of this statement.
7 Schalk 2001a: 38–39.
8 Kapferer 1997.
9 *Journal of Buddhist Ethics* 2003, vol. 10, and Dīgalle (ed.) 2003.
10 I have previously applied the term fundamentalism to political Buddhism, see Schalk 1997.
11 http://selections.gov.lk/2004/index.html.
12 Schalk 1990. For the special totalitarian character of this imagined Buddhist state see Schalk 2001a, especially pp. 58–59.
13 See Schalk 1986b and 1988.
14 Seneviratne 2002.
15 http://selections.gov.lk/2004/index.html.
16 For the history of this term see Schalk 2004.
17 Schalk 2002.
18 *Vīra carita* 1985.
19 *Vīra carita* 1985: 22.
20 See Schalk 2003.
21 For this see Schalk 2003.

22 Schalk 1988.
23 For the *Īḻavar* conception of secularism see Schalk 2001a.
24 Schalk 2001b, Schalk *et al.*, 2002b and 2002c.
25 Schalk 2003.
26 Schalk 2004.
27 Akuratiye Nanda 2003.
28 Akuratiye Nanda 2003.
29 Bengamuvē Nālaka Thera 2003.
30 Premasiri 2002. The title in the publication is slightly modified.
31 See Schalk 2002b: 35–39.
32 This passage has been highlighted by many like Bechert 1988; Schalk 1986a; Obeyesekere 1988, and more recently Breitfeld 2001.
33 Dhammavihari 2003.
34 Dewaraja 2002.
35 Paranavitana (ed.) 1970: cii.
36 For this see Schalk 1998.

Bibliography

Akuratiye Nanda (Ven.) (2003) 'An Analysis of the Selected Statements Issued by the Mahanayakas on the North-East Problem of Sri Lanka', *Journal of Buddhist Ethics,* 10. Available online at http://jbe.gold.ac.uk/bath-conf.html (accessed 10 April 2004).

Bartholomeusz, T. (1999) 'First Among Equals: Buddhism and the Sri Lankan State', in I. Harris (ed.), *Buddhism and Politics in Twentieth-Century Asia*, London and New York: Pinter, pp. 173–93.

Bechert, H. (1988 [1966]) *Buddhismus, Staat und Gesellschaft in den Ländern des Theravada-Buddhismus*, vol. 1, Grundlagen, Ceylon (Sri Lanka) and Wiesbaden: Otto Harrassowitz.

Bengamuwē Nālaka Thera (2003) 'The Origins of Tamil Racism and its Evolution', *Journal of Buddhist Ethics,* 10. Available online at http://jbe.gold.ac.uk/bath-conf.html (accessed 10 April 2004).

Breitfeld, S. (2001) *Das singhalesische Nationalepos von König Duṭṭhagāmaṇī Abhaya*, Berlin: Dietrich Reimer.

Harris, Ian (ed.) (1999) *Buddhism and Politics in Twentieth-Century Asia*, London and New York: Pinter.

Dīgalle, Mahinda (ed.) (2003) *Budusamaya saha śrīlaṃkāvē janavārgika ghaṭiṭanaya.* Saṃskāraka Dīgalle Mahinda himi, Koḷamba: Norvē bauddha saṃgamaya.

Dewaraja, L. (2002) 'Religious and Ethnic Amity in Pre-Modern Sri Lanka', Paper Presented at the New Year Celebrations of the Sri Lanka Federation of University Women, 20 April 2002. (Distributed by the Author during 'Buddhism and Conflict in Sri Lanka, An International Conference', Friday 28 June to Sunday 30 June 2002, Bath Spa University College, Bath, UK.)

Dhammavihari, Ven. (2003) 'Recording, Translating and Interpreting Sri Lankan Chronicle Data', *Journal of Buddhist Ethics,* 10. Available online at http://jbe.gold.ac.uk/bath-conf.html (accessed 10 April 2004).

Journal of Buddhist Ethics (2003) Vol. 10. Available online at http://jbe.gold.ac.uk/10/schalk-sri-lanka-conf.html.

Kapferer, B. (1997) *The Feast of the Sorcerer. Practices of Consciousness and Power*, Chicago and London: University of Chicago Press.

Kemper, S. (1991) *The Presence of the Past: Chronicles, Politics and Culture in Sinhala Life*, Ithaca: Cornell University Press.
Obeyesekere, G. (1988) *A Meditation on Conscience*, Colombo: Social Scientists Association.
Paranavitana, S. (ed.) (1970) *Inscriptions of Ceylon* 1. *Early Brāhmī Inscriptions*, Colombo: Department of Archaeology.
Phadnis, U. (1976) *Religion and Politics in Sri Lanka*, New Delhi: Manohar.
Premasiri, P.D. (2002) 'The Place for a Righteous War in Buddhism', *Journal of Buddhist Ethics*, 10. Available online at http://jbe.gold.ac.uk/bath-conf.html (accessed 10 April 2004).
Rahula, W. (1974) *The Heritage of the Bhikkhu*, New York: Grove.
Schalk, P. (1981) [Review of H. Bechert], 'Buddhismus, Staat und Gesellschaft in den Ländern des Theravada-Buddhismus', *Lanka*, 6: 42–45.
——(1986a) 'Landets söner. Om nutida buddhistisk historieskrivning och konflikten mellan singhaleser och tamiler i Sri Lanka', *Häften för kritiska studier*, 1 (19): 24–41.
——(1986b) 'Buddhistische Kampfgruppen in Sri Lanka', *Asien. Deutsche Zeitschrift für Politik, Wirtschaft und Kultur*, 21: 30–62.
——(1988) '"Unity" and "Sovereignty". Key Concepts of Militant Buddhist Organisations in the Present Conflict in Sri Lanka', *Temenos*, 24: 55–87.
——(1990) 'The Lankan Mahasangha's Concept of a Dharmacracy and Society', *Radical Conservatism: Buddhism in the Contemporary World, Articles in Honour of Bhikkhu Buddhadasa's 84th Birthday Anniversary*, Bangkok: International Network of Engaged Buddhists, pp. 354–59.
——(1997) 'Kette ohne Anfang und Ende. Die Welt der Fundamentalisten in Sri Lanka ist hermetisch gegen Kritik versiegelt', *Der Überblick. Zeitschrift für ökumenische Begegnung und internationale Zusammenarbeit*, 33 (March): 83–88.
——(1998) 'Twisted Cross: The Religious Nationalism of the German Christians', *Studia Theologica*, 52: 69–79.
——(2001a) 'Present Concepts of Secularism among Ilavar and Lankans', Zwischen Säkularismus und Hierokratie: Studien zum Verhältnis von Religion und Staat in Süd-und Ostasien, *Acta Universitatis Uppsaliensis, Historia Religionum* 17, Uppsala: ACTA, pp. 37–72.
——(2001b) 'Buddhism among Tamils in Ilam', *Religio et Bibliotheca. Festskrift till Tore Ahlbäck* 14.3, Red. Nils G. Holm *et al.*, Åbo: Åbo Akademis Förlag, pp. 199–211.
——(2001c) 'Political Buddhism among Lankans in the Context of Martial Conflict', *Religion, Staat, Gesellschaft, Zeitschrift für Glaubensformen und Weltanschauungen*, 2 (2): 223–42.
——(2002a) 'Ilavar and Lankans. Emerging Identities in a Broken-up Island', *Journal of Asian Ethnicity*, 3 (1): 47–62.
——*et al.* (2002b) 'Buddhism among Tamils in Pre-Colonial Tamiḻakam and Īḻam, 2002. Part 1. Prologue, The Pre-Pallava and the Pallava period', *Acta Universitatis Upsaliensis; Historia Religionum 19*, Uppsala: ACTA.
——*et al.* (2002c) *Buddhism among Tamils in Pre-Colonial Tamilakam andĪlam*, Part 2. The Period of the Imperial Cōḻar, in Tamiḻakam and Īḻam. *Acta Universitatis Upsaliensis; Historia Religionum 20*, Uppsala: ACTA.
——(2003) 'Relativising Simhalatva. A Historical Analysis of Semantic Transformations of the Concept of *dhammadīpa*', *Journal of Buddhist Ethics*, 10. Available online at http://jbe.gold.ac.uk/bath-conf.html (accessed 10 April 2004).

——(2004) Īḻam < sīhaḷa? Assessment of a Derivation. *Acta Universitatis Upsaliensis; Historia Religionum 25*, Uppsala: ACTA.

——(ed.) (2005a) 'Im Dickicht der Gebote. Studien zur Dialektik von Norm und Praxis in der Buddhismusgeschichte Asiens', *Acta Universitatis Upsaliensis, Historia Religionum 26*, Uppsala: ACTA.

——(2005b) '"Buddhistische Götterkulte in Lanka – eine Normabweichung?". Im Dickicht der Gebote. Studien zur Dialektik von Norm und Praxis in der Buddhismusgeschichte Asiens', *Acta Universitatis Upsaliensis, Historia Religionum 26*, Uppsala: ACTA, pp. 253–86.

Seneviratne, H.L. (1999) *The Work of Kings: The New Buddhism in Sri Lanka*, Chicago and London: University of Chicago Press.

Seneviratne, M. (2002) 'The PA: Therminally Ill', *The Island*, Internet Edition, Features, 4 November 2001. Available online at http://origin.island.lk/2001/11/04/featur06.html (accessed 27 July 2002).

Sinhala Urumaya Policy [No date given] Public letter entitled *Sinhala Urumaya Policy* sent as attachment by *Sihala Urumaya*, 655, Elvitigala Mawatha, Colombo 5.

Tambiah, S.J. (1986) *Sri Lanka: Ethnic Fratricide and the Dismantling of Democracy*, Chicago: University of Chicago Press.

——(1992) *Buddhism Betrayed? Religion, Politics, and Violence in Sri Lanka*, Chicago and London: University of Chicago Press.

Vīra carita. Anagārika Dharmapāla tumā (1985) Vol. 1–2. Nugegoḍa: Kurunäägala Taruṇa Bauddha Saṃgamaya.

7 Religion and violence

The historical context for conflict in Pakistan

Ian Talbot

The last two decades of the twentieth century saw mounting intra-Muslim and inter-religious violence in Pakistan. The former was characterized by Sunni–Shia[1] sectarian conflict, the latter by violence against the religious minorities of Christians, Ahmadis, Hindus and Sikhs. Sunni-Shia conflict saw leading clerics and activists assassinated in tit-for-tat killings as were professionals from the 'rival' communities. There was large-scale tribal sectarian warfare in such areas as the Shia dominated Upper Kurram Agency. Bitter fighting in September 1996 resulted in 100 deaths and scores more injuries. In such cities as Karachi, Lahore and Peshawar innocent worshippers were increasingly attacked. In all, bomb blasts, assassinations and machine-gun attacks on places of worship resulted in 581 deaths and over 1,600 injuries in the period 1990–1997.[2]

Inter-religious violence also increased during this period. Thirteen Christian churches were burnt down down in Khanewal in southern Punjab in February 1997.[3] The remaining Hindu temples in Karachi were attacked in the aftermath of the Babri Masjid's December 1992 demolition in India. The Ahmadi community simultaneously faced individual acts of violence and persecution as a result of the Blasphemy Ordinance.[4] The most celebrated blasphemy case, however, was the Salamat Masih and Rehmat Masih trial. This generated international attention not only because of the guilty verdict handed down by the Sessions Court and later overturned by the Lahore High Court, but because Salamat was a minor and another of the Christians accused, Manzoor Masih, had been shot dead after an earlier court appearance. There is evidence that blasphemy charges have been brought to pay off old rivalries, or to assist in land-grab activities. It seems that attacks on minority communities in both India and Pakistan are sometimes occasioned by the desire to acquire the valuable land on which mosques, churches and graveyards are located.

There was nothing inevitable about this tide of violence, nor was it intrinsic to Pakistani Islam. During this period, lawlessness of all kinds increased. In 1998, 325 criminal offences were reported in the population unit of 100,000. This compared with only 180 offences in 1966.[5] Sind and Punjab possessed the worst crime records. Murders in the Punjab rose from under 2,000 per annum in 1966 to 5,000 in 1998. There was bitter ethnic conflict in Karachi throughout much of the 1980s and 1990s[6] that claimed more lives than did sectarian violence.This chapter seeks to provide a contextualization for moving beyond simplistic associations of religion with violence in Pakistan. It argues that their linkage is historically contingent and focuses on key moments, institutions and individuals. The chapter looks first at the colonial legacy and then at the changes in Pakistan's politics arising from the Islamization of the Zia era. (1977–1988). The continuing influences of this period are traced during the restored democracy of the 1990s.[7] Finally, the changes arising from the installation of General Musharraf's regime in October 1999 and the impact of 9/11 are considered.

The colonial inheritance

During the British Raj there was a sharpening of religious identity and its politicization. These processes are known in the Indian context as communalism. Conflict if not violence was its likely outcome in the circumstances of competition for scarce resources and political patronage from the colonial rulers. Hindu nationalist and Muslim nationalist works regard communalism as a primordial natural 'given'. Indian nationalist writers, on the other hand, have explained its existence in terms of British political divide and rule policies.[8] More sophisticated accounts, such as that provided by Gyanendra Pandey,[9] link the Raj's legitimization needs with its communalist reading of Indian society. Katherine Prior[10] and Chris Bayly[11] have challenged the easy assumption that communalism is a product of the colonial era. They maintain that the regional states of the Sikhs, Marathas and Bhumihar Brahmins of Benares, which succeeded the Mughals, actively patronized religion in their public ceremonial as part of their assertion of independence, while at the local level there was increasing competition between a declining Muslim service gentry and rising Hindu merchant classes. Whatever we may think of this argument, it is clear that there were existing 'fault-lines' for the creation of nineteenth-century communal identities.

A number of scholars have discussed the impact on identity of the colonial census from 1881 onwards. The censuses were not of course about curiosity for its own sake, but in 'Saidean'[12] terms about the 'expropriation' of knowledge in order to better sustain the imperial edifice. Census enumeration not only forced individuals to identify themselves with a religious, caste or tribe category, but made them aware of the numbers of their fellows. This became important with the gradual spread of political representation from the 1880s onwards, for numbers count in a democracy. Multiple identities and fluid boundaries were reduced to religious categories which were easily understandable to British 'outsiders'. The essentialization of community by the census operations is brought out most clearly in the following statement from Denzil Ibbetson who supervised the 1881 enumeration in the Punjab. 'Every native who was unable to define his creed', he declared, 'or described it by any name *other than that of some recognised religion* (emphasis added), was held to be classified as a Hindu.'[13]

It was not only colonial agency that sharpened community boundaries. Religious revivalism and reformism exerted a major impact. Harjot Oberoi[14] has examined how the 'enchanted universe' of pluralistic Punjabi 'folk religion' was transformed by the reforming activities of the Singh Sabha movement. This created a khalsa-orientated Sikh identity which emphasized the trope of martyrdom and eighteenth-century conflict with the Mughals. The Arya Samaj similarly laid the basis for a neo-Hindu identity in which belief in revealed doctrine and conversion were Semitic borrowings. Muslim revivalism operated alongside these competitors as well as in the context of what was seen as an alien Christian ruling presence. The loss of Muslim political power which had always been seen as crucial for creating the conditions for 'right behaviour' had been felt in North India as early as the career of the great Sunni revivalist, the Delhi scholar Shah Wali-Allah (1703–1762). He established the basis for later reformers with his criticisms of Shia doctrines, emphasis on the duty of *jihad* (holy war) and his hostility to the popular Islam of the Sufi shrines. Sufism survived the attacks of later reformers by purging itself of some of its syncretic elements and organizing itself in the Barelvi school of '*ulama* (religious scholars). Shah Wali-Ullah's son Shah Abd al-Aziz (1746–1824) declared the northern areas of the subcontinent under British influence, but not East India Company Rule to be *dar al-harb* (i.e. an abode of war in which Muslims could launch a *jihad*). This scholastic ruling was followed in more practical terms by Saiyid Ahmad Bareilly (1786–1831) who waged a *jihad* against the Sikhs in the Frontier districts from 1827. The struggle was continued by his deputies after his death in 1831. Saiyid Ahmad Bareilly was influenced by the Islamic reform movement of Muhammad Ibn Abdul Wahhab in Arabia. The British attributed direct 'wahhabi' influence to their series of military conflicts in the Frontier in the 1850s and 1860s with *mujahadin* (warriors engaged in holy war).

Uprisings by well-armed Pakhtun tribesmen in which religious symbols played a major mobilizing role continued throughout the colonial era. The last revolt led by a Muslim holy man, the Faqir of Ipi[15] commenced as late as 1936 in Waziristan. Guerrilla fighting persisted into the1940s. Pakistan thus inherited a region in the tribal agencies in which enemies of the state, such as the Faqir of Ipi could live a shadowy existence in the border caves and in which there was a long tradition of *jihad* led by charismatic militant religious leaders. Contemporary press comment on al-Qaeda's activities in the area rarely refers to this historical context. Yet it helps to explain the problems the Army faced when it was deployed, for the first time in Pakistan's history, in June 2003 in the Federally Administered Tribal Areas to flush out the remnants of al-Qaeda and Taliban fighters.

The Deoband movement was the most influential of the nineteenth-century Islamic reformist movements. Its founders Muhammad Qasim Nanautvi (1833–1877) and Rasghid Ahmad Gangohi (1829–1905) sought to sustain a reformed Sunni Islam apart from the colonial state.[16] Their teachings were institutionalized in 1867 in a *dar-ul-ulum* (establishment for higher religious learning) at Deoband, a country town in the Saharanpur district of the United Provinces some hundred miles north-east of Delhi. Many Deobandis opposed the Pakistan movement because it would result in a 'worldly' rather than 'religious' government.

The Jamiat-ul-Ulema-e-Islam (JUI) founded in November 1945 by a leading Deobandi *alim*, (religious scholar) Shabbir Ahmad Uthmani, however, supported the Pakistan movement. Since independence, the JUI has sought to Islamicize Pakistani society. It has built up support in Pashtun areas of the Frontier and Baluchistan. As we shall see later, the JUI was connected with the creation of the militant sectarian organization the Sipah-e-Sabha Pakistan (SSP) in the mid-1980s, and a decade later possessed close ties with the SSP's even more militant offshoot the Lashkar-e-Jhangvi (LJ) and also with the Taliban. Members of these groups had attended its *madrassahs* in the North West Frontier Province of Pakistan and in southern Afghanistan, including the famous Deobandi Haqqaniyah *madrassah* at Akora Khattak in the Peshawar district run by Maulana Sami ul Haq. By the mid-1980s, 60 per cent of its students were Afghans.

By the beginning of the twentieth century, the Ahl-e-Hadith had emerged as a more puritanical reformist movement than that of Deoband. It wielded less influence, in part because of its sectarian outlook, but also because it controlled fewer religious institutions. A reworking of the Ahl-e-Hadith tradition to lay more emphasis on *jihad* has provided the philosophical underpinning for the Lashkar-e-Taiba. This militant 'terrorist' group from its headquarters at Muridke near Lahore and its training bases in Afghanistan sought from the late 1980s to wage an international *jihad*.

While the Deoband and Ahl-e-Hadith movements represented reformist responses to colonial rule, the Islamist position was taken up by Jamaat-e-Islami (JI). Its founder in 1941, Sayed Abul Ala Maudoodi emphasized not just individual moral reform, but the need to acquire political power.[17] JI opposed the Pakistan movement because it regarded the establishment of a secular Muslim nation-state as blasphemous. Maudoodi clearly articulated this attitude in the work, *Tehreek-e-Azadi-e-Hind* which was published in 1942. Five years later he migrated from India in order to reconstruct the new state on a truly Islamic basis.

During the colonial era, reformist Sunni organizations engaged in bitter polemics with Sufis, Ahmadis and Shias. Clashes between Sunnis and Shias in the future Pakistan areas, however, were confined almost entirely to the tension-filled days of the Muharram festival, when Shias publicly mourn the death of Ali's son and his companions. They were on a much smaller scale than in such United Provinces cities as Lucknow, where there were a series of violent clashes in the early 1930s. Friction arose regarding procession routes and the Sunnis' recitation of *Madh-e-Sahabah* (praise for the companions of the Prophet) in response to Shia denigration of the first three Caliphs of Islam. Indeed one possible explanation for a surge of sectarian violence in Pakistan is the partition-related migration of populations from areas that possessed a more violent tradition. The key differences arise, however, from the ending of state sectarian neutrality during the Zia era, the transformation of a ritual-based conflict to one based around political identity and the emergence of what has been termed a 'proxy war' between Iran and Saudi Arabia on Pakistan's soil.

The Ahmadi movement which was founded in March 1899 rose out of the soil of nineteenth-century Islamic reform.[18] The movement was at first in the forefront of Muslim defence against the attacks of the Hindu revivalist Arya Samaj. It increasingly became the target for Muslim critics as its founder Mirza Ghulam Ahmad (1835–1908) not only identified himself with the promised *madhi* who would conquer the world for Islam, but claimed to be a *nabi* (messenger) of God. Such claims to revelation challenged the fundamental Islamic belief that Muhammad is the last of the prophets.

The Ahmadis established their headquarters at Qadian which was Mirza's birthplace and henceforth they were also known as Qadianis. '*Ulama* from a number of schools issued *fatwa* (religious edicts, opinions) against them. The Ahrar movement rose to prominence in the Punjab during the 1930s in part because of its implacable hostility to the Ahmadis. The first anti-Ahmadi riots in the post-independence era occurred in Lahore in 1953. It was only in 1974, during Zulfiqar Ali Bhutto's Government, however, and following pressure from Jamaat-e-Islami, that the Ahmadis were declared as non-Muslims. In April 1984 Zia issued an ordinance which made it a criminal offence for Ahmadis to 'pose' as Muslims, to 'preach or propagate by words either spoken or written' and to use Islamic terminology or Muslim practices of worship. Militant Islamists were henceforth encouraged to bring charges against Ahmadis for simply exercizing their religious beliefs. Symptomatic of the atmosphere of hatred which was engendered was the shooting of a mild-mannered physics professor, Nasim Babar, on the Quaid-e-Azam University Campus in Islamabad in October 1994, due apparently to his Ahmadi religious faith.

Communalism remained stronger than sectarianism, however, throughout the colonial era. Communal violence increased in India during the closing decades of British rule. It must be understood in terms of local contests for power and standing rather than merely in terms of 'bigotry' or 'fanaticism'. Just as in the great communal bloodletting at the time of the subcontinent's partition, it contained elements both of spontaneity and political organization. By the 1930s, communal riots were endemic in many of the Punjab's cities, earning the province the epithet of the 'Ulster of India'.[19] Violence was more frequently Hindu–Muslim, than Sikh–Muslim in character. There was little antagonism between Muslim and Christian communities during the colonial era. Contemporary persecution of Christians in Pakistan stems from their identification with 'anti-Muslim' Western policies in such places as Israel, Iraq, Bosnia and Kashmir. The tiny minority Hindu community has suffered similar scape-goating at times of Indo-Pakistan tension.

Pakistani Islam continues to be dominated by the reform movements of the colonial era. Contemporary '*ulama* political parties and their militant offspring are linked with the institutions and ideas which emerged in this period. The emphasis on educational reform and an activist individual commitment to Islam has also continued. The controversies between orthodox Islam and the heterodox Ahmadi movement have been similarly perpetuated in the contemporary era. The Sunni–Shia conflict has also intensified with the substitution of a religiously 'neutral' colonial state by one which, since the 1980s, has been increasingly identified with Sunni Islam. The emphasis on the duty of *jihad* raised by Shah-Wali Ullah in the context of eighteenth-century Muslim political decline has also taken on a new dimension in the contemporary globalized world.

The Zia era and the rise in sectarian violence and religious militancy in Pakistan

The Zia-ul Haq regime of (1977–1988) represented a key moment in the rise of sectarian violence and religious militancy in Pakistan. Zia sought to legitimize his military rule by co-opting Islamic parties through a domestic process of Islamization and internationally by involvement in the *jihad* against the occupying Soviet forces in Afghanistan. It is from this period that the spread of *madrassah* education proceeded apace. This has been a crucial element in providing support for *jihadist* and sectarian groupings. The encouragement of *madrassahs* was both a response to the collapse of the state education system and part of the Islamization process. During 1983/84 alone nearly 12,000 such schools were opened. The *madrassahs* not only provided free education, but meals and clothing. In addition to these material attractions, they provided the status of a religious education. Unfortunately, there was no external control on their curriculum with the result that many propagated an increasingly violent sectarian and *jihadist* version of Islam.[20] Many mosque schools were funded from abroad either from Saudi Arabia or Iran as the two countries competed for influence in Pakistan. The advantage lay with the Saudis as Zia emphasized a Sunni interpretation of Islam rooted in his own Deobandi tradition. Islamization came to be seen as a state-sponsored Sunni Islamization that resulted in growing conflicts with the Shia community over such issues as the compulsory giving of *zakat* (alms) following the 20 June 1980 Zakat Ordinance. Indeed Zia may have emphasized Islamization not only to legitimize his regime, but to challenge Iran's leadership of a worldwide Islamic resurgence in the wake of the overthrow of the Shah in 1979 by the Ayatollah Khomeini.

The Iranian Revolution profoundly influenced Pakistan's Shia minority. A new generation of religious leaders emerged who espoused Khomeini's activism and pan-Islamic views. They abandoned the Shia tradition of political quietism.[21] The assassination of one of the new generation's most prominent figures, Allama Arif Hussain al-Husaini, who had adopted many of Khomeini's teachings while studying in *madrassahs* in Iran and Iraq, was the catalyst for increasing violence. The post-revolutionary Iranian regime funded new mosques and cultural centres in Pakistan as well as providing scholarships for study in the leading *madrassahs* of the holy city of Qom. The funds flowing into Pakistan from Iran and later from Lebanese Shias were countered by the patronage of Sunni institutions by Saudi Arabia and Iraq during its bloody eight-year conflict with Iran from 1980 onwards. Increased Shia self-assertion inevitably resulted in conflict with the Zia regime which was supervising a state-sponsored Islamization process that emphasized the reformist tradition of Sunni Islam.

It was in the context of Shia opposition to the Zakat Ordinance that the Tehrik-e-Nifaz-e-Fiqh-e-Jafria (TNJF) was founded in April 1979 in order to protect the Shias' separate religious identity. Shia protest forced the Zia regime to grant exemption from *zakat*. This enraged upholders of Sunni orthodoxy, some of whom began to deny that Shias were true Muslims. Allama Ahsan Elahi Zaheer, Chief of the Ahl-e-Hadith denounced Shia Islam as a heresy and accused Shias of being Zionist agents in his book published in 1980 entitled, *Shias and Shi'ism*.[22]

The Sunni cause received financial support from the state and Saudi Arabia. Funds flowed to *madrassahs* which expanded rapidly especially in the Frontier and Punjab. The number of *madrassahs* in the latter province rose from 1,320 in 1988 to 2,521 in 1997.[23] Many of these were linked with the JUI. Second, support was given to sectarian organizations such as the SSP. They drew recruits from the *madrassahs* as well as from veterans of the Afghan conflict. Shias forcefully responded to the Sunni violence. Following the assassination in 1988 of the TNJF leader Allama Arif Hussain al-Husaini, the organization spawned the militant splinter group Sipah-e-Muhammad (SM). In the early 1990s it engaged in armed conflict with its Sunni rivals.

The Islamization process also marginalized the religious minorities. The most vulnerable of the minority communities, the Ahmadis, suffered the most from the amendment of the Pakistan Penal Code. Finally, The Zia era's Islamization process increased not only intra-Muslim conflict, between Sunnis and Shias, but also that between Barelvis and Deobandis. This took the form both of a confrontation over the management of mosques and shrines in May 1984[24] and at a deeper level between the state's legalistic imposition of Islam and the humanist traditions of Sufism. Highly suggestive of the different conceptions of Islam was the successful legal challenge by the custodian of Baba Farid's famous Sufi shrine at Pakpattan to the ban on pigeon-flying in Lahore early in 1981.[25] This practice along with kite-flying had been banned on the grounds that they violated the sanctity and privacy of women. The keeping of pigeons, however, was associated with many great Sufi saints and was a familiar feature of the leading shrines.

Significantly the Sufi *Pirs* of Sind played a leading role in the struggle against the Zia regime waged by the Movement for the Restoration of Democracy in August and September 1983. The regime, however, suppressed the movement and would have survived if Zia had not been killed in a plane crash on 17 August 1988. Nevertheless, Islamization had not solved Pakistan's identity problems. It had divided rather than united the country and had laid bare the deep-rooted differences among the '*ulama*.

The regional dimension of contemporary communal and sectarian violence in Pakistan

In international affairs as well as domestically, the Zia regime's identification with Islamic causes marked an important turning point. The roots were laid for the Pakistan state's alliance with militant groups committed to the cause of *jihad*. The ties with what after 9/11 would be termed international terrorists were established by the Inter-Services Intelligence (ISI), the intelligence wing of the Army. It rose to prominence during the Afghan struggle. Throughout the period of restored democracy in the 1990s it operated as almost a state within a state.

The Afghan War and its aftermath

The Afghan conflict that followed the Soviet occupation on 28 December 1979 left four important legacies for the rise of sectarian violence in Pakistan. First, the leakage of weapons intended for the *mujahideen* resulted in the growth of what has been termed the 'Kalashnikov culture' in Pakistan. This enabled militant sectarian organizations to readily take on a paramilitary character. Cities such as Karachi were so awash with weapons that these could be hired out for the day. The fire-power of sectarian groups far exceeded that of a corrupt and demoralized police force. The weaponization of Pakistani society explains why conflicts were so bloody. In the increasingly anarchic city of Karachi, the SMP and SSP fought pitched gun battles. An assault on the Masjid-e-Akbar on 7 December 1994 left eight dead including the city chief of the SSP.[26]

Second, the Afghan War created links between elements of the Pakistan Army, the Inter-Services Intelligence, and Islamic militants. This provided the latter with invaluable training. It also ensured a degree of immunity if they turned from *jihad* to wage sectarian violence within Pakistan. The existence of safe houses and networks of sympathizers organized around mosques and their attendant *madrassahs* also explains how massacres, assassinations and 'terrorist' outrages could be carried out with apparent impunity.

Third, the collapse of the state in Afghanistan created the conditions in which military training camps could be established. These were initially used by Saudi- and American backed *mujahideen*. They were later to be taken over by the Taliban, *jihad* groups such as Lashkar-e-Taiba and the Harkat-ul-Ansar (later renamed as the Harkat-ul-Mujahideen) and by sectarian militant groups such as SSP and LJ.

The Hizb-e-Islami of Gulbuddin Hekmatyar was the most favoured of the Afghan *mujahideen* groups by the Americans and the Pakistani authorities. Hekmatyar received weapons, communication equipment and training provided by the US Central Intelligence Agency and the Inter-Services Intelligence Agency of the Pakistan Army. The Jamaat-e-Islami also patronized him. The Jamaat's links with the Muslim Brotherhood ensured financial support from the Middle East. Hekmatyar's failure to stabilize Afghanistan after the Soviet withdrawal and the eventual fall of the Najibullah regime in 1992, precipitated Pakistan's sponsorship of the Taliban two years later.[27] It is important to note that this occurred following the restoration of democracy, during Benazir Bhutto's first ministry. The Taliban's emergence as a fighting force in September 1994 owed much to the support of the ISI. The Pakistan Army had also provided logistical support in the struggle with the warlords and the Northern Alliance. Some more Islamically minded officers were sympathetic to the Taliban experiment, but support was primarily given for strategic reasons. These centred around Pakistan's desire to have access to Central Asia through a pliant Kabul regime and through its bases in Afghanistan to secure 'strategic depth' against India.

Fourth, Sunni extremism within Pakistan was encouraged by the Taliban's rise to power. Many of the Taliban shared Pushtun ethnic and religious ties with Pakistani militants. They had been educated in the same network of *madrassahs* in the North West Frontier Province. They shared a commitment to Sunni orthodoxy and a hostility to the Shias. Such writers as Ahmed Rashid have revealed how in these circumstances, the Taliban 'exported' extremism.[28] The Islamic order that was established in Afghanistan provided a 'role model' for a theocratic state in which the *sharia* would be enforced along the puritanical lines of the Deoband school. Sunni militants dreamed one day of the Talibanization of Pakistan. Mullahs gathered outside the Lahore High Court during the hearing of the petition against the Blasphemy Law death sentence of Salamat and Rehmat Masih chanted, '*Kabul ke baad Islamabad ... Taliban, Taliban*' (After Kabul, Islamabad ... Taliban, Taliban).[29]

The Kashmir conflict and its contemporary evolution

The Kashmir dispute has dominated Indo–Pakistan relations since independence. The subcontinent's insecure strategic environment has severely limited legal cross-border trade. Moreover, Pakistan as the weaker of the rivals has distorted its economy to keep up the arms race. The subsequent starving of funds for human development has created the conditions for militancy. These have been further strengthened by the perpetuation of hostile stereotypes of the 'other' community/country as a result of the more than a half century of animosity regarding Kashmir. The profound influence of the military and the security services in Pakistan is rooted in the ongoing Indo–Pakistan Cold War. The consequent undermining of civil society has removed a barrier to religious extremism.

The 1989 *intifada*[30] marked a new phase in the Kashmir conflict. This spontaneous uprising was a result of the increased alienation from the Indian state of a new and much better educated generation of Kashmiris. Its catalyst had been the rigging of the 1987 assembly elections in order to deny power to the Muslim United Front. Increasingly, '*Mehmaan Mujahideen*'[31] (Guest Mujahideen) fought alongside older indigenous militant groups such as the secular nationalist Jammu and Kashmir Liberation Front and the Jamaat-e-Islami affiliate Jamiat-e-Tulba. These 'guest' militants included Arab veterans of the Afghan War, who infiltrated the line of control from their bases in the Tribal areas of Pakistan and from Azad Kashmir. It was the large-scale infiltration from Pakistan, supported by regular army forces, that prompted both the 1999 Kargil conflict and the military stand-off in the summer of 2002. *Mehmaan Mujahideen* fought in such organizations as Al-Faran,[32] the Harkat-ul-Ansar[33] (which from

1997 was annually reported by the US State Department as a terrorist organization), the Lashkar-e-Taiba[34] and Jaish-e-Mohammad.[35] These groups were to develop ties with Osama bin Laden's al-Qaeda network.

The Kashmir *jihad* like the earlier Afghan *jihad* strengthened Islamic militancy within Pakistan. Activists moved between *jihad* and sectarian organizations. The latter used the same camps in Afghanistan and Azad Kashmir as the *jihad* groups. Pakistan army instructors and ISI operatives provided their training. The cooperation of the Pakistan Military with Islamic militant groups which had begun during the Afghan War was thus continued. By the fateful date of 11 September 2001, a nexus of transnational *jihad* and sectarian groups had emerged in which there were close ties with the Pakistan military. Indeed in his training of Afghan *mujahideen* and in his planning of the Kargil operation, Musharraf was at the heart of the army's post-1979 strategic alliance with *jihad* groups designed to counterbalance India's regional supremacy.

The restored democracy 1988–1999

Zia's death paved the way for the restoration of democracy.[36] In November 1988, Benazir Bhutto had become Pakistan's youngest prime minister and the first woman to hold this position. She raised the hopes of increasing governmental legitimacy and of addressing the inequalities born of gender and religious minority status. Unfortunately, these expectations were dashed during not only her tenure of office, but that of her bitter rival Nawaz Sharif.[37] Any criticism of either leader must recognize the difficulties which they encountered. Foremost among these was the post-Zia political entrenchment of the Army and the intelligence services. This power was greatest over defence expenditure and the control of security and foreign policy, especially with respect to Afghanistan and Kashmir. Attempts by the civilian leaders to extend their authority usually resulted in their dismissal by the President working at the army's behest.

The political leaders' room for manoeuvre was further constrained by the economic downturn. The slowing economic growth rate of the 1990s resulted in an increase in poverty. Whereas one in five families was living in poverty at its outset, the proportion at the end was one in three.[38] The costs of debt financing, poor economic governance, military expenditure and low tax yields starved resources for human development. Military expenditure at 4.5 per cent of the GDP is more than twice the total expenditure on public education.[39] The United Nations Development Programme's 1999 Human Development Report ranked Pakistan 138 out of 174 countries. It recorded that 62 per cent of adults were illiterate and only 45 per cent possessed access to health facilities.[40] Demographic pressures and rapid urbanization exacerbated low resource allocation. The economic crisis provided the background to growing political instability. Pakistan lurched from crisis to crisis. Oppositions denied ruling parties any legitimacy and governments used selective accountability to intimidate their opponents. Parliament was at worst a bear-pit, at best the fountainhead of patronage politics, with legislation being restricted to presidential ordinance.

Militant Islamic groups thrived in this unstable political situation. Moreover, there is evidence that the security agencies kept sectarian and ethnic violence on the boil in order to excuse the dismissal of governments that were becoming too independent, on the grounds of their failure to handle the law and order situation. Nawaz Sharif initially possessed much closer ties with Sunni *'ulama* parties than did Benazir Bhutto who continued the PPP's traditional links with Shias. During her second government (1993–96) she turned to JUI to bolster her Islamic legitimacy, while simultaneously forming a tacit alliance with the militant Shia organization Sipah-e-Muhammad. Ironically it was the more Islamically oriented Muslim League of Nawaz Sharif in its second administration (1997–99) that took the first faltering steps to curb the militants. The threat that sectarian violence would get out of control, together with his more secure political base encouraged Nawaz Sharif in August 1997 to pass the Anti-Terrorism Act. Special courts were established to accelerate the justice process and to increase the chances of prosecution. Their existence, however, failed to prevent the Lashkar-e-Jhangvi perpetrating the infamous Mominpura massacre of 25 Shias in Lahore in January 1998. When the government attempted to crack down on the Lashkar-e-Jhangvi and the Sipah-e-Sahaba, militants from these organizations on 3 January 1999 unsuccessfully attempted to assassinate Nawaz Sharif by placing a bomb under the Bhobattian Bridge, Raiwind Road, Lahore along which he was travelling.[41]

President Pervez Musharraf's Pakistan

Musharraf's accession to power following the coup of 12 October 1999 that removed Nawaz Sharif further diplomatically isolated Pakistan. Sanctions already in place following the nuclear tests of May 1998 were increased. The Pakistan economy was already in a parlous condition because of its structural problems arising from low taxation and investment, lack of transparency, poor human capital and an overblown defence budget. The debt stood at $38 billion (£26 million) with the foreign exchange reserves at just $1.5 billion. Musharraf sought to present his coup as reactive and his regime as socially liberal and reformist in order to encourage overseas investment. He pointedly took the title of Chief Executive rather than Chief Martial Law Administrator. The volte-face in policy after 9/11 involving the abandonment of the Taliban and a playing down of support for international *jihad* groups, despite the risks this involved, occurred due to the weak economic background.

Less well known is the fact that even before 9/11 Musharraf had begun to take some tentative steps towards curbing militant groups. The Lashkar-e-Jhangvi (Jhangvi army) and Sipah-e-Mohammad were banned by the Pakistan Government on 14 August 2001. The effect of 9/11 was to force Musharraf to move much more quickly and decisively than he would have wished in banning militant organizations such as Harkat al Ansar. His action has created many enemies. Indeed it appears that members of the Jaish-e-Mohammad organization that had been banned following the 13 December 2001 terrorist attack on the Indian Parliament were behind the failed suicide bomber attacks on his car some two years later. The decision to jettison the policy of support for Taliban and the international *jihad* groups and to fully cooperate with the US war on terror was not Musharraf's alone. It was made on 14 September following a seven-hours' meeting of the Corps Commanders and other members of the military hierarchy. Although Musharraf replaced so-called hardliners like Lt General Mehmood Ahmad and DG ISI General Muzaffar Hassan Usmani with junior officers loyal to himself, the army as an institution accepted Musharraf's pragmatic response to the post-9/11 situation. Talk of a counter-coup by disgruntled Islamist officers ignores both the discipline of the army and its unified chain of command. Musharraf's fellow officers accepted that Pakistan had no alternative. If it had refused to join in the war of terror, its nuclear assets would have been put at risk, its economy would have been ruined and India would have been assured of a hegemonic position within the region.

In the immediate aftermath of the Pakistan Government's alignment with the Western led coalition against terrorism there were attacks on churches and NGOs which were a 'soft' target for extremist groups. Innocent worshippers were massacred in a church at Model Town A, Bahawalpur on 28 October 2001. Such attacks multiplied in 2002. Pakistan became the victim of terrorism designed to undermine the pro-Western policies of the Musharraf regime. Five persons were killed, including a US diplomat's wife and daughter, following a grenade attack on 17 March 2002 on the Protestant International Church in Islamabad's diplomatic enclave.[42] Further attacks followed on the Christian Missionary School at Murree (5 August), the chapel of the Christian Hospital at Taxila (9 August) and the Karachi offices of the Christian Welfare Organisation, Peace and Justice on 25 September. Earlier in June there was a huge car bomb blast outside the US Consulate in Karachi that claimed eight lives.[43] Despite the crackdown on such extremist groups as Lashkar-e-Jhangvi and Jaish-e-Mohammad, there was growing evidence of cooperation between banned groups in Pakistan and al-Qaeda and Taliban fugitives from Afghanistan. The Pakistan Government claimed to have arrested around 300 of the latter during the opening six months of 2002. But there was evidence that the outrage outside the Karachi Consulate was an al-Qaeda financed operation. An attack early in December on the Macedonian Consulate in Karachi was also linked with al-Qaeda.[44] The attempt to investigate such linkages resulted in the kidnapping and murder of the Wall Street journalist Daniel Pearl.[45] In mid-July, the Anti-Terrorism Court sitting in Hyderabad Central Jail sentenced the British-born militant Sheikh Omar[46] to death in the Pearl matter on murder, conspiracy and abduction charges. Further evidence of the Government's intent regarding terrorism was demonstrated by its cooperation with the FBI and the US military in the hunting down of al-Qaeda forces along the Afghan border. Pakistan's first ever military intervention in the Waziristan tribal area took place in support of the US Mountain Lion Operation. The deaths of civilians who were caught in the crossfire with militant groups intensified the controversy surrounding it within Pakistan.

The 2002 Pakistan elections

The post-9/11 context explains the unexpected political breakthrough of the MMA (United Council of Action) in the North West Frontier Province (NWFP) in the October 2002 general elections.[47] Its component members that included Jamaat-e-Islam and Jamiat-ul-Ulema-e-Islam had never captured more than a handful of seats in the past. The MMA outflanked nationalist and secular opponents by decrying the presence of US bases in Pakistan in pursuit of the war on terror along with the bombing raids in Afghanistan. It emerged with 44 out of the 99 seats in the NWFP Provincial Assembly and 53 National Assembly seats. Some commentators feared that its control of the police and civil administration in the sensitive frontier areas would undermine the effectiveness of the military operations against al-Qaeda groups and Taliban remnants. In reality, the army actions continued unhampered when ordered to do so by Islamabad. The consequence of the MMA breakthrough lay in another direction, namely that of creating the circumstances for a constitutional deadlock throughout much of 2002.

The MMA successes trimmed the majority of the Musharraf loyalist Pakistan Muslim League (Q) Government of Mir Zafarullah Khan Jamali.[48] The MMA formed a provincial government in the Frontier under the leadership of the 42 year old Akram Durrani, but sat with the opposition mainstream parties the Pakistan Peoples' Party (PPP) and Pakistan Muslim League (N) in the National Assembly. The PPP was not only locked out of power at the Centre, but also in Sind where it had emerged as the largest party. The elections reversed the trend in the 1990s towards a two-party system. While the side-lining of the PPP and the PML (N) was to Musharraf's liking, the MMA's decision to join with them on the one point issue of opposition to the Legal Framework Order resulted in a constitutional deadlock throughout 2003.

The Legal Framework Order controversy[49]

The Legal Framework Order (LFO) of 21 August 2002 had been introduced by General Musharraf to ensure that whatever the outcome of the polls, a 'guided democracy' would be instituted in Pakistan. The MMA's decision to join the PPP and PML(N) to oppose the LFO meant however that parliament did not supinely accept the executive ordering of democracy. The LFO had restored to the President the authority to dissolve the National Assembly and 'relieve' the prime minister and cabinet of their functions. The former Prime Minister Nawaz Sharif had removed this power in April 1997 by the 13th Amendment to the Constitution. The LFO had also introduced a National Security Council, on which the service chiefs would be represented, to serve as a forum for discussion of matters relating to democracy, governance and interprovincial harmony.

The opposition objected that amendments to the Constitution enshrined in the LFO had not received the necessary two-thirds majority parliamentary assent. The Government response was that the LFO had become part of the

Constitution because the Supreme Court ruling of May 2000 that upheld the October 12 1999 coup authorized General Musharraf to make constitutional amendments needed for his reforms. The struggle widened to one of enforcing parliamentary supremacy. The protests against the LFO were thus also linked with Musharraf's simultaneous occupation of the posts of President and Chief of Army Staff. Moreover, his legitimacy as President was questioned because it was based on the controversial 30 April 2002 Referendum.[50] The disputes were ultimately not about constitutional niceties, but about the extent and terms on which the army's influence would be institutionalized in the political process.

After months of deadlock right at the end of 2003 when the MMA voted with the government ensuring the necessary two-thirds' parliamentary majority for the 17th Constitutional Amendment to pass into law. The MMA had managed to extract seven concessions and claimed that parliamentary supremacy had been asserted by incorporating the LFO into the Constitution in this way. In reality however the 17th Constitutional Amendment did little more than soften some of the undemocratic features of the LFO. Musharraf further legitimized his position by safely negotiating a vote of confidence. The vote was however less than a ringing endorsement following the abstention of the MMA and the boycott of the Alliance for the Restoration of Democracy (ARD) and its smaller allies. The President was nevertheless pleased to secure the 56 per cent majority. The vote gave him a more legitimate position in which to work for a rapprochement with India on the sidelines of the 12th South Asian Association for Regional Cooperation conference hosted by Islamabad on 4 January 2004.

Musharraf's apologists drew comfort from the outcome to the constitutional deadlock. It was portrayed as a safeguard against instability and a guarantee of Pakistan's development as a moderate Islamic state. Opponents viewed the situation rather differently. They claimed that it further retarded the maturing of the political process and perpetuated the weak institutionalization and opportunism that has been the hallmark of Pakistan's political development since independence. This was further evidenced by Jamali's 'forced resignation' and replacement by another Musharraf loyalist in June 2004.

The first half of 2004 had been punctuated by further religious linked violence. The Pakistan state had continued fighting 'foreign' *jihadist* forces in South Waziristan. Karachi had been the scene of two devastating sectarian suicide bomb attacks against mosques in early May and June. Such dramatic episodes should not obscure the fact that religious violence involves not only a physical, but a psychological dimension. This has especially damaged the minorities' esteem and sense of self-worth. One example of this is the stigmatizing of Christians as 'sweepers'. Many Christians do carry out this low status job, but it has become a stereotype for the whole community. Christians also receive derogatory treatment because of the 'freedom' of their women and their possession of liquor permits. Hindus are stereotyped by the term *bania* (moneylender).

Wall chalking and posters are often inflammatory in their attacks on minorities, especially on the Ahmadis. The Pakistan official passport application form contains a statement which not only reiterates *khatam-e-nabuwwat* (finality of the Prophethood) but denigrates Mirza Ghulam Ahmad's claims to be a *Nabi* (Prophet). The Ministry of Religious and Minorities Affairs possesses an inscription which reads, 'of course Islam is the best religion in the eyes of God'.[51] The minorities' inequality has been reinforced by Islamic Laws such as the Qisas and Diyat Ordinance regarding blood money, the Law of Evidence and the fact that non-Muslims are excluded from the highest offices of the state. This institutionalizes their sense of alienation from the mainstream and their powerlessness. Even wealthy minorities lack social status, while poorer members of the communities live in a constant state of vulnerability. This explains why many Ahmadis, Hindus and Christians who are Muslim converts do not openly profess their beliefs.

Conclusion

This chapter has uncovered the context for the contemporary religious violence in Pakistan. While beliefs such as in the finality of the Prophet, the justification for *jihad* and the sanctity of the Qur'an are directly linked with much of the contemporary turmoil, these are historically contingent, rather than intrinsically linked to Islam. The colonial era saw the emergence of the Deoband School of '*ulama*, and its political offshoot which wields great influence in contemporary Pakistan. Jamaat-e-Islami similarly came into existence in this period. The Zia era marked another important watershed. It both encouraged an exclusivist attitude to citizenship and created dangerous ties between the military establishment and armed Islamic militant groups. These alliances were the result of the Pakistan state's security, strategic and political interests in its ongoing conflict with India. Economic marginalization, poverty and ignorance ensured a steady stream of recruits for the alluring visions of the *jihadist* cause.

Even before 9/11, however, the dangers of the state's patronage of militant Islamic groups were becoming evident with the rise of sectarian violence within Pakistan. This also stemmed from the contest for influence between Saudi Arabia and Iran. Both countries financed *madrassahs* and activists. The events of 9/11 heralded a dramatic transformation in Pakistan's regional security and strategic policy. Despite the anxieties of Western commentators, the country's internal politics have been far less affected. The army remains a unified and disciplined organization committed to its own understanding of the national interest. It has been influenced by Islamization since the Zia era, but it remains a professional force that is unlikely to engage in adventurism in the name of Islam. The restoration of close professional ties with the US military has lain at the heart of its interests. The army institutionally is committed both to the war on terror and the current rapprochement with India. Such policies would survive Musharraf's demise or his retirement. Musharraf has, however, sought to secure maximum US protection by emphasizing his personal role in these policy directions.

The Pakistan state's dramatic reversal of its support for the Taliban after 9/11 and for foreign groups involved in the Kashmir *jihad* following the 2002 military stand-off with India, has not, however, brought about an immediate diminution of sectarian violence. Groups that had developed links with al-Qaeda sought to destabilize the Musharraf regime because of its 'front-line' status in the 'war on terror'. Assassination attempts against its leading figures and sectarian killings remain their preferred mode of operation.

Notes

1 Shias comprise around 20 per cent of the population. For further details of their situation see Malik 2002.
2 Nasr 2002: 85.
3 The violence appeared to be caused by a police vendetta rather than through bigotry. A number of leading local policemen had been suspended following an earlier incident in which a Bible had been desecrated (*Dawn* (Karachi), 9 February 1997).
4 Section 295-C of the Penal Code provided for the death penalty or life imprisonment for committing blasphemy against the Holy Prophet. In October 1990 the Federal Shariat Court ruled that death was the only punishment for blasphemy. The Ahmadis have also fallen foul of Ordinance XX of 1984 which added sections 298-B and 298-C to the Pakistan Penal Code. This provided for three years' imprisonment for the use of epithets and practising of rights peculiar to Islam by non-Muslims. Cases have been brought even on such issues as wearing a ring inscribed with Quranic verses. For details see Mehdi and Rizvi 1995: 46–54.
5 See Nadeem 2002: 97.
6 See Talbot 2000: 259 & ff. for an overview.
7 This could be understood as a 'controlled democracy'. The elected governments of Benazir Bhutto (1990 and 1996) and of Nawaz Sharif (1993) were dismissed by the President in 'constitutional coups'. Nawaz Sharif's second government was replaced by General Musharraf following the coup of 12 October 1999.
8 See Prasad 1946; Kabir 1943; Mehta and Patwardhan 1942.
9 Pandey 1989.
10 Prior 1990
11 Bayly 1985: 177–203.
12 Ever since the publication in 1978 of Edward Said's seminal study *Orientalism* some scholars have recognized that European Orientalist knowledge, classification, definition and representation of non-Western societies was more about the power to control than about intellectual curiosity.
13 *Census of India Report, 1881* Vol. 1, p.19.
14 Oberoi 1994.
15 For details see Warren 2000.
16 See Metcalf 1982.
17 See Nasr 1996.
18 See Lavan 1974.
19 See Talbot 1988.
20 In 2002 President General Pervez Musharraf's government introduced an ordinance to make the imparting of sectarian hatred and militancy in *madrassahs*, a crime punishable by two years' rigorous imprisonment. It also drew up a three-year project to provide government funds and technical assistance for the widening of the curriculum to include 'modern' general subjects. Foreign aid would be subject to the approval of Federal and Provincial *madrassah* boards and if it came from a government source would have to also be cleared by the Interior Ministry (*Dawn* (Karachi) 21 June 2002).

21 This was rooted in part in the concept of *taqiyyah* (dissimulation) to avoid persecution. Husayn was seen as a martyr rather than a role model of revolt. Khoemini presented him as an exemplar of revolutionary defiance.
22 Zahab 2002: 126.
23 Dorronsoro 2002: 167.
24 Talbot 1999: 251.
25 Ibid.
26 *Newsline* (Karachi) March 1995 p. 24.
27 See Marsden, 1998.
28 Rashid 1999: 22–35.
29 Hussain 1995: 22 &ff.
30 See Ganguly 1997.
31 Ganguly 2002: 180.
32 Al-Faran was implicated in the murder of the Norwegian tourist Hans Christian Osto in 1996.
33 This organization was founded in 1993 and two years later was involved in a bloody clash with Indian security forces at a famous Kashmiri sufi shrine at Charar-e-Sharief. HUA was renamed as Harkat-ul Mujahideen following its being identified as a terrorist organization by the US State Department. Harkat-ul Mujahideen's leading figure Fazlur Rehman possessed close ties with Osama bin Laden. The organization in its new manifestation was listed as a terrorist organisation by the USA.
34 For further details see Shafqat 2002: 131–149.
35 Jaish-e-Mohammad was an offshoot of Harkat-ul Mujahideen. It appears that Brigadier Abdullah, head of the Kashmir department of the ISI helped to establish the organization in January 2002. Omar Sheikh was one of its prominent members. Jaish-e-Mohammad claimed responsibility for the suicide bomb attack on the State Assembly in Srinagar on 1 October. This initiated the round of tensions that culminated in military stand-off and nuclear brinkmanship.
36 Talbot 2002: 284–285.
37 Talbot 2002: 310.
38 Social Policy and Development Centre 2001: 2.
39 Ibid.: 15.
40 Nadeem 2002: 49.
41 The bomb exploded too early for its target. Three passers-by lost their lives and considerable damage was done to the bridge.
42 Talbot 2003: 201.
43 *Dawn* (Karachi) 14 June 2002.
44 *Dawn* (Karachi) 6 December 2002.
45 See Bakhtiar 2002: 32 &ff.
46 For details of his career, see Gunaratna 2002: 210–215.
47 See Talbot 2003: 204 &ff.
48 Jamali was the first Baloch to become Pakistan Prime Minister.
49 For further details see Talbot 2004: 36–42.
50 *Dawn* (Karachi) 2 May 2002.
51 Malik 2002: 22.

References

Bakhtiar, I. (2002) 'Pearl and After', *Herald* (Karachi), 32 &ff.

Bayly, C.A. (1985) 'The Pre-History of "Communalism"? Religious Conflict in India 1700–1860', *Modern Asian Studies,* 19 (1): 177–203.

Dorronsoro, G. (2002) 'Pakistan and the Taliban: State Policy, Religious Networks and Political Connections' in Jaffrelot, C (ed.), *Pakistan: Nationalism without a Nation?* New Delhi: Manohar, pp. 161–179.

Ganguly, S. (1997) *The Crisis in Kashmir: Portents of War. Hopes of Peace,* Cambridge: Cambridge University Press.

——(2002) 'The Islamic Dimensions of the Kashmir Insurgency' in Jaffrelot. C (ed.), *Pakistan: Nationalism without a Nation?* New Delhi: Manohar, pp. 179–195.

Gunaratna, R. (2002) *Inside Al Qaeda: Global Network of Terror,* London: Hurst.

Hussain, Z. (1995) 'Islamic Warriors', *Newsline* (Karachi), 22 &ff.

Jaffrelot, C. (ed.) (2002) *Pakistan: Nationalism, without a Nation?* New Delhi: Manohar.

Kabir, H. (1943) *Muslim Politics, 1906–1942,* Calcutta: Gupta, Rahman, Gupta.

Lavan, S. (1974) *The Ahmadiyah Movement: Past and Present,* Delhi: Manohar.

Malik, I.H. (2002) *Religious Minorities in Pakistan,* London: Minority Rights Group International.

Marsden, P. (1998) *The Taliban: War, Religion and the New Order in Afghanistan,* London: Hurst.

Mehdi, T. and Rizvi, M. (1995) 'The Price of Faith', *Newsline* (Karachi) April, 46–54.

Mehta, A. and Patwardhan, A. (1942) *The Communal Triangle in India,* Allahabad: Kitabistan.

Metcalf, B. (1982) *Islamic Revival in British India: Deoband, 1860–1900,* Princeton: Princeton University Press.

Nadeem, A.H. (2002) *Pakistan: The Political Economy of Lawlessness,* Karachi: Oxford University Press.

Nasr, S.V.R. (1996) *Mawdudi and the Making of Islamic Revolution,* New York: Oxford University Press.

——(2002) 'Islam, the State and the Rise of Sectarian Militancy in Pakistan' in Jaffrelot, C. (ed.), *Pakistan: Nationalism without a Nation?* New Delhi: Manohar, pp. 85–115.

Oberoi, H. (1994) *The Construction of Religious Boundaries: Culture, Identity and Diversity in the Sikh Tradition,* Chicago: Chicago University Press.

Pandey, G. (1989) 'The Colonial Construction of "Communalism". British Writings on Banaras in the Nineteenth Century', in Guha, R. (ed.), *Subaltern Studies* Vol. 6, Delhi: Oxford University Press.

Prasad, R. (1946) *India Divided,* Bombay: Hind Kitabs.

Prior, K. (1990) 'The British Administration of Hinduism in North India 1780–1900', Unpublished Ph.D. thesis, Cambridge: Cambridge University.

Rashid, A. (1999) 'The Taliban: Exporting Extremism', *Foreign Affairs,* 78, 6: 22–35.

Shafqat, S. (2002) 'From Official Islam to Islamism: The Rise of Dawat-ul-Irshad and Lashkar-e-Taiba', in Jaffrelot. C (ed.), *Pakistan: Nationalism without a Nation?* New Delhi: Manohar, pp. 131–149.

Social Policy and Development Centre (2001) *Social Development in Pakistan. Annual Review 2000: Towards Poverty Reduction*, Karachi: SPDC.

Talbot, I. (1988) *Punjab and the Raj 1849–1947,* New Delhi: Manohar.

——(1999) *Pakistan: A Modern History,* London: Hurst.

——(2000) *India and Pakistan,* London: Arnold.

——(2003) 'Pakistan in 2002: Democracy, Terrorism and Brinkmanship', *Asian Survey,* 43, 1: 198–208.

——(2004) 'Pakistan in 2003: Political Deadlock and Continuing Uncertainties', *Asian Survey,* 44 (1): 36–43.

Warren, A. (2000) *Waziristan: The Faqir of Ipi and the Indian Army. The North West Frontier Revolt of 1936–37,* Karachi: Oxford University Press.

Zahab, M.A. (2002) 'The Regional Dimension of Sectarian Conflicts in Pakistan' in Jaffrelot, C. (ed.), *Pakistan: Nationalism without a Nation?* New Delhi: Manohar, pp. 115–131.

8 The 2002 pogrom in Gujarat

The post-9/11 face of Hindu nationalist anti-Muslim violence

Christophe Jaffrelot

Introduction

Violence between Hindus and Muslims is a structural feature of Indian society. One finds its traces very early in the country's history,[1] a fact that can drive the analyst to explain the phenomenon by referring to the incompatibility of Hindu and Muslim cultures.[2] However, those historians interested in the phenomenon have always emphasized the economic dimension of the rivalry between Hindus and Muslims, which springs from conflicts about real estate or commercial competition.[3] Among sociologists and political scientists, this approach has found favour with many authors more or less inclined to Marxist categories.[4]

The interpretation of violence between Hindus and Muslims that I have suggested is very different.[5] It emphasizes the role of politics in two complementary aspects, the impact of a militant ethno-religious ideology and the exploitation of communal issues by political parties.

Indeed, research on communal riots in India after 1947 suggests that these riots largely originate from a distorted idea of 'the Other' among Hindus who, though representing an overwhelming majority, often perceive the Muslims as a 'fifth column' threatening them from within Indian society. The main representative of the Hindu nationalist movement, the Rashtriya Swayamsevak Sangh (RSS, The Association of National Volunteers) was founded in 1925 in reaction to the Khilafat movement in which the first Hindu nationalists saw a pan-Islamic threat. After independence, Hindu–Muslim riots became one *classicus locus* of Indian politics largely because the Hindu nationalist parties – the Jan Sangh and then the Bharatiya Janata Party (BJP) – resorted to anti-Muslim violence to polarize the electorate and solidify the Hindu 'vote bank'. This process culminated in the Ayodhya movement through which the Sangh Parivar – the 'RSS family', i.e. the network of organizations developed by the RSS, including the BJP – reclaimed one of the mosques of Uttar Pradesh, a north Indian State, the Babri Masjid by claiming that it was built on the birthplace of Lord Ram. This movement was marred by recurring riots which reached their climax in 1992 when Hindu nationalist activists destroyed the Babri Masjid.

This explanatory model of Hindu–Muslim riots combining ideological and electoral dimensions was verified again in the light of the Gujarat riots of 2002.

Indeed, these riots also commit us to reconfirm the role of the Hindu nationalist politicians. The latter has to be weighted even more heavily in Gujarat, for they held political power in that province. This state of things explains the rather exceptional intensity of the Gujarat riots. This time, Hindu–Muslim violence was not so much a reflection of the routinized logic of communal riots in India, but rather the result of an organized pogrom with the approval of the state apparatus of Gujarat acting not only with the electoral agenda in mind, but also in view of a true ethnic cleansing. Besides, the intensity of the riots has also demonstrated that this kind of violence has triggered a feedback in society even among groups hitherto less inclined to ethnic nationalism, such as, for example, the tribals. But there is an effect of yet another political strategy at work, which reminds us of the ideological core of our explanatory model: the more and more thorough diffusion of Hindutva in Gujarat in reaction to a fear of Jehad.

Godhra, 27 February 2002: a riot provoked

Gujarat has long been known for its communal violence.[6] The riot in Ahmedabad in 1969, which left approximately 630 dead, remained the most serious riot in India after Partition until the Bhagalpur riot, 20 years later, which was part of the wave of clashes between Muslims and Hindus from the Ramjanmabhoomi movement set on building a Hindu temple on the Babri Masjid site in Ayodhya. But this same movement also brought Gujarat to the fore: throughout the 1980s to 1990s, this state counted the most riot victims per inhabitant. In 1990, L.K. Advani's *Rath Yatra* sparked riots that left about 220 dead in this state. In 1992, the demolition of the Babri Masjid also set off a wave of violence that killed 325 people, mostly Muslims. The heightening of this phenomenon in the 1990s already reflected nationalist Hindu activism. The clashes in 2002 must also be analysed as a political phenomenon.

Violence broke out on 27 February in Godhra, a district headquarters in eastern Gujarat. Fifty-seven Hindus were killed, including 25 women and 14 children, who were burned alive aboard the Sabarmati Express. The train was carrying back from Faizabad (Uttar Pradesh) nationalist Hindu activists who had travelled to Ayodhya to build a temple dedicated to the god Ram on the ruins of the Babri Masjid. A campaign to build this temple had been instigated by the Vishva Hindu Parishad (VHP), a key element of the Sangh Parivar, within the context of the election campaign in Uttar Pradesh, where the BJP was attempting to retain power by all possible means. The undertaking had once again been postponed through central government mediation and the judges' vigilance, a recurrent process since the demolition of the Babri Masjid in 1992, which had increasingly frustrated the *kar sevaks* (literally 'servers-in-action'), Hindu nationalist activists who had come to Ayodhya to erect the temple.

Those who were originally from Gujarat and were returning home aboard the Sabarmati Express had gathered together in a few coaches. They chanted Hindu nationalist songs and slogans throughout the entire journey, all the while harassing Muslim passengers. One family was even made to get off the train for refusing to utter the *kar sevaks*' war cry: '*Jai Shri Ram!*' (Glory to Lord Ram!). More abuse occurred at the stop in Godhra: a Muslim shopkeeper was also ordered to shout '*Jai Shri Ram!*' He refused, and was assaulted until the *kar sevaks* turned on a Muslim woman with her two daughters. It seems that one of them was forced to board the train before it started going again.

The train had hardly left the station when one of the passengers pulled the emergency chain. It was yanked several times, until the train came to a halt in the middle of a Muslim neighbourhood inhabited by Ghanchis, a community from which many of the Godhra street vendors hail. According to Hindu nationalist activists, hundreds of Muslims surrounded the coaches occupied by the *kar sevaks* and attacked it with stones and torches. Coach S-6 caught fire, killing 57 people.[7] But the Justice UC Banerjee Commission, a one-man commission which had been appointed in September 2004 by the Union government, held that the fire which occurred aboard the Sabarmarti Express at the Godhra railway station was accidental and started from inside. This assessment was first spelled out by this former Supreme Court judge in his interim report submitted in January 2005 and was confirmed in the final report one year later in March 2006.

Whatever the initial cause,[8] the aftermath of the events clearly showed that the violence reached unprecedented proportions because of the political strategy employed by Hindu nationalists.

From riot to pogrom: state-sponsored violence

Narendra Modi, the BJP Chief Minister in Gujarat, is a former cadre member in the RSS which spawned the Hindu nationalist movement, and where most of the VHP and BJP leaders began their career. Whereas Godhra District Collector, on 27 February, had spent the day explaining that the incident was not premeditated, Modi declared that very evening that it was a 'pre-planned violent act of terrorism'.[9] And that very evening too, on the government's orders, the bodies of those who had died in Godhra were taken to Ahmedabad for a *post-mortem* and public ceremony. The arrival of the bodies at the Ahmedabad station was broadcast on television, causing considerable agitation among the Hindus, all the more so since the bodies were exhibited merely covered with a sheet. The following day, the VHP organized the shutdown of the city (*bandh*) with the support of the BJP. This mobilization established the conditions for a Hindu offensive in Ahmedabad.

However, in addition to Godhra and Ahmedabad (two cities with histories steeped in communal strife),[10] other towns in Gujarat where such riots had not developed previously experienced clashes. On the evening of 28 February, Gandhinagar, the capital of Gujarat, located 30 km from Ahmedabad, was the scene of Hindu–Muslim rioting for the first time in its history. Twenty-six towns in all were subject to curfew. Ahmedabad and Godhra saw the most serious clashes, with 350 and 100 victims respectively in early March, according to official figures. After these two cities came Mehsana (50 dead) and Sabarkantha (40 dead).

Reviewing the sequence of events, even in a condensed version, gives an idea of the power of destruction that came over Gujarat during those few days. On 28 February, in Ahmedabad, in the Naroda Gaon and Naroda Pattiya areas, an armed hoard of several thousand people attacked Muslim houses and shops, killing 200. Six other neighbourhoods in the city were subject to similar attacks on a lesser scale. Three other districts, Vadodara, Gandhinagar and Sabarkhanta, were host to comparable violence. In the latter district, several settlements were the scene of clashes. Elsewhere, too, but to a lesser degree, the previously spared rural areas were involved. The next day, on 1 March, mainly rural districts were added to the list of hotspots: Panchmahals, Mehsana, Kheda, Junagadh, Banaskantha, Patan, Anand and Narmada. On 2 March, Bharuch and Rajkot, which had yet to be affected by communal violence, were hit in turn. On the 4 March, riots broke out in Surat, a town that had seen considerable Hindu–Muslim violence in the 1990s and was much less affected this time.

Premeditated and coordinated clashes

The clashes in Gujarat could not have spread so quickly and taken on such proportions unless they had been orchestrated by well-organized actors and the attackers' plan had been prepared prior to the events in Godhra. As early as 28 February, 24 hours after the attack on the Sabarmati Express, and shortly after Modi's repatriation of the bodies had caused such extreme distress, the VHP *bandh* degenerated into an orgy of violence: nothing was left to chance; it was a far cry from the spontaneous rioting Modi later described to excuse the Hindus.[11]

Actually, everything went according to a military-like plan in Ahmedabad and elsewhere.[12] The troops were perfectly disciplined and incredibly numerous: groups of attackers often included thousands of men. These squads generally arrived in the Muslim neighbourhoods by truckloads. They wore a basic uniform – the RSS khaki shorts and a saffron headband – and carried daggers and pitchforks as well as bottles of water to quench their thirst en route. The lists that the ringleaders had in hand attest to the premeditated nature of the assault: these indicated Muslim homes and shops, some of which bore Hindi names, thereby proving that investigation had actually been undertaken beforehand to ascertain the owner's identity. These lists – on computer print-outs – had obviously been drawn up on the basis of voter registration lists.

That the entire plan had been carefully organized can also be inferred from the assiduous use the aggressors made of cellular telephones. They apparently reported regularly to a central headquarters and received their instructions from this same centre. It is not entirely impossible that these headquarters had been set up simply in the police stations of the towns involved, or of the state itself, because a number of Hindu nationalist leaders took up residence there throughout the period of violence. Several senior civil servants – on condition of anonymity – admitted to National Human Rights Commission investigators that on 28 February, the Gujarat Interior Minister and Health Minister directed the advance of the assailants from the 'City police control room' of Ahmedabad[13]'. At the same time, the Urban Development Minister had set up his headquarters in the Gujarat 'State police control room' in Gandhinagar. All gave the police forces orders not to intervene.

The attackers were organized and well equipped. This was obvious in the use of gas cylinders that they had shipped to their attack sites. The typical scenario of this new-style violence involved looting Muslim shops then blowing them up with these makeshift but extremely powerful bombs. Not only do these operations show carefully planned organization, but they also indicate official state support. It would be impossible to transport that many men (and gas cylinders) with that many trucks without the benefit of state logistic support. Above all, the protected nature of the clashes over days, weeks, and even months can only be explained by active government cooperation.

This bias was tested beforehand by the Hindu nationalist activists, after their leaders had given them assurances: they set fire to a few automobiles in the vicinity of police stations to make sure their schemes could be carried out with no fear of punishment. This was almost always the case, given that the leaders of the party in power, the BJP, had quickly occupied central police headquarters. The administration was paralyzed. But in any event, since their rise to power in Gujarat, Hindu nationalists had already penetrated deep into the state apparatus, starting with the police. Hence the standard response they gave to the Muslims who called them to their rescue: 'We have no order to save you'.[14]

Local BJP and VHP leaders were out in the streets alongside the attackers. Victims of their violence gave names and descriptions about which there can be no mistake. On the basis of these, the editor-in-chief of *Communalism Combat*, a secularist publication, revealed that charges had been filed against a BJP MP and four city councillors.[15] No tangible effective action was taken.

An indication that the government wanted to see the clashes last was that the army, which was already in the vicinity on 1 March – 12 columns with 600 men were stationed at the time in Ahmedabad and other hotspots in Gujarat – was not sent to the places where it could have been the most useful. Aside from a few '*flag marches*', it had to settle for remaining on stand-by because allegedly no 'official' was available to accompany the troops.

The state partiality also appeared in the treatment inflicted on the Muslims who took shelter in refugee camps. At the height of the violence, there were as many as 125,000 refugees in these camps. Officially, they still numbered 87,000 in April 2002, 66,000 of them in Ahmedabad alone. In three months, the government registered the return home of 73,500 refugees (52,500 in Ahmedabad) to pretend that law and order had been restored and that elections could be held. In any case, the authorities never took the necessary steps to help the refugees: most of the aid came from Muslim NGOs.

Clashes in rural Gujarat: the communalization of tribal zones

Riots between Hindus and Muslims have traditionally been an urban phenomenon. This was all the more true in Gujarat where there are, moreover, proportionally more Muslims in cities than in the countryside (the share of Muslims living in rural areas is only 42 per cent in Gujarat compared to 65 per cent for the national average).[16] Yet the violence in 2002 spread to the villages and so, in many cases, to villages where very few Muslims resided. The districts of Mehsana and Gandhinagar, for instance, which have only 6.6 per cent and 2.9 per cent Muslim residents respectively according to the 2001 census, were heavily affected, even in the rural areas.

This singularity can be largely explained by the fact that the small Muslim minority is made up mainly of shopkeepers and moneylenders: unlike their coreligionists in the rest of India, the Muslims have a small, fairly successful economic elite in Gujarat. This social class is primarily from the Bohra, Khoja and Memon castes. In many villages, these groups own several businesses and are the main moneylenders (*sahukar*), to whom peasants become indebted, sometimes to pay their daughter's dowry, sometimes to buy seed for the year. These Muslims were one of the attackers' prime targets. Often this target was pinpointed by Hindu nationalist activists who had come from the city. They exploited the peasants' resentment toward this small economic elite; they raised their hopes of financial reward in the form of looting shops. This has led Dipankar Gupta to interpret the spread of rioting to rural areas in Gujarat as due mainly to economic reasons.[17] The study conducted by Bela Bhatia in Sabarkantha partly corroborates this analysis. The author in fact observes a shift in the violence from cities to villages between 28 February – the date when the cities of Khedbrahma and Bhilodas were hit – and the evening of 1 March, when it spread to the villages.[18] The agents of this spread were Hindu nationalist activists from the city or nearby towns. These *tolas* (groups), whose members were wearing the saffron-coloured headband and chanting anti-Muslim slogans, entered the villages on tractors or in jeeps. Most of them were from the Patel caste – a caste of landed peasants who had prospered in farming before going into trade and industry to such an extent that the urban economy in Gujarat today is as much in their hands as those of the traditional merchant castes in the region. These assailants proved to be perfectly organized: divided into three groups, *todwavalla* (those who were destroying), *lootwavalla* (those who were looting) and *baadwavalla* (those who were burning), they went through several villages. In all, 2,161 houses, 1,461 shops, 71 workshops and factories and 38 hotels were looted and entirely or partly destroyed in the district of Sabarkantha. In addition, 45 places of worship underwent the same fate, which suggests that beyond the purely economic aspect, the violence reflected xenophobic feelings. In fact, one of the most repeated slogans was: '*Muslai ne gaam ma thi kado*' (Run the Muslims out of the village), a slogan chanted by local villagers as well as activists from outside the village.

Altogether, over 1,200 villages were affected, particularly in the districts of Panchmahals, Mehsana, Sabarkantaha, Bharuch, Bhavnagar and Vadodara. In this latter district, the army had to be called in on 5 March. Some 2,500 Muslims from 22 different villages were evacuated and moved to refugee camps. These villages no longer had a single Muslim according to the District Magistrate.[19]

But the most surprising development still, lies elsewhere: of the villages involved, many of them were in the tribal zone, the eastern '*tribal belt*', bordering Madhya Pradesh, from Ambaji to Narmada. Never before had there been such massive participation of indigenous peoples (*adivasis*) in the anti-Muslim riots alongside Hindu nationalist activists.

This phenomenon has usually been interpreted by local observers in the same way villager involvement has, the *adivasis* being a subgroup of them. Bela Bhatia's study in Sabarkhanta – a district where tribes make up 17 per cent of the population – thus leads her to conclude that the *adivasis* 'were used by upper caste and class Hindus in their program against the Muslims'.[20] Testimonies gathered by Bhatia in the field among Muslim survivors even made excuses for the aggressions the *adivasis* perpetrated, considering that it was not surprising to see them loot Bohra, Khoja and Memon shops, given the drought they had long suffered and the atmosphere created by the riot.

Election-oriented violence

The government's involvement in Hindu–Muslim violence – a fact that largely explains its exceptional scope – is part of an unavowed but easily reconstructed political strategy. There is great suspicion that the BJP, and the Hindu nationalist movement on the whole, honed this strategy between 1989 and 1991 when their activists worked at provoking anti-Muslim riots as election time approached. This violence in effect polarizes society along a religious line of cleavage, which generally leads the Hindu majority, with a heightened sense of Hindu identity, to vote more in favour of the BJP. This explains the correlation between the election calendar and the cycle of riots. Steven Wilkinson has thus shown that 'both riots and deaths do tend to cluster in the months before elections, and then drop off sharply in the months after an election is held'.[21]

This analysis began to lose some of its relevance in 1993 when the BJP was defeated in state assembly elections in Madhya Pradesh, Himachal Pradesh and Delhi precisely due to excessive violence: too many riots tend to cancel out the impact of what is gained in terms of votes, because even the Hindu elite suffers from the anarchy resulting from repeated violence and curfews. Shopkeepers and industrialists – from whom the BJP traditionally draws a lot of support – are particularly at risk when violence is heavy and drawn out. The violence of the 1992–93 riots following the demolition of the Babri Masjid in Ayodhya on 6 December 1992 exceeded anything India had yet experienced since Partition. Afterward, the BJP was also dissuaded from using riots as a strategy by the mere fact of its rise to power in New Delhi in 1998, since it was henceforth responsible for public order and it had to accommodate coalition partners who did not share its ideology. However, this new rule of conduct was challenged by many party activists and cadres as the BJP was declining. At the end of the 1990s, the party in fact started losing local and state elections one after the other. The most radical members then suggested doing away with the moderate official line and returning to a strategy of ethno-religious mobilization, of which communal violence was a key element, so as to win the elections again.

In Gujarat, elections were not scheduled until 2003, but the rioters' high level of organization suggests that the Hindu nationalist movement was already preparing for this date with strong-arm tactics. Nothing could be more logical. First, the state was accustomed to pre-election riots (between 1987 and 1991, 40 per cent of the 106 Hindu–Muslim riots that afflicted Gujarat took place at election time).[22] Second, the BJP had stacked up repeated electoral setbacks here as elsewhere: in December 2000, the party lost two cities in municipal elections (one of which was Ahmedabad) out of the six it had held up to then, and above all, it was marginalized in nearly all the *zila parishads* (district councils) whose elected officers were being renewed at the same time.[23]

The Sangh Parivar thus used Godhra as an opportunity to unleash violence upon which it hoped to capitalize during early elections. It was to provoke early elections that Modi decided to recommend that the governor – S.S. Bhandari, another RSS activist – dissolve the Gujarat assembly on 19 July. At the same time, he resigned as Chief Minister, while remaining at the helm to handle routine proceedings. And he immediately set about calling for early elections. These tactics were all the more shocking since the violence had far from subsided everywhere.[24]

In such conditions, James Michael Lyngdoh, Chief Election Commissioner, who visited 12 of the state's districts between 31 July and 4 August, was reluctant to organize any poll, especially since many voters, a vast majority of them Muslims, were still living far from their homes in refugee camps. So Modi and the BJP strove to demonstrate that calm had been restored, leading them first to hurriedly close the refugee camps or lower the number of their occupants reported in official statistics, and argue that in accordance with article 174 of the Constitution, the time between dissolving the assembly and holding new elections could not exceed six months. National BJP leaders – starting with deputy prime minister L.K. Advani – joined in the call for early elections. Given the objections of the Election Commission, which preferred that President's Rule be declared because the election could not be organized under proper conditions and because, in this case, article 174 did not apply, the BJP brought the case before the Supreme Court. The Court refused to express an opinion, referring to the Election Commission's decisions. In early November, the Commission set a date for the elections to begin on 12 December.

On 8 September, Modi relaunched the campaign he had started in the immediate aftermath of the violence, in preparation for the elections. He then undertook a tour of the state that was highly reminiscent of L.K. Advani's Rath Yatra in 1990. Like this huge political pilgrimage that left from the Somnath Temple in Gujarat, Modi's Gaurav Yatra (Pilgramage of Pride) left from the Bhathiji Maharaj Temple in Phagval (Kheda district). This tour instantly met with great popular success. On 9 September in Himmatnagar, for instance a huge crowd gathered along the roadside and at the place where Modi was to hold his rally, which he did not even reach until 2 a.m.

Throughout this entire tour, Modi's speeches were peppered with anti-Muslim references. In Becharaji, he referred to Muslims as abiding by the motto '*hum paanch, hamare pachchees*' (We are five – an allusion to Muslim polygamy – we will have 50 children – an open criticism of the high Muslim birth rate that many Hindus fear). The VHP distributed thousands of copies of this speech. The BJP and the VHP carefully divided up the work: Modi was bound by the Election Commission's model code of conduct obliging political parties to maintain a certain reserve, whereas Togadia, VHP international general secretary, used all means at his disposal: he held 220 rallies during the election campaign, taking 'jehadi terrorism' as his main target. The VHP not only handed out CDs describing the massacre in Godhra, but also had T-shirts printed stating: 'We will not allow our area to be converted into Godhra'.

The Election Commission was obliged to react. It demanded that Modi take the necessary steps to end the Vijay Yatra – Victory Pilgrimage – that the VHP had begun in mid-November. Modi had Togadia and 42 other VHP militants arrested when their movement set off on 17 November from a temple in Ahmedabad. The VHP initiated another movement called 'Jan Jagaran', a mass awareness campaign. The government settled for denying Togadia access to Panchmahals of which Godhra is the district headquarters. Many suspected that this gesticulating fooled no one: Modi and Togadia had divided up the work for an extremely aggressive election campaign.

Not only was the BJP campaign rife with anti-Muslim references, but it was also based on an obvious equation between Islam and terrorism. One of the BJP's television commercials began with the sound of a train pulling into a station, followed by the clamour of riots and women's screams before the ringing of temple bells was covered by the din of automatic rifle fire. After which, Modi's reassuring countenance appeared, hinting to voters that only he could protect Gujarat from such violence. The BJP Election Manifesto pledged to train Gujarat youth, particularly those living on the Pakistani border, in anti-terrorist tactics. Self-defence militia would be set up in border towns where large numbers of retired servicemen would be brought in. Special gun permits would be issued to the lifeblood of a nation under siege. Not only to the BJP did Muslim mean terrorist, but the equation went a step further by establishing an equivalence between 'Muslim' and 'Pakistani' as well: any adept of Islam was potentially a fifth-column Pakistani. This explains the attention devoted to attacks against Musharraf in Modi's election campaign. He, for instance, declared at a rally in Ahmedabad on 1 October – for 'Anti-Terrorism Day': 'India will continue to refer to him as Mian Musharraf. If the pseudo-secularists don't like it, they can go and lick Musharraf's boots. I dare him to send more terrorists to Gujarat, we are prepared this time. *Arey mian, taari goli khuti jashe* (*Mian*, your bullets will get exhausted)'.[25]

Modi spared no efforts throughout his campaign to spread this anti-Muslim security-based obsession which developed in the specific context created by the 9/11 events but also by the attack of the Indian parliament in December 2001. He covered 4,200 kilometres during the Gaurav Yatra, which began on 8 September

Communalism
propaganda
Xenophobia
racism
} sparked the violence and Human Rights Violations

and ended at the same time as the election campaign. He held 400 rallies in 146 of the state's 182 constituencies. He did what he could to discredit his main opponent, the Congress, accusing it in particular of being the 'mother of terrorism' during a rally in Bhuj on 4 December. The outcome was in his favour: 63 per cent of the registered voters took the trouble to go out and vote and the BJP garnered a majority of seats for the third time in a row (unprecedented elsewhere in India) with a record score of 126 seats out of 182 (compared to 117 in 1998) and about 50 per cent of the votes cast. As for the Congress, it won only 51 seats (2 fewer than in 1998 despite a slight increase in votes, 38 per cent compared to 34 per cent). Only the violence made this landslide possible: the BJP won 42 out of the 50 seats in the three districts most heavily affected by this violence, Panchmahals, Dahod and Vadodara. This is what allowed it to transcend caste cleavages and attract the Hindu masses. An exit-poll mentioned for instance that while 76 per cent of the upper castes and 82 per cent of the Patels voted for the BJP, Other Backward Classes (OBC) castes supported this party too – between 54 and 61 per cent according to the *jati*.[26] Another survey showed that 59 per cent of the respondents did not wish to have someone from another community as a neighbour, indicating just how deep the divide is and calling forth explanations other than mere electoral tactics on the part of politicians.[27]

The communalization of a society and the jehad syndrome

The political strategy of a movement solidly entrenched in the state apparatus and desperate for electoral gains is not enough to explain the scope and intensity of the violence in Gujarat. These methods must be placed in a broader context: that of a reactivation of the Hindu majority's inferiority complex caused by Islamist attacks, and, more generally speaking, that of the communalization of the state of Gujarat and its society.

Since the 1990s, Gujarat has become the main stronghold of Hindu nationalists, to such an extent that today it is the state where the BJP is in power for the longest period, a situation which enabled the party to reshape the administration. One of the BJP government's favourite targets was the police. Muslim police officers have systematically been barred from executive positions. Of the 65 'IPS Officers' (Indian Police Service) on active duty in the state in 2002, only one of them still fulfilled such a role as Deputy Superintendent of Police. All the others had been transferred to railway surveillance, organization of computer-training programme, etc.[28] At the same time, a vast number of Hindu nationalist activists and sympathizers were recruited by the Gujarat Home Guards, a form of municipal police in important cities of the state.

In addition to the police, the state machinery seems to have been infiltrated by Hindu nationalists and to have bowed to BJP influence. Otherwise how could one explain that the rioters had access to documents that could only come from the state administration? They were thus able to identify, and torch, a shop in Ahmedabad that did not have a Muslim name but of which 10 per cent of the capital was owned by a Muslim, as well as a factory owned by a Hindu who had just secured a contract in the Middle East. The aggressors could not have identified these targets without documents supplied by the administration.

Hindu nationalist control over the state apparatus is a determining factor in explaining the violence in Gujarat, but the collective psychology is an equally significant variable.

The new dominant ideology: Hindutva against jehad

In August 2002, a survey conducted among a sample of 17,776 citizens spread over 98 parliamentary constituencies showed that for a relative but nearly absolute majority of respondents, the Gujarat riots were not due to the state government or Hindu nationalists or even to local rabble-rousers, but to 'Muslim fundamentalists' and Muslims aggressors from Godhra (29 per cent and 20 per cent of the answers respectively).[29] Moreover, many of the respondents rated Modi highly, ranking him in second place among the Chief ministers in terms of popularity, with 45 per cent of favourable opinions (compared to 22 per cent six months earlier in a similar survey).[30]

The notion that the Hindus were in a position of self-defence and that Islamism was the guilty party can be explained by the context on 13 December 2001, when a suicide commando gained entry to the Lok Sabha, killing 15 people. This tragic event which targeted the core of the polity of India has been its 9/11 in a way. But other, less publicized attacks happened elsewhere, including in Jammu and Kashmir where a massive explosion killed 50 people in front of the state assembly of Srinagar on 30 September 2001.

These attacks reactivated the feeling of vulnerability Hindus have experienced toward Muslims periodically throughout the twentieth century:[31] in the 1920s, the Khilafat movement gave rise to the first Indian Muslim show of pan-Islamism and in return triggered the creation of the RSS during a series of communal riots; in the 1980s, Islamic proselytism, which appeared in a more fundamentalist light since the Iranian revolution, fuelled a Hindu nationalist counter-mobilization – which ended up focalizing on the Ayodhya incident – and several riots; the terrorist attacks of 2001 made the same impact since they enabled the Hindu nationalist movement to capitalize on the feeling of some threat. A tract distributed during the riots opened with this characteristic assertion: 'Today the minority community is trying to crush the majority community'.[32] Another declaration, made by the Bajrang Dal (the VHP's paramilitary branch), began the same way: '50 years after independence it appears that Hindus are second [class] citizens of this country. Religious conversions, infiltration terrorism and bomb blasts have surrounded Hindustan'. This feeling of insecurity is justified a little further on by designating a culprit: 'Jehad is being carried out in order to establish an Islamic state in Hindustan'.[33]

A VHP tract distributed in Ahmedabad goes into detail on this point:

> America found Laden alone too much whereas we have in our lanes and by-lanes thousands of Ladens[...]and two lakhs [200 000] mullah-maulvis who poison one lakh [100 000] madrassas and mosques day and night with terrorist activities. Organisations like SIMI [a Muslim student union], Lashkar-e-Toiba [a Pakistani Islamist movement active in Kashmir and other places in India] and ISI [the Pakistani secret service] with the support and help of Pakistan, are carrying on terrorist activities. They train lakhs of terrorists in thousands of institutions. They have formed an army of single, unemployed Muslim youth of India by paying high salaries.
>
> The terrorist and traitorious Muslims of this country get weapons from more than 50 Muslim nations to carry out their religious war. They are supplied with AK-56 and AK-47 rifles, automatic machine guns, small canons, rocket launchers and several kilos of RDX.[...]When Pakistan attacks India, the Muslims living here will revolt.[34]

Which led Pravin Togadia to comment: 'What is happening in Gujarat is not communal riots but people's answer to Islamic Jehad'.[35] A leaflet distributed by Bajrang Dal activits during the Gujarat riots went one step further since it requested the Hindus to 'reply in the same language that is used for Jehad'.

This strategy of stigmatizing and *imitating* the Other, who, by his assumed strength, represents a danger to the Hindus has been the brand mark of Hindu nationalism since its inception.[36] For long it fuelled an ethnic nationalism that did not preclude community cohabitation: Muslims were required to pledge allegiance to the majoritarian Hindu culture, even publicly assimilate it, although they could continue to practise their religion in private. But a new juncture was arrived at in 2002 in Gujarat. Then, the nationalist Hindu discourse openly advocated elimination of the Muslims.

Toward ethnic cleansing: sadism and savagery

Over and above the geographic and social extent of the violence, the intensity and savagery of the rioting of Gujarat is what was most striking. The countless accounts gathered by spontaneous NGO investigations and more official inquiries all concur: never has Hindu–Muslim violence reached such extremes in both the systematic nature and duration. This analysis could leave things at that and drape a veil of discretion over these unbearable scenes, but instead of shying away from this violence, it must be told. Putting a damper on the survivors' accounts would boil down to denying what for some could have been their last wish: to recount the unspeakable. What happened? Entire families were electrocuted in their houses, which were first flooded by the murderers. Children were forced to drink kerosene before a match was set to their mouths. Fetuses were cut from the bellies of pregnant women and held up to see. Women, again, were gang raped before being mutilated and burned alive before their children's eyes. No one was safe. Not even former Ahmedabad MP, Ahsan Jafri, a Muslim of the Congress Party. Holed up in his home, he repeatedly called the police for help as the hoards besieging him continued to grow. Dragged outside and delivered up to public condemnation, he was covered with wax and burned alive along with his brother-in-law, the latter's wife and their two sons.

As it is now obvious, women were not spared by the rioters, on the contrary. For example, in the mass grave dug by the Naroda Pattiya victims in Ahmedabad, 46 of the 96 bodies buried there were women. And never had communal violence reached such heights of sexual cruelty vis-à-vis women. Among the Hindus, it harks back to an ancient obsession: Muslims have always appeared more virile to them, partly because of their diet (meat-eating) and their ritual animal sacrifices. Hindu women themselves tend to see Muslims as threats. As explained by Nonica Datta, 'The imaginary suspicion of the Muslim as an aggressor and a sexual predator continues to haunt the Hindu nationalist's psyche',[37] including that of women who sympathize with this ideology. The widespread practice of gang rape in the course of clashes in Gujarat no doubt reflects a desire to equal and even surpass Muslims in the sex act. But there is much more than that. First, the desire to dishonour and destroy an entire community by raping and torturing its women, which of course also aims to destroy their reproductive capacity[38] – a method akin to the rationale of ethnic cleansing.

Another tract distributed during the riots of Gujarat, bearing the title 'Jehad' and written in Gujarati in the form of a poem is most edifying in this respect:[39]

> The people of Baroda and Ahmedabad have gone berserk
> Narendra Modi you have fucked the mother of miyas [derogatory term for Muslims]
> The volcano which was inactive for years has erupted
> It has burnt the arse of miyas and made them dance nude
> We have untied the penises which were tied till now
> Without castor oil in the arse we have made them cry
> Those who call religious war, violence, are all fuckers
> We have widened the tight vaginas of the 'bibis' [term referring to married Muslim women]
> Now even the adivasis have realised what Hinduism is
> They have shot their arrow in the arse of mullahs
> Wake up Hindus there are still miyas left alive around you
> Learn from Panwad village [a village in Panchmahals district that was the scene of serious rioting] where their mother was fucked
> She was fucked standing while she kept shouting
> She enjoyed the uncircumcised penis
> With a Hindu government the Hindus have the power to annihilate miyas
> Kick them in the arse to drive them out of not only villages and cities but also the country.

The violence in Gujarat, due to its very geographic scope and unbearable intensity, in fact marks the first example of ethnic cleansing targeting Muslims since India's Partition in 1947: the aim here was not only to loot and destroy private property, even if such events also took place, but indeed to murder and run off those perceived as intruders. In Sabarkantha, Hindus of Khetbrahma, the district headquarters, after having emptied the place of its Muslim inhabitants, wrote on a sign at the entrance to the town: 'Muslims not allowed'.[40]

A tract distributed in Gujarat during the riots says it plainly:

> We do not want to leave a single Muslim alive in Gujarat.[...]Annihilate Muslims from Bharat[...]when there were kings, the Muslim kings forced Hindu brethren to convert and then committed atrocities against them. And this will continue to happen till Muslims are exterminated.[...]Now the Hindus of the villages should join the Hindus of the cities and complete the work of annihilation of Muslims.[41]

This obsessive desire to eradicate Islam from India also explains the many attacks against Muslim places of worship. Though it is widely thought that the official figures regarding the casualties of the Gujarat riots and these destructions have been underestimated, they provide some valuable indications: between 27 February and 1 April, the official number of Muslim victims was 536 and Hindus, 95; the number of Muslim wounded was 1,143, Hindus, 529. (These figures are considerably lower than those published by *Muslim India*, which reports the total number killed in Gujarat as 1,071 and wounded, 1,973).[42] In fact, the total number of casualties was most certainly over 2,000 dead. As for places of Muslim religion, they were attacked at least as repeatedly as Muslim shops, an indication that these symbolic targets were also of major importance. Altogether, 527 mosques, madrasas, cemeteries and other *dargahs* were damaged or destroyed.[43] Most places of worship that were demolished were 'replaced' by a statue of Hanuman and a saffron-coloured flag.

The very fact that communal violence in Gujarat acquired such large proportions forces us to resort to explanations other than the instrumentalist one: the Hindu activists were not only trying to polarize the society according to a religious line of cleavage; nor did the rioters target the Muslims only for looting. Their actions were overdetermined by an obsessive fear of the Muslim 'Other' and an uncontrollable desire to annihilate Islam. The systematic dimension of the pogroms is an indication of the unprecedented responsiveness of society to this deep-rooted xenophobia. In a way, the pervasiveness of this feeling was evident from the incredible passivity of all actors in the public sphere, with the exception of a few NGOs and newspapers. The debate organized at the Lok Sabha shows to what extent anti-Muslim violence has become part of everyday life and how much the political class has become accustomed, or even sympathetic, to this fact. The regional parties which had joined the BJP-led ruling coalition under the condition that the BJP should moderate its Hindu nationalist rhetoric because they were sworn secularists and counted Muslims among their electoral supporters (such as the Telugu Desam Party) protested only as a matter of form. It is mainly for this reason that one can agree with Ashis Nandy's statement that 'The Gujarat riots mark the beginning of a new phase in Indian politics'.[44] The violence in Gujarat reflects the dissemination of hatred of the 'Other' that had never before reached such intensity or had ever been so widespread – extending even into the tribal areas, a place to test these assertions.

The militant Hinduization of the adivasis

It is a limited interpretation to view the riots as spreading to the tribal zones only because Hindu nationalist activists from the city exploited the *adivasis* by luring an impoverished community jealous of Muslim merchants' wealth with the mirage of looting their riches. Such an analysis disregards how the *adivasis* appropriated the riots. If, at the start, the violence came from the outside, was exported, so to speak, by city-dwelling activists, the *adivasis* devised their own version of it. This process was particularly obvious in the first tribal village in Gujarat to be affected, Tejgadh, in the district of Panchmahals. There again, the first shops were torched by outsiders, but 'once the first attack was over, other villagers joined in on their own with no further need for instigation and the looting continued', writes Ganesh Devy, who observed the riots in the field for the most part.[45] To Devy, from that point on it was clear that rioting 'was not included in the master plan of violence'. It became 'leisurely': one or two shops were torched every day. Twelve days after the outbreak of violence, one house was burned down, then another the next day, and another the day after: 'It was cold-bloodedness in slow-time. This ritual quality was a clear indication that at this end of the Gujarat riots, the theme of communalism was taking a back seat, having been taken over by the norms of tribal culture'. This process of tribal takeover was even more clearly illustrated in Panwad, a village 30 kilometres from Tejgadh where about 200 *adivasis* took part in the violence, armed with their ceremonial bows and arrows.

Although Devy is convincing when he temporizes the instrumentalization of the *adivasis*, his emphasis on the influence of visible marks of tribal culture during the violence poses a problem. Outer signs of culture, such as bows and arrows, are not enough to make the violence the expression of that culture. Actually, the *spontaneous* involvement of the *adivasis* in the rioting reflects the Hinduization of their culture under the influence of a campaign led by the RSS, VHP, BJP and especially the Vanavasi Seva Sangh (*Vanavasis*' Service Association).

This organization is one of the regional branches of the Vanavasi Kalyan Ashram created in 1952. The very name of this 'ashram' for the welfare of 'forest (*vana*) dwellers' translates both the vision that Hindu nationalists have of tribals and the strategy they have developed towards them. Hindu nationalists refer to tribals as 'those who live in the forest' (*vanavasis*) rather than 'those who were there first' (*adivasis*), simply because to them, 'first' among the people of India can only be Hindus. But the *vanavasis* are nevertheless a target group, for the Hindu nationalists are determined to compete within this milieu against Muslim and Christian missionaries.

They first sought to pit tribals against Christians to counter the latter's evangelizing efforts among these animist tribes, which had met with a degree of success since the nineteenth century: the conversion rate of tribals to Christianity was particularly high in the Chhattisgarh tribal belt where the RSS set up the Vanavasi Kalyan Ashram (VKA) in 1952. Its strategy of gaining access to the tribes was simply to imitate the Christian missionaries' approach, which owed its popularity to its social work, most commonly in the form of free schooling and access to medical care by opening dispensaries. The VKA duplicated this technique by attempting to inculcate nationalist Hindu ideology in schools it opened in Chhattisgarh and later elsewhere. The organization in fact set up branches in nearly all states in India over the years, a development confirmed by the name change to *Bharatiya* Vanavasi Kalyan Ashram in 1977.

In Gujarat, this movement was known as Vanavasi Seva Sangh (*Vanavasis*' Service Association). The name well reflects its primary vocation: social work. There, as in other places, the VSS strove to attract tribals by duplicating the missionaries' charity strategies, at the same time stigmatizing Christians all the better to Hinduize them. Their most ordinary form of Hinduization involved free distribution of statuettes of Lord Ganesh, to encourage the tribals to worship him. Another, strategy was to build temples devoted to Hanuman all over *adivasi* villages.

In the end, Devy is obliged to remark that 'the VSS and the BJP have achieved a measure of success in providing the tribals a political agenda of hatred'. So tribal culture has indeed been altered under the influence of Hindu nationalist propaganda. One must emphasize the receptivity of certain Bhils to Hindu nationalist ideas in the districts of Panchmahals and Sabarkantha, through propaganda from the RSS and its sister organizations. As a matter of fact, other tribes refer to these tribals somewhat ironically as '*Ramayana Bhils*', a name coined from the great classic in Hindu literature, the *Ramayana*.

The last communal violences are bound to accentuate this trend, not only because Muslims – from whom tribals used to borrow funds – do not trust *adivasis* as much as before, but also because these *adivasis* have realized that they could draw dividends from riots in terms of looting and exerting power.[46] For Lobo, the *adivasis* are even more attracted to Hindutva than before, and their culture has been irreversibly affected. Indeed, more than one third of the Scheduled Tribes have voted for the BJP during the Gujarat election according to the Centre for the Study of Developing Societies (CSDS) exit poll.

Conclusion

If Hindu nationalist propaganda prospers, as we believe it does, on the instrumentalization of an increasingly widespread Hindu sense of insecurity, the rise in terrorist attacks attributed to Islamic militants is in danger of rekindling Hindu activism and fuelling a literally infernal spiral of which the Muslims will ultimately be the victims.

The violence in Gujarat has already put the Muslims in this state in an unbearable situation. Since Partition no riot had yet equalled this pogrom, either in the number of victims or the savagery of the violence; no government had to this extent sided with the assailants – to the point of becoming an aggressor itself; no administration, from the bureaucracy to the police, had ever shown such open complicity with the attackers. Whom can the Muslims turn to? The media? The English language press – whether it is national or regional – demonstrated its support and criticized the abuses, but the Gujarati press continually fanned the fire. For instance, on 1 March the daily newspaper *Sandesh* published an entirely fabricated story claiming that two Hindu women in Godhra travelling on the same train as the *kar sevaks* had been attacked by Muslims, raped, mutilated, then murdered.[47] The story proved to be unfounded.

Alone and traumatized, the Muslim community became entrenched in camps forming ghettos and continued to be harassed by the police after the riots. When Nivedita Menon came to Ahmedabad from Delhi, like so many other human rights and minority rights activists, she recounted that in June

> every day the police would raid Juhapura, the Muslim ghetto, to try to round up 'suspects', they would be resisted by the residents, there would be police firing, and the papers were full of front-page photographs of 'Muslim mob marching towards Juhapura police station'. The photograph clearly showed an unarmed, peacefully marching demonstration.[48]

And Menon added: 'Every Hindu knows full well that what was perpetrated there is beyond human endurance. They have looked into the void – will there not come a moment when the void will look back?'[49]

The moment of '*Muslim backlash*' finally arrived in September 2002. On the 23rd, a makeshift bomb hidden in a bus in Ahmedabad wounded five. But the most spectacular operation took place the next day, on 24 September, in Gandhinagar, when two armed men entered the Akshardham Hindu temple, a huge complex that can accommodate up to 5,000 worshippers. With AK-56s they shot at everything that moved and launched grenades, killing 28 people. They holed up in the temple until a National Security Guard commando flushed them out the next morning. Three members of the police forces were killed in the siege.

Modi immediately declared that the terrorists were from Pakistan but the fact that it was an act of vengeance was made clear by the notes found in the two men's pockets, in which they claimed, in Urdu, to belong to a group called 'Tehreek-e-Kasas' (Movement for Revenge). Addressing 'thousands of conscienceless enemies of the Muslim of India', they declared: 'We will never rest in peace if we do not take revenge for the killings of our people'.[50]

This act is indicative of the risk of escalation India may face if the Muslims are still subjected to unbearable abuse. Till now Gujarat has not been brought back to normalcy. Not only are riots still a recurring phenomenon – in Vadodara, a riot killing eight persons occurred in May 2006 after the Municipal Corporation decided to demolish a *dargah* – but in riot-hit areas of 2002, there's no *status quo ante*. Dealing with the villages which had been affected by the 2002 communal clashes, A.A. Engineer wrote recently:

> Those who have returned live in fear and total isolation. No one talks to them, no one invites them, no one even looks at them. So scorned they find it difficult to live there. Villages are small units of population and quite interdependent. In big cities one can live in such a situation but not in small villages.[51]

A ray of hope may come from the judiciary. The Gujarat government had closed down all the cases soon after the events, arguing that there was no evidence. But the Supreme Court has reopened more than 2,000 of them. The guilty men now need to be punished, otherwise Gujarat may never fully recover from this trauma.

Notes

1 See, for example, the description of Ibn Battutta dating from the fourteenth century (Ibn Battutta (1969) *Voyages d'Ibn Battuta*, Paris: Anthropos, p. 80).

2 Louis Dumont is not far from a culturalist reading of this kind when evoking 'l'hétérogénéité sociale définitive des deux communautés' (see *Homo Hierarchicus*, (1966) Paris: Gallimard, p. 382).

3 See in particular, C. Bayly (1995) 'The Pre-history of "Communalism"? Religious Conflict in India, 1700–1800', *Modern Asian Studies* 19 (2): 190–191.

4 See, for example, I. Ahmed (1984) 'Political Economy of Communalism in Contemporary India', *Economic and Political Weekly*, 2 (6): 903–906 and A.A. Engineer (1984) 'The Causes of Communal Riots in the Post-partition Period in India', in A.A. Engineer (ed.), *Communal Riots in Post-independence India*, Bombay: Sangam Books, pp. 33–41.

5 See C. Jaffrelot (1996) *The Hindu Nationalist Movement and Indian Politics*, New York: Columbia University Press.

6 Between 1970 and 2002, Gujarat experienced 443 Hindu–Muslim riots.

7 See, for more details, S. Varadarajan (ed.) (2002) *Gujarat: The Making of a Tragedy*, New Delhi: Penguin India.

8 The Hindu nationalists naturally offer a different interpretation. In 2004 I found a very revealing publication in the bookstore of the RSS headquarters in Delhi. It reads:

> On the 27 Feb. 2002, innocent, unarmed *karsevaks* including women and children were burnt alive in the S-6 compartment of Sabarmati Express. From information available so far, the whole episode was preplanned. Had the train reached there as per its scheduled time, it was planned to burn the whole train near village Chanchelav. A mob of 2000 strong men with petrol bombs, enough quantity of kerosene, can not be mustered all at once. As per the investigating agencies, it is felt that the threads of all this operation appear to be pointing towards ISI [Inter Services Intelligence – the Pakistani military intelligence service] involvement here.[...]

The mastermind behind this plan are those people of terroristic mentality who had the courage to carry out an attack on the Parliament House. Their intention was not only to burn the *karsevaks* but in a wider effect, they wanted to spread unrest in the country and to destabilize it through insurrections within the country. The army be required to be shifted from the Indo-Pak boarders and to tarnish the international image of Bharat as also to increase the inimical rift between the Hindus and Muslims. All this was a wisely planned action.

(*Godhra: Terrorism Unmasked* (2002) Ahmedabad: Vishva Samdav Kendra, p. 1.)

9 Quoted by *Communalism Combat* (March/April 2002) 8 (77–78): 12.

10 With 1,119 victims of Hindu–Muslim riots between 1950 and 1995, up to then Ahmedabad ranked just behind Bombay (1,137 dead) in this grim classification. It most likely took the lead in 2002. (See A. Varshney (2002) *Ethnic Conflict and Civic Life: Hindus and Muslims in India*, New Haven/London: Yale University Press, p. 7.)

11 He even justified the most violent doings among them with these words: 'The violence in Godhra was communal violence, the violence after that was "secular violence"'.

12 The VHP president in Gujarat in fact stated that the Muslims' shops in Ahmedabad were divided up the morning of 28 February. He added that the most active thugs in the violence were Waghri untouchables – which recalls the use of untouchables as real mercenaries during previous riots in the 1980s; the 'payoff' came in the form of looting Muslim shops (http://www.rediff.com 12 March 2002).

13 The National Human Rights Commission's interim report, interim order and final report on Gujarat are reproduced in J. Dayal (ed.) *Gujarat 2002. Untold and re-told stories of the Hindutva lal* vol. 1, Delhi, Media House, 2003 pp. 182–231.

14 See Human Rights Watch (April 2003) *India, 'We have no order to save you': State Participation and Complicity in Communal Violence in Gujarat*, 14 (3).

15 Letter of Teesta Setalvad to Election Commission of India, 26 July 2002. E-mail communication.

16 Hindu–Muslim riots for a long time remained basically an urban phenomenon in Gujarat and elsewhere: from 1950 to 1995, 80 per cent of the victims of all the rioting in Gujarat were in Ahmedabad and Vadodara (Varshney, op. cit., p. 7).

17 D. Gupta, 'The Limits of Tolerance: Prospects of Secularism in India After Gujarat', Prem Bathia Memorial Lecture, 11 August 2002.

18 B. Bhatia, 'A Step Back in Sabarkantha', *Seminar* n° 513. Available at http://www.india-seminar.com/2002/513/513%20bela%20bhatia.htm

19 These figures come from a confidential report of the National Human Rights Commission, following its March 2002 investigation in Gujarat.

20 Bhatia, op.cit.

21 Steven I. Wilkinson (Winter 2000) 'Froids calculs et foules déchaînées. Les émeutes intercommunautaires en Inde', *Critique Internationale*, (6): 132.

22 K.M. Chenoy *et al.* (April 2002) *Gujarat Carnage 2002: A Report to the Nation*, p. 19.

23 For more details, see G. Shah (2002) 'Contestation and Negociations. Hindutva Sentiments and Temporal Interests in Gujarat Elections', *Economic and Political Weekly*, 30 Nov.: 4838–4843.

24 Several months after the paroxysm of late February to early March, skirmishes were still claiming victims: on 21 April, the death of a policeman in Ahmedabad led to acts of vengeance – six Muslims were shot down by men in uniform. On 20 July, the day after the assembly was dissolved, two people were killed and

14 others wounded by stone-throwing and police gunfire, again in Ahmedabad. On 13 August, still in Ahmedabad, sporadic clashes wounded three. On 17 September, violence again broke out in Borsad (a small town in Anand district) after a Muslim motorcyclist accidentally hit a young Hindu. Shops owned by Muslims were torched in retaliation. The riot left one dead and 13 wounded. The town had to be put under curfew. On 29 September, a makeshift bomb exploded, wounding one person in Godhra. On 2 October, the festivities organized to celebrate Gandhi's birthday (Gandhi Jayanti) gave rise to violence in Bhavnagar (where the police had to open fire to disperse the attackers), Vadodara and Piplod, where police forces had to use teargas. On 6 October, the police again had to intervene, leaving two wounded, after Hindu–Muslim clashes. On 15 October, a makeshift bomb exploded in a bus in Godhra, wounding six. The following day another bomb went off in a bus in Lunawada (Panchmahals district), wounding two people.

25 D. Desai (2002) 'That Missing Healing Touch', *Outlook*, 10 Oct.
26 S. Kumar (January 2003) 'Gujarat Assembly Elections 2002. Analysing the Verdict', *Economic and Political Weekly*, 25: 275.
27 *India Today*, 16 December 2002, p. 27.
28 *Communalism Combat*, op. cit., p. 119.
29 *India Today*, 26 August 2002, p. 33.
30 Ibid.: 42.
31 For more details, see C. Jaffrelot (1996) *The Hindu Nationalist Movement and Indian Politics, 1920s to the 1990s*, New York, Columbia University Press.
32 Quoted in *Communalism Combat*, op. cit., p. 136.
33 *Communalism Combat*, op. cit., p. 137.
34 *Communalism Combat*, op. cit., p. 77–78
35 *Asian Age* (Delhi edition), 2 April 2002.
36 C. Jaffrelot, *The Hindu Nationalist Movement*, op. cit.
37 N. Datta (2002) 'On the Anti-Muslim Ethos of Hindu Women in Gujarat', *Muslim India*, 237 (Sept.): 408.
38 T. Sarkar (2002) 'Semiotics of Terror. Muslim-Children and Women in Hindu Rashtra', *Economic and Political Weekly*, (13 July): 2872–2876.
39 Ibid.
40 K. Balagopal (2002) 'Reflections on "Gujarat Pradesh" of "Hindu Rashtra"', *Economic and Political Weekly*, (1 June): 2119.
41 Ibid.: 135.
42 *Muslim India* (2002) no. 235, July, p. 305.
43 Ibid.: 305.
44 A. Nandy (2002) 'Obituary of a Culture', *Seminar*, no. 513. Available online at http://www.india-seminar.com/2002/513
45 G. Devy, 'Tribal Voice and Violence', *Seminar*, no. 513. Available online at http://www.india-seminar.com/2002/513
46 N. Lobo (2002) 'Adivasis, Hindutva and Post-Godhra Riots in Gujarat', *Economic and Political Weekly*, (30 Nov.): 4848.
47 Chenoy *et al.*, *Gujarat Carnage 2002*, op. cit., p. 5.
48 N. Menon, 'Surviving Gujarat', e-mail communication.
49 Ibid.
50 D. Desai (2002) 'Temple Terror', *Outlook*, 7 Oct.
51 A.A. Engineer (2006) 'They Hate Us, We Fear Them: The Situation in Gujarat', csss@vsnl.com (accessed 2 March 2006).

Part 3

Theory – framing the religion and violence debate

9 A categorical difference

Communal identity in British epistemologies

Peter Gottschalk

Bifurcated scholarship

Until recently, Anglophone scholarship on South Asian cultures suffered from a stark epistemological apartheid. Historians specialized in the ancient (Hindu) period, medieval (Muslim) era, or modern (British and post-independence) time. Sociologists and anthropologists researching in the Subcontinent often chose between Hindu or Muslim groups of communities. Meanwhile, historians of religions steered their graduate students to specialize in a single tradition: Hinduism, Islam, Buddhism, Sikhism, etc. Each of these came with prerequisite languages and a prescribed literature: Sanskrit and a vernacular language for Hinduism; Arabic, Persian, and probably Urdu for Islam.[1] Through a Darwinian process of natural selection by the academic environment, job candidates whose linguistic training differed from these expectations often found their applications shelved by department search committees.

Not surprisingly, these institutional and personal bifurcations of South Asia created a sense of different cultural worlds defined by mutually exclusive religious traditions. Although the interaction of different 'communities' at inter-religious sites (e.g. Sufi tombs) and as evidenced in certain literature (e.g. Kabir's poetry) drew some attention, most scholars considered these to be unusual clefts in the Himalayan barrier mountains that defined each mutually exclusive and often hostile 'tradition'. At times, hostility toward the other tradition could be discerned in the scholar's voice itself, motivated as it often was by a sympathetic aesthetical attraction to or personal association with Hinduism or Islam. The violent birth of independent Pakistan and India seemed to inevitably give catastrophic definition to this divide even as it partitioned what until then had been largely composite communities of Punjab and Bengal.

Happily, a rising surge of scholarship has challenged this image and worked to demonstrate not only the many places of shared culture, practice and belief but also the fallacy of relying so heavily on a singularly religious definition of South Asian societies. The publication of David Gilmartin and Bruce Lawrence's edited volume *Beyond Turk and Hindu* in 2000[2] signalled the gathering effort of more than a dozen scholars to mutually challenge this long-enduring paradigm. This effort was echoed soon thereafter in *Surprising Bedfellows*, edited by Sushil Mittal.[3]

Despite this and other hopeful signs, much of the Anglophone scholarship on South Asia – written by both indigenous and foreign authors – struggles to craft new paradigms that sidestep the pitfalls of the old ones even as the political forces of religious exclusion, despite occasional setbacks, continue to strengthen. Success, however, it can be argued, relies on an understanding of the historical origins of the earlier paradigm of a bifurcated South Asia and its institutional roots.

The origins of religious enmity have been fiercely debated in scholarship. However, much of this literature has either accepted or failed to challenge the central epistemological assumption regarding South Asian cultures that has ruled many of the ways of understanding South Asians. Because of the dominance of the classification paradigms of the natural sciences, South Asian societies have historically been engaged using but one set of mutually exclusive, clearly defined categories that have ignored the elastic, indefinite, multi-dimensional and contextually shifting identities assumed by the peoples of the Subcontinent. Because of the globalization of Western epistemologies, these classification systems have been replicated and seemingly confirmed in the other corners of empire.

If violence involves the forceful injury of one by another, then the impact of these western classification systems, embedded in hegemonic systems of knowledge and impelled by the inertia of imperialism, served as an epistemological violence that would, over time, help amplify pre-existing possibilities for social tension into unprecedented paroxysms of religious violence.

Between continuities and discontinuities

News reporting, works of fiction, visual imagery and scholarship have all been used in attempts to depict the horrors of communalist violence. Besides their unfortunate topic, they also usually share an awareness of their implicit failure to communicate not only the gruesome violence too often inflicted but also the depths of fear generated, the lifelong traumas instilled, the enduring insecurities engendered. The terror-filled tragedies of Punjab in 1947, Delhi in 1984, Bhagalpur in 1989 and Gujarat in 2002, have impelled much scholarship as well. The magnitude of these tragedies promotes attention, while simultaneously reinforcing prevalent perceptions of India as an inherently religious and, thus, deeply divided nation balancing on the edge of chaos.

Scholarship on communalism, as many of the contributions in this volume demonstrate, has attempted to approach this seemingly intractable phenomenon from a number of directions, reflecting the complex dynamics at work. Most prominently perhaps, many researchers have gravitated to one of two sides regarding communalism's origins, one side finding it in pre-modern conditions and the other in the British imperial experience. In many respects, this debate has taken on many of the hues of various post-colonial intellectual debates, establishing two sides, both with deep investments beyond the immediate argument.

Gyanendra Pandey's seminal *Construction of Communalism in Colonial North India* (1990) laid out many of the foundational arguments for its origins in British rule. At its heart, Pandey's book considers the narrative of a religiously divided people and their propensity to communal violence as a construction of British administrators intending to legitimate their rule. Fundamental in Pandey's work, and the works of similarly minded authors, is not only a suspicion of the modes and products of knowledge deployed by Europeans during their imperial projects, but also an awareness of their persuasive power among South Asians which has continued to be felt decades after the decline of the colonial state. At times, this scholarship attempts to acquit South Asian cultures of the allegations used by Europeans to justify their paternalistic domination of a people 'not yet ready' for self-determination by impeaching the motivations for this judgement.

It would be easy to portray those who defy this perspective, who find continuities in communal relations from the pre-British to British period of rule, as furthering the imperial portrayal of an inherently divided people in need of Western secular models to accomplish national unity. Furthermore, some critics argue that claims for 'continuities' stem from a static and essentialist view of South Asian cultures. However useful these cautions, much scholarship regarding religious identities preceding the arrival of the British demonstrates more sophistication than these critics allow. The best of this work explores the variable importance of religious identity in the shifting contexts of social life. Cynthia Talbot, for instance, has argued convincingly that middle-period Kakatiya state records portrayed neighbouring states in religious terms only in specific political contexts while in other situations other identifications were used to depict those states.[4] Phillip Wagoner, meanwhile, has demonstrated through two examples how elites in pre-British Deccan lived in a fluid environment fashioned according to religious ideologies demanding conformity to protocol while accepting religious diversity.[5]

Significantly, these works neither deny the roles of religion in cultures nor essentialize all aspects of these cultures as religious. As importantly, many of these scholars recognize the multiple identities at work. That is to say, they understand that individuals associate with diverse communities and, through these, negotiate the various social contexts in their everyday lives. However more sophisticated a picture these approaches offer, they do not disclaim the existence of religiously motivated (or, at times, religiously defined) violence before the British arrival.

This essay takes a position between continuity and discontinuity – perennial communalism and British constructions – by arguing that, although some continuities of identity categories existed, the completeness of the overall matrix of interrelated epistemologies employed by the British provided both the *context* of knowing and the categories that shaped the *content* of knowing. This irrevocably refashioned many indigenous ways of understanding South Asian populations and religions. Many examples of literature, inscriptions, histories and other materials demonstrate the formal and informal social classification schemas operative in middle-period South Asia. What differentiated the British systems in India from their predecessors was the establishment of a universal set of social categories that became instrumental in government rule and South Asian self-understandings throughout the Subcontinent and the primacy of religious identity as the first order of classification in multiple epistemologies. That is what I believe many studies have overlooked, although many of the classifications that the British deployed derived from indigenous categories, the *model* of classification they used, its derivation from the natural sciences, and its affirmation through a matrix of globalized epistemologies was unique and uniquely transformative.

Issues of continuity and discontinuity, inflected with similar meta-concerns as the debate on the origins of communalism, have also troubled scholarship on systems of knowledge in South Asia. Scholars such as Arjun Appadurai,[6] C.A. Bayly[7] and Norbert Peabody[8] argue for a continuity of information-gathering strategies in contrast with the work of Ronald Inden[9] and Nicolas Dirks[10] who emphasize discontinuity.[11] Although the persistence and adaptation of a range of indigenous South Asian epistemologies cannot be overlooked, neither can the profound and global impact of Western ways of knowing that established a universal standard for many fields of scientific research, nationalist representation and information exchange. Although these ways of knowing have had their own arc of development – and one cannot overlook the influence in that development of their involvement in various European imperial projects – they represent not only a legacy of the previous patterns of Western political domination but an expression of contemporary Western hegemony.

Categories of scientific difference

During the nineteenth century in particular, a range of epistemologies coalesced into academic disciplines that combined together to comprise what Chris Bayly has termed a matrix of knowledge.[12] The individual epistemologies of this matrix developed to mutually confirm the results of and reinforce the authority of one another while maintaining control over specific subjects. The astounding breadth of this matrix becomes apparent as one considers the overwhelming panoply of systems of knowing deployed by the imperial British in their Indian territories alone – topography, botany, demography, ethnology, sociology, archaeology and historiography (to name but some) – and the vast assortment of materials produced to communicate the knowledge they produced such as gazetteers, maps, histories, drawings, census reports, zoological specimens, museums and botanical gardens.

Each of these disciplines generated a specific classification scheme to order the vast assortment of data it collected. And each turned first to the natural sciences for examples of classificatory method. After all, the mind-staggering variety of new plants and animals that European voyages of discovery, commerce and conquest brought to Europe's attention required some type of sorting out to be managed and analysed. In fact, all forms of knowledge rely on some sort of classification. (Take a look around any room and bring to mind the different categories of objects associated with the mundane classification 'furniture'.)

So, for instance, Francis Buchanan in his early nineteenth-century report on Indian animals based on what he found in the Barrackpur menagerie, which he managed in 1803–1805,[13] begins the description of each animal with its Linnaean designation. Carl Linnaeus (1707–1778) established the system of naming animals according to their classification as both species and families. An individual animal came to be associated with a species if it shared a unique and essential quality that defined that species. The same held true for the membership of a species to a genus, a genus to an order, and so on. Of course, the actual classifications Buchanan relied upon to describe animals differed from those he used to describe the land, habitations and people during his walking surveys of Bengal and Bihar (1807–1814). However, the classificatory paradigm would remain the same. This was true even in the analysis of foreign cultures that offered taxonomic problems not encountered among the objects of other studies.

In South Asia as in many other parts of the world, the British (like other imperial Europeans) not only encountered plants and animals on their voyages that appeared new to them, but cultures too. The previously dominant biblical paradigm of a world divided between the three sons of Noah dispersed, respectively, to the three known continents (Europe, Asia and Africa), could not accommodate the 'new' peoples of the 'discovered' continents of Australia and the Americas. Earlier observations lacked the epistemological discipline and shared categories to help with the interpretation of the rapidly accumulating data. As folklorist William Crooke lamented in 1873, 'My difficulty has arisen not so much from deficiency of material, as in the selection and arrangement of the mass of information, which lies scattered through a considerable literature, much of which is fugitive'.[14] He, like many of his contemporaries, looked to scientific classificatory schemes for a model of his own.

Much would change between the time of Buchanan's first-hand observations and Crooke's gleaning of others' recorded observations for the sake of his studies of folklore and religion. Reflecting the earliest efforts of the British to know their conquered territories, the East India Company (EIC) dispatched their servant Buchanan (and his contemporary Colin Mackenzie) to 'survey' what they had brought under their control at the end of the eighteenth and beginning of the nineteenth centuries. The Directors of the EIC instructed Buchanan that 'Your inquiries should be particularly directed to the following subjects', which included topography, the condition of the inhabitants, religion, natural productions, fisheries, antiquities, domestic animals, and the fine and common arts.[15] No small task. By the end of the nineteenth century, no one person would be entrusted with such a multitude of topics since increasingly specialized disciplines developed that focused on ever narrower topics while establishing more highly esoteric classification systems. Despite this diversity, the various classificatory schemas drew on the Linnaean classification paradigm as an ideal model. Overall, as the disciplines developed, they did so in mutual awareness of one another. Practitioners of newer fields of investigation drew on the conclusions of more firmly established disciplines to substantiate their work while, at the same time, attempting to demonstrate their credentials as consistent with the scientific method.

Much of the responsibility for the changes that occurred between the eras of Buchanan and Crooke lay with the rebellion of 1857. The great misperception of the submissiveness of the sepoys and the failure of intelligence regarding the population made apparent the general lack of information about Indians among the British. They, therefore, launched multiple new efforts of knowing South Asians in order to better achieve the political control that British economic interests demanded. New institutions such as the Census of India, the Archaeological Survey of India and the Linguistic Survey of India took their places alongside previously existing projects such as the Trigonometrical Survey of India. Meanwhile, disciplines borrowed the models of representation offered by other fields in their efforts to communicate their findings. So, for example, historians relied on the growing body of archaeological relics to supplement documentary evidence even as demographers represented their findings on maps provided by surveyors. Specialized studies like Crooke's replaced the generalist observations of Buchanan and Mackenzie's surveys and each relied on its own Linnaean-influenced system of classifying its data. An understanding of the dynamics of classification in general is necessary in order to understand the significant qualities of this particular system.

Taxonomist Ramkrishna Mukherjee has described three operations that categorizing systems perform. First, they place a person, idea, or object into a class of other people, ideas, or objects that share at least one trait. Second, they distinguish variations of that trait and group individuals accordingly. And, finally, the system arranges the classes relative to one another.[16] In the case of Linneaus' biological taxonomy, all individual living beings represent an enormous field of entities that are, therefore, sorted into genus (e.g. *Felis*) according to a common trait or set of traits (e.g. cat characteristics). Because variations exist among the members of the genus, another classification level, species, sorts members according to those characteristics, so that orange cats with black stripes are given a unique label, *Felis tigris*, and distinguished in name from those not sharing this trait. The system, therefore, differentiates tigers from lions, lynxes and housecats while placing them into relation with one another as members of the genus *Felis*. Simultaneously, the genus label relates them more distantly to ground sloths as cohabiters of the category *animals* that distinguishes them from plants and bacteria.

Central to the Western scientific model of classification is the understanding that an individual belongs to one category only. Ambiguity should not exist. This is why, for example, Buchanan wrestled over the classification of the cheetah. He wrote

> The name Cheeta, which signifies spotted, is also commonly given to the Leopard and is indeed still more usually applied to the spotted deer or axis. It cannot therefore be considered as a proper specific name, although by the Europeans and Musulmans of India it has been considered as such.

> Kendua, so far as I can learn, is a proper specific name and I therefore shall employ it to distinguish this animal; for the name hunting Leopard also is improper, as at least two other species of the Feline genus are employed in this amusement.[17]

He discards 'hunting Leopard' as an adequate category because it contains more than one species.

Meanwhile, this example demonstrates another critical component of scientific classification: a unique characteristic inherent in all members of the class that *essentially* defines that class. Buchanan, therefore, disregards the name 'Cheeta' for a class of felines since its general association with 'spotted' applies to non-feline animals too. Part of the reason he rejects the label 'hunting Leopard' is that Indians use more than one species in their hunts, and so the name does not identify a characteristic unique to that one genus. He requires a name that exactly refers to a spotted feline and so prefers the Bengali name 'Kendua Bagh' because of its specific identification.[18]

Through these deliberations, Buchanan demonstrates his dedication to the classificatory ideals Mukherjee details. (1) He places leopards and Kendua in the same genus of *Felis,* separating them from deer and other mammals. (2) He distinguishes variations of the identifying traits of felines, and groups spotted ones into the species Kendua. (3) By arranging certain species as sub-categories of a specific genus, Buchanan implicitly establishes a closer relationship among these species than to those belonging to another genus. In Buchanan's day, this arrangement was based on shared physiological qualities, while post-Darwinian biologists base their classifications on evolutionary derivation. However, the British reliance on the scientific system of classification had its most profound impact not in the study of native animals but in the investigation of Indian societies.

Table 9.1

order	Mammalia		
genus	Felis		Deer
species	Kendua	Leopard	Spotted deer

Religion as *the* categorical difference

Although the disciplines emerging in the nineteenth century may have all borrowed to one degree or another from the model of scientific classification, it was bound to have a more significant effect in social sciences. The reason is obvious: whereas the Kendua's self-perception and understanding of other animals remained unaffected by its designation as *Felis kendua* by British authorities, Indians had their own self-identifications and social associations that were influenced and interrupted by British classifications. This was particularly true because of the British proclivity to collapse most social categories onto a single plane of identity: religion. Just as British scientists sought to fit all creatures onto a single taxonomy and establish the precise relationship of each group (defined by essential characteristics) to one another, so specialists in Indian societies attempted to determine the exact place of social relationship in order to clarify the complex social interactions of everyday life. Because the imperial government controlled the ruling bureaucracy, determined privileges for certain groups and influenced the Indian perceptions of South Asian cultures, the importance of their taxonomy was not inconsequential. The British fixation on religion also said as much if not more about them as about those they hoped to categorize.

As some scholars have argued, no similar concept to the British notion of religion existed in South Asia before their arrival. Terms like *dharm* and *din* simply did not carry the same connotations as *religion*. Talal Asad has rightly explained that this was the case because the European concept of religion is partly defined by the counter-notion of the secular. That is to say, religion could be conceived as a distinct realm of ideation and behaviour only with the positing of a non-religious realm. Prior to the secularization (originally meaning the appropriation by the state) of church lands in the midst of the Protestant Reformation, Europeans did not use any equivalent term to today's 'religion' since there existed no separate social or political milieu that was strictly 'non-religious'. This is not to claim that everything was religious in the contemporary sense but only that there was no need to declare certain spaces or communities as *not* religious.[19]

This situation – and the definition of 'secular' – changed over the course of the Protestant Reformation and the subsequent 'wars of religion'. Just at the time that rationalism took intellectual root in Europe, Europe bled from brutal conflicts that were legitimated by religious claims and infused with religious fervour but more often than not motivated by political and economic considerations. These conditions concatenated to create both the political model of a secular state distinct from religious institutions and a secular public sphere ideally dominated by rational thought rather than religious passion.

This model became particularly integral to the developing notion of nationalism in which the state no longer commanded loyalty through the person of the divinely ordained king or queen but through its claim to represent all citizens. Reflective of the variable understandings and expressions of secularism, the British government still allied with a state church (something the constitutions of the USA and India would forbid).[20] Moreover, a teleology came to be integrated into this political vision that made the move from monarchism to nationalism a matter of progress. Of course, a transition was still underway among the British as the monarchy at home maintained a place of political prominence and Queen Victoria would be proclaimed Empress of India in 1877. Nevertheless, great efforts were made to promote the notion of a shared identity among a 'British' citizenry that was supposedly reflected by the government (a proposition not always accepted by many among the Scots, Welsh and, particularly, the Irish).

The British who arrived in South Asia often unfavourably depicted the states and societies there as hopelessly religious and, therefore, vulnerable to the same superstitions, priestly subterfuge, intellectual oppression, religious intolerance and political tyranny that they imagined they had successfully escaped. They operated under an implicit categorical system that defined different types of societies and valued them relative to one another according to the success each had demonstrated in achieving some measure of modernity. So, for instance, the British census did not include a question regarding religion anywhere in the British Isles (except in Catholic-majority Ireland) because it was considered an intrusion on the freedom of religious conscience for the state to make this query. Yet the question was central to most of the demographic categories in all censuses in India after the census of the northwest provinces of Bengal in 1853. A practice that seemed natural in India appeared egregious at home because of assumptions about the historical stage of each society.

It is of no small consequence that, in juxtaposition to these secularist perspectives, many Britons working in South Asia operated under a definitively Christian paradigm, analysed the indigenous people accordingly and understood the British government as a Christian one. Biblical categories commonly informed this paradigm with humanity divided into idolaters, Jews and Christians. Some devout Christians valued Muslims above Hindus, if for no other reason than because Muslims believed (rightly, in their eyes) in one God and avoided the idolatry of Hindus. However, their rejection of Jesus as the Son of God necessarily relegated them to a status below that of Christians. In this vein, R.G. Hobbes, former soldier and servant of the government of Agra, wrote hopefully in his 1852 manuscript for a later published travelogue:

> Heathenism is dying, and few Pagodas will now be erected, but we trust the day will ere long arrive when Christian Churches, beautiful, solemn, and magnificent, shall rise amid the crumbling ruins of mosques and idol-temples; and when the Dwelling-House, if it have not the strength and dignity, shall at least be neat and commodious.[21]

Many missionaries would alter the valuation, placing Hindus above Muslims because, for all their professed monotheism and regard for Jesus (as a prophet), Muslims proved notoriously difficult to proselytize. Thus, on the spectrum of salvation, Muslims negated their monotheistic advantage by increasing the distance between themselves and the Truth through their intransigence.

Table 9.2

	Societies	
Indian		*British*
(+)		Secular
(–) Hindu	Muslim	

Table 9.3

Religions		
Indian		*British*
(+)		Christianity
	(monotheistic) Islam	
(–) (heathen) Hinduism		

Of course, many South Asians resisted these conclusions, although in their effort to do so they often relied on the same teleological and taxonomic framework. Christian missionary valuation of these categories according to their place on a timeline especially elicited different defences from different groups. Muslims, following much older Islamic traditions of comparative religion, understood themselves as the most advanced because their revelation occurred the most recently and as a self-conscious correction of revelations now hopelessly flawed because their receiving communities had imperfectly maintained them. Some Hindus responded by revaluing their uncontested primaeval status into a positive since theirs was the *adi* ('original') religion, if not revelation.

Whether they relied on a secularist or Christian paradigm, most Britons who depicted South Asians did so with firm reliance on religious categories of difference. Both paradigms also fostered the image of a social world defined by inherent tension and potential violence. Medieval European competition with Mediterranean Muslims still informed the popular Christian image of Muslims as fanatically violent and intolerant. James Tod, amateur historian and political agent to the Western Rajput states, described the 'eight centuries of galling subjection by [Muslim] conquerors' whom he characterized as 'barbarous, bigoted, and exasperated foes'.[22] Meanwhile, secularists considered both the religious nature of native rule and the presumably constant conflict between Hindu and Muslim princes as leading to inevitable warfare. Many Britons made events like Mahmud Ghaznavid's sacking of the Somnath Temple emblematic of all Hindu–Muslim political relations. But such conclusions were over-generalized. Even the Mughal emperor Aurangzeb, the poster child of Muslim chauvinism with his re-application of the *jizya* tax on Hindus and supposed mass destruction of temples, has been found to have continued a tradition of patronizing various temples even as he engaged in another Indic tradition of demolishing those associated with the political legitimation of his vanquished foes.[23] This is not to say that middle-period Muslims may not have understood themselves as different from those they described as Hindus, as the occasional application of the *jizya* demonstrates. However, there appears little evidence of a pervasive and persistent self-exclusion from all interrelations, let alone the notion of imminent and inevitable conflict between two mutually antagonistic 'communities', found among many Muslims and Hindus today.

The British use of the Linnaean classificatory paradigm to order their understanding of people fossilized these perceptions of both religion and religions in South Asia. As previous scholarship has demonstrated, the primacy of religious identification and universal surveys of the populations required all individuals to declare their 'religion' according to British-established categories.[24] Or, in the terms of this essay, according to *one* category. As Benedict Anderson explains: 'The fiction of the census is that everyone is in it and that everyone has one – and only one – extremely clear place. No fractions'.[25] Just as the feline cheetah had no choice but to fit into the category *Felis kendua* and no other, so Indian individuals had the multiple dimensions of their identities flattened and the multiple interactions overlooked.

However, it must not be overlooked that some British officials did recognize and describe spaces and activities shared by Hindus and Muslims. T.C. Hodson, culling census records for the first three decades of the twentieth century, noted a number of these occasions. For example, the report for the Indian census in 1931 noted that: 'Bengal affords a number of instances of border line sects such as that of the Bhagwania or Satyadharma community, recruited both from Hindu and Muslims, though even within the sect there is no intermarriage' and 'The Nayitas of Malwa share in equal degree the Muslim and Hindu religious beliefs. Worshipping Ganesh as well as Allah, using Hindu names and dress and observing Hindu festivals'.[26] Note, however, that these conflicting examples of Muslims acting and believing according to 'Hinduism' (a term unknown before the nineteenth century) and *vice versa* fail to upset the categories of Hindu and Muslim. These groups remain stranded on some borderline that appears to be defined more by the investigator than the community.[27] This is why these observations tended to be discussed as mere aberrations from a norm defined by strict difference instead of examples that might challenge the reigning categorical presumptions.

Meanwhile, the policies and infrastructure of the British government altered the societies they hoped to stabilize. British administrators disrupted earlier patterns of political patronage for religious sites that were not restricted to those places in accord with the court's religious affiliation. So, for instance, as Mridu Rai has demonstrated, British officials convinced their Sikh Dogra allies to refashion their self-image according to a strictly religious identity and, as a result, to curtail their patronage of Sufi and other shrines that previously had promoted a shared regional identity.[28] Meanwhile, the development of educational institutions throughout the Subcontinent inculcated both the paradigm of Western science and social classifications of Indian populations at the same time that the emerging mass printing market more widely disseminated these views through an increasingly literate population. Finally, the evolution of representational politics led to the reinforcement of these identities through efforts at mass mobilization that aimed at the largest groups described by demographic studies: Hindus and Muslims.[29]

It would be an overstatement to presume that all Indians envision their diverse social contexts according to British classification systems. Many undoubtedly live their everyday lives without resort to anything resembling the highly structured and overwhelmingly rigid taxonomies introduced by the British. Indeed, as Roy Wagner has said:

> although many of us eat apples, oranges, pears and grapes, it may well only be a relatively small group of us who wish to develop and use the higher order, analytical category 'fruit' as a means for organizing all these various foods under one classification.[30]

Indeed, if any of us reflects on the variable of everyday social interactions in which we commonly engage, can we really explain each and every category that plays its part as we interact with friends, family, lovers, enemies, acquaintances, fellow baseball fans, commercial competitors, etc.?

In sum, then, the British did not construct *ex nihilio* the categories of *Hindu* and *Muslim*. Nor was it simply their application of them in policy and study that fostered communalism. Rather, it was both the impact of their official policies and their influence on indigenous expectations regarding the dynamic of those identities – the totality of the religious nature of social categories and their antagonistic mutual exclusion of one another – that has had such an enduring effect not only on social relations in the Subcontinent but also on scholarship from and about there.

An example from current scholarship outlines both the step-by-step dynamics of exclusivist classification among violent communalists and demonstrates the danger for scholars investigating communalism of capitulating to communalist logic by allowing religious categories to eclipse other social categories that may be operative in an individual's life.[31] Psychoanalyist Sudhir Kakar, summing up his interviews with participants and victims of communalist violence in Hyderabad, explains that:

> For the outbreak of violence, the communal identity has to swamp personal identity in a large number of people, reviving the feelings of love connected with early identifications with one's own group members and the hate toward the out-group whose members are homogenized, depersonalized and increasingly dehumanized.[32]

This passage offers a key insight into the metamorphosis possible in the qualities of a category. Homogenization requires erasure of difference among members of the category through uniformity to a certain essential characteristic or characteristics. This suggests that, before the activation of their hate, communalists recognize both differences among members of the out-group and possibly attributes they share with some of them. However, communal hatred erases the possibility of commonality by redefining all members of the out-group according to essential characteristics (homogenized). When the possibility of variance from this stereotype vanishes, the communalist can act against any member of that social category because they are no different (i.e., no less guilty) than any other (depersonalized). The communalist reaches the ultimate extreme when all possibility of sharing common human qualities is lost ('You dog!' 'You scum!') which, of course, frees them of all constraint ('dehumanized').

But Kakar falls into a trap when he refers to the group of 'one's own group members' in the singular. This suggests, as do other passages in the book, that the individual balances her or his personal identity with a singular group identity that is defined by their religious community. Furthermore, Kakar appears to echo the secularist suspicion of religion: the religious group constantly threatens to submerge the individual, erasing their individuality and subsuming them to its latent violence. In so doing, the author reflects the British expectation (so foreign to many middle-period South Asians) that individuals belong to one social category alone, that that category is essentially religious and strictly defined and that it inherently exists in tension with other religious social categories. Undoubtedly Kakar accurately describes the process by which the communalist dehumanizes the other while focusing more intently on the in-group.[33] However, he ignores what this refocusing is likely to now omit from the communalist's vision: the possibility of a member of the out-group belonging to one of the multiple social groups to which most individuals belong: the *muhalla*,-*jati*, village and nation, not to mention religious organizations, devotional groups, sports teams and other communities. In order for affiliation, association and even empathy to be lost, there must have been some with which to begin.

Most of today's Anglophone scholarship echoes Kakar's secularist assumptions. Little attention has been directed to either the religious influences or secularist premises about religion in imperial British epistemologies because so much of the present work remains unreflective about its implicit appropriation of this heritage (the work of Richard King stands among the few exceptions). This perhaps helps explain the prevalence of popular apprehension in the West about a coming or current 'clash of civilizations' most notably between 'secular' nations (like the USA) and 'religious movements' (like the Iranian revolution). The remarkable success of the global European empires in ordering the peoples under their control according to paradigms fitting their imperial ambitions can be measured by the near universality of the Gregorian calendar, Western medicine and European science. No doubt many non-European systems continue to operate, but most of these do so in competition with the hegemonic epistemologies that, among many changes, successfully colonized indigenous epistemologies with such concepts as *religion* and the natural science-based classificatory systems that they inherently include. In Japan, Korea and China, as Don Baker has shown, European political pressure and Christian missionaries not only established the category of religion but also created conditions in which Shintoism and various 'new religions' became established as religions.[34]

Meanwhile in South Asia, *Hinduism* would evolve as a word (and as a recognized religion) for the first time in the nineteenth century while the millennia-old term *dharma* would be reconceptualized once more so that it could offer an indigenous equivalent to the English *religion*. Adapting to the new conditions that imagined a public sphere without religion, South Asians created a new term to describe a supposedly ancient reality and adapted a familiar term to fit an increasingly implicit category. The fact that so many South Asians made claims for the antiquity of *Hinduism* when the name was coined only recently reflects both the persuasiveness and significance of British epistemologies. The fact that many scholars will identify ***dharma*** as a Hindu word despite its common use by Muslims in parts of India demonstrates the depth of the classificatory schism that scholarship has too often reinforced.

Notes

1 See King's useful reflections on this theme in his 1999: 64–72.
2 Gilmartin and Lawrence 2000.
3 Mittal 2003.
4 Talbot 2000: 295–96.
5 Wagoner 2003.
6 Appadurai 1993.
7 Bayly 1996
8 Peabody 2001.
9 Inden 1990.
10 Dirks 2001.
11 For an insightful comparison of Cohn and Bayly's perspectives, see Pinch 1999.
12 Bayly 1996: 22.
13 Kaye 1937: 580.
14 Crooke 1873: vi.
15 Buchanan 1934: i–iv.
16 Mukherjee 1993: 7.
17 Hamilton n.d.
18 Buchanan made a point of relying on local names when a pre-existing English or Latin term did not exist.
19 Asad 1993.
20 van der Veer 2001: 16.
21 Hobbes 1852.
22 Tod 1829: xiv.
23 Eaton 2000.
24 Cohn 1996.
25 Anderson 1991: 166.
26 Hodson 1937: 82.
27 Shail Mayaram investigates this ambiguity in outsiders' classification of one particular community, the Meo, in her 1997 monograph.
28 Rai 2004: 66–79.
29 Appadurai 1996: 130–133.
30 As quoted in McCutcheon 2001: 83
31 Chandra 1984: 12.
32 Kakar 1996: 192.
33 Kakar 1996: 46.
34 Baker 1997.

Bibliography

Anderson, B. (1991) *Imagined Communities: Reflections on the Origin and Spread of Nationalism*, New York: Verso.

Appadurai, A. (1993) 'Number in the Colonial Imagination', in *Postcolonial Predicament: Perspectives on South Asia*, Carol Breckinridge and Peter van der Veer (eds), Philadelphia: University of Philadelphia Press.

——(1996) *Modernity at Large: Cultural Dimensions of Globalization*, Minneapolis: University of Minnesota Press.

Asad, T. (1993) 'The Construction of Religion as an Anthropological Category', in *Genealogies of Religion: Discipline and Reasons of Power in Christianity and Islam*, Baltimore: John Hopkins University Press.

Baker, D. (1997) 'World Religions and Nation States: Competing Claims in East Asia', in *Transnational Religion and Fading States*, Susanne Hoeber Rudolph and James Piscatori (eds), Boulder: Westview Press, pp. 144–172.

Bayly, C.A. (1996) *Empire and Information: Intelligence Gathering and Social Communication in India, 1780–1870*, Cambridge: Cambridge University Press.

Buchanan, F. (1934) *An Account of the Districts of Bihar and Patna in 1811–1812*, Patna: Usha.

Chandra, B. (1984) *Communalism in Modern India*, New Delhi: Vikas.

Cohn, B. (1996) *Colonialism and its Forms of Knowledge: The British in India*, Princeton: Princeton University Press.

Crooke, W. (1873) *The Popular Religion and Folklore of Northern India*, Vol. 1, New Delhi: Munshiram Manoharlal.

Dirks, N. (2001) *Castes of Mind: Colonialism and the Making of Modern India*, Princeton: Princeton University Press.

Eaton, R. (2000) 'Temple Desecration and Indo-Muslim States', in *Beyond Turk and Hindu: Rethinking Religious Identities in Islamicate South Asia*, David Gilmartin and Bruce B. Lawrence (eds), Ginesville: University of Florida Press, pp. 246–281.

Gilmartin, D, and Lawrence, B. (eds) (2000) *Beyond Turk and Hindu: Rethinking Religious Identities in Islamicate South Asia*, Gainesville: University of Florida Press.

Hamilton, F. (n.d.) MSS Eur D 94, Oriental and India Office Collection, London, no. 30.

Hobbes, R. (1852) *Scenes in the Cities and Wilds of Hindostan*, Vol. 1, unpublished manuscript.

Hodson, T. (1937) *India: Census Ethnography, 1901–1931*, New Delhi: Government of India Press.

Inden, R. (1990) *Imagining India*, Oxford: Blackwell.

Kakar, S. (1996) *The Colors of Violence: Cultural Identities, Religion, and Conflict*, Chicago: University of Chicago Press.

Kaye, G. (1937) *India Office Library Catalogue of Manuscripts in European Languages: Vol. II. Part II: Minor Collections and Miscellaneous Manuscripts*, London: His Majesty's Stationery Office.

King, R. (1999) *Orientalism and Religion: Postcolonial Theory, India and 'The Mystic East'*, New York: Routledge.

Mayaram, S. (1997) *Resisting Regimes: Myth, Memory and the Shaping of aMuslim Identity*, Delhi: Oxford University Press.

McCutcheon, R. (2001) *Critics not Caretakers*, Albany: State University of New York Press.

Mittal, S. (ed.) (2003) *Surprising Bedfellows: Hindus and Muslims in Medieval and Early Modern India*, New York: Lexington Books.

Mukherjee, R. (1993) *Classification in Social Research*, Albany: State University of New York Press.

Pandey, G. (1990) *The Construction of Communalism in Colonial North India*, Delhi: Oxford University Press.

Peabody, N. (2001) 'Cents, Sense, Census: Human Inventories in Late Precolonial and Early Colonial India', in *Comparative Studies in Society and History*, 43: 4.

Pinch, W. (1999) 'Same Difference in India and Europe', in *History and Theory* 38/3: 389–407.

Rai, M. (2004) *Hindu Rulers, Muslim Subjects: Islam, Rights, and the History of Kashmir*, Delhi: Permanent Black.

Talbot, C. (2000) 'The Story of Prataparudra: Hindu Historiography on the Deccan Frontier', in *Beyond Turk and Hindu: Rethinking Religious Identities in Islamicate South Asia*, David Gilmartin and Bruce B. Lawrence (eds), Gainesville: University of Florida Press.

Tod, J. (1829) *Annals and Antinquities of Rajast'han or, the Central and Western Rajpoot States of India*, New Delhi: Rupa & Co.

van der Veer, P. (2001) *Imperial Encounters: Religion and Modernity in India and Britain*, Princeton: Princeton University Press.

Wagoner, P. (2003) 'Fortuitous Convergences and Essential Ambiguities: Transcultural Political Elites in the Medieval Deccan', in *Surprising Bedfellows: Hindus and Muslims in Medieval and Early Modern India*, Sushil Mittal (ed.), New York: Lexington Books, pp. 31–54.

ɔbal fiduciary

ıg the violence of religion

Mandair

Religion as response/the response of religion

There is a certain aporia that marks Indian thinking about the relationship between violence and religion. Perhaps the clearest manifestation of this aporia is the way in which Indians have attempted to engage the political through a mode of identification that once did not exist, yet which today is brought to life through a response to the word 'religion'. Indeed the aporia can be visualized in terms of the relationship between 'religion' and 'response', such that religion not only informs the Indian response to the political, but that religion is also the response that gives form to the Indian experience of political modernity. Given that an aporia refers to an experience that is simultaneously possible and impossible, this aporetic response would be one which, on the one hand, accepts without resistance the translatability of the term 'religion', and at the same time resists what is encompassed by the term 'religion'.

I begin by citing the problem of aporia not only because it constitutes a peculiarity of Indian decolonization that post-colonial scholarship by and large has failed to understand due to its lack of a sufficiently nuanced theory of religion, but also because it enables a mode of critique that cuts through the artifice of subjective versus objective methodology in which the latter is ultimately privileged. Such then is the nature of aporia which on the one hand constitutes an experience that I share with fellow Indians (that historically there is no exact equivalent for 'religion' from within the vocabulary of Indian languages), and on the other hand constitutes the method of my investigation (that it is now a matter of historical interest that Indians have responded to the call of this word). The nature of the aporia reveals its modus operandi, namely the elision of subjective versus objective, in another way. Consider for example those Indian Marxists and leftist Gandhians who continue to reject the term 'religion' in favour of its secular other, the argument being that there will always be a colonial violence associated with the term 'religion'. Or those on the Indian right (the Bharatiya Janata Party (BJP), Sangh Parvar, Akalis, etc.) who have accepted what the term signified in the name of tradition and are represented as perpetrators of violence in the name of religion. It would also be necessary to implicate scholars of religion on both sides of this divide because, by and large, and especially in the name of academic immunity ('neutral observation') they have also responded to religion, and in responding have not remained immune to its influence. There are of course notable exceptions who have pointed out that the term religion is the product of a particular culture (the Euro-Christian West) that Indians like other non-Western cultures do not possess this word, and that it is misguided to map and allow oneself to be mapped in terms of the religion/secular divide (Balagangadhara 1994; King 1999). *Yet the response has still taken place.* Nevertheless this response not only remains singular (since its apparent variations can be traced back to a single source: 'religion') it also cannot be regarded as wrong or right. Rather its aporetic nature beckons towards a different way of encountering the term 'religion', one that might hold open the questionable nature of religion, indeed, for South Asians, the idea of 'religion' as a question that precedes any possible response.

With this in mind let me turn to what might seem an unlikely source for insights relevant to the South Asian context, namely, Jacques Derrida's peculiarly oblique meditations on violence and religion. From seemingly different angles Derrida argues that religion and violence are intrinsically connected to the question of law and the (im)possibility of experiencing justice (Derrida 1992). Thus every time an Indian responds to the word religion s/he is obliged to speak (whether in English or Hindi) in another's language, breaking with her own and in so doing give herself up to the other. 'In this obligation the violence of an injustice has begun when all members of a community do not share the same idiom throughout. For all injustice supposes that the other, the victim of the languages' injustice, is capable of a language in general', that the other is a subject capable of responding and insofar, a responsible subject (Derrida 1992: 18). Furthermore, Derrida argues, to address oneself to the other in the language of the other is the impossible condition of all justice since I can speak the language of the other only to the extent that I am able to appropriate it according to the law of an implicit third, an appeal to a third party who suspends the unilaterality or singularity of all idioms, implying thereby the element of universality, and specifically here the implied translatability/universality of the term religion (Derrida 1992: 17). Accordingly, every time an Indian responds, quite responsibly, either: 'I am Hindu/Hinduism is my religion', or whether one rejects this response in favour of a purely secular enunciation, what is never questioned, because it is always assumed, is the concept of religion operating in this case, indeed, the relation between religion and conceptuality. In responding one will always have conformed to a certain law according to which the meaning and concept of religion is universally known and accepted without resistance.

A strange scenario: Indian's have no exact word for religion yet they cannot avoid answering to its call. As Derrida notes

> [t]here is no common Indo-European term for what we call religion, no omnipresent reality that is religion. There has not always been nor will there always and everywhere be *something*, a thing that is *one and identifiable*,

> identical with itself, which whether religious or irreligious, all agree to call 'religion'.
>
> (Derrida 1998: 36)

Why then do Indians continue to respond? And respond precisely in terms of something that is identifiable and one? More to the point why do they feel obliged to respond in conformity with a law? To feel obliged is already to have interiorized that law, to have imposed the law on oneself, to have introjected as a self-censorship, the visible projection of which would be the response or enunciation: 'I am Hindu/Hinduism is my religion' or 'I am a secular Indian'. The law itself is never seen. It is simply assumed. Indeed to make visible the law which obliges one to respond to religion would entail a trespass against the law, a violation of a meaning that all are supposed to know, whence its universality. Clearly, though, a universal that needs to be shown in evidence is no longer a universal since not everybody will have assented to its meaning.

Prior to even questioning religion, therefore, what needs to be interrogated is the invisible link or law that connects, on the one hand, religion as the response that conforms to the enunciation of an identity ('I am Hindu/Sikh', etc.), and on the other, the violence that results not from simply not-responding, but from a response that resists conforming to the law that demands identity and identification.[1] Elsewhere Derrida refers to this law as an interdict. The interdict works by preventing a certain kind of speech from being articulated, instead specifying access to certain identifications, while in that very moment actively repressing other identifications. Moreover, the interdict does not simply work at the level of language. It is the language of law: Language as Law. Though Derrida does not reveal his source, his notion of the interdict is indebted to Lacan's concept of the Unconscious structured like a language.[2] The relationship between religion and response can therefore be recast in a Lacanian frame as follows. By responding to the word religion in the form of a religious identity ('I am Hindu', 'Hinduism is my religion') the Indian believes s/he has already mastered the meaning of religion through a normal acquisition of English. But according to Lacan one cannot acquire language, one merely accedes to it, which means that one willingly agrees to submit to it as Law, such that one is first mastered by language. If the legitimate meaning of religion appears as an identity which is repeated as the same thing, always one and identifiable, then violence is a force which acts legitimately to remove this active repression that reproduces the universal meaning of religion with Indians.

Contrary to the dictionary definition, therefore, violence is not necessarily unlawful – an unwelcome entry into an otherwise peaceful public realm. There can be such a thing as a *lawful* violence, one that *resists* the active repression that determines the meaning of religion-as-identity. Two kinds of force are at work here. The first kind of force is effected by language-as-law where an Indian speaker in acceding to the word religion actively represses certain identifications of religion. In this case the repressive force of the law isn't manifested as the signifier 'violence' but as the signifier 'religion' which carries the meaning 'non-violence'. The second kind of force is effected when we become conscious of the law. Becoming conscious of self-censorship enables the removal of repression through questioning the inevitability of the meaning of religion as 'non-violence'. It would then be possible to entertain the idea that religion is simultaneously violent and non-violent.

Yet few Indians today would stop to think that they are actively repressing anything whenever they use the word 'religion'. Are Indians not sufficiently versed in English to understand the proper meaning of the term religion? As free agents today, are they not capable of entering into a dialogue about religion even if it happens to be conducted in the language of the ex-colonizer? And even if the language of dialogue belongs to the ex-colonizer, has not the world's general understanding of the word 'religion' expanded because of this dialogue? Indeed as a result of this dialogue is it not the case that everyone can now assent to universally recognizable objective realities called Hinduism, Sikhism, etc. which form part of the world religions? It is precisely when Indians confidently and without resistance make this transition from a singular response to the *word* 'religion' to its pluralized form that circulates globally as part of discourse of '*world* religions' that Derrida's meditations on the indissociability of religion and response (where the response *is* religion and religion *is* the response) becomes especially pertinent to the South Asian experience.

Derrida identifies the link between religion-as-response (the *word* 'religion') and the discourse of '*world*-religions' through the notion of the 'interdict'. Though rarely considered, the notion of the interdict is indirectly supported by recent research on colonial and pre-colonial India conducted in the form of detailed micro-studies. As a result of these studies it is now increasingly recognized that when Indians enunciate identity in terms of strictly defined religious traditions, it forms part of a history of response to the colonizer's demand for Indians to equivocate the concept religion, and that this enunciation-response mimics a colonial gesture which was effected through the institution of the Anglo-Vernacular (AV) mission schools during the nineteenth century (Mandair 2007). The avowed aim of this gesture was to give back to Indians, as a gift, or to enable Indians to rediscover their original religion(s) and their mother-tongue(s), which they were perceived to have lost during their fall from a Golden Age, a fall caused by the mixing of races, religions and languages, with the resultant long history of despotism and foreign domination that continued until the redeeming advent of British rule (Halbfass 1988; Lincoln 1999; Van der Veer 2003; Sugirtharaja 2003). As Ashis Nandy and others have convincingly argued, the enunciative response of the native elites can be considered the outcome of a process of cultural and psychological transformation during their encounter with British imperialism (Nandy 1983). Since these are adequately covered elsewhere I shall do no more than mention in all but the most cursory fashion, some of the key mechanisms of these transformations:

(a) The imposition of English as the language of the master, the one who makes the rules and enforces the law, and insofar, the *official* language of India (King 1994; Krishnaswamy and Burde 1998).

(b) The establishment of a vast network of Anglo-Vernacular mission schools as the institutions in which the law was imprinted onto the native elites and internalized through a regime of translation consisting of set procedures for simultaneously learning English and inventing a mother tongue (Dalmia 1996; Niranjana 1991; Viswanathan 1998). This regime of translation and the system of learning implicit within it becomes the privileged site for the operation of the language event that Derrida calls the interdict: the repression of a certain type of speech. As Derrida notes (albeit in the somewhat different context of colonial Algeria) the interdict as inscription of English as law/self-censorship, is almost always a 'pedagogical mechanism', something that happens at school, namely an enunciation, a response, the emergence of a speaking subject (Derrida 1996: 37).

(c) As a result of the interdict the speaking subject who emerges from subjection to the regime of translation at the heart of which is the 'pedagogical mechanism', articulates a distinct mother tongue ('my own language', the national language) and a determinate religion ('my own religion'), corresponding in socio-political terms to the emergence of boundarified vernacular languages (Hindi, Urdu, Punjabi) and strictly religious identities (Hindu, Muslim, Sikh).[3]

This was a religio-linguistic situation that had not existed prior to colonialism, and which laid the epistemic foundations for the English-educated elites to enter into 'dialogue' with Western thought. The result of this 'dialogue' was to effect a fundamental departure from pre-colonial 'Indic' ontologies with a concomitant accession to the ontology of modernity (Mandair 2007). A good example of this departure is the shift in paradigms of language and religion from the broadly non-dualistic paradigm characteristic of South Asian cultures (which recognizes the material as well as the cognitive properties of language and grounded in a notion of the One that resists representation and conceptualization in terms of ego-centric consciousness which automatically generates subject/object, self/other binaries) to the dualistic paradigm of Western modernity which privileges the referential meaning grounded in ontotheological notions of a transcendent Being or transcendental consciousness (Mandair 2006). Stated differently, this break corresponds to the repression of the *hetero*logies of non-dual One, a repression which in turn gives birth to the subject capable of responding in terms of a *mono*logic identity.

The conclusions of these micro-studies appear to endorse the idea of a break with Indic ontologies effected through Anglo-Vernacular education. Nevertheless, due to their presumption of objectivity which entails knowing in advance the meaning of religion, their analyses, broadly speaking, fall short of revealing the key mechanism responsible for the break. This mechanism is the insidious link between religion and translation, or the idea that religion and translatability are interchangeable concepts. In the colonial context English simultaneously signifies the Law and the language of the Law. The presence of

English therefore imposes a regime of translation that operates through the mechanism of the interdict. In this case the interdict would enforce something like the following rule: that religion is always and everywhere translatable, and that translatability (which here denotes not so much semantics but the creation of an exchange economy of colonial desire and the consequent transactions between colonizer and colonized) is inherently religious. Effectively the interdict represses the heterological Indic ontologies. It prohibits them from being articulated. If articulated they would count as unlawful.

The connection between religion and the principle of translatability (which I have likened to the work of the interdict) has rarely been questioned and almost not at all in the context of colonial or post-colonial India probably because, as attested to by evidence of recent history, Indians have continued to reciprocate – in the sense of finding equivalents for – terms such as religion, God, faith from within their conceptual resources through a process that seems entirely natural and transparent, namely, the response. By interrogating the response, however, the very focus of the question shifts in a different direction: how or why one consents to such an exchange when one does not have an equivalent thing to exchange in the first place? Which begs the question as to how one subsequently enters into the economy of exchange? And why this agreement or giving of consent appears natural, as nothing extraordinary?

For Derrida the very fact that we require language to speak to the other, and for the other to respond, means that speaking/responding is unavoidable insofar as it constitutes the possibility of the social bond or what might be regarded as the minimal form of community: the self *in relation to* an other (the not-self). Thus, one cannot give, or even think of giving, an equivalent thing/word in exchange for the word-thing called 'religion' until there is first of all an agreement already in place, a given-word, a sworn faith, without some kind of testimonial pledge, a legal binding that invokes the sacred (Derrida 1998: 26). What is really going on within such an invocation, Derrida warns us, is that we are already speaking Latin:

> [B]efore even envisaging the semantic history of testimony, of oaths, of the given word (indispensable to whomever hopes to think religion under its proper or secularized forms) before even recalling that some sort of 'I promise the truth' is always at work, and some sort of 'I make this commitment before the other from the moment that I address him, even and perhaps above all to commit perjury' we must formally take note of the fact that *we are already speaking Latin*. We make a point of this in order to recall that the world today speaks Latin (most often via Anglo-American) when it authorizes itself in the name of religion.
>
> (Derrida 1998: 26)

What Derrida seems to suggest here goes beyond the issue of Latin's linguistic hegemony. Rather the reference to Latin is a pointer towards a structure around which an entire tradition (religious, cultural and political) continues to gravitate.

At the core of this structure there is enshrined a sacred principle, an 'a priori ineluctable' or inescapable presupposition: that at the very moment of our coming to speech, at the very moment that an 'I' addresses or responds to another 'I' (and therefore to an *other*), the self engenders the figure of God as a witness, 'quasi-mechanically' as it were (Derrida 1998: 27). The very emergence of our speech presupposes that God can be called upon as a witness, albeit the supreme witness, who testifies to the legality or correctness of the self's relation to an other, indeed to the inviolability of a distance that must separate self and other. According to this model of language, speech begins by assuming the presence of God, that is to say, his existence, which undergirds his absence or non-existence. Without God, or with a God who is non-existent, there is no absolute witness and therefore no ground for a proper relationship between self and other. With God, or a God who exists, we have the existence of a third who guarantees even the minimal social bond between self and other, even when, and perhaps most importantly, the self/I commits perjury, when I lie to the other, or when the pledge is at its most secular. Derrida refers to this structure which reduces God to a 'transcendental addressing machine' (i.e. God is invoked as supreme, transcendent One, but he can still be called upon at will and put to good use) as the *fiduciary* (Derrida 1998: 27).

Quite simply the fiduciary can be regarded as a performative experience of the act of faith, without which there can be no address to the other. Constituted on the 'soil of bare belief' (Derrida 2001: 65) the fiduciary not only underlies everything to do with religion or the religious, but equally, the economic rationality of capitalism and all techno-scientific discourse (Derrida 1998: 28). Yet contrary to the prevalent idea that belief/faith is central to all religions, Derrida argues that the fiduciary is rooted in a peculiarly Christian concept of the world. As such the fiduciary can only be spoken of universally in relation to other cultures through the phenomenon of Latinity and its globalization, or *globalatinization* to use Derrida's neologism (Derrida 1998: 43; Derrida 2001: 66). *Globalatinization* refers to a process which today helps Christianity to retain its hegemony due to the conceptual apparatus of international law, global political rhetoric and multiculturalism. It can be seen as the global re-Christianization of the planet through the discourse of atheistic secularism. Wherever this conceptual apparatus dominates it speaks through the discourse of religion. As a result religion is peaceably imposed (or violently self-imposed) on all things that remain foreign to what this word designates.

Though not always obvious the basic procedure of globalatinization repeats a mechanism that was put into play at the micro-cosmic level in the Anglo-Vernacular school, a mechanism variously described as the manufacture of consent (Chomsky), native-informancy (Spivak) or mimicry (Bhabha). I cite these three names more as a way of highlighting a fact that tends to be underplayed by intellectuals of the Left, namely, the inseparability of contemporary globalatinization even in its most secular forms from the value tradition of Christianity. One must note here that although Nietzsche and Heidegger who connected the death of God (atheism) with the Christian values, had already forseen this event,

Derrida seems to go much further in pointing out the implications of globalatinization and/or the translatability of religion for non-Christians. Indeed, what he seeks to problematize with the term globalatinization is the almost desperate struggle of non-Christians religions when they attempt at the same time to Christianize themselves and to defend themselves against Christianity, which is precisely what was happening in the AV schools of nineteenth-century India. Thus, 'even as non-Christian religions try to resist mimicry by underscoring their differences with Christianity, these religions seem to become ever more Christian in their forms, in their discourse, in their manifestations' (Derrida 2001: 73).

An interesting and revealing example of this problem was a recent comment by the Archbishop of Canterbury, Rowan Williams, noting that non-Christian religions (signifying, thereby, Buddhism, Hinduism and Sikhism, rather than Islam which seems to have an accepted place in the high table of dialogue between the three Abrahamic religions) ought to make more effort to articulate their differences from Christianity. What the comment suggests is not so much a plea for greater diversity, but an exasperation with other religions' mimicry of the Christian conceptual framework, their ability to use comparative frameworks such as the world religions discourse, created in the first place by a long line of Christian thinkers, in order to acquire for themselves a measure of the global legitimacy of Christianity. Rowan Williams' comment is not a solitary reaction but part of a broader Christian intellectual movement whose most eloquent exponent is the group calling itself Radical Orthodoxy.[4] The foremost exponents of this group mounted a strong challenge to the supremacy of secularism and its attendant globalization by reclaiming the position and status of theology as 'queen of the sciences'. However, closer scrutiny of their arguments reveals a barely suppressed nostalgia for a return to the era of Christendom, or the political supremacy of Christianity.

Viewed from this perspective the neologism globalatinization questions what is going on when an Indian says: 'Hinduism/Sikhism/Buddhism is *my religion*' or when one presents oneself on an international stage to claim that 'my religion has been violated'. One can only say 'my religion' (implying the link to self and to its repetition as the same) in a Christian manner. To do so would be to 'inscribe oneself in a political and ideological space dominated by Christianity' and to enter into the struggle for recognition/equivocation between nations in which the putatively 'universal' value of the concept of religion already derives its meaning from Christianity.

In the South Asian context the role of the fiduciary and its link to constitutional law is clearly illustrated by the recent representations of 'religious' conflict between Hindus and Muslims (Ayodhya 1992, Gujerat 2002), Hindus and Sikhs (Punjab, New Delhi 1984) and Buddhists and Hindus (Sri Lanka). Despite their different geographical and cultural contexts, it would not take great powers of advocacy to show parallels between the representation of these conflicts in the global media during the 1980s and 1990s and the representation of religious violence in the US media post-9/11. For one thing both India and the USA are large democratic states with legal constituencies framed in the name of secularism but governed in reality by overwhelming religious majorities – Christian in the case of the USA, and Hindu in the case of India. Moreover, the main ideological vector in US and Indian media and academia during the 1980s and early 1990s with regard to the representation of religious violence largely echoed state policy not only by attributing violence to some enemy of the state (turbaned and bearded Sikhs or Muslim fundamentalists with regard to India, Muslims with regard to the USA) but by narrating and displaying the spectacle of violence as a deviation of these troublesome minorities from the 'truth' of the religions they purport to represent, where 'truth' is contained in some kind of a fiduciary structure. Of course, the 'truth' of these religions, as the media and academia are so keen to portray, is peace or non-resistance to the state law. It is the ultimate measure of a religion's compatibility with democracy. Clearly, what is elided in this representation is that the definition of religion in terms of peace/non-resistance is in fact a legal definition. It is framed by a juridical process that has predetermined the definition of religion as a renunciation of violence, and violence as a deviation or fall from religion's truth.

As Michael Hardt and Antonio Negri argue in their recent work on war and democracy, the state with its overwhelming material advantage reserves for itself the exercise of violence as legal (Hardt and Negri 2004: 25). All other social violence (and especially 'religious' violence that deviates from its truth) is illegitimate. Although the state's legitimation of violence is grounded in the structures of law, an adequate notion of legitimate violence is in turn dependent on the law's claim to morality. Violence is legitimate if it can be morally justified, but illegitimate if its basis is immoral (Hardt and Negri 2004: 29). This is of course a circular argument, for the claim to morality of Law is itself justified by the state's presentation through media of an enemy with its attendant threat of indeterminate chaos. Ultimately, then, it is the presence of the enemy that legitimates the violence of the state. The figure of the enemy functions as a 'schema of reason' which sketches out in advance the very horizon on which self and other are constructed. What is interesting here is the nature of the schema that connects the representation of chaos–religion–enemy. Chaos names that which has fallen from the state of order; the guarantor of order is the state of divine stasis exemplified by the truth of religion; the enemy is the figure of chaos which deviates and tempts into deviation from religion. The schema serves, as Hardt and Negri rightly point out, to demonstrate the state's need to maintain security. Hence the state monopolizes violence in order to constantly secure the peace. More insidiously though, this schema helps the state to manipulate a knowledge about the fiduciary structure of religion and religious identity in order to manufacture violence and then switch it off at will.

One of many such examples of this ability to switch violence on and off is the Indian state's careful crafting of the image of 'Sikh terrorism' around the personality of the militant cleric Sant Jarnail Singh Bhindranwale. As the head of the Damdami Taksaal, Bhindranwale was initially brought into Punjabi politics by Congress aides in order to divide the popular support base of the dominant Sikh political party, the Akali Dal. Although Bhindranwale soon discovered the Congress's true motives and turned against his former promoters, party officials soon found a new role for him. By representing him in the media as the archetypal 'Sikh fundamentalist' – bearded, turbaned, and fully armed in contravention of the state's prohibition against firearms, and therefore akin to Islamic militants – Congress found an effective way of undermining a key component of the BJP's campaign strategy during the early 1980s in which the BJP projected itself as the only party that championed the cause of the Hindu majority thereby eroding Congress' popular support. The presence of Bhindranwale and the 'Punjab problem' conveniently allowed the state to manufacture a figure of the Sikh fundamentalism as the 'enemy within' which colluded with the 'foreign hand' of Pakistan to undermine the unity of the Indian nation. Following the death of Bhindranwale and his supporters at the hands of the Indian Army in 1984, the state machinery continued to project Punjab as a chaotic or 'disturbed region' infested with Sikh terrorists whose resistance was evidence of a deviation both from the essentially peacefulness of Sikhism as well as from a key principle of the democratic state, namely, that it alone exercised a legal mandate to deploy violence for the protection of the peaceful majority.

In hindsight what remains most disturbing about the 'Sikh problem' is not so much the number of people who were killed over a twelve-year period (approx. 250,000), nor even the controlled precision with which the state allowed the chaos of insurgency to proliferate before brutally and clinically exterminating it almost at will. What continues to disturb is the way in which the Indian state exercised complete understanding of the fiduciary, and therefore machine-like, nature of religion and religious identity. That is to say, the way in which, once confronted with the figure of the 'enemy', Hindus reacted by differentiating themselves from it, while Sikhs were forced into a dilemma. *Either* to reject this 'enemy' thereby (i) affirming that militancy is a deviation from 'true' Sikhism and (ii) renouncing the right to resist the state (a principle historically and theologically inscribed in Sikh tradition). *Or*, to identify with the 'enemy' thereby (i) affirming that Sikhism itself is not a true religion and by nature incompatible with democracy and (ii) affirming that Sikhs and Sikhism can never rightfully belong within the ambit of the Indian nation, hence justifying separatism which inevitably invites state violence. The moral of the story is that as long as people respond to the demand for religion in a predictable way, the state continues to keep its finger on the fiduciary structure of religion. Consequently the fiduciary can be turned on or off at the whim of the state and milked not only to produce violence when and where needed, but also to legitimate state violence by creating a *spectacle* of violence in the eyes of international law.

However, for Sikhs the story does not finish there. The events of 9/11 and the US media's massive and overt sensitization of a largely ignorant American mindset with the imagery of Bin Laden as the turbaned terrorist, created an unexpected and deadly problem of mistaken identity for innocent Sikhs living in the USA and Europe. Mistaken for Muslims, Sikhs were targeted in a spate of hate crimes culminating in the murder of several innocent Sikhs. In effect the media had skillfully deployed the fiduciary structure of religion by creating a fundamental divide between the Christian West and the 'Axis of Evil' represented by Islam/Al Qaida (the one was identified by default with the other). Ironically, in the aftermath of 9/11 Sikhs were forced to rely on the very fiduciary structure that had caused the problem. In a frenetic wave of community mobilization Sikhs went out of their way to 'dialogue' with their Christian and Jewish neighbours in order to explain not only that they were *not* Muslim, but more precisely that they shared the same fundamental values as Christians.

The fiduciary's cultural bias: *violence in the name of love*

A surprising indicator of the Christian underpinnings of the global fiduciary is the recent appropriation of contemporary theory by theologians and vice versa the appropriation of theology by militantly secular theorists. Theologians have appropriated contemporary theory not only to successfully dispute the atheistic underpinnings of modern secular thinking in the social sciences, but to revitalize religious and theological reflection in the Christian and Judaic traditions. More surprising, however, is the return of political theory to its religious roots. Exemplified by the recent work of Slavoj Zizek, a scholar whose thought is rooted in the legacy of Marxist theory, the net effect of this return is to have legitimized the use of phenomena from these particular traditions as resources for critical thinking not only about religion as such, but about the political. However, what is really interesting about Zizek's recent work is an underlying anxiety about contemporary globalization that it shares after 9/11 with intellectuals of the Christian right such as Radical Orthodoxy.

If one looks closely at Zizek's recent writings it would appear that the focus has shifted from a critique of the religious right in America and elsewhere, to an aspect of globalization normally not given much credence by political science or political theory, namely the contemporary clash between civilizations defined primarily by their allegiance to one or another religion. Weighing heavily on Zizek's mind it seems is the potential access of *other* religion*s* to the European mindset as a result of globalization. The real danger is not so much the Americanization of the planet but what lurks behind it, namely, the whole medley of 'New Age Mysticisms' and 'paganisms' – effectively code words for Indian and Chinese spiritualities – which because of American globalization are given increasingly greater access to the Western/European market (Zizek 2004: 32–33). In other words, 'New Age Mysticisms' pose a danger by exploiting the political void created by a post-modernist America allied with Third World cultures in order to export their ideologies of non-involvement and disinterested action. Consequently for Zizek the '[t]arget on which we should focus ... is the very ideology which is proposed as a potential solution – for example Oriental spirituality (Buddhism) with its "gentle", balanced, holistic, ecological approach' (Zizek 2003: 25). For Zizek these ideologies serve as examples of yet another Third World or 'premodern society', which have nothing to offer in the way of intellectual or religio-cultural solutions in any present or future global problems because the contributions to human development were long since exhausted, which is precisely why they can only ever be regarded as 'premodern societies'. This fear is expressed even more forcefully in his recent book on the US–Iraq war where he pleads for a 'renewed leftist Eurocentrism':

> To put it bluntly: do we want to live in a world in which the only real choice is between American civilization and the emerging Chinese authoritarian–capitalist one? If the answer is no, then the true alternative is Europe. The third world cannot generate a strong enough resistance to the ideology of the American Dream; in the present constellation only Europe can do that.
>
> (Zizek 2004: 33)

Although it is not immediately obvious, Zizek's designation of 'premodern societies' can be traced to a tradition of Occidentalism based on a particular concept of religion deployed by Hegel, Marx and Husserl in which premodern designates those cultures that have yet to achieve a level of elevation or transcendence that is the hallmark of history and historicism. Its no surprise then to see Zizek elsewhere using terms such as pagan, New Age Mysticism as metaphors of the threat of Eastern nihilisms further weakening Europe (Zizek 2001). The upshot of Zizek's argument is this: (i) whereas 'Christian love is a violent passion to introduce a Difference, a gap in the order of being, to privilege and elevate some object at the expense of others' the 'Buddhist stance is ultimately one of Indifference, of quenching all passions that strive to establish differences', consequently insofar as the 'violent Love' of Christianity establishes the order or the act and therefore the domain of the political, it is the essential part of the European legacy worth fighting for (Zizek 2000). (ii) Other religions, especially pagan/premodern religions, their disclaimers notwithstanding, are also based on the structure of belief. Secretly, Zizek argues, we are all believers and Asian spiritualities, far from espousing an ego-less and heterological standpoint which might be a stumbling block for global capitalism, in fact form a perfect ideological supplement to it. The sophistication of his analyses notwithstanding, Zizek's political theory inherits from its intellectual predecessors, such as Hegel, Augustine, Marx and Husserl, the conceptual violence that imposes itself through a belief in the absolute translatability of religions, and stemming from this, a framework for creating a stereotype of the other. This in turn enables the possibility of comparing and calculating the contemporary worth of cultures. Only through the logic of the stereotype and the comparative schema that results from it at his disposal could Zizek so confidently call for a 'renewed left Eurocentrism' rooted in a Christian legacy and able to withstand the ideological contamination from pagan cultures and 'premodern societies' like India and China.

Space prevents fuller engagement with Zizek in this essay. It will suffice simply to counter Zizek with a question posed by Derrida, the simplicity of which belies its potential for reversing the conceptual violence *imposed* by the translatability of religion, the global fiduciary, belief in belief, and as I have argued above, *self-imposed* by Indians through a certain response to religion. Derrida argues that the very point at which globalatinization appears to assert total hegemony, also reveals its greatest weakness. If this hegemony is dependent on a belief in the unhindered translatability of religion, Derrida poses the question: '*What if religio remained untranslatable?*' (Derrida 1998: 30). Stated otherwise, what if one were not to respond to the demand for the equivocation of religion? What if Indians were to exercise a certain undecidability in the process of translating received traditions according to a mechanism which automatically inserted into a global circulation as proper representatives of several determinate (world) religions?

To pose the *un*translatability of religion is not to halt the history of colonial translation of religion, or to pretend that it never happened, nor to ignore its very tangible consequences so evident in Indian responses. Rather it is to circumvent the ideological relay whereby translation happens automatically. For Indians to pose the question as to whether *religio* might remain untranslatable is to allow the emergence of a religiosity-without-religion, one might say, determined not by the figure of the self (with its attendant politics of identity) but by the figure of the other. For such a religiosity even to be expressed would require different categories capable of shedding light on cultural singularities rather than universals. Or perhaps different universals not subservient to a fiduciary, nor to overdetermined distinctions between religion and violence/secularism/politics. I would like to venture a notion here that for Indians to entertain this possibility would be to retrieve and reinvent modes of perception, epistemologies and possibilities for thinking religion as determined primarily by the relation to the other, which since colonialism has been repressed under the sign of the nation. Yet to reinvent this would be far from a nostalgic return to an imagined *pre*-modern society. Rather it would be for Indians to feel confident about asserting ancient and very practical notions of freedom based of the non-dual One (not the One of monotheism but a paradoxical One which allows the co-existence of the one of non-ego and ego) which creatively cultivates impermanence through a certain weakening of the ego as the ground of social relations, so that one could say in response to the demand for modernity and modernization, that being is firstly being-with, or that ego sum is firstly ego cum. Love for the other, another name for this primordial interconnectedness of the self to *everything* that is not-self, and therefore the essential vacuity of the self, has long been the starting point for pervasive strands in Indian thought and social ethics. For Occidentalists such possibilities will no doubt evoke deep-rooted fears of the return of anarchistic Eastern nihilisms, and the fear of losing control of the devices have so far prevented the threat of paganisms, pantheisms and mysticisms infecting the heart of Europe and the West. It is precisely such a fear that allows political theorists such as Zizek to elevate Christianity over the merely determinate religions, *in the name of love*, by claiming in effect that Christianity is the only true religion of love, or that the ultimate secret of Christian love is the loving attachment to the Other's (i.e. God's) imperfection. The real injustice here is that for Indians such ideas stem naturally from the paradoxical notion of the non-dual One, yet their attempts at cultural representation based on such ideas has historically provided the perfect proof for their exclusion from modernity and human progress. Inclusion always entailed having to respond to religion.

Notes

1 Particularly instructive here is Martin Heidegger's argument in *The Principle of Reason* (1991).

2 Lacan (1991).

3 I am well aware that prior to the arrival of the British there was a broad demarcation between Muslim and non-Muslim ('Hindu'). The literature on this is well established (see for example Thapar 1997). However, while the Muslim/'Hindu' divide has connotations of the religious, it does not exactly correspond to religion as a *universalizable concept* being deployed by Europeans in the nineteenth century, which is also informed by an ideology of language as I go on to explain in this article. Otherwise we would have to admit that the concept of religion means exactly the same thing in Muslim India as it did in colonial British India and thereafter, which it clearly does not.

4 Recent works include: (1998) *Radical Orthodoxy*, John Milbank, Catherine Pickstock and Graham Ward (eds), London and New York: Routledge; (1999) *Post-Secular Philosophy: Between Philosophy and Theology*, Philip Blond (ed.), London and New York: Routledge.

Bibliography

Balagangadhara, S.N. (1994) *The Heathen In His Blindness: Asia, the West and the Dynamic of Religion*, Leiden: E.J. Brill.

Blond, Philip (1998) *Post-Secular Philosophy: Between Philosophy and Theology*, London and New York: Routledge.

Dalmia, Vasudha (1996) *The Nationalization of Hindu Traditions: Bharatendu Harischandar and 19th Century Benares*, New Delhi: Oxford University Press.

De Vries, Hent and Weber, Sam (eds) (2001) *Religion and Media*, Stanford: Stanford University Press.

Derrida, Jacques (1992) 'Force of Law: The "Mystical Foundation of Authority"' in *Deconstruction and the Possibility of Justice*, Drucilla Cornell, Michel Rosenfeld, David Gray Carlson (eds), London and New York: Routledge.

——(1996) *Monolingualism of the Other; Or, the Prosthesis of Origin*, Stanford: Stanford University Press.

——(1998) 'Faith and Knowledge: The Two Sources of "Religion" at the Limits of Reason Alone', in *Religion*, London: Polity Press.

——(2001) 'Above All, No Journalists' in Hent De Vries and Sam Weber (eds) *Religion and Media*, Stanford: Stanford University Press.

Derrida, Jacques and Vattimo, Giani (eds) (1998) *Religion*, London: Polity Press.

Halbfass, Wilhelm (1988) *India and Europe: An Essay in Philosophical Understanding*, New Delhi: Motilal Banarsidas.

Hardt, Michael and Negri, Antonio (2004) *Multitude: War and Democracy in the Age of Empire*, New York: Penguin Press.

Heidegger, Martin (1991) *The Principle of Reason*, trans. Reginald Lily, Bloomington, IN: Indiana University Press.
King, Christopher (1994) *One Language, Two Scripts: The Hindi Movement in Nineteenth Century North India*, New Delhi: Oxford University Press.
——(1999) *Orientalism and Religion: Post-Colonial Theory, India and the 'Mystic East'*, London and New York: Routledge.
Krishnaswamy, N. and Archana S. Burde (1998) *The Politics of Indians' English: Linguistic Colonialism and the Expanding English Empire*, New Delhi: Oxford University Press.
Lacan, Jacques (1991) 'The Function of Language in Psychoanalysis', in *Speech and Language in Psychoanalysis*, trans. and ed. Anthony Wilden, Baltimore: Johns Hopkins University Press.
Lincoln, Bruce (1999) *Theorizing Myth: Narrative, Ideology and Scholarship*, Chicago: University of Chicago Press.
Mandair, Arvind (2006) 'The Politics of Non-Duality: Reassessing the Work of Transcendence in Modern Sikh Theology', *Journal of the American Academy of Religion*; Oxford: Oxford University Press (forthcoming).
——(2007) 'Mono-Theo-Lingualism: Derrida and the Disorientation of Indian Identity' in *(dis)-locations*, a special issue of *Social Identities: Journal of Race, Nation and Culture*, Carfax, forthcoming 2007.
Milbank, John, Pickstock, Catherine and Ward, Graham (1999) *Radical Orthodoxy*, London and New York: Routledge.
Nandy, Ashis (1983) *The Intimate Enemy: Loss and Recovery of the Self Under Colonialism*, New Delhi: Oxford University Press.
Niranjana, Tejaswini (1991) *Siting Colonialism: History, Post-Structuralism and the Colonial Context*, Berkeley: University of California Press.
Thapar, Romila (1997) 'Syndicated Hinduism', in Gunther Dietz Sontheimer and Hermann Kulke (eds), *Hinduism Reconsidered*, New Delhi: Manohar.
Sugirtharajah, Sharada (2003) *Constructions of Hinduism*, London and New York: Routledge.
Van der Veer, Peter (2003) *Imperial Encounters: Religion and Modernity in India and Britain*, Princeton and London: Princeton University Press.
Viswanathan, Gauri (1998) *Outside the Fold: Conversion Modernity and Belief*, New Delhi: Oxford University Press.
Zizek, Slavoj (2000) *The Fragile Absolute – or, Why is the Christian Legacy Worth Fighting For?*, London and New York: Verso.
——(2001) *On Belief*, London and New York: Routledge.
——(2003) *The Puppet and The Dwarf: The Perverse Core of Christianity*, Cambridge, MA: MIT Press.
——(2004) *Iraq: The Borrowed Kettle*, London and New York: Verso.

11 The association of 'religion' with violence

Reflections on a modern trope

Richard King

> Our conceptions of the world face the predicament of turning into ideologies the moment that they forget their own historicities.
>
> (Dirlik 2000: 84).

> Understanding the system of ideology that operates in one's own society is made difficult by two factors: (i) one's own consciousness is itself a product of that system, and (ii) the system's very success renders its operations invisible, since one is so consistently immersed in and bombarded by its products that one comes to mistake them (and the apparatus through which they are produced and disseminated) for nothing other than 'nature'.
>
> (Lincoln 1996: Thesis 10).

> The point is rather that the Enlightenment must examine itself.
>
> (Adorno and Horkheimer 1972: xv).

It is a commonly held view that 'religion' has a particular association with violence. Consider, however, a few salient facts and statistics about the contemporary world in which we live. In 2005 between 62 to 65 per cent of the world's total military budget was spent by five ostensibly 'secular' nation-states (the USA, the UK, France, Japan and China).[1] Of these five states, one in particular – the United States of America – has a military budget that accounts for almost half of the total global spending on the military (47 per cent in 2004). This is almost *10 times* the amount spent by the next biggest spenders (the United Kingdom and France, both on 5 per cent). According to proposed spending plans for 2007, the US government will spend $1.2 billion a day, that is almost $14,000 per second, on its military budget.

Consider a different, but, in my view, equally pertinent set of statistics relating to another sphere of modern 'secular' activity – the rapidly expanding global economy. In the year 2000 while the sales of the top 200 multinational corporations constituted over a quarter of the world's total economic activity, these companies employed less than 1 per cent of the world's total workforce. The combined sales of these top 200 companies are *18 times* the size of the combined annual income of the 1.2 billion people living in 'severe' poverty.[2] In an interview with the British newspaper *The Independent* on 20 June 2005, Jeffrey

Sachs, the Columbia University professor, economist and special advisor to the UN Secretary General Kofi Annan, made the following sobering remark to the interviewer:

> Every day, your newspaper could put on its front page, 'More than 20,000 people died yesterday because of extreme poverty'. Every day. And every single one of those deaths is preventable. It's not just something that just happens, like rain. It is something that we can change in a short period of time.
>
> (*Independent* 20 June 2005)

In a world characterized by an increasing concentration of wealth in the hands of a small percentage of the world's population and mass consumption levels in the 'developed world' reaching an unprecedented scale, the continued death of thousands of people in conditions of extreme poverty *every single day,* while others live in conditions of unparalled affluence, is surely the most scandalous example of ongoing systemic violence in human history. Yet we hardly ever hear about it. Place this gruesome statistic alongside the untold suffering and deaths caused by a century of world wars and genocides, few of which have an easily identifiable 'religious' dimension, and one wonders why the recurring issue of mass-mobilized forms of violence is so often seen to be a problem specifically associated with 'religion'. My suggestion in this paper is that the mainstream discourse on 'religion and violence' and the emphasis that has been placed upon this as a recurring problem of human history is the secularist equivalent of a 'lone gunman theory'. By focusing one's attention upon the apparently intolerant, dogmatic and socially disharmonious aspects of purportedly identifiable entities known as 'the religions', our attention is distracted from asking deeper, structural questions about violence as a condition of modern, 'everyday' life and about the involvement of human beings in the performance of such violence – whether grounded in (so-called) 'secular' or 'religious' forms of life. Whether intended or not (and I would concede that in many cases this is unreflective and unintentional) the way that the debate about violence has been framed effectively insulates the institutional forms, organizations and ideologies that govern modern ('secular') life from critical interrogation.

'Religion' as *doxa*

This volume of papers has been particularly concerned with South Asian traditions in both their ancient and contemporary forms and their complex relationship to the performance, justification and condemnation of acts of violence. In a broader cultural and intellectual context, these discussions have systematically been framed within a broader discursive context concerned with the global question of 'religion and violence', of which there is now a growing literature, both popular and academic. It is important, given this wider hermeneutic context, to examine the debate over 'religion and violence' and locate it within its own historical and cultural context. Only then will we be in a position to appreciate some of the specificities and issues involved in understanding 'the South Asian experience'.

This paper will take a step back from this discussion and ask some critical questions about the theoretical framework that underlies the 'religion and violence' debate in general. This analysis will be carried out through an examination of the work of two prominent scholars of religion who have published on this topic, namely, Mark Juergensmeyer (UC Santa Barbara) and Bruce Lincoln (University of Chicago). Both are highly respected academics and have not only produced scholarly work of extremely high quality but also made significant contributions to their respective fields of expertise. Both however, in slightly different ways, deploy a universalized category of 'religion' that ends up dulling rather than sharpening our attention to the particularities under discussion in the 'religion and violence' debate. This paper should not be read in any sense as an attempt to diminish the substantial contribution that both scholars have made to the academic body of knowledge, but is rather an attempt to tease out some of the cultural tropes at work in the field of study as a whole through an examination of two key contributors to the debate.

Like virtually all of the authors who have written on this theme, the work of Lincoln and Juergensmeyer carries forward certain cultural assumptions and tropes about the relationship between something called 'religion' – which both scholars see as a clearly identifiable phenomenon in the world – and a propensity for intolerance and acts of violence. I will attempt to demonstrate in this paper that both authors base their work upon prevailing Euro-American assumptions about the nature of religion and its association with conflict. These assumptions can broadly be classified as 'secularist' in tenor since they reflect the way that the debate about 'religion' has unfolded in a post-Enlightenment context (though this does not preclude the occurrence of such tropes in the work of more 'theologically' inclined defences of 'the religious' that have been precipitated by such critiques.)

The prevailing assumption that runs throughout the literature on this subject, whether addressed from a theological or 'insider' perspective or from a social scientific or historical point of view, reflects a wider 'common-sense' view of history in the Western world, which assumes that 'religion' and violence have had a long and murky history of association with one another. Consider for instance the following opening remarks by Stephen J. Stein in his 2002 review of recent literature on this theme:

> Religion and violence have never been strangers, nor are they in the contemporary world. Popular and scholarly attention to the troubling relationship between the two is fostered almost daily by media accounts of religiously influenced violence in seemingly every quarter of the globe. Muslims and Jews in the Middle East, Protestants and Catholics in Northern Ireland, antiabortionists in the United States, and anticultists in a variety of nations – these are the familiar examples of such conflict. ...

> None of this is terribly mysterious. Religion has often (maybe always) operated in close proximity with violence, either as the object of, or the motivator of violence.
>
> (Stein 2002: 103)

What has made these assumptions so prevalent and uncontested is the fact that they remain deeply entrenched as key components of the myths of origin of modern 'secular' nation-states such as the United States of America and France. In so far as this is the case, such assumptions remain powerful and convincing tropes within dominant Euro-American constructions of 'modernity' and remain not only largely beyond question for those influenced by such myths, but also barely conscious in their operation. In this sense the underlying discourse of religion at work here represents a good example of what Pierre Bourdieu called a *doxa*, that is:

> the coincidence of the objective structures and the internalized structures which provides the illusion of immediate understanding, characteristic of practical experience of the familiar universe, and which at the same time excludes from that experience any inquiry as to its own conditions of possibility.
>
> (1990: 25–26)

For Bourdieu, a *doxa* occurs when a particular taxonomic system presents itself as corresponding to 'nature' – the way things really are, rather than as a culturally constructed artifice. It is constituted by that which is taken for granted in a specific social setting, that which remains literally unquestionable because its arbitrary and socially constructed origins have been occluded. *Doxa* forms the unquestioned truth or authority that frames the very possibilities of thought itself – the stage upon which orthodoxies and heterodoxies can be played out according to a set of rules and assumptions that none of the participants question (Bourdieu 1977: 164–71). According to Bourdieu, challenges to *doxa* require not only a crisis of some sort but also that those who have been dominated and interpellated by such assumptions develop the 'material and symbolic means' to challenge this construction of the real. The view that all of the major macro-traditions of the world (with the exception of the European Enlightenment tradition) are examples of a single genus 'religion', and that they therefore share certain characteristics with Christianity (the archetypal religion in all of these debates) is, I would suggest, a fundamental *doxa* of modernity. As Daniel Dubuisson has argued:

> Created by the West, enshrined in Western epistemology, and central to its identity, the concept of religion eventually came to be the core of the Western worldview. Since this notion is intrinsically linked to all the philosophies, complementary or competing, that have been invented in the West, the West cannot, at the risk of its own disintegration, do without it,

> because these global conceptions would then decompose into scattered or juxtaposed fragments. ... Would not abandoning the idea of religion be the equivalent for Western thought of abdicating part of its intellectual hegemony over the world?
>
> (2003: 94)

The denaturalization of the concept of 'religion' is a fairly recent consequence of the intellectual and cultural crisis that has occurred in the West in the late twentieth century as a result of the end of European colonialism. The rising challenge to the hegemony of Occidental theory has been slowly making an impression on all disciplines in the modern academy in a series of waves (post-modernism, post-structuralism, post-colonialism). It should come as no surprise then to discover that some of the most significant early contributions to unmasking the doxic status of the category of religion in the modern world have been from scholars of non-European origin (see Asad 1993 and Balagangadhara 1994).

Once one considers the discourse of 'religion' to be a fundamental *doxa* of Euro-American modernity one begins to see how different ideological positions involved in this debate engage in a struggle for supremacy based upon an underlying complicity about their object of study. For the secularists religion tends towards zealotry, intolerance, dogmatism and conflict. For apologists of religion, this is only the case when religious ideals have been misappropriated for other ends or when 'religion goes bad'. There are various intermediary positions that one can take on this debate, but what they all have in common is first, the assumption that the complex macro-traditions that are classified by the universal category of 'religion' (however differently this term may be defined by each author) can all be denoted by implication when this term is employed in debates, and second, that 'religion' does not (and cannot) denote its opposite – those dimensions of life and ideologies that are to be classified as 'secular'. These assumptions, rendered invisible by the framing of debate in terms of a series of 'competing possibles', establish a censorship, which, as Bourdieu argued, is far more radical than one that is based upon a simple orthodoxy. Indeed, the construction of an orthodoxy and various competing heterodoxies only serve to crowd our intellectual space with oppositional views that create the illusion that all options are being explored. In this way, such debates actually '*delimit the universe of possible discourse*' (Bourdieu 1977: 169).

Thus, before one is able to consider the question of violence and, say, South Asian traditions (the theme of this volume), one must confront a prior epistemological issue, namely what traces and assumptions are being carried forward when we use terms such as 'religion' and 'violence' in these contexts. Generally speaking, debates about 'religion and violence' assume, often uncritically, that these categories are unproblematic and 'straightforward' and can be universally applied in quite distinct cultural and historical situations. However, the history of the usages of both of these terms and their specific association with each other in the modern (by which I mean here, post-Enlightenment) world should be as much the subject of critical analysis as the case studies that we are so routinely offered of this apparently universal phenomenon.

The association of religion with conflict in Euro-American modernity

Contemporary debates about religion and violence in the West often focus upon the question of the possibility of a just or holy war, particularly after the attacks upon the World Trade Center in New York in September 2001. Western commentators have struggled to understand the motivations of the hijackers, particularly their willingness to die in the pursuit of their goals. It is not clear, however, that there is a specific and necessary correlation between suicide missions and 'religious traditions'. Robert Pape (2005) notes for instance that the pioneer and world leader in suicide attacks is an overtly secularist movement – the Marxist Tamil Tigers of Sri Lanka. Similarly, Diego Gambetta notes that:

> Contrary to a widespread belief, the majority of [suicide missions] have been carried out by secular rather than religious organizations. This suggests that if special and exalted motivations to self-sacrifice are involved, religious beliefs and preaching are not the only way to induce or to exploit them.
>
> (2005: viii–ix)

The attacks of 11 September 2001 on the United States of America by a small but well-organized group of radical Islamists however has breathed new life into the now well-established association of religion and violence and brought this issue into the forefront of public discussion. In a contemporary Western context this is usually framed according to the following clash of tropes about 'the religious': Do religions justify and cause violence or are they more appropriately seen as forces for peace and tolerance? In the context of secular forms of modernity, religion has been represented by some as a primary cause of social division, conflict and war, whilst others have argued that this is a distortion of the 'true' significance of religion, which, when properly adhered to, promotes peace, harmony, goodwill and social cohesion. On the one hand some writers suggest that religion is a primary producer of conflict and violence. For others this is only the case when 'religion becomes evil' (Kimball 2002).

A good example of the tension between these two tropes can be found in the work of Mark Juergensmeyer, perhaps the leading scholar in the study of religion and violence in the modern world. In a series of books (most notably, *The New Cold War? Religious Nationalism Confronts the Secular State* (1993) and *Terror in the Mind of God. The Global Rise of Religious Violence* (2000)) Juergensmeyer, examines what he perceives to be an alarming global rise in religious violence in recent years. His 2000 book (re-issued with a new preface after the events of 11 September 2001), is full of detailed analysis and important empirical data. It is based upon extensive interviews and, in some cases, unprecedented access to individuals involved in various forms of ideologically motivated violence. His analysis of this data, however, is severely skewed by his recourse to an uncritical notion of 'the religious'. The author expresses puzzlement that 'bad things are done by people who otherwise appear to be good – in cases of religious terrorism, by pious people dedicated to a moral vision of the world' (2000: 7). This perplexity reflects a popular understanding of 'religion' that relates it to the development of moral values within society and harmonious influences upon the behaviour of its individual adherents. The intrinsic moral goodness of religion is a constant theme throughout Juergensmeyer's work and is reiterated (for instance) in his concluding remarks in *Terror in the Mind of God*, where the author expresses the hope that religion can act as a 'moral beacon' to provide a 'cure' for contemporary religious violence:

> Religion gives spirit to public life and provides a beacon for moral order. At the same time it needs the temper of rationality and fair play that Enlightenment values give to civil society. Thus, religious violence cannot end until some accommodation can be forged between the two – some assertion of moderation in religion's passion, and some acknowledgement of religion in elevating the spiritual and moral values of public life. In a curious way, then, the cure for religious violence may ultimately lie in a renewed appreciation for religion itself.
>
> (2000: 243)

Juergensmeyer's response to 'the rise of religious violence' is to propose an accommodationist secularism, deriving from the values of the European Enlightenment, as the basis for mediating the problems of 'religious violence' in the contemporary world. This, of course, immediately raises the question of whether the liberal values of the Euro-American Enlightenment are really capable of mediating the competing claims of cultural traditions and ideologies on a worldwide scale. Global social and economic inequalities, many of them a direct historical consequence of the colonial reconfiguration of the globe by those same 'enlightened' Europeans (and now Americans), remain in place despite the rhetoric of the Western liberal tradition. Whilst secular forms of liberalism have significantly reconfigured the terrain and opened up opportunities for resisting oppressive regimes with the emphasis that they have placed upon individual human rights and freedoms, they have also sat rather too easily with colonialist agendas. It has proved far too easy to justify colonial aggression and domination under the cover of the spread of 'Western liberal values' and the claim to be exporting civilization and 'democracy' abroad.

Failure to acknowledge the murky history of complicity between Western secular liberalism and the colonial project however, continues for as long as one specifically associates violence and aggression with 'religious' worldviews rather than as a recurring feature of human ideologies in general (including Western secular liberalism). It may be argued that this has been an unfortunate feature of Western liberal regimes in the past, but that the colonial era has now ended.

Unfortunately, the claim that Western liberalism, once purged of unpleasant associations is really a force for good, utilizes the same strategy of exclusion that is deployed by defenders of 'the religious'. On this view liberalism in itself is good, and should not be confused with 'liberalism gone bad'. Sadly, even attempts to consign the complicity of Western liberal discourse with colonial oppression to the dustbin of history does not sit easily with the current geopolitical situation in which we find ourselves at the beginning of the twenty-first century with the rise of a neo-liberal world order that seems intent on spreading its empire far and wide and the ongoing expression of military might by powerful Western nations in places such as Afghanistan and Iraq.

In the contemporary post-Cold War context there remains a widely perceived sense of social, economic and cultural injustice in relations between the West and the rest, a situation exacerbated in recent decades by the rise of neo-liberal forms of capitalism and a growing, rather than decreasing, gulf between rich and poor which is only likely to foster further examples of insurgency and violence.[3] Scholars discussing what they see as a resurgence of 'religious violence' have generally ignored such factors, partly because of an insufficiently critical engagement with dominant constructions of 'globalization' and its apparently wholesome and redemptive trajectory. They are also oriented away from such analysis by the assumption that, as a secular and economic phenomenon, contemporary global capitalism is beyond the remit of their discussion. The attack on the World Trade Center in New York in September 2001 was horrific and unjustifiable but it is surely of great significance that the choice of target was an iconic emblem of American/global capitalism. Clearly those who carried out and planned the attack saw this as an opportunity to speak to the sense of social and economic injustice felt by many in 'the Muslim world' in its relations with major Western powers such as the USA. European (and more recently American-driven) colonialism has also been a significant historical factor in the contemporary rise of 'religious violence' across the globe. This colonial history, however, remains largely invisible to scholars such as Juergensmeyer, for whom an Enlightenment-centred (and largely American) view of history appears to be the only way forward,[4] since from such a perspective it becomes difficult to interrogate the darker side of Western secular modernity, which as Anibal Quijano (2000) has pointed out, is experienced as 'coloniality' by those outside the privileged domain of 'the First World'.

Crucial to the generic nature of the debate about 'religion' and violence is an uninterrogated and ahistorical construction of 'the religious'. A significant body of scholarly literature has now emerged since the 1990s that has called into question the universalization of this category from a variety of different perspectives.[5] As I have argued in *Orientalism and Religion* (1999), modern uses of the term 'religion' carry with them the cultural and historical traces of European Christian theological debates and, at least since the Enlightenment, the framing of 'the religious' as a universal category of world history to be firmly distinguished from more recent 'secular' ideologies. Indeed, it is important to appreciate that modern notions of 'the religions' were forged in an ideological context framed by the rise of secular humanism. The concept of religion carries forward cultural tropes that reflect its largely Christian history, but as a feature of Western constructions of modernity it remains essentially the product of a secularist conception of history.

Broadly speaking, 'secularization' – that complex series of processes related to the disestablishment of the Christian Church as a hegemonic force in European and American polities, is not, as is so often claimed, the death of religion but rather the very moment of its birth. It is during the Enlightenment that 'religion' became objectified as systems of belief and practices. This was only possible because the 'sacred canopy' of medieval Christendom had fragmented after the Protestant Reformation leading to a 'denaturalization' of a 'divinely ordained' social and political ordering of reality. The theocentric conception of the cosmos that had dominated in the medieval period also became increasingly displaced by an anthropocentric or humanistic vision of history. The invention of 'the religions' in the modern sense of the term is a consequence of these social processes and reflects the conceptual distillation of a clearly distinguishable human phenomenon – the 'historical religions' – from a wider cultural dynamic. As John Bossy (1982) has suggested, the abstraction of something called 'the religions' (as well as their deployment as a category of universal history) would have been impossible before the social and political transformations of late sixteenth-/early seventeenth-century Europe. I will not dwell any further upon the debate about the historical construction of the religious as a category at this juncture because of limitations of space but instead refer the interested reader to the relevant literature on this topic. What emerges, however, from a serious consideration of these works is that one cannot apply the term 'religion' and its close correlates in a cross-cultural context without at least engaging reflexively with the history of the term and the multiple traces and resonances it carries in the contemporary Euro-American *imaginaire*. Failure to engage with the historical and culturally specific tropes of the 'religion and violence' debate constitutes not only a failure to recognize the Euro-American mindset which frames such discussions, but is also an abdication of the responsibility to apply the same degree of historicization (that is so often applied to the non-Western traditions under examination), to one's own primary categories of analysis.

How exactly then does the use of a 'catch all' category such as 'religion' aid us in understanding ideologically rooted acts of violence in the contemporary and ancient worlds? Clearly as a site of comparative analysis the *modern* concept of religion (which is nothing if it is not a *comparative* category – that is a conceptual site through which an imaginative act of comparison takes place) allows one to bring together apparently disparate cultural and historical phenomena into a single overarching framework. This has enabled those deploying this term to generate cross-cultural and transhistorical statements about otherwise widely divergent traditions and epochs. However, we should remain highly suspicious of the easy deployment of this category, particularly as it has been used in the 'religion and violence' debate, precisely *because* of its largely taken-for-granted status. The belief that there are 'religions' out there in the world is so culturally embedded in the modern imagination that it has become a 'common-sense' category or *doxa* to use Pierre Bourdieu's term. However, as Clifford Geertz (1983: ch.4) has suggested, 'common-sense' is that which in its very taken-for-granted status requires the most rigorous interrogation.

The modern concept of 'religion' carries with it certain key assumptions about the world that are, as we shall see, ultimately grounded in a hegemonic Euro-American myth about the origins of 'modernity' and the birth of the secular nation-state. These assumptions are not ideologically neutral but rather are encoded according to a specifically European history of the world. This history reflects an extended series of conversations or 'cultural wars' in medieval and early modern Europe between various competing forms of Christianity as well as between Christianity and other traditions (usually classified at the time as Jewish, 'Mohammedan' and 'pagan' or 'heathen'). More recently these controversies also incorporated the clash between 'secular' or humanistic movements and the fragmentation of the socio-political world of Christendom. These conflicts played a significant role, for instance, in the colonization of 'the New World' and have become enshrined in the foundational myths of origin for those nations that emerged from the revolutionary movements of the Enlightenment such as the United States of America and France. This has left a strong cultural imprint and suspicion of 'the religious' based upon a particular reading of European history that focuses upon 'the Wars of Religion' as the primary cause of social strife and factionalism. Important though these events have been, in planetary and macro-historical terms, such clashes have been decidedly local disputes, which only appear universal in import because of the way in which they have spilt over onto a global canvas as a consequence of the European colonial reconfiguration of much of the planet in the last few centuries. Failure to appreciate the provincial origins (and traces) of the concept of religion in general and of the 'religion and violence' debate in particular, constitutes one of the most significant *theoretical* obstacles to any attempt to examine not only human propensities towards violence (regardless of whether this is framed as 'religious' or not) but also a broader, non-Eurocentric account of human history that takes account of its diversity and complexity.

How then is the term 'religion' operationalized within the 'religion and violence' debate? Juergensmeyer (2000: 10) characterizes the religious in terms of three features:

1. a transcendentally grounded moralism
2. the ritual intensity with which such acts are committed
3. images of struggle and transformation and concepts of a cosmic war between good and evil.

These features are fairly standard generalizations about 'the religious' in academic and journalistic literature on the subject. Another contributor to this debate, Bruce Lincoln, suggests a similar model of the religious involving the following four characteristics:

> (a) a discourse that claims its concerns transcend the realm of the human, temporal, and contingent, while claiming for itself a similarly transcendent status; (b) a set of practices (ethical, ritual, and sometimes also aesthetic) informed and structured by that discourse; (c) a community organized around the discourse and its attendant practices, whose members regulate their identity with reference to them; and (d) an institutional system that regulates discourse, practices, and community, reproducing and modifying them over time, while still asserting their eternal validity and transcendent value. Whenever any of these components plays a role of some seriousness within a given conflict, one ought to acknowledge that the conflict has a religious dimension.
>
> (1998: 65)

In his book *Holy Terrors* (2003), Lincoln reiterates the centrality of his 'four domains' of the religious. Moreover, he suggests, 'discourse becomes religious not simply by virtue of its content, but also from its claims to authority and truth' (2003: 5) and again 'religion begins with a discourse that constructs itself as divine and unfailing, through which deeds – any deeds – can be defined as moral' (2003: 16). The contrast between the human and the divine here make it absolutely clear that for Lincoln religion implies not only the postulation of these two categories but their explicit polarization. This characterization of the religious of course fits theistic (especially monotheistic) traditions, but it is not clear that it maps at all well in a broader global context.

The various features of 'the religious' highlighted by Juergensmeyer and Lincoln are in fact both too broad *and* too narrow to pick out the global phenomena that they wish to discuss. On the one hand such characterizations can equally apply to a whole host of apparently secular ideologies or movements in the modern world. The struggle for democracy, human rights, free-market capitalism, 'the American way of life', Communism, etc., all involve reference to some kind of transcendental signifier or value. These transcendental referents (whether identified as capital, nation, liberty, etc.) correspond to a set of ideals or values that remain as intangible, out of reach and 'incontestable' as the claims made on behalf of so-called 'religious' values and ideals. They are also similarly anchored in institutions, rituals and social practices that normalize and legitimate their own existence and authority. Contemporary proponents of capitalist neoliberalism – the current orthodoxy of the 'new world order' of globalization – continually imbue their own ideological claims with a magical air of incontestability. A regular mantra of the dominant 'transnational capitalist class' (Sklair 2001) – from corporate leaders to major politicians – is that 'there is no alternative' to globalization (which they read as both an ineluctable force of history and as an economically driven process). This feature of capitalist ideology in the post-Cold War context is increasingly being recognized by some scholars as exhibiting precisely the kinds of features that scholars such as Lincoln and Juergensmeyer associate exclusively with 'the religious' (see Cox 1999; Hopkins 2001; Loy 2002; Carrette and King 2005; Deutschmann 2001). This aspect of capitalism was perhaps first noticed by Walter Benjamin in 1921 in his originally unpublished fragment 'Capitalism as Religion':

> A Religion may be discerned in capitalism – that is to say, capitalism serves essentially to allay the same anxieties, torments, and disturbances to which the so-called religions offered answers. . . . Capitalism is a religion of pure cult, without dogma.
>
> (Benjamin 1996 [1921]: 288–89)

Juergensmeyer's second point – that religious acts are carried out with 'ritual intensity', hardly picks out any clearly identifiable phenomena that we can describe as religious. This characterization builds upon older medieval uses of 'religious' which imply a firm adherence to one's faith (as in taking up a monastic life of 'holy orders'). Even today, when someone undertakes an activity with great resolve and determination we say that they are doing it 'religiously'. This 'cultic sense' of the term (as Jonathan Z. Smith (1998b: 270) describes it), connotes the idea of wilful and unwavering commitment and predisposes one to associate 'religiosity' with ritual repetition, zealotry and extremism. However, since one can 'be religious' in this general sense about anything (from mowing the lawn to looking both ways before crossing the road), in analytic terms it provides no help at all in pinpointing a specifically 'religious' dimension to certain practices. In fact, if anything, everyday usage suggests quite the opposite – namely that one can 'be religious' about a whole host of activities that have nothing to do with 'the religions'.

In a similar fashion, organized acts of violence and aggression carried out by apparently secular nation-states can be just as intense in their ritualized commitments as 'religious' ones, and can similarly polarize the world in terms of a primordial battle between good and evil (in George W. Bush's infamous words about the 'global war on terrorism' – 'you are either with us or you are against us'). This is a point well noted by Lincoln in his analysis of the common Manichean structure to Bush and Bin Laden's rhetoric, but in the case of the American President this is linked by the author to George W. Bush's well-publicized Christian allegiance. This is an easy target and allows Lincoln to continue pressing his case about the dangers of 'the religious' for civic society. It also ignores the continuity of Bush's stance with a broader civic tradition of American exceptionalism, which frequently utilizes a Manichean rhetoric and identifies the USA as the primary driving force of modernity and freedom in the world.[6] Moreover, as William Cavanaugh (2004: 31) notes in his own critique of the discourse of 'religion and violence', the question 'What you would be prepared to kill for?' offers stark empirical evidence that nationalism is a far greater incitement to violence in contemporary America than Christianity.

> What percentage would be willing to kill for their country? Whether we attempt to answer these questions by survey or by observing American Christians' behavior in wartime, it seems clear that, at least among American

> Christians, the nation-state – Hobbes' 'mortal god' – is subject to far more absolutist fervor than 'religion'. For most American Christians, even public evangelization is considered to be in poor taste, and yet many consider it their duty to go to war against whomever the president deems necessary.
>
> (Cavanaugh 2004: 31)

On the other hand, Lincoln and Juergensmeyer's accounts of the religious are also too narrow. Virtually all of the examples that Juergensmeyer uses to illustrate his points in *Terror in the Mind of God*, come from the Jewish, Christian and Islamic traditions and his explanation of the rationale behind such acts invariably appeals to a Manichean cosmic war between good and evil, notions of a struggle between martyrs and demons and a 'satanization' of the other (e.g. 2000: 163). These tropes are not so easily mapped onto the traditional categories of many of the South Asian traditions that Juergensmeyer refers to by implication. Indeed, the main example deployed in the book as an example of contemporary Buddhist violence is the Japanese sect Aum Shinrikyo. This movement is a small-scale and highly eclectic mixture of Buddhist, Śaivite, millenarianist Christian and New Age elements and is hardly representative of the Buddhist tradition as a whole. In making this point I should stress that I am not seeking to romanticize Asian traditions as somehow exempt from the charge that they have been involved in the legitimation and incitement of appalling acts of violence throughout their histories. My point is rather that it does not aid us in understanding these processes to label such traditions as 'religious'. There are a number of obvious examples, for instance, of Buddhist involvement in, and justification of, violent acts, both historical and contemporary (a point noted by Juergensmeyer in his 1993 work; see also Victoria 1997, 2003, Bartholomeusz 2002, and articles by Gethin and Schalk in this volume), but these are rarely dwelt upon by Juergensmeyer in his sweeping account of global terrorism in *Terror in the Mind of God*. Similarly, if one is seeking images of a battle for righteousness against evildoers one need look no further than Indian epics such as the *Mahābhārata*, (again something that Juergensmeyer at least discusses in his 1993 work, but is missing from *Terror in the Mind of God* which focuses exclusively upon the contemporary context). However, despite these clear instances of the complicity between South Asian traditions and the justification and incitement of violence, we should reject very clearly any suggestion that such examples express something 'essential' or even 'essentially religious' about 'Hindu culture' or South Asia, for this is to ignore the heterogeneity of South Asian history. As Lincoln notes:

> Every macro-entity that gets called a 'religion' – Buddhism, Islam or Christianity, for example – has countless internal varieties and subdivisions, each of which undergoes its own historic process of development and change.
>
> (2003: 8)

Indeed, we discover from Lincoln that 'no practices are inherently religious and any may acquire a religious character when connected to a religious discourse that constitutes them as such' (Lincoln 2003: 6). Despite this, Lincoln fails to dwell upon the possibility that the converse might also be the case – namely that the ideologies that are conventionally labelled 'secular' (including his own Enlightenment-grounded tradition of critique) might also exhibit qualities (such as intolerance and intellectual hubris) that the author otherwise associates with 'the religious'.[7] Again, developing one line of argument from Lincoln's analysis, one might ask if it is more appropriate in some instances to classify 'macro-traditions' such as Buddhism, Islam and Christianity – traditions that in their very heterogeneity also include a great deal that is pluralistic and 'tolerant' – as inclusive of trends within them that are more 'secular' than 'religious' (in the sense defined by Lincoln's 'four domains'). The reason that these theoretical possibilities are not explored in any depth by the author, I would suggest, is that to do so would disrupt the stability of the 'secular/religious' dichotomy in a way that would challenge Lincoln's own project, which is, as I read him, to offer a critique of 'the religions' (as he conceives them) based upon their transcendental claims to absolute authority.

The irony of the accounts offered by Juergensmeyer and Lincoln, which in this regard are generally representative of the 'secularist' strand in the 'religion and violence' debate, is that they replicate a Manichean-style dualism of their own in the form of an uncritical and universalized dichotomy between the secular and the religious, and the explicit privileging of ideologies associated with the former not only as adequate and appropriate explanatory accounts of 'the real world' on the one hand but also as a framework for mediating cultural and ideological differences on a global scale on the other. Thus, a key element in both authors' characterization of the religious is their assumption that religions provide secondary interpretations of reality that build upon the more solid (more 'real'?) foundations of social, economic and political events. Juergensmeyer argues, for instance that:

> religious ideas have given a profundity and ideological clarity to what in many cases have been real experiences of economic destitution, social oppression, political corruption and a desperate need for the hope of rising above the limitations of modern life.
>
> (Juergensmeyer 2000: 242)

Here 'real experiences' are equated with the social, economic and political dimensions of life to which religious ideologies 'add' clarity and meaning. Again, elsewhere in the study (Juergensmeyer 2000: 161), the author sets up a dichotomy between 'religious images' on the one hand and 'real life situations' on the other. Similarly, for Lincoln, religious discourse is a worldly (*read*: social/economic/political) discourse that attempts to portray itself as 'other-worldly'. For Lincoln, dissent from this position, as in the claim that such analysis is reductionist, 'is meant to silence critique' (Thesis 12 of Lincoln's *Theses on Method*). This rebuttal of all criticism from traditions that do not accept Western social scientific categories as given, means effectively that Lincoln himself silences any criticism that does not conform to the canons of his own historicism. This reflects a tension in Lincoln's method between an acceptance of human fallibility on the one hand and a rejection of traditions of criticism that are not grounded in the secularist traditions of the European Enlightenment. This is encapsulated in Lincoln's 'Theses on Method' (1996) in the tension between his tenth and twelfth theses:

> Understanding the system of ideology that operates in one's own society is made difficult by two factors: (i) one's own consciousness is itself a product of that system, and (ii) the system's very success renders its operations invisible, since one is so consistently immersed in and bombarded by its products that one comes to mistake them (and the apparatus through which they are produced and disseminated) for nothing other than 'nature'.
>
> (Thesis 10)

> Although critical inquiry has become commonplace in other disciplines, it still offends many students of religion, who denounce it as 'reductionism'. This charge is meant to silence critique. The failure to treat religion 'as religion' – that is, the refusal to ratify its claim of transcendent nature and sacrosanct status – may be regarded as heresy and sacrilege by those who construct themselves as religious, but it is the starting point for those who construct themselves as historians.
>
> (Thesis 12)

Thesis ten is a classic statement of reflexivity. It is a recognition that there is no position from nowhere. Everyone, including the author, has blind spots deriving from their own cultural background and conditioning and this prevents us from seeing the world in an unmediated fashion. Thesis twelve, however, classifies any challenge to Lincoln's own Enlightenment-rooted historicism from a rival intellectual tradition as 'the silencing of critique'. In this context Lincoln seems to fall foul here of what I would call 'Bourdieu's paradox' (so named because it has become one of the classic criticisms of Bourdieu's conception of 'reflexive sociology'). In Bourdieu's case this involved the claim on the one hand that we are all caught in culturally specific webs of signification from which we cannot extricate ourselves (hence the need for reflexivity) and the contrary claim that only the sociologist is in a position to see these conditions and work to overturn them. This paradox is not insurmountable as long as one is prepared to accept that the sociologist's reflexivity is a relative rather than an absolute achievement, and on these terms I think it could be argued that Bourdieu manages to sidestep such a critique. In the case of Lincoln, however, it is not clear that he would be prepared to give up his exclusivist claim that materialist/social scientific accounts of reality (deriving from the humanistic philosophies of the European

Enlightenment) are both *more true* than any other (the 'religious' ones) and also *more capable of embodying tolerance* of differences. As a result virtually every other intellectual tradition in human history is framed as inferior to the humanistic traditions of Western modernity. The underlying burden of this ideology (and let us be clear that it *is* an ideology like all of the others) is to ensure that 'secular' and 'religious' discourses are not analysed on a level playing field – as different, and sometimes competing, ideologies or explanations of the world.

The consequence of this stance is that for Lincoln well-established social-scientific categories, deriving as they do from the specific cultural experiences of Northern Europeans and their American brethren, are naturalized and privileged over the categories of all other worldviews (which have already been interpellated and subalternized according to Lincoln's normative construction of 'the religious'). From this perspective all philosophies that do not express themselves according to the styles, traditions and categories of critical reflection that have been established by the secularist ideologies and disciplines of the European Enlightenment are assigned a subordinate or derivative status as explanations of the world. Indeed, for both Lincoln and Juergensmeyer 'religious' worldviews appear to operate at a secondary level as culturally specific and 'imagined' responses to the real world (of social, economic and political processes).

Thus, a similar sociologism[8] can be found in Juergensmeyer's work when he discusses attitudes towards death within the various 'religions':

> the Jewish notion of raising the dead, the Christian and Muslim notions of heaven and hell, the Roman Catholic notion of purgatory, the Buddhist idea of levels of consciousness (and in the Mahayana tradition, heavenly mansions), and the Hindu theory of karmic cycles of reincarnations – all of these offer ways of avoiding what humans know to be a fact: eventually they will die.
>
> (Juergensmeyer 2000: 158)

In this sweeping list, no account is taken, for instance, of the importance within Buddhist traditions of a contemplative recognition of the inevitability of one's own death or the traditional Hindu, Buddhist and Jain understanding of transmigration as a cycle of re-deaths (*punarmṛtyu*). Rather the impression is given that all religious traditions turn us away from a realization of the reality of death. This of course is precisely the rhetorical function of universalized terms like 'religion' in these contexts – to classify *by implication*. Again, one might ask why modern capitalism is not included in this list, since it also encourages individuals as consumers to avoid an awareness of the inevitability of their own death by promoting the pursuit of a bewildering array of consumable and 'life-enhancing' products that will provide you with *nirvana* in the here and now. Juergensmeyer, following the theories of Ernest Becker, implies that religion denies mortality and that he, as the secular social scientist, is in a privileged position to understand the reality of death.

Frequently one finds scholars relying on what one might call a 'base-line' definition of religion as belief in some kind of transcendental reality or being, beyond the material world. This for instance, is clearly the stance taken by Lincoln (1996: 225) who argues that religion is 'that discourse whose defining characteristic is to desire to speak of things eternal and transcendent with an authority equally transcendent and eternal'. The spirit of Edward B. Tylor (1832–1917) of course, hovers behind such definitions of the religious, with the emphasis placed upon *belief* in some form of supernatural, spiritual or transcendental being or reality beyond the material world of the here and now. Such definitions of the religious, however, privilege 'secular' or materialist presuppositions in at least two regards. First, such a construction of the religious is clearly 'theory-loaded' (Braun 2000: 11), since it presupposes that it already knows what constitutes the (materialist and historical) 'here and now' from which the transcendental pretensions of the religions are subsequently projected. What precisely counts as the world 'out there' and what counts as 'the supernatural', however, constitutes one of the fundamental points at issue when different ideological constructions of reality confront each other. To define the 'religious' as that which claims to be more than it is (that is as postulating a *transcendent* authority that goes beyond its actual and *immanent* historical instantiation) is to presume the falsity of the systems being discussed and privileges materialist accounts of reality as 'given'.[9] One is entitled to ask what makes so-called 'secularist' accounts of the world any less involved in webs of cultural signification than so-called 'religious' accounts of reality. How exactly do secular social scientists learn to wrench themselves out of their own cultural conditioning – by lifting themselves up by their own bootstraps perhaps? The point of my rhetorical question, of course, is to highlight the *transcendentalist* nature of the historicist claim to have left behind (i.e. transcended) religious claims of transcendence. In such an account the cards have already been stacked in favour of a secularist worldview before the game even begins.

The supreme irony of such a position is that it is a materialist, 'secular', and historicist account of the world that is thereby granted transcendental authority – in that only from this perspective is one authorized to speak about cultural and historical contexts beyond their own milieu. The secularist claim to be able to speak about and mediate all rival claims is thus exposed as one of the very same 'bootstrap theories' or ontotheologies that are being criticized for being 'religious' – that is for claiming a totalizing, universal and transcendental authority. This is not easily seen because it is occluded by the use of the discourse of 'religion' to insulate certain ideologies (humanist/materialist ones) from critical engagement alongside the rest. The (post-Feuerbachian) projectionist claims being made here by scholars such as Lincoln also predispose us to read 'the religious' as being somehow characterized by absolutist appeals to an unquestionable authority. This is clearly not the case for many of the traditions and movements that one might label 'religions' in conventional and popular parlance and is more a feature of self-contained, totalitarian or closed ideological systems in general. Such systems may or may not postulate ontologically transcendent or 'supernatural' realms in the narrow sense implied by Lincoln's Tylorian definition of the religious, but an exclusive focus upon these (through the deployment of the category of 'religion') only succeeds in insulating secularist ideologies from the same level of critical analysis. Such a move (and its investment in a particular construction of 'the religious' as a foil to the secular) remains crucial to Lincoln's approach. However, once one challenges the necessary association of 'religion' with absolutist claims to authority, two possibilities emerge. First, that so-called 'secular' ideologies can also lead to totalitarian impulses (something that would be easy to demonstrate from even a cursory glance at twentieth-century history) and second, that tolerance of diversity (and the rejection of absolutism) can be expressed from 'within' a 'religious' tradition (see Asad 1993: Chapter 6 for an interesting discussion of this). This is crucial in demonstrating that modern materialist ideologies do not monopolize the values of tolerance, humility and fallibilism.

Furthermore, it is not even clear that the Tylorian claim that religion is associated with the postulation of an *ontologically* transcendent reality or supernatural being will suffice as a definition of the subject-matter. First, it does not fit all of the cases that are popularly taken to be examples of 'religions' (consider for instance the Buddhist position that, as Nāgārjuna puts it, 'there is not the slightest difference between *saṃsāra* (this world) and *nirvāṇa* – the goal of liberation', *Madhyamaka-Kārikā* 25.19–20). Second, such constructions of the religious ignore the possibility that in a contemporary 'secularized' and scientific context, the transcendental has not disappeared, it has simply gone underground. After the apparent 'death of God', the so-called 'religious impulse' (which as we have seen for Lincoln seems to imply some kind of absolutist claim to authority) is likely to manifest itself in new and surprising ways, reflecting not only considerable local variations but also the cultural dominance of natural scientific explanations of the cosmos. This indeed may be a consequence of secularization when viewed as a process of differentiation (Casanova 1994). Conceding much of the traditional cosmological and metaphysical ground of explanation to the sciences, post-Enlightenment forms of 'religiosity' may well express themselves in a way that conforms to a scientific explanation of the world. This may make them appear decidedly 'secular' when in fact this is merely a reflection of the reconfiguration of the 'field of the religious' (if one insists on using this concept) or the 'metaphysical' in a post-scientific context. We should not be surprised therefore to find behavioural patterns, practices, beliefs and authority claims that might traditionally have been associated with 'the religions' (in Lincoln's terms), manifesting themselves in new apparently 'secular' and 'post-metaphysical' forms (as David Martin (1998: 40–41) has suggested). The modern authority of the natural sciences in a 'secularized' context has fundamentally transformed the ideological field in which fundamental world-views, 'religions' (or 'cosmographic formations' as Dubuisson (2003) calls them) are now able to express themselves. One way of putting this would be to say that in certain contexts modern (and 'postmodern') secular ideologies, may themselves turn out to be 'religions' (again in Lincoln's sense of the term).

Given that humans inspired by avowedly secularist ideologies have been responsible for some of the most terrible atrocities and genocides of the twentieth century, one is entitled to ask why violence and intolerance continue to be associated with 'the religions' in particular and at the expense of seeing a similar complicity between violence and so-called 'secular' ideologies. Indeed, such are the problems involved in attempting to maintain a hard and fast distinction between the religious and the secular that I would suggest that we avoid this particular dichotomy as much as possible, since it simply does not aid us in understanding societies that do not easily conform to the social pattern that emerged in European and American societies influenced by Christian and Enlightenment-derived philosophies of the world. Moreover, in the context of the 'religion and violence' debate, the dichotomy between the secular and the religious has served to bolster the interests of two key constituencies involved in the controversy – the secularists and the religionists. Both have something to gain by maintaining and reproducing the language of 'religion' in this debate.

Much of the contemporary impetus behind the very idea that there is a sharp difference in type between 'the secular' and 'the religious' itself originates from within the interpretive framework of one particular ideological perspective – which, for want of a better word, we might label 'secularism'. The historical relationship between constructions of 'the religious' and 'the secular' is far too complex to allow such a simple dichotomy to be deployed usefully, for as Talal Asad has noted:

> The secular ... is neither continuous with the religious that supposedly preceded it (that is, it is not the latest phase of a sacred origin) nor a simple break from it (that is, it is not the opposite, an essence that excludes the sacred). I take the secular to be a concept that brings together certain behaviours, knowledges, and sensibilities in modern life. To appreciate this it is not enough to show that what appears to be necessary is really contingent – that in certain respects, 'the secular' obviously overlaps with 'the religious'. It is a matter of showing how contingencies relate to changes in the grammar of concepts – that is, how the changes in concepts articulate changes in practices ... the secular is neither singular in origin nor stable in its historical identity, although it works through a series of particular oppositions.
>
> (Asad 2003: 25)

Rather than focusing upon 'the problem of religion and violence', as if this reflected some sort of intrinsic or essential 'religious' quality that some ideologies possess and others do not, I suggest that one would do better to examine apparently 'secular' and 'religious' worldviews side by side. Only then are we likely to gain a greater comparative understanding of the human propensity to carry out ideologically rooted and 'communal' acts of violence upon each other.

One of the features that Juergensmeyer identifies as a characteristic of 'religious' acts of violence is the 'symbolic' and dramatic aspect of acts of 'religious terrorism', reflecting the sense in which they refer to something 'beyond their immediate target' (2000: 123). This is used by the author to suggest that such acts relate to 'other-worldly' or 'transcendental' goals. However, there is perhaps a more prosaic reason why groups like Aum Shinrikyo and al-Qaida engage in highly symbolic acts of violence and this has little to do with the purported 'religious' or transcendental nature of their goals. If the act is not an example of state-sponsored 'terrorism' (such as an attack on a sovereign nation or a bombing campaign on a civilian population) but is rather carried out by a relatively small-scale and disempowered group then there is little choice but to carry out highly *symbolic* acts of violence, since this is the most effective way of drawing widespread public attention to one's cause when faced with a radical asymmetry of power.[10] Juergensmeyer's point presumably is that the message or goal motivating the act transcends the particular focus of that attack, but this hardly makes such goals 'otherworldly' in nature (2000: 217). The implication drawn by Juergensmeyer about the 'otherworldly' nature of such acts is misleading. That this dichotomy between 'religious' and secular' uses of 'performance violence' cannot be maintained becomes clear, even on Juergensmeyer's own terms, when he acknowledges that the 'religions' (as he understands them) do not have a monopoly on such symbolic acts (2000: 216–17). As one frequently finds in literature on this theme, Juergensmeyer assumes before his analysis begins that religion and war have a long history of association (2000: 156) but this is hardly surprising given that the phenomena that he pinpoints as 'religious' relate to civilizations and traditions with long-standing and complex histories. The twentieth century has been scarred by the violent oppression of people by a number of totalitarian regimes (most notably Nazism and Stalinism) and two bloody world wars. The twenty-first century has begun in a similarly belligerent fashion. Are these wars religious in nature? To frame this point in a different way, is the problem of violence in human history one that is best laid at the door of *homo religiosus* or of *homo sapiens* in general? How does referring to this history in terms of 'religions' do anything other than insulate certain societies, institutions and ideologies (usually labelled 'secular') from a comparable degree of critical interrogation? As Talal Asad has suggested:

> The point that matters in the end, surely, is not the justification that is used (whether it be supernatural or worldly) but the behaviour that is justified. On this point, it must be said that the ruthlessness of secular practice yields nothing to the ferocity of (the) religious.
>
> (1993: 236)

Although Lincoln engages with Asad's critique of the universalization of 'religion' in *Holy Terrors*, he sidesteps the more radical implications of Asad's thesis by suggesting that all language (not just the construction of 'religion') 'is the historical product of discursive processes' (Lincoln 2003: 2) and by focusing on that aspect of Asad's critique that targets an extreme and privatized conception of 'the religious'. This, however, domesticates Asad's general critique of the concept of religion and also ignores the colonial issues that arise when one applies an Occidental concept that has played a crucial role in the identity-construction of the modern 'West' as a fundamental category in the study of non-Western civilizations and traditions. What we have in the deployment of the category of religion in these contexts is the projection of an 'insider category' from Lincoln's own cultural tradition, a notion that has a long and complicated history in the West and its application in cultural domains where, until comparatively recently, it had no role to play. This would not necessarily be a problem if it were not for the ideological baggage that the term 'religion' carries with it and the work it continues to do in fostering a sense of the distinctiveness and 'modernity' of Western civilization. This is all the more surprising since Lincoln asserts at this point in his discussion that 'the end result of our definitional labors ought to problematize and not normalize, the model that prompted their inception' (2003: 2).

Even more strikingly, at no point in *Terror in the Mind of God* does Juergensmeyer interrogate the concept of religion that is, of course, so crucial to his analysis. This is unfortunate because one of the issues here is precisely that of determining how – that is through what processes – certain institutions, traditions and civilizations have become characterized as 'religions' during the period of European colonial rule. To give an example, consider David Scott's work on Śri Lanka. Scott highlights the role of the British Colebrooke–Cameron reforms of the 1830s in re-structuring indigenous subjectivities and institutions, thereby creating an Anglicized middle-class elite in Śri Lanka and providing the conditions for the emergence of new reform-oriented trends such as Dharmapāla's modernist-oriented Buddhism. As Scott notes:

> Concepts like 'religion', 'state', and 'identity', are treated ahistorically insofar as they are made to refer to a set of timeless social-ideological formations as defining (or as *defining in the same way*) for say third-century inhabitants of the island as for contemporary Sinhalas. This conceptual/ideological projection of the present into the past (as a hermeneutic of the present) is possible only because these categories – religion, state, and so on – are the authoritative and normalized categories through which Universal History has been written, and through which the local histories of the colonial and postcolonial worlds have been constituted as so many variations on a common theme about the progressive making of modernity.
>
> (2000: 288–9)

The transformation of Sinhalese 'Buddhism' into a 'religion' in the modern sense of a total belief-system with clear (and largely closed) boundaries that differentiate it from other religions is a complex process. It was bound up with the activities of Christian missionaries (and their insistence that the native 'confess their faith' as a means of contestation and conversion to Christianity). It was also propelled by the colonial re-structuring of civil society and education, the impact of European scholarship on 'Buddhism' upon indigenous subjectivity and the activities of groups like the Theosophists in defending what they saw as 'the Buddhist faith' of the Śri Lankan people (Lopez 1998). Through all of these factors (which cannot be explored here in any detail), not only was something called 'Buddhism' born (translating indigenous notions of *bauddhāgama* and *bauddha-śāsana* in the process) but this 'Buddhism' entered the colonial regime of knowledge as a 'religion' and a 'faith' amenable to a universalized discourse of 'world religions' that, as Tomoko Masuzawa (2005) has shown, only really emerged in the early twentieth century. This context severely complicates our attempts to analyse 'communal' and 'religious' violence in Śri Lanka. Similarly, as Arvind Mandair and Balbinder Bhogal have argued in this volume, European colonialism has played a crucial role in the construction of modern Sikh subjectivities. The issue here is not just that Western power has influenced the historical formation of the modern 'religions' of South Asia, but that the very characterization of the history of South Asian civilization (and by extension the rest of the 'non-Western' world) in terms of Euro-American notions of 'the religious' is itself problematic (King 1999; Peterson and Walhof 2002), see also Peter Gottschalk's contribution to this volume, pp. 195–210).

Moreover, once one begins to question the usefulness of the concept of 'religion' as a way of understanding ideologically rooted acts of violence, one might also ask why conflicts in South and West Asia are so often conceptualized differently from those involving Western nations. Why, as Peter Gottschalk has asked, is the American–Vietnamese war *never* represented as a clash between Christian and Buddhist civilizations, or the Quebeçois secessionist movement in Canada not seen as a Catholic struggle against a Protestant dominated nation, whilst South Asian cultures are so often represented in terms of a clash between *Hindu* and *Muslim,* or *Sinhalese Buddhist* versus *Hindu Tamil* (Gottschalk 2000: 12)? Is it that 'the religious' is supposed to have a greater significance in South Asian constructions of identity and community or is it rather that the supposedly 'religious dimension' of such phenomena has been over-determined in such accounts? To what extent is the *description* of violence in South Asia as 'religious' itself a product of the discursive transformations of these traditions in the modern world under the influence of European colonialism and orientalism?

To begin to answer some of these questions one must first understand the historical roots of the contemporary association of 'religion' with violence in Euro-American cultural contexts.

'The Wars of Religion' as part of the myth of origin of the nation-state

The modern association of violence with 'the religions' became firmly embedded in European (and early American) societies during the Enlightenment, where the underlying principles of modern liberalism were born. According to the secular myth surrounding the birth of the nation-state that most of us have inherited, the conflictual and violent nature of medieval Christian factions (often called 'The Wars of Religion') could only be resolved by some form of disestablishment of the Church and the State. By challenging the traditional social, moral and philosophical authority of the Church, European and North American intellectuals sought to establish a framework for society and politics that avoided the religious conflicts of previous centuries. The most popular solution was to relegate the religious to the private sphere of life – to clearly demarcate it from the public realms of politics, science, philosophy and economics. This modern myth about the triumphant birth of the secular nation-state is deeply embedded in the consciousness of most Europeans and Americans. Thus, Bruce Lincoln (1998: 66) can declare, without any need for justification that 'The modern nation-state was created, in large measure, as a check against the violence and destruction unleashed in religious conflicts of this sort'.[11]

The taken-for-grantedness of this account of history obscures a considerably more complex understanding of the historical conditions under which the modern nation-state emerged. While it may have been the Protestant Reformation that broke the sacred canopy of medieval Christendom, thereby opening up the space for the emergence of proto-nation states (Philpott 2001), social turbulence during this period (called retrospectively the 'Wars of Religion') can just as easily be read as the product of the conflict between old and new regimes of regional power in early modern Europe. It is these regional power struggles, brought about by the fracturing of medieval Christendom that culminated in the sanctification of the sovereignty of the nation-state at the Peace of Westphalia in 1648. This coincides with the emergence of the modern concept of 'religion' as an identifiable phenomenon (Bossy 1982; Harrison 1990). The reification of this concept, I would argue, has played a crucial role in normalizing the sacred mythology of the modern 'secular' nation-state.

According to William Cavanaugh (1995), the modern (one might even say 'secular') concept of religion and its association with discord and violence emerged in this period primarily as a means of displacing the violence associated with the end of feudalism and the birth of the modern nation-state. Cavanaugh argues, therefore, that the story conveyed in conventional historical accounts 'puts the matter backwards':

> The 'Wars of Religion' were not the events, which necessitated the birth of the modern State; they were in fact themselves the birthpangs of the State. These wars were not simply a matter of conflict between 'Protestantism' and 'Catholicism', but were fought largely for the aggrandizement of the emerging State over the decaying remnants of the medieval ecclesial order. I do not wish merely to contend that political and economic factors played a central role in these wars, nor to make a facile reduction of religion to more mundane concerns. I will rather argue that to call these conflicts 'Wars of Religion' is an anachronism, for what was at issue in these wars was the very creation of religion as a set of privately held beliefs without direct political relevance. The creation of religion was

> necessitated by the new State's need to secure absolute sovereignty over its subjects.
>
> (Cavanaugh 1995: 398)

The Westphalian solution initiated the birth of the modern nation-state, with its clear territorial boundaries and the notion of national sovereignty. In Northern Europe the divergent Christian allegiances of citizens in the newly emerging nation-states were to be protected by 're-locating' them to the private sphere. The Enlightenment secularist model of course has also led to a prevailing belief in Northern Europe and its former colonies (including the USA) that politics and religion should not be mixed. I would like to highlight two consequences that have followed from this particular configuration of the religious. First, the Western liberal assumption that religion and politics represent two separate realms of human life has become a major stumbling block in Western attempts to understand the phenomenon of 'religious nationalism'. Once modern Western renderings of the secular/religious divide are accepted as the normative paradigm, examples of politically active and religious authority become easily predisposed to the image of the manipulative and opportunistic ideologue.[12] Groups that accept the secular authority of such a figure thus become represented as subject to some form of mass religious indoctrination. One does not have to look far to find contemporary examples of such a paradigm at work in Western representations of religions in the various mass media. In contrast to such reductionist approaches, we should, as Peter van der Veer argues, 'take religious discourse and practice as constitutive of changing social identities, rather than treating them as ideological smoke screens that hide the real clash of material interests and social classes' (van der Veer 1994: ix).

A second consequence of the secularist assumption that politics and religion are separate realms has been to perform a cognitive separation of acts of violence carried out by nation-states from acts of violence carried out in the name of 'religion'. The continued exclusion of acts of war and other state-sponsored acts of violence carried out by modern 'secular' nation-states in debates about violence and 'terrorism' is a reflection of the conceptual difficulties that secular nationalist discourse has in looking beyond its own Euro-American cultural horizons. The modern secular nation-state was formed in a Euro-American context, where its very legitimacy was bound up with a denial of the violence associated with its own birth. In this context, forged in the crucible of Enlightenment anti-clericalism, the category of 'the religious' has becomes the primary foil, the point of conceptual displacement and the epistemological 'dumping ground' for secular modernity's own dark side. Similarly, the assumption that violence only occurs when 'religion becomes evil' (Kimball 2002), trades upon a conception of 'the religious' which divests the traditions so classified of their complexity and historical complicity in acts of oppression and violence.

What 'secularist' critics and 'religionist' defenders share in common in this debate is an investment in the production of a discourse of religion that can be easily deployed to justify not only their own institutional location as 'experts of religion' (of varying points of view) but also to bolster their particular ideological stake in the debate (whether 'pro-religious', 'anti-religious' or somewhere in-between). Lincoln, for instance, raises the stakes to the highest level when considering those who might dare to question that the secularism that emerged from the European Enlightenment is the only model possible for successfully mediating pluralities in society: 'When one rejects the Enlightenment's values en masse and dispenses with its model of culture, one risks not just a return of the repressed, but novel Wars of Religion' (Lincoln 2003: 61). In the face of such a challenge and in anticipation of such a charge, it is important that I reiterate that there is no sense at all in which the arguments in this paper constitute a rejection of 'Enlightenment values en masse' (many of which I share and hold dear), as if such a thing were even possible for a Western scholar like myself working in the academy and committed to its traditions of critical and disciplined inquiry. However, I think it behoves us as human beings to acknowledge that open-ended, tolerant and critical thinking of the kind valued by Lincoln and others (including myself), is *not* solely the provenance of the secular humanists of the European Enlightenment, and that a critique of absolutist claims to truth can be grounded in intellectual traditions other than the secularist hermeneutic of suspicion initiated by Marx, Freud and Nietzsche. To suggest otherwise is to do no less than assert the inherent superiority of modern Western civilization.

In this regard, in the post-9/11 world we have seen an unholy alliance between left- and right-wing thinkers. Moreover, the Enlightenment tradition of critical thought (which is itself heterogeneous) can also be applied reflexively to itself. Such moves undermine the exclusivist claim that 'only we have the answers'. It is important therefore to acknowledge the historicity of Enlightenment values and concepts (including ironically the historicity of historicism itself!)[13] as well as maintain a sense of humility when tempted to make totalizing and universalist claims about reality. Failure to perform this act of reflexivity in such contexts is to assert the privileged status of a secularized Enlightenment account of human history, or, in other words, to turn it, as Adorno and Horkheimer cautioned, into a new kind of totalizing myth. None of this precludes an acknowledgement of the tangible social achievements and practical advantages of adopting Western-style secularism, or what we might call (to use Lincoln's terms) a pluralistic and 'minimalist' approach to macro-traditions, but it is not clear to me why non-Western (and so-called 'religious') traditions cannot also serve as the basis for developing pluralistic, tolerant and inclusivist models of society. One might still wish to appeal to the ways in which models of society emerging from the European Enlightenment have promoted a democratically oriented culture of tolerance and some measure of protection for minorities, but again, one does not need to be a secular humanist to uphold such values. It is also important that we confront the darker side of Euro-American constructions of 'modernity/coloniality' (Quijano 2000) rather than shield these aspects from critical engagement by the normalization of an unexamined and secularist construction of 'religion'. Indeed, I would argue that those who wish to defend the merits of an Enlightenment-inspired 'secularist' position are better served on a global scale if they take seriously the fact that this is only one of a number of potential responses to the issue of mediating conflicts and divergent truth-claims in contemporary societies. One size may not fit all. The alternative in our new age of 'Empire', unfortunately, would seem to be to endorse a kind of *Pax Americana* by default.

The tragic irony of a secularist position that privileges its own standpoint as *uniquely* positioned to promote tolerance, pluralism and protection of the minorities in modern society is that, in the attempt to exclude 'religious' discourse from the public arena, the pluralistic ground upon which the secularist position stands becomes itself undermined. As William Connolly (1999) has argued, the sheer intensity of secularist resistance to traditional (so-called 'religious') dogmatisms can often lead to an unacknowledged immodesty of its own and a failure to acknowledge the possibility of what he calls 'asecular, non-theistic perspectives' that promote reverence, ethics and a civil society. The blind-spot of secularism occurs when it sets itself up as the authoritative centre of public discourse. Without decentering itself, secularism serves only to breed further opposition – thereby reproducing the very threat that it is designed to exclude. Thus, the secularist prophecy about 'religion' becomes self-fulfilling! The reproduction of authoritarian and fundamentalist discourses is of course the real danger of the binary logic at work in attempts to clearly differentiate 'religious' from 'secular' worldviews. If the options are so drastically reduced that 'you are either with us or against us' (to echo the words of George W. Bush) then the pluralistic vision that supposedly grounds a secularist vision of public life becomes undermined by an inability to take seriously the possibility of Christian, Buddhist, Hindu and Islamic correlates to the 'Western secular model'. As framed by Connolly, the key question (and response) becomes:

> Is it, again, possible to refashion secularism as a model of thinking, discourse and public life without lapsing into the 'opposite' view that 'Christianity' or 'the Judaeo-Christian tradition' must set the authoritative matrix of public life? Not if you think that the world comes predesigned with these two options alone. . . . *If* the objective [however] is to project your own perspective into the fray while also decentering the political imagination of the ensconced contestants so that each becomes an honored participant in a pluralistic culture rather than the authoritative embodiment of it, *then* the positive possibilities expand.
>
> (1999: 6)

To conclude, we would do well to try playing a different language game from the one that has characterized the 'religion and violence' debate. Such approaches must take seriously the fact that not all civilizations and traditions are mere correlates or carbon copies of European Christianity and that they are therefore not condemned (by virtue of belonging to the same genus – 'religion') to replicate the historical patterns of violence that have been laid at the feet of 'religion' in modern Euro-American accounts of history. To change the debate, however, requires an acknowledgement that we have all been framed. The major 'macro-traditions' of the world, by virtue of their status as 'great civilizations', extend over a vast cultural, geographical and temporal range. Since they represent such a vast heterogeneity of movements, trends, beliefs and practices they can be characterized both as vehicles of violence on the one hand and of social harmony and moral selflessness on the other. It all depends upon the evidence that one chooses to highlight and the lenses one is wearing.

Despite, the enormous conceptual problems involved in attempting to maintain a strict dichotomy between 'religious' and 'secular' worldviews, the discourse of 'religion and violence' has proved so popular precisely because it serves such powerful and deeply embedded interests. The overall effect of accounts of world history that rely on an uncritical deployment of the category of 'religion' is to reinforce an Orientalist vision of the world that posits 'the West' (however that putative entity may be defined) as a beacon of hope, tolerance, democracy and rationality in a world otherwise beset by the dark forces of superstition, intolerance and irrationality. The self-congratulatory rhetoric of such Euro-American tropes of course is exactly mirrored in the anti-Western rhetoric that has emerged, for instance, in Islamist portrayals of a decadent and irreligious West. This is a dangerous rhetorical game that we should be seeking to displace rather than escalate. Both stances, however, are challenged once one challenges the universalization of the discourse of religion upon which both positions rest. As Daniel Dubuisson (2003) has argued, such a critique goes to the heart of Western imperial power, since the universalized category of religion has played such a crucial role in the West's assertion of its own distinctiveness and superiority. Finally, failure to challenge this Euro/Americo-centric account of the world not only sets a paradigmatic limit on our attempts to understand ideologically rooted acts of violence in their complexity and diversity, but also does a violence to the cultures and civilizations of the non-Western world that it so actively frames.

Notes

1 This statement requires some qualification. The USA, France and Japan have a constitutional separation of church and state. China remains, ostensibly at least, a socialist country, ruled by the Communist Party of China. Although there are a small number of state-regulated churches and temples, meaning that in practice there is no formal separation of church and state, the secularist ideology of the ruling party severely restricts the role of 'religion' in public affairs. The United Kingdom has as its formal head of state a monarch, who is also the head of the Anglican Church. There is therefore an established church. However, the United Kingdom is in many respects a highly 'secularized' and multicultural society, with the Anglican Church having little more than a formalistic and ritual function with regard to the affairs of state. In their differently inflected fashions all exhibit a broadly 'secularist' approach to governance.

2 See Anderson and Cavanaugh (2000).

3 For an insightful but biting critique of contemporary neoliberalism and the violence it reaps upon societies, see Giroux (2004) and Brennan (2003).

4 Indeed, Juergensmeyer's work assumes a Western (mostly North American audience) and at times appears to express the view that Enlightenment tolerance can only go so far, before lapsing back into some kind of *Pax Americana*:

> If we were to compile a list of those characteristics of religious nationalism *we* cannot live with and those *we* can live with, the first list must be quite lengthy. It would surely include the potential for demagoguery and dictatorship, the tendency to satanize the United States and to loathe western civilization, and the potential to become violent and intolerant. Most Americans, including myself, would agree that these are indeed *unacceptable* characteristics in any nation that wants to be part of the global community, and *we should not have to live with them.*
>
> (1993: 195, my italics for emphasis).

5 These works include: Cantwell Smith (1962); J.Z. Smith (1978, 1982, 1998); Despland (1979, 1999); Asad (1993); McCutcheon (1997); Dubuisson (2003); Fitzgerald (2000); Bossy (1982); Biller (1985); Harrison (1990); Despland and Vallee (eds) (1992); Cavanaugh (1995); Feil (1986, 1997); David Chidester (1996); Balagangadhara (1994); King (1999); Peterson and Walhof (eds) (2002); Masuzawa (2005).

6 Thus Eric Foner, a professor of history at Columbia University argues that Americans sometimes have the tendency to see enemies not just as opponents but as evil. Linked to that is the belief that America is the world's last best hope of liberty, so that those who oppose America become the enemies of freedom. Foner suggests that this is

> an unfortunate recurring pattern in American history. ... We have a tendency in times of war to adopt a Manichean vision of the world. It's a state of mind that makes us demonize the enemy and leads to a failure to see dissent as anything but treason.
>
> (Cited in Robert F. Worth, 'Truth, Right and the American Way; A Nation Defines Itself By Its Evil Enemies', *New York Times*, 22 February 2002)

7 That this position can be derived from Lincoln's work can be seen for instance in *Myth, Cosmos and Society* (1986: 164) where he suggests that 'an ideology – any ideology – is not just an ideal against which social reality is measured or an end toward the fulfillment of which groups and individuals aspire' but in fact also acts to persuade members of that group 'of the rightness of their lot in life, whatever that may be, and of the total social order'. Here all ideologies – whether secular or religious – it appears can function as religions in the later sense of Lincoln's 'four domains'.

8 I am using the term 'sociologism' here in the sense in which it is used by Talal Asad, that is as referring to the widespread scholarly belief that 'religious ideologies are said to get their real meaning from the political or economic structure, and the self-confirming methodology according to which this reductive semantic principle is evident to the (authoritative) anthropologist and not to the people being written about' (Asad 1993: 198–199). It should be clear from my arguments throughout this paper and elsewhere (e.g. King 1999) that the 'religionist' position (by which I mean the counter-claim, most often associated with the phenomenology or 'history of religions' school, that there is an autonomous realm known as 'the religious') is equally problematic. Both positions are products of a Euro-Occidentalist view of the world.

9 One might argue that the underlying cosmologies of these worldviews do not necessarily presuppose a 'spiritual' or transcendental realm in the classical (that is 'pre-Enlightenment') sense of some kind of ethereal existence beyond the material 'here and now'. However, to construct 'religion' in this fashion is to use the term to denote *all* metaphysical systems that pre-existed or have yet to be reformulated by the rise of modern science and the various humanistic philosophies of the European Enlightenment. In other words, 'religion' comes to denote any worldview that does not conform to the metaphysics of contemporary materialism in positing the sole reality of the material world. This approach privileges secularist philosophies (with 'religion' being defined in a circular manner as that which is not secularist). Such constructions not only privilege metaphysics and discourse as the ground for defining what is and is not religious but also obscure the fact that materialism is itself only one of a number of metaphysical interpretations of reality.

10 It is clear for instance from Jason Burke's work on al-Qaida (2003, 2004) that bin Laden's movement has always been a small-scale network of radical Islamists. Initially involved in fighting a guerrilla war to 'liberate' Afghanistan from Soviet rule (with the aid of the USA), they have been concerned more recently with challenging what they saw as decadent rulers in the Middle East (such as the Saudi Arabian monarchy and the secular dictatorship of Saddam Hussein in Iraq) and also seeking to overthrow Western imperialist interests in that same region. The loose cadre of radicals surrounding Osama bin Laden (apparently first portrayed as a tight and coherent organization known as 'al-Qaida' by the FBI in 1998) have become emboldened and swelled in their ranks by the high-profile attacks of 9/11 and subsequent US military reactions to those attacks, such as the invasions of Afghanistan and Iraq. 'Al-Qaida' as a global label has now become an 'Islamic franchise' for a variety of radical Islamist groups responding to what they see as American-led imperial intervention in the Middle East on the part of certain Western nations.

11 See Lincoln, *Holy Terrors* (2003: 56–57) for a classic example of the Enlightenment secularist account of the 'Wars of Religion' that underlies Lincoln's approach.

12 One consequence of this distinction has been to foster a suspicion amongst Westerners that any linkage of the two realms reflects a 'merely rhetorical' use of religious discourse to mask some underlying political, ideological or 'worldly' intention. This is a form of simplistic reductionism. This approach presupposes that religion and politics can, and indeed should, be distinguished and that the political dimension is the more fundamental of the two. The political meta-discourse is thus given ultimate explanatory status, explaining what has been hidden from view by religious discourse.

13 In making this point I am reminded of Bourdieu's declaration (2004) that to fulfill its own condition a reflexive sociology must also be a 'sociology of sociology' – that is, reflect upon its own socially constructed nature.

References

Adorno, Theodor and Horkheimer, Max (1972) *Dialectic of Enlightenment*, New York: Herder and Herder.

Anderson and Cavanaugh (2000) *Top 200: The Rise of Global Corporate Power*, New York: The Institute for Policy Studies.

Asad, Talal (1993) *Genealogies of Religion: Discipline and Reasons of Power in Christianity and Islam*, London: John Hopkins University Press.

——(2003) *Formations of the Secular. Christianity, Islam, Modernity*, Stanford, CA: Stanford University Press.

Balagangadhara, S.N. (1994) *'The Heathen in His Blindness': Asia, the West and the Dynamic of Religion*, Leiden: E.J. Brill.

Bartholomeusz, Tessa J. (2002) *In Defense of Dharma: Just-War Ideology in Buddhist Sri Lanka*, London and New York: RoutledgeCurzon.

Benjamin, Walter (1921) 'Capitalism as Religion' in Marcus Bullock and Michael W. Jennings (eds) *Selected Writings: Volume 1913–1926*, London: Belnap Press, 1996, pp. 288–289.

Biller, Peter (1985) 'Words and the Medieval Notion of "Religion"', *Journal of Ecclesiastical History*, 36 (3): 351–369.

Bossy, John (1982) 'Some Elementary Forms of Durkheim' in *Past and Present*, 95 (May): 3–18.

Bourdieu, Pierre (1977) *Outline of a Theory of Practice*, Cambridge: Cambridge University Press.

——(1990) *Logic of Practice*, Stanford, CA: Stanford University Press.

——(2004 [2001]) *Science de la science et la reflexivité*, Edition Raisons d'Agir; English trans. Richard Nice, *Science of Science and Reflexivity*, Chicago: Chicago University Press, 2004.

Braun, Willi (2000) 'Religion' in Willi Braun and Russell T. McCutcheon (eds) *Guide to the Study of Religion*, London and New York: Cassell, pp. 3–20.

Brennan, Teresa (2003) *Globalization and its Terrors: Daily Life in the West*, London: Routledge.

Burke, Jason (2003) *Al-Qaida, Casting a Shadow of Terror*, London: I.B. Tauris.

——(2004) *Al-Qaida: The True Story of Radical Islam*, London: I.B. Tauris.

Carrette, Jeremy and King, Richard (2005) *Selling Spirituality: The Silent Takeover of Religion*, London and New York: Routledge.

Casanova, José (1994) *Public Religions in the Modern World*, Chicago: University of Chicago Press.

Cavanaugh, William T. (1995) 'A Fire Strong Enough To Consume the House: "The Wars of Religion" and the Rise of the State' in *Modern Theology*, 11, 4 (October): 397–420.

——(2004) 'Killing in the Name of God' in *New Blackfriars*, 85: 510–526.

Chidester, David (1996) *Savage Systems: Colonialism and Comparative Religion in Southern Africa*, Studies in Religion and Culture, Charlottesville, VA: University Press of Virginia.

Connolly, William E. (1999) *Why I am Not a Secularist*, Minneapolis: University of Minnesota Press.

Cox, Harvey (1999) 'The Market as God' in *The Atlantic*, (March): 18–23.

Despland (1979) *La Religion en Occident: Evolution des idées et du vécu*, Héritage et projet, 23, Montreal: Fides.

——(1999) *L'émergence des sciences de la religion. La monarchie de Juillet: un moment fondateur*, Paris: L'Harmattan.

Despland, Michel and Gérard Vallee (eds) (1992) *Religion in History: the Word, the Idea, the Reality*, Waterloo, ONT: Wilfred Laurier University Press.

Deutschmann, Christoph (2001) '"The Promise of Absolute Wealth": Capitalism as a Religion?' in *Thesis Eleven*, 66 (August): 32–56.

Dirlik, Arif (2000) *Postmodernity's Histories: The Past as Legacy and Project*, Lanham, MD: Rowman and Littlefield.

Dubuisson, Daniel (2003 [1998]) *L'Occident et la religion: Mythes, science et idéologie*, Editions Complexe; English trans. William Sayers, *The Western Construction of Religion: Myths, Knowledge and Ideology*, Baltimore, MD: John Hopkins University Press.

Feil, Ernst (1986) *Religio: die Geschichte eines neuzeitlichen Grundbegriffs vom Frühchristentum bis zur Reformation*, Forschung zur Kirchen- und Dogmengeschichte, 36, Göttingen: Vandenhoeck and Ruprecht.

——(1997) *Religio II: die Geschichte eines neuzeitlichen Grundbegriffs zwischen Reformation und Rationalismus (ca. 1540–1620)*, Forschung zur Kirchen- und Dogmengeschichte, 70, Göttingen: Vandenhoeck and Ruprecht.

Fitzgerald, Timothy (2000) *The Ideology of Religious Studies*, Oxford: Oxford University Press.

Gambetta, Diego (ed.) (2005) *Making Sense of Suicide Missions*, Oxford: Oxford University Press.

Geertz, Clifford (1983) *Local Knowledge: Further Essays in Interpretive Anthropology*, New York: Basic Books Inc.

Giroux, Henry A. (2004) *The Terror of Neoliberalism: Authoritarianism and the Eclipse of Democracy*, Boulder, CO: Paradigm Publishers.

Gottschalk, Peter (2000) *Beyond Hindu and Muslim*, Oxford and New York: Oxford University Press.

Harrison, Peter (1990) *'Religion' and the Religions in the English Enlightenment*, Cambridge: Cambridge University Press.

Hopkins, Dwight (2001) 'The Religion of Globalization' in Dwight, N. Hopkins, Lois Ann Lorentzen, Eduardo Mendieta and David Batstone (eds) *Religions/Globalizations: Theories and Cases*, Durham, NC and London: Duke University Press.

Juergensmeyer, Mark (1993) *The New Cold War? Religious Nationalism Confronts the Secular State*, Berkeley and Los Angeles: University of California Press.

——(2000) *Terror in the Mind of God. The Global Rise of Religious Violence*, Berkeley and Los Angeles: University of California Press.

Kimball, Charles (2002) *When Religion Becomes Evil*, New York: HarperSanFrancisco.

King, Richard (1999) *Orientalism and Religion: Postcolonial Theory India and 'the Mystic East'*, New York and London: Routledge.

Lincoln, Bruce (1986) *Myth, Cosmos, and Society: Indo-European Themes of Creation and Destruction*, Harvard: Harvard University Press.

——(1996) 'Theses on Method' in *Method and Theory in the Study of Religion*, 8 (3): 225–227.

——(1998) 'Conflict' in Mark C. Taylor (ed.) *Critical Terms for Religious Studies*, Chicago: University of Chicago Press, pp. 55–69.

——(2003) *Holy Terrors. Thinking About Religion After September 11*, Chicago: University of Chicago Press.

Lopez Jr, Donald (1998) 'Belief' in Mark C. Taylor (ed.) *Critical Terms for Religious Studies*, Chicago: University of Chicago Press, pp. 21–35.

Loy, David (2002) *A Buddhist History of the West: Studies in Lack*, Albany, NY: State University of New York Press.

McCutcheon, Russell (1997) *Manufacturing Religion: The Discourse on* Sui Generis *Religion and the Politics of Nostalgia*, Oxford: Oxford University Press.

Martin, David (1998) *Does Christianity Cause War*, Oxford: Oxford University Press.

Masuzawa, Tomoko (2005) *The Invention of World Religions Or, How European Universalism Was Preserved in the Language of Pluralism*, Chicago and London: University of Chicago Press.

Pandey, Gyanendra (1992) 'In Defense of the Fragment: Writing About Hindu-Muslim Riots in Indian Today' in *Representations* 37, Special issue: *Imperial Fantasies and Postcolonial Histories* (Winter): 27–55.

Pape, Robert (2005) *Dying to Win: The Strategic Logic of Suicide Terrorism*, New York: Random House.

Peterson, Derek and Darren Walhof (2002) *The Invention of Religion: Rethinking Belief in Politics and History*, New Brunswick, NJ and London: Rutgers University Press.

Philpott, Daniel (2001) *Revolutions in Sovereignty: How Ideas Shaped Modern International Relations*, Princeton, NJ: Princeton University Press.

Quijano, Anibal (2000) 'Coloniality of Power, Eurocentrism and Latin America' in *Nepantla*, 1 (3): 533–580.

Scott, David (2000) 'Toleration and Historical Traditions of Difference' in *Subaltern Studies* XI: 288–289.

Sklair, Leslie (2001) *The Transnational Capitalist Class*, Oxford: Blackwells Publishers Inc.

Smith, Wilfred Cantwell (1962) *The Meaning and End of Religion*, Minneapolis: Fortress Press.

Smith, Jonathan Z. (1978) *Map is not Territory: Studies in the History of Religions*, Leiden: Brill.

——(1982) *Imagining Religion: From Babylon to Jonestown*, Chicago: University of Chicago Press.

Stein, Stephen J. (2002) 'The Web of Religion and Violence,' in *Religious Studies Review*, 28: 103–108.

van der Veer, Peter (1994) *Religious Nationalism. Hindus and Muslims in India*, Berkeley, Los Angeles, London: University of California Press.

Victoria, Brian (1997) *Zen At War*, New York: Weatherhill.

——(2003) *Zen War Stories*, London and New York: RoutledgeCurzon.

Worth, Robert F. (2002) 'Truth, Right and the American Way; A Nation Defines Itself By Its Evil Enemies', *New York Times*, 22 February.

Index

Note: References to endnotes are indicated by page number, followed by 'n.' and note number (191n.23).

Related titles from Routledge

Religions of South Asia

Edited by Sushil Mittal and Gene R. Thursby

South Asia is home to many of the world's most vibrant religious faiths. It is also one of the most dynamic and historically rich regions on earth, where changing political and social structures have caused religions to interact and hybridise in unique ways. This textbook introduces the contemporary religions of South Asia, from the indigenous religions such as the Hindu, Jain, Buddhist and Sikh traditions, to incoming influences such as Christianity, Judaism and Islam. In ten chapters, it surveys the nine leading belief systems of South Asia and explains their history, practices, values and worldviews. A final chapter helps students relate what they have learnt to religious theory, paving the way for future study.

Entirely written by leading experts, *Religions of South Asia* combines solid scholarship with clear and lively writing to provide students with an accessible and comprehensive introduction. All chapters are specially designed to aid cross-religious comparison, following a standard format covering set topics and issues; the book reveals to students the core principles of each faith, compares it to neighbouring traditions, and its particular place in South Asian history and society. It is a perfect resource for all students of South Asia's diverse and fascinating faiths.

ISBN10: 0-415-22390-3 (hbk)
ISBN10: 0-415-22391-1 (pbk)

ISBN13: 978-0-415-22390-4 (hbk)
ISBN13: 978-0-415-22391-1 (pbk)

Available at all good bookshops
For ordering and further information please visit:
www.routledge.com

Related titles from Routledge

Imagining Hinduism

A Postcolonial Perspective

Sharada Sugirtharajah

Imagining Hinduism examines how Hinduism has been defined, interpreted and manufactured through Western categorizations, from the foreign interventions of eighteenth and nineteenth-century Orientalists and missionaries, to the present day. Sugirtharajah argues that ever since early Orientalists 'discovered' the ancient Sanskrit texts and the Hindu 'golden age', the West has nurtured a complex and ambivalent fascination with Hinduism, ranging from romantic admiration to ridicule. At the same time, Hindu discourse has drawn upon Orientalist representations in order to redefine Hindu identity.

As the first comprehensive work to bring postcolonial critique to the study of Hinduism, this is essential reading for those seeking a full understanding of Hinduism.

ISBN10: 0-415-25743-3 (hbk)
ISBN10: 0-415-25744-1 (pbk)

ISBN13: 978-0-415-25743-5 (hbk)
ISBN13: 978-0-415-25744-2 (pbk)

Available at all good bookshops
For ordering and further information please visit:
www.routledge.com

Related titles from Routledge

Muslims

Their Religious Beliefs and Practices
Third edition
Andrew Rippin

Praise for previous editions:

'Every page of it is a delight. ... not sacrificing subtlety and historical accuracy and a highly readable style.'
Vera B. Moreen, *Department of Religious Studies, Franklin & Marshall College*

'... probably the best general account of what Muslims believe.'
Robert Irwin, *Guardian*

This concise and authoritative guide provides a complete survey of Islamic history and thought from its formative period to the present day. It examines the unique elements which have combined to form Islam, in particular the Qu'ran and the influence of Muhammad, and traces the ways in which these sources have interacted historically to create Muslim theology and law, as well as the alternative visions of Islam found in Shi'ism and Sufism.

Combining core source materials with coverage of current scholarship and of recent events in the Islamic world, Andrew Rippin introduces this hugely diverse and widespread religion in a succinct, challenging and refreshing way. Using a distinctive critical approach which promotes engagement with key issues, from fundamentalism and women's rights to problems of identity and modernity, it is ideal for students seeking to understand Muslims and their faith.

The improved and expanded third edition now contains brand new sections on twenty-first century developments, from the Taliban to Jihad and Al-Qaeda, and includes updated references throughout.

Library of Religious Beliefs and Practices
Series editors: John Hinnells and the late Ninian Smart

ISBN10: 0-415- 34882-X (hbk) ISBN13: 978-0-415-34882-9 (hbk)
ISBN10: 0-415-34888-9 (pbk) ISBN13: 978-0-415-34888-1 (pbk)

Available at all good bookshops
For ordering and further information please visit:
www.routledge.com

eBooks – at www.eBookstore.tandf.co.uk

A library at your fingertips!

eBooks are electronic versions of printed books. You can store them on your PC/laptop or browse them online.

They have advantages for anyone needing rapid access to a wide variety of published, copyright information.

eBooks can help your research by enabling you to bookmark chapters, annotate text and use instant searches to find specific words or phrases. Several eBook files would fit on even a small laptop or PDA.

NEW: Save money by eSubscribing: cheap, online access to any eBook for as long as you need it.

Annual subscription packages

We now offer special low-cost bulk subscriptions to packages of eBooks in certain subject areas. These are available to libraries or to individuals.

For more information please contact webmaster.ebooks@tandf.co.uk

We're continually developing the eBook concept, so keep up to date by visiting the website.

www.eBookstore.tandf.co.uk